Régulation Theory

The French *régulation* school established itself with the analysis of the era of Fordism, the post-Second World War period of development of mass production and mass consumption, and its crises. *Régulation* theory has developed a set of concepts, methods and models in conjunction with the long-term lessons of history and systemic comparative studies. It explains that the historically and geographically variable structure of each economy gives rise to its own economic and social cycles and crises. The modes of *régulation* vary in different countries and time periods because the economies are embedded in a dense network of social and political relations and institutions.

Updated and translated from the bestselling *Théorie de la régulation: l'état des savoirs*, this book provides an exhaustive overview of the subject. It traces the theory and empirical developments, making them available to English-language readers for the first time. Since *régulation* theory was created in the 1970s it has continued to evolve in new directions, including theories of the state, money, macroeconomic formalisations of various growth regimes, sector-based analysis, future alternatives to Fordism and contributions to a general theory of institutions. The volume shows that it is an active research programme adapted specifically to the analysis of a period with extensive structural transformations, political changes and dramatic crises. It proposes an ambitious programme for a fully fledged, institutionally grounded and historically embedded economic theory.

Nearly forty specialists from a variety of disciplines and of European, American, Latin American and Japanese origin come together to provide a concise article on each topic, which includes the basic concepts, principal results and current research areas.

Robert Boyer is an Economist at CEPREMAP, Research Director at CNRS and Professor at the Ecole des Hautes Etudes en Sciences Sociales in Paris. He is the author and editor of several books, including *Japanese Capitalism in Crisis* with Toshio Yamada (Routledge 2000) and *States against Markets* with Daniel Drache (Routledge 1996). **Yves Saillard** is an Economist and Researcher at CNRS and the Institut de Recherche Economique sur la Production et le Développement at the University of Grenoble.

Régulation Theory

The state of the art

Edited by Robert Boyer and Yves Saillard

Translated by Carolyn Shread

London and New York

First published 1995
as *Théorie de la régulation: l'état des savoirs*
by Editions La Découverte & Syros
9 bis rue Abel Hovelacque, 75013 Paris, France

English translation published 2002
by Routledge
11 New Fetter Lane, London EC4P 4EE

Simultaneously published in the USA and Canada
by Routledge
29 West 35th Street, New York, NY 10001

Routledge is an imprint of the Taylor & Francis Group

© 1995 Editions La Découverte & Syros;
translation © 2002 Taylor & Francis

Typeset in Times New Roman by
Florence Production Ltd, Stoodleigh, Devon
Printed and bound in Great Britain by
T.J. International Ltd, Padstow, Cornwall

British Library Cataloguing in Publication Data
A catalogue record for this book is available from the British Library

Library of Congress Cataloging in Publication Data
Théorie de la régulation. English.
  Régulation theory: the state of the art = Théorie de la régulation:
  l'état des savoirs / edited by Robert Boyer and Yves Saillard;
  translated by Carolyn Shread.
    p. cm.
  Text in English.
  Updated.
  Includes bibliographical references and index.
  1. Economic policy. 2. Capitalism. 3. Equilibrium (Economics)
  I. Boyer, Robert II. Saillard, Yves. III. Title.
  HD87.T44513 2001
  338.9–dc21   2001019500

ISBN 0–415–23721–1 (hbk)
ISBN 0–415–23722–X (pbk)

Contents

Figures

Tables

Contributors

Jaime Aboites, Professor at the Autonomous Metropolitan University, Xochimilco, Mexico.

Michel Aglietta, Professor at the University of Paris X, Researcher at CEPII and at the Banque de France.

Gilles Allaire, Director of Research at INRA.

Bruno Amable, Professor of Economics, University of Paris X, Researcher at CEPREMAP.

Christine André, Director of Research at CNRS, Researcher at CEPREMAP.

Maurice Baslé, Professor at the University of Rennes I, Researcher at CERETIM (CNRS).

Georges Benko, Assistant Professor at the University of Paris I.

Hugues Bertrand, Professor at the University of Paris VII.

Bernard Billaudot, Professor at the University of Grenoble, Researcher at IREP-D.

Robert Boyer, Director of Research at CNRS, Researcher at CEPREMAP, Professor (Directeur d'Etudes) at EHESS.

Bernard Chavance, Assistant Professor at the University of Paris VII, Researcher at the Centre d'études de modes d'industrialisation, CEMI-EHESS.

Allan Coban, Associate Professor at the Hundred Flowers University, Massachusetts.

Benjamin Coriat, Professor at the University of Paris Nord, Researcher at the Centre for Research in Industrial Economics, CREI.

Robert Delorme, Professor at the University of Saint Quentin in Yvelines, Researcher at CEPREMAP.

Giovanni Dosi, Professor at the University of Pisa.

Olivier Favereau, Professor at the University of Paris X, Researcher at FORUM.

Jean-Pierre Gilly, Professor at the University of Toulouse, Researcher at LEREP.

Robert Guttmann, Professor at Hofstra University, New York.

Michel Hollard, Professor at the University of Grenoble, Researcher at IREP-D.

Yasuo Inoué, Professor in the Faculty of Economic Sciences, University of Nagoya.

Michel Juillard, Assistant Professor at the University of Paris VIII, Researcher at CEPREMAP.

Alain Lipietz, Member of the European Parliament, Researcher at CEPREMAP.

Frédéric Lordon, Researcher at CNRS, Researcher at CEPREMAP.

Luis Miotti, Associate Professor at the University Paris XII–Villetaneuse.

Lars Mjøset, Research Director of Comparative Studies, Institute of Social Research, University of Oslo.

Amédée Mollard, Director of Research at INRA, Researcher at IREP-D.

Henri Nadel, Assistant Professor at the University of Paris VII, Director of the Groupe d'étude et de recherche sur le travail, les techniques et le développement.

Bernard Pecqueur, Assistant Professor at the University of Grenoble, Researcher at IREP-D.

Pascal Petit, Director of Research at CNRS, Researcher at CEPREMAP.

Carlos Quenan, Researcher at Caisse centrale de coopération économique and at IHEAL, Paris.

Bénédicte Reynaud, Director of Research at CNRS, Researcher at CEPREMAP.

Yves Saillard, Researcher at CNRS, Researcher at IREP-D.

Jacques Sapir, Professor at the Ecole des hautes études en sciences sociales, Researcher at the Centre d'études des modes d'industrialisation, CEMI-EHESS.

Christian du Tertre, Assistant Professor at the University of Paris IX, Researcher at IRIS, Paris Dauphine.

Bruno Théret, Director of Research at CNRS, Researcher at IRIS-TS, University Paris Dauphine.

Jean-François Vidal, Professor at the University of Paris–Sceaux.

Marie-Claire Villeval, Director of Research at CNRS, Researcher at Economie des changements techniques (ECT).

Toshio Yamada, Professor in the Faculty of Economic Sciences, University of Nagoya.

Abbreviations

CEMI	Centre d'études des modes d'industrialisation
CEPAL	Commision Economica para America Latina y el Caraibe
CEPII	Centre d'études prospectives et d'informations internationales
CEPREMAP	Centre d'études prospectives d'économie mathématique appliquée à la planification
CERETIM	Centre d'études et de recherches sur l'entreprise, la technologie, les institutions et la mondialisation
CNRS	Centre National de la Recherche Scientifique
CREI	Centre de recherche en économie industrielle
CT	Convention theory
EMS	European Monetary System
ERIC	L'état relationnel intégré complexe
EST	Extended standard theory
EVA	Economic value added
FORUM	Fondements des organisations et des régulations de l'univers marchand
GREMI	Groupe de recherche européen sur les milieux innovateurs
IHEAL	Institute des hautes études de l'Amérique latine
IMS	International monetary system
IREP-D	Institut de recherche économique sur la production et le développement
IRIS	Institut de recherche et d'information socio-économique
IRIS-TS	Institut de recherche et d'information socio-économique, travail et société
LEREPS	Laboratoire d'études et de recherches sur l'économie, les politiques et les systèmes sociaux
LEST	Laboratoire d'économie et de sociologie du travail
MREE	Mode de relation entre l'état et l'économie
NIE	New institutional economics
RT	*Régulation* theory
SSA	Social structure of accumulation
ST	Standard theory
URPE	Union of radical political economists

1 Introduction

Robert Boyer

Régulation theory has encountered two main obstacles to achieving wide-spread international recognition. The first is a purely semantic difficulty: in British and American texts, written in English, the French term *régulation* is confused with 'regulation' (*réglementation* in French); furthermore, as a result of conservative deregulation strategies, English usage of the term 'regulation' has experienced a revival. However, *régulation* theory is not concerned with this area of investigation at all. While *régulation* theory originated in France, it was subsequently enriched by studies of many other countries, and was then faced with a major difficulty in the translation of its founding concept. In the words of Michel Aglietta, one of the founding fathers of *régulation* theory, it involves 'the analysis of the way in which transformations of social relations create new economic and non-economic forms, organised in structures that reproduce a determining structure, the mode of production'. In short, *régulation* theory offers an analysis of capitalism and its transformations, which is entirely the opposite of the purely microeconomic approach of regulation (in the English sense), concerned with the optimum type of control for natural monopolies and collective services by public authorities. After reading this collection of essays the reader will undoubtedly understand this major difference.

But this linguistic obstacle is not the only impediment to the dissemination of *régulation* theory. The second difficulty is that in practice English language readers have had access to only a few texts, which were already outdated, on the basis of which they made their critiques, which were often apt, but which did not take into account subsequent developments in research. To put it in the simplest terms, *régulation* theory proposed an interpretation of growth in the post-Second World War period which was based on the instituting of an unprecedented regime: Fordism. A series of misunderstandings and ill-founded critiques have subsequently arisen which this book seeks to clarify and refute.

An oft-cited theory, based on an unfamiliar body of work

Régulation theory is commonly criticised on account of its functionalism, its exclusive reference to Fordism, its limited capacity to analyse crises, inadequate treatment of politics and inability to specify what exactly post-Fordism entails. All these criticisms arise from a purely partial access to the large body of research that has been carried out internationally following the first generation of research. While this collection of essays offers a response to these objections, it is nevertheless important to address these sources of misunderstanding in the context of this introduction.

Is régulation *theory a functionalist theory?* This is to misconstrue the central question for regulationist research, which, in fact, is constantly involved in an examination of geographical and historical variations in the institutional arrangements that define capitalist economies. The central issue for *régulation* theory is the viability of a set of institutionalised compromises when there is no *a priori* reason why they should define a stable accumulation regime.

Is Fordism the only issue for the theory? This question confuses an important theoretical result with founding concepts, methods or ability to explain and interpret a range of phenomena far wider than economic growth during the 1960s. The breadth of the conceptual and methodological research presented in this book should convince readers of the need to modify this opinion. This is particularly the case given that many more results have been produced over a long period by a second and even third generation of research.

Is *régulation* theory a conciliatory analysis of perpetual *capitalism*, since it would be without contradiction? Not at all, given that the concept of Fordism emerges from observation of the limits of the post-war growth regime at the time when it entered a structural crisis. In more general terms, all accumulation regimes and modes of *régulation* are affected by a series of disequilibria and conflicts that eventually destabilise them. The theory's relevance does not derive from an analysis of stabilised regimes, but rather from its capacity to detect and anticipate probable sources of crisis: *régulation* and crises are linked as intimately as two sides of a coin.

It is claimed that *régulation* studies provide *mere descriptions*, which although interesting, have no theoretical consequences. This is to forget the starting point of this approach, namely extended critical consideration of Marxist and macroeconomic theories (Kaleckian rather than Keynesian) in the light of the lessons of economic history in the long term as well as in the context of contemporary transformations. It also underestimates its contributions to institutional and historical macroeconomics, presented in Part III. The results obtained are worthy of comparison with the results of most contemporary major research programmes.

'But no *post-Fordism* has emerged!'. . . and the theory is therefore false, claim other critics. This grants this approach the same normative status as neoclassical theory. Yet the interest of *régulation* theory is precisely its ability to determine many different accumulation regimes and potential modes of development in response to political conflicts and compromises with regard to results which are difficult to anticipate from the perspective of pure economic theory. The variety of national trajectories, discussed in Part V, confirms this general hypothesis, while changes in relevant levels of *régulation* (sector, region, zones of economic integration, the global system) have become the increasingly frequent object of research studies, the most important of which are presented in Part IV.

But there remains a criticism that is still more devastating and to which this book aims to respond, namely that *régulation* theory *does not contribute anything new* in regard to contemporary developments in neoclassical theory, particularly in the area of research into the role of institutions.

An antidote to the abstraction of contemporary neoclassical research

The 1980s and 1990s witnessed unprecedented developments in *methodological individualism*, starting in the field of economics and then propagated throughout most related disciplines, including sociology, political science and even social and economic history (cliometrics). Analysis of the institutions of capitalism attracted the attention, for example, of transaction cost theory. It should, however, be recognised that methodological individualism is better suited to defining local organisations and institutions than to analysing the founding institutions structuring contemporary society. It is not easy to grasp the dynamics of an economic system on the basis of bilateral interactions between individuals divested of all social and political substance. Yet this was the somewhat Promethean project adopted by many in the social sciences. In contrast, *régulation* theory adopts a well-tempered 'hol-individualism', on the basis of which it considers collective actors and institutions, which are viewed as pre-existent – in other words, formed by a historical past. It is thereby able to define the result of interactions between individuals who are always socialised through a complex network of norms, customs, rules, beliefs and membership of many different groups.

A second striking tendency is that of basing economic science solely on *axioms*: studies in this field must always remain connected with the three important founding hypotheses of *pure economics*, an area of research which prides itself on its self-defined boundary and its complete separation from related social sciences.

The first axiom is that all human actions obey a *universal principle of rationality*. In the field of economics the fiction of a *homo economicus* guarantees the universality of this type of behaviour. Thus fundamentally, all economies subscribe to the same model as a result of the invariability in the basic unit of the *homo economicus*. No wonder empirical analyses, such as international comparisons, run up against difficulties of interpretation! But the concept of irrationality due to a cultural residue, a sort of archaism, rapidly removes this lacuna from neoclassical theory. In doing so the theory loses much of its explanatory power, since it turns out that it is a general theory but that it can never be applied precisely nor falsified.

The conjunction of a series of individual behaviour patterns is rendered compatible through recourse to a second axiom – the *concept of equilibrium* – which describes the viability of a society, or, rather, an economy, composed of units that are moved only by individual interests, understood in the strict sense. Here we find an *ex post* compatibility in a series of rational calculations that constantly measure the costs and benefits of each decision. In contemporary economic research, the hypothesis of rationality is extended to the calculation of projection over a distant long term, sometimes as far as to descendants. From this point on, the intertemporal equilibrium thus obtained eliminates all historicity or event, since in every period individuals merely fulfil the optimum plan determined in the initial moment, give or take a few random perturbations. It is ironic that this theory, which assumes a complete knowledge of interactions and thus of economic mechanisms, reached its apogee in the 1970s, just when leading economists and the best informed experts proved incapable of making the slightest forecast without it being immediately belied. The kinematics of the rational economic mechanism replaced the density of historical time to the point where its dependence on axioms became an additional obstacle to understanding those highly troubled times marking the entry of the Fordist regime of growth into crisis.

Finally, in these theories economic agents interact through *the sole intermediary of a group of interdependent markets*. It is as if contemporary neoclassical economists take an ideal, proposed by Walras and Pareto in a context of pure economics, at face value. In this theory, the law, organisations, the state, trade associations, unions and collective conventions are merely dross signalling various imperfections that are responsible for most of the ills from which economies suffer, for example, unemployment, inflation or the public budget deficit. It is no surprise that the common recommendation is to dissolve these institutions so as to reduce them to markets or contracts based on a principal/agent model. The Anglo-Saxon theory of optimum regulation (as opposed to *régulation*) is not so very different from this. However, it is the exact opposite of French and European *régulation* theory, which deals with the dynamics of an economy with a wealth of institutions and organisations that do indeed interact through markets, but which are by no means limited to this type of interaction.

If we consider any theory holding the three preceding axioms a neoclassical theory,* it would be quite wrong to claim that *régulation* theory contributes nothing new to an understanding of contemporary economies. (Asterisks refer to the glossary on pp. 334–45.)

The four pillars of *régulation* theory

The intellectual dominance of neoclassical theory is not inevitable. It is possible to construct alternative theories that are more respectful of the limits of rationality and the embedded nature of economic phenomena in societies endowed with different social relations from the structural transformations that have permanently influenced the periods of expansion and crisis in capitalism. *Régulation* theory is one such alternative. It has sought to develop a set of concepts and methods that permit the analysis of structural change as well as periods of rapid and regular growth.

This research programme has been gradually established on the basis of four founding hypotheses.

1   The field of analysis must be reconstructed so as to constitute relevant units integrating economic logic, the preservation of the social bond and the importance of politics in the transitory solutions to the conflicts that emerge constantly in all socio-economic orders. *Régulation* theory seeks to benefit from the *contributions of related disciplines* such as history, sociology and political science, from which it is willing to draw some conclusions as working hypotheses.
2   *Régulation* theory offers precise definitions of the times and places where it is legitimate to postulate the adequacy of these basic concepts for the phenomena for which they account. The general relevance of the theory is not derived from an axiomatic source, it comes instead from the *gradual generalisation* of its basic concepts, tools and results over long historical periods and in increasingly diverse geographical areas. This book presents the state of *régulation* theory after almost three decades of research based on progressively wider times, places and issues.
3   A third founding hypothesis is the fundamental *historicity* of the process of development in capitalist economies. In the capitalist mode of production, organisational, social and technological innovation become a permanent feature, creating a process whereby socio-economic relations experience transformations that are sometimes slow and controlled but at other times brutal, beyond the analysis and control of contemporaries. While the hypothesis of rational expectations makes the consequences of decisions to be taken tomorrow present in the here and now, a historical approach sees the future as depending on largely unintentional strategies in the present. The desire of pure economic theory is to be founded on a break with the dross of history, but as a process, history sifts through the relevance of economic theories . . . and very few pass the test. The challenge offered by *régulation*

theory is thus to historicise economic theories, for theories are the daughters of history and not vice versa.

4   Neoclassical theory makes use of many *ad hoc* hypotheses to account for unemployment at one moment, at another for technical change, uncertainties in the construction of Europe, or reform difficulties in Soviet-type economies. On the other hand, *régulation* theory tries to explain as many of the stylised facts that emerged from the 1950s to the early twenty first century as possible using *the same set of hypotheses*. A paradox then arises: *régulation* theory is more unified and comprehensive in its construction and results than neoclassical theory; by contrast, while it is methodologically homogeneous, the conclusions of neoclassical theory are thoroughly contradictory.

A theory for troubled times

What are the main questions that must be answered by all economic theories, including *régulation* theory? Throughout this work, the reader will find different explanations and interpretations of the major stylised facts marking the 1980s and 1990s.

A first question concerns *the universality and invariability of macroeconomic theories*. Examples that make the regulationist message more convincing in the early 2000s than in the past are: the contrast between growth patterns in North America, Europe and Japan; differences in crises affecting Latin American economies in the 1980s and South East Asian economies in the 1990s; and, more generally, doubts about the application of the single structural adjustment programme proposed by the IMF. Each growth mode and form of economic cycle must be related to the institutional architecture of that particular time and place. Furthermore, the success of a *régulation* mode can trigger a slow process of structural transformation that in some cases results in the breaking down of macroeconomic regularities. This is one of the definitions of a structural crisis and is one of the key concepts of *régulation* theory. Part III provides tools and models to serve as a starting point for institutional and historical macroeconomics.

A second question deals with defining the processes that enable an economy to *overcome structural crises*. *Régulation* theory emphasises the major rupture separating episodes characterised by a stable growth regime from the break-up of previous patterns that occurs during structural crises. At that point, it would be erroneous to extrapolate a previous economic determinism that by definition no longer influences the general dynamics of the system. It then depends on strategic behaviour patterns reflecting the innovations of the time. But it would be equally wrong to believe that the simple interaction of individual rational strategies suffices to reveal more favourable new rules of the game that would enable an economy to overcome a crisis. One of the lessons of history is that, to overcome the strategic uncertainty and indivisibility that govern the emergence of a new social and economic order, it is frequently necessary to enrol or create groups to defend and promote collective interests and to call on the intervention of political authorities at any level, from local to transnational. Hence there is no automatic mechanism governing the process of emerging from major crises. This therefore acts as an invitation to reclaim the vocation for political economy, as the joint analysis of economics and politics.

A third question concerns the *level* at which contemporary *régulation* modes operate. In response to a frequent objection to analyses of Fordism,* which referred essentially to a national scale, Part IV considers transformations in the autonomy of national governments. Financial deregulation and rapid increases in innovation have destabilised the monetary policies of the 1970s and have taken an element of decision-making away from governments. In turn, this change has affected the management of budgetary policy, and more generally, relations between the state and the economy. In a similar manner, the oligopolistic competition previously dominating the level of the individual nation state has been eroded by rapid developments in foreign trade, direct investment and the creation of free trade zones or areas of economic integration. Consequently, the three institutional forms* – the monetary regime,* relations between the state and the economy* and forms of competition* – are partly governed at a supranational level, rather than directly and exclusively from within the nation state. In parallel with this, forms of regional or sector-based organisation have become more important. The configuration of the contemporary economy is thus very different from the one that prevailed under Fordism, and this fact is fully taken into account by the research studies presented in this book.

As for discussions of globalisation, the book highlights the question of the *convergence of economies* towards the same, single institutional configuration that is reputedly the most efficient. Part V presents an array of national case studies which conflict with a naïve view of the end of history, marked by convergence towards democratic, market-based capitalism. While the United States has been exploring an accumulation regime characterised by modest productivity gains and the extension of inequalities since 1971 and until 1995, Japan continued to define an alternative organisational form even after the financial crisis of the 1980s. France and Sweden have followed yet another trajectory, one which in France is marked by the predominance of the role of the state – even during the period of privatisation – and in Sweden by the importance of partnerships between labour and management. The hypothesis of institutional convergence is ruled out even more thoroughly by a comparison of the different developments of Latin America, South East Asia or the countries of Central and Western Europe.

One final question, which is extremely important, concerns the *conditions of the emergence and viability of a market economy*. In this regard, the extreme difficulties experienced by Russia and the length of the process at work in the other countries that were previously under a Soviet-type regime emphasise the relevance of a central result of *régulation* theory. In periods of structural crisis, the emergence of a viable configuration is not automatic and generally does not result from a 'big bang'. The success of a new mode of development requires a slow, contradictory process during which representations, ideologies, skills, locations and ways of life and production are newly adjusted, often when one generation is replaced by the next. In these terms, Russia will act as a testing ground for institutionalist theories: the hypothesis about the selection of institutions according to the efficiency criterion is clearly disproved. Concurrently, in the old 'socialist' countries new forms of capitalism are being created which no doubt will be very different from the model initially targeted by leaders when they decided to adhere to the general principles of the market and democracy.

However, a critical reader might quite legitimately raise the objection that, since the time of interest in the work of Douglas North and Ronald Coase, the renewal of institutionalist theories and attempts to apply the theory of rational choice to institutional economy, virtually all contemporary research has, in any case, adopted the areas of interest of *régulation* theory.

It is with a view to answering this objection that the book concludes with Part VI, which is devoted to comparisons with related theories such as the old American institutionalist theories and the radical school of social structure of accumulation (SSA). The possibility of an alliance between evolutionary theories and models and the regulationist approach should also be considered. French researchers are often asked whether convention theory provides the microeconomics which *régulation* theory lacks and vice versa. Does not *régulation* theory offer the macroeconomics needed by convention theory? These questions lead to the research agenda that lies ahead for *régulation* theory.

Régulation theory has grown from adolescence to maturity. This work presents the history of this transition and compiles a complete list of concepts as they have developed over the course of time. Above all it emphasises the major results obtained by a network of researchers, well beyond the context of France and Europe, encompassing America and Asia as well.

The reader must decide whether the results have been worth the effort. If the reader's overall perspective is modified, even slightly, by reading the analyses presented here, then the hopes and intentions of the editors and contributors to this work will have been fulfilled.

Reading guide

Every reader will decide for himself the best way of approaching the book. The contents list may be used to consult the chapters of greatest interest,

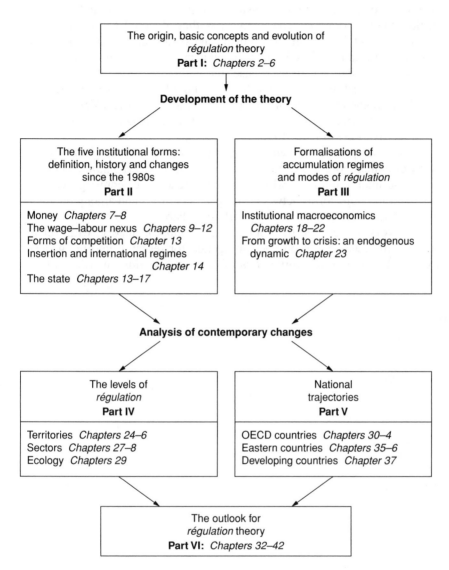

The origin, basic concepts and evolution of
régulation theory
Part I: *Chapters 2–6*

Development of the theory

The five institutional forms:
definition, history and changes
since the 1980s
Part II

Money *Chapters 7–8*
The wage–labour nexus *Chapters 9–12*
Forms of competition *Chapter 13*
Insertion and international regimes
Chapter 14
The state *Chapters 13–17*

Formalisations of
accumulation regimes
and modes of *régulation*
Part III

Institutional macroeconomics
Chapters 18–22
From growth to crisis: an endogenous
dynamic *Chapter 23*

Analysis of contemporary changes

The levels of
régulation
Part IV

Territories *Chapters 24–6*
Sectors *Chapters 27–8*
Ecology *Chapters 29*

National
trajectories
Part V

OECD countries *Chapters 30–4*
Eastern countries *Chapters 35–6*
Developing countries *Chapter 37*

The outlook for
régulation theory
Part VI: *Chapters 32–42*

Figure 1.1 The structure of the book

or the index may be used to trace a particular theme across the various
contributions. The developments in the basic concepts of *régulation* theory
are summarised in Chapter 5.

One might also follow the order of the parts and chapters, which are
intended to connect in a logical fashion (Figure 1.1). The book opens with
a retrospective account of the formative influences on the theory in its
present state: the structuralist reinterpretation of Marxism, the *Annales*

school of social and economic history, German historicism and American institutionalism (Part I). The analysis is then devoted to presenting the origins, content, impact and theoretical stakes associated with the five institutional forms at the basis of the different accumulation regimes and modes of *régulation* (Part II). In each case, the authors describe the hypotheses which distinguish their approach from methodological and fundamentalist neoclassical theory,* present the theoretical and empirical developments which have taken place over the last twenty years, and conclude by offering interpretative keys for the 1990s.

These concepts are applied to macroeconomic questions (Part III), to a study of contemporary transformations in the levels of *régulation* (Part IV) and to an interpretation of why, despite the renewal of convergence theories, national trajectories between European countries and among the major zones of the triad remain so very different (Part V).

The work concludes by connecting *régulation* theory with related currents of research and outlines an agenda for research into the genesis, role, evolution and transformations of economic institutions (Part VI).

Part I

A review of *régulation* theory

2 The origins of *régulation* theory

Robert Boyer

This research programme was initiated in the context of the intellectual climate and economic situation of the early 1970s. At that time, the social sciences were under the influence of Marxism and structuralism, but there were also signs of the revival in methodological individualism that, some fifteen years later, has utterly transformed the questions, methods and research agenda of most disciplines. The field of economics is exemplary of this trend: in the 1980s and the 1990s its scientific credentials were measured solely in terms of the hypotheses of rationality and equilibrium.

A critique of the theories of equilibrium and reproduction

The regulationist movement originates in a rigorous and radical critique of neoclassical theory. Its critique is based on a postulation of the self-regulating character of market economies (Aglietta, 1976) and the abandoning of an erroneous interpretation of the disequilibria and contradictions which marked the end of the Golden Age ('trente glorieuses') (Boyer and Mistral, 1978, 1981). But does this necessarily imply the adoption of traditional Marxist terms and approaches? Both historical and theoretical factors suggest that such is not the case. The original historical research on which *régulation* theory is based emphasises the long-term transformations of the American and French forms of capitalism. This research invalidated orthodox Marxist theory, for example the theory that attributes a central role to the state in the extension of monopolist capitalism during the inter-war period.

The structuralist reinterpretation of Marx analyses only the conditions for the reproduction of capitalism, without attributing sufficient importance to the transformations that were necessary to enable this surprising resistance to economic crises and conflicts (Lipietz, 1979). The notion of *régulation* is precisely what allows us to study the contradictory dynamics of the transformation and permanence of a mode of production (Aglietta, 1976). A second essential aspect is that from the start the research programme is guided by a recognition of the progressive deregulation of the processes which had led to the belief in rapid growth as automatic and guaranteed. Where most economists saw the turbulence of a prosperous economy, regulationists diagnosed the onset of a structural crisis.

Twenty years later, the intellectual climate has altered radically: the social sciences have diffracted amongst a myriad of disciplines and areas of specialisation by an explosive division that obscures the extent of the crisis they are undergoing. Economics has exported into related disciplines, such as sociology, law and political science, the *nec plus ultra* of its methods and postulates, for example, methodological individualism, rationality, equilibrium and efficiency. These research programmes present models which are increasingly specialised and sophisticated, but which do not however offer an account of the phenomena dominating the news: persistent unemployment, recurrent financial crises and an inability to convert innovations into sources of growth. Thus the transformations that influence national economies, as well as the international regime, are more evident now than they were in the 1970s. And yet theorists insist on formulating their theses from a stationary environment where nothing can surprise fully rational agents who interact through the sole intermediary of pure and perfects markets (Lucas, 1984). Consequently any transformations that occur are simply considered random shocks.

Analysing the growth and crises of an economy endowed with a wealth of institutions

Régulation theory emphasises a central hypothesis from which it derives two important conclusions. These features are found over and above the many different sub-programmes and research groups which make up *régulation* theory (Jessop, 1989). First, economic actors interact on the basis of a series of institutions, rules of the game and conventions that imply so many situated rationales (Orléan, 1994). It would therefore be illusory to try to explain contemporary developments on the basis of a set of principles valid for all times and in all places. It is therefore important to examine the nature of the institutions that really exist in contemporary economies and to challenge the traditional instrumentalist argument which accepts too readily that it is enough to act 'as if', deriving what may prove to be true consequences from false premises (Amable *et al.*, 1995).

In fact, the findings of historical and comparative studies have more or less confirmed this historical and geographical variability in the modes of adjustment of economic variables, in other words for the mode of *régulation* (Mazier *et al.*, 1993; Berger and Dore, 1996). Apart from the series of phases of economic boom followed by recession, this theory also led to an early diagnosis, at the time of the first oil shock, of the break-up of the sources of growth during the post-war period and the onset of a period of structural crisis. During this type of episode, the repetition of adjustments implied by the mode of *régulation* tends to destroy, destabilise or bypass founding institutional forms. This affects previous patterns of regularity and a structural crisis is measured by the radical uncertainty it introduces with regard to the expectations of the best-informed economic agents.

This formulation accords with many observations from the 1980s and 1990s. For instance, policies intended to reduce unemployment tended to aggravate it; instead of encouraging a return to full employment, competitive disinflation perpetuated a vicious circle of slow growth; attempts to re-institute an international order fostered the desire for protectionism and deflationary pressures, rather than enabling a return to shared and rapid growth among the various countries. What a contrast to most contemporary economic theories! By adhering to the sole criterion of conformity to the founding axioms of equilibrium and rationality, these theories were unable to explain the major phenomena at the heart of economic policy without frequently resorting to a varying series of *ad hoc* hypotheses, depending on the theory and phenomena under consideration.

It is paradoxical that while the hegemony of the neoclassical methodology that was supposed to produce a cumulative research programme prevailed, its results were more contradictory than ever. In contrast, *régulation* theory expanded its methodological tools – giving the impression of explosive division – and yet simultaneously produced a set of conclusions which were noticeably convergent and which have been undergoing a process of refinement since the early 1970s. The intention of this book is to share this perspective with the reader – just so long as he or she prefers realistic hypotheses and relevant conclusions to aestheticism and axioms! In all economic situations, the advantages and difficulties of the regulationist research programme derive from a desire to analyse and understand how the founding institutions of a social order and an economic dynamic are altered. Most economists are looking for a 'good model', one that will be valid for all times and in all places. Their hope is that as soon as politicians adopt this model then all problems – European unemployment, the move to a market economy in the east or international monetary deregulation – will be miraculously solved. After engaging with the arguments presented in this book, the unique message of the *régulation* theory emerges: that every society displays the economic evolution and crises that correspond to its structure. Just as the post-war model of growth, Fordism, was unprecedented, so was its crisis. It could be redoubled only by the conjunction of institutional innovations channelling a market logic that, once unleashed, is potentially explosive. This is one of the guiding threads of the research undertaken over the past twenty-five years.

The *régulation* theory cauldron

This research focuses on a second characteristic of the problematic. In the 1980s and 1990s there was a reinforcement of disciplinary frontiers, with

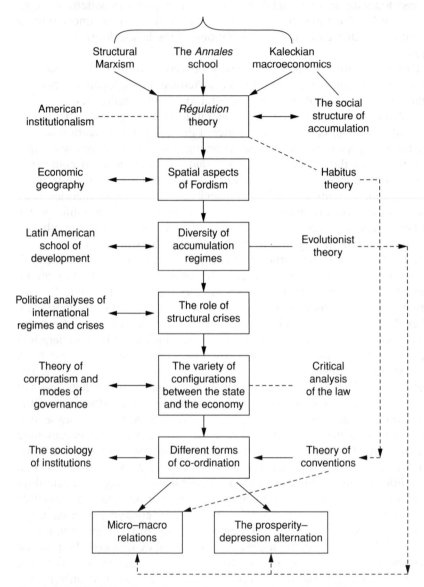

Figure 2.1 Régulation theory's genealogy and sources of inspiration

each social science trying to establish its own foundations more firmly, in spite of declarations of interdisciplinarity. Thus the 'new economic history' (Témin, 1973) always applies the logic of *homo economicus* to contexts or historical periods that are very different from our own, apparently making a virtue of anachronism. Likewise, the economic analysis of the law transfers the goals and behaviour of *homo economicus* to the legal realm (Posner,

1981). The economist expects to find the microeconomic foundations of all the phenomena he observes, including social and macroeconomic phenomena. The research programme of an extended standard theory (to employ the terminology of Olivier Favereau, 1989a) is thus related to an intensive use of a few founding principles and instigates a complete break with pure economics with regard to the interactions of politics, culture and economics that are at the core of modern societies.

In contrast to this, *régulation* theories originate in the juxtaposition and transformation of a collection of tools and different approaches (Figure 2.1). From Marxist theory, they retain an interest in long-term evolution without, however, accepting the grandiose, erroneous dynamic piously admired by Marx's successors. From heterodox macroeconomics, which is more Kaleckian than Keynesian, *régulation* theories agree with the assumption that full employment and a strong, stable rate of growth are the exception rather than the rule. This research develops the methods and teachings of the *Annales* school: if every society has the economic context and crises corresponding to its structure, then it is important to analyse how the different stages of industrial capitalism affect economic cycles and major crises (Bouvier, 1989). From law and political science, *régulation* theory adopts the idea that institutional forms are 'an intermediary between forces', in other words, they result from conflicts between social groups arbitrated by political and legal processes. 'The rules and legal institutions . . . are not merely a cover for pre-existing economic relations, they in fact enable their conception and development' (Lyon-Caen and Jeammaud, 1986: 9).

But legal formalisations must be replaced in relation to practices, for the existence of a rule does not imply that it is respected, since it interacts with the *habitus*, which is by nature uncertain and vague (Bourdieu, 1986). Although *régulation* theory makes few explicit references to them, the concepts of *habitus* and field are well suited to its project. They establish a link between social and individual dimensions by showing their interpenetration: 'The collective is deposited in each individual in the form of enduring dispositions such as mental structures' (Bourdieu, 1980: 29). Investment, in other words the desire to act generated by the relation between a field and a *habitus,* is 'the historical effect of the agreement between two forms of the social: in objects, through the institution and in bodies, through incorporation'. An identical formation for the relation of institutional forms to individual and collective behaviour is found in *régulation* theory. Finally, structure implies a number of conflicts and thus an endogenous dynamic that refutes the idea that a structural analysis is essentially static: 'The permanent battle within the field is its motor. We see, incidentally, that there is no antinomy between structure and history and that which defines the structure of the field . . . is also the principle of its dynamic' (Bourdieu, 1980: 200). This vision is also found in the analysis of the gradual transformation of modes of *régulation,* up to the threshold at which its structural stability collapses and it poses the question of the redefinition of institutional forms, which themselves presume the recomposition of a great many fields and *habituses.*

In other words, both the origin and the dynamic energy of *régulation* theories derive from an *extensive culture*, on the margins of various disciplines within the social sciences, even if economics is the dominant field. As economic activity is embedded within a collection of social, political and legal relations and value systems, there would be no point in wielding the scalpel in the hope of finding the form of a pure economics. Instead it is a matter of establishing the boundaries of the phenomena studied according to interrelated sub-systems, which capture the principal interactions between spheres that supposedly belong to distinct disciplinary fields. In this sense, *régulation* theory has in its origins a multidisciplinary vocation that extends today among a network of researchers borrowing from different academic disciplines whose boundaries are thereby redefined.

Thus the path of French researchers is parallel to the one taken by the American Social Structure of Accumulation radicals. The SSA theorists combine Marxist intuitions and heterodox macroeconomics with the intention of examining their hypotheses and conclusions by means of modern econometric techniques. Like *régulation* theorists, the radicals attempt to explain the move from growth to crisis by a shared set of hypotheses (Bowles *et al.*, 1986). Likewise, some specialists in the political sciences have explored the interactions between politics and economics in relation to strategies for emerging from major crises and have shown a variety of national configurations in this matter (Boismenu and Drache, 1990; Boismenu and Jalbert, 1991). Others in this field have analysed the emergence and operation of international regimes (Krasner, 1983; Keohane, 1984). The economic geographers have studied spatial transformations associated with each major development model and have cast light on the key issue of new productive systems which might replace Fordism (Scott, 1988a; Storper and Scott, 1989). In Latin America, economists influenced by the analyses of the Commision Economica para America Latina y el Caraibe (CEPAL), have developed various critiques, some of which share the notion of the coexistence of different styles of development beyond dependence on an international system (Pinto, 1976; Sunkel, 1990). An original branch of *régulation* theory at the intersection of these two traditions has emerged from this (Ominami, 1986).

One area of research linking sociologists, historians and political scientists has considered the relevance of concepts of corporatism, as well as focusing on replacing the market and the state within the group of coordination procedures that govern economic and political activity (Hollingsworth *et al.*, 1994; Hollingsworth and Boyer, 1997). More recently, the theory of conventions has proposed an ambitious construct which gives an account of the many reasons for action and coordination (Boltanski and Thévenot, 1991; Favereau, 1989b; Boltanski and Ciapello, 2000).

Finally, the contemporary evolutionary research programme is concerned with the reasons for alternations in phases of prosperity followed by depression, with great attention paid to technical systems (Freeman, 1982). The phases of long-term growth appear to result from the compatibility of a technical system with an institutional organisation, while structural crises are seen as the expression of their divorce (Perez, 1983). More recently, evolutionists have created the notion of a national system of innovations to take into account the interlocking nature of the technological, social and economic factors from which innovation originates (Nelson, 1993). Some correspondences between the nature of innovation systems and modes of *régulation* then become apparent (Amable *et al.*, 1997). The project of other researchers is to explain the microeconomic origin of the macroeconomic patterns which define a mode of development (Dosi *et al.*, 1988). This has become an important theme of *régulation* theory.

Thus *régulation* theory is part of a galaxy of research in the social sciences which it interacts with extensively, for example in borrowing and transforming concepts, importing hypotheses and the exploration of similar or related questions. The establishment and increasing success of international associations with an interdisciplinary vocation bear witness to the emergence of a scientific community within which the paradigm of *régulation* theory is able to develop today. It is all the more essential therefore for it to be reconsidered in the light of earlier projects.

Avoiding the errors of the past

In so far as this type of attempt to construct an alternative to pure theory is not new, it is important to draw on past experiences for guidance; this is the purpose of the chapters that follow.

Why did German historicism not establish a school? Is not the American institutionalist movement an unrecognised ancestor of *régulation* theory, and would it not benefit from exploring some of the areas of concern identified by Veblen, Commons or Mitchell (Chapter 3)?

How far is the Marxist filiation still present in contemporary research? Can *régulation* theory do without a theory of value and has it managed to identify the institutional determinants of profit and accumulation (Chapter 4)?

If the retrospective research which launched *régulation* theory was strongly inspired by the *Annales* tradition, did it in return stimulate contemporary research in economic history (Clio, 1995; Verley, 1995)? Is it a matter of simple descriptions reinforcing a pre-established 'vision' or, on the contrary, has the accumulation of case studies permitted a revision of hypotheses and basic concepts?

It is not enough, however, to avoid the errors of the past, it is also necessary to create a coherent construct from elements that are equally varied, or at least to establish various compatible formulations of the issues to be studied. The final two chapters therefore offer a concise presentation of the principal concepts of *régulation* theory and an analysis of themes and results considered over the last twenty-five years. A research programme is at work; it remains for the reader to judge its creative capabilities and relevance.

3 Acknowledged and unacknowledged institutionalist antecedents of *régulation* theory

Maurice Baslé

The origins of a research programme are often distant. They may be acknowledged, thus constituting an early heritage, or they may remain unacknowledged, as mere 'antecedents'. Our purpose here is to initiate a debate through a 'rational reconstruction in the present' of the hypothetical heritage or the lines of possible relation of French *régulation* theory to the institutionalist approaches of a selection of early economists. This does not provide an exact comparison and it is therefore necessary to identify the similarities and differences between French *régulation* theory and the theories that in retrospect appear to be its antecedents.

The analysis of the five major institutional forms by French *régulation* theory has interesting antecedents in the work of German and American institutionalists, although they have now been partly superseded. Of course, these are not the only antecedents that could be mentioned. There are countless precursors from many different countries in terms of the tools of French regulationists. Our selection for the purpose of this chapter is based partly on the fact that some are no longer of interest today owing to impasses they came up against or errors they contain, while others are still respectable, but are of little use. The examples cited here are chosen because despite their flaws they are undoubtedly worthy of reconsideration simply because they may save time for young economists attracted by recent developments in the instruments of economic analysis. We shall provide only a selection of references in this context; the panorama is far from complete and constitutes a research programme in itself.

The antecedents and impasses of nineteenth-century scientism and historicism

Nineteenth-century scientism and historicism have been strongly criticised. Daniel Villey states bluntly: 'the German historicists drew up inventories, catalogues, chronological tables and dictionaries, but wrote no real works to speak of' (Villey, 1954). The expression 'jack of all trades, master of none' might summarise this critique. It is not a new critique, since already in the nineteenth century Menger had addressed it to the economists who were considered to be too historicist or overly concerned by economic analysis of the law and institutions. Later it reappeared in the standard critique of the American institutionalist economists during the period 1920–30. The criticism is still levelled today against *régulation* theory by orthodox economists and methodologists. The recurrence of this criticism is obviously of concern: does the economic thought of the French *régulation* school have antecedents among German historicists or institutionalists? The next question is then: did it learn nothing from earlier disagreements about method?

A rereading of the assumptions of German historicism and institutionalism will enable us to understand and define perspectives on the value of the criticisms currently levelled against the French *régulation* school.

From 1840, Roscher (1815–94) and Hildebrand (1812–78) initiated the German economists' historicism ('the old historical school') on the basis of 'the fruitful alliance of the four major moral sciences which should support one another: philosophy, history, the law and political economy' (Roscher, 1857). At this time economics was experiencing great difficulty in emerging as an autonomous entity. As Adolph Wagner himself mentioned later, the old historical school had too great a tendency to 'disregard the difference between the concrete history of economic facts and political economy, be it specialised or in the practical form of economic policy. It did not even differentiate between the object, method and presentation of economic history and theory (theoretical economic policy)' (Wagner, 1904).

Not until the time of the second German historical school of Karl Knies (1821–98) did an improved monetary theory appear (Knies, 1873–9; Barkai, 1989) and only then did Gustav Schmoller (1838–1917) outline a true public economics. Schmoller's approach is still primarily historical; it also adopts a global perspective (in terms of the national economy) and is truly institutionalist. Schmoller linked together technical modifications, evolution of mentalities and institutional change. Schmoller defined an institution as an

> arrangement at a particular point in the life of a community. An institution answers specific needs, having achieved an existence and form of development of its own, which acts as a context or frame of action for successive generations over hundreds or thousands of years. Examples of this are property, slavery, serfdom, marriage, tutelage, the market, money and industrial freedom. Each and every institution has a set of habits and rules of morality, custom and rights. These aspects of the institution share a common core or goal and are self-supporting, constituting a system, having taken part in a shared practical and theoretical form of development, and are solidly anchored in the life of the community. They act as a typical form, constantly drawing live forces into its sphere of influence.
>
> (Schmoller, 1905–7)

The German institutionalist approach has frequently been criticised on various grounds. These doubts emerged early on. For Menger, Roscher and the German historical school were characterised by vague political economy and subdivisions in the fields of their science. Menger believed that the subdivisions were necessary. He thought them necessary for historical and statistical sciences (which describe and measure phenomena and are consequently empirical and realistic, producing 'empirical laws'); for economic theory (which identifies general aspects of phenomena, relations and 'exact laws'); and for practical economic sciences and those applied to a 'national economy' (which clarify the principles of economic policy actions). The criticism is therefore obvious: Roscher did not perceive the true relation between economic history and the fields of economic theory and applied economics correctly. According to Menger, we should not think that historical analysis is the only starting point for economic theory on account of the induction, generalisations or comparisons that it gives rise to. Furthermore, Menger finds the scientific approach and the holistic or organic approach to certain phenomena too vague (for example, Hildebrand's attempt to discover the laws of development of the national economy). Finally, in Menger's view, the programme of the German historical school was overly influenced by ideological considerations and by too many assumptions in relation to economic policy (relevant only to Germany's economic and geographical particularities, for instance its late nineteenth century 'backward capitalism'). Menger's criticism was directed at all the approaches common in political economy at that time: positivism (A. Comte or J.S. Mill) and the rationalist, pragmatic and constructivist explanation of business development (for example, Smith's explanation of equilibrium through the invisible hand). It also shared the claim that all economic analysis can be derived from history, as in the work of Roscher, Knies, Hildebrand and Schmoller, or even Marx.

Menger maintained a perspective of methodological individualism in economic theory, as well as a belief in 'exact laws': starting with a survey of the simplest individual behaviour, he proceeds by composition to the most complex aspects. In his view it is only thus that one can understand individual interactions and the genesis of the institutions, generally considered non-intentional or 'organic', which regulate these interactions. It is not by induction, but only in this way that one can obtain exact, 'natural' laws, in other words, strict laws for 'typical ideal' phenomena and regular patterns in the succession of phenomena which are difficult to identify in reality. These laws are the relations between structures of mental representation, since everything starts with the representation and judgement (determined subjectively by the individual) of the economy's operation. The conflict in methods that became a recurrent issue therefore starts with Menger as standard-bearer. Menger's perspective was entirely antithetical to that of the first and second German historical schools and anticipated several criticisms that were later levelled against the French *régulation* school.

But the apparent recurrence of this critique may be misleading. First, because it would be wrong to retain only this antithetical relation between two economic analyses of institutions. There is no great difference between Schmoller's 'embodied objective methods' or his 'maxims of what experience and the wisdom of the ages have determined in terms of the rational and fair treatment of relations to the practical' and Menger's 'organic institutions' (and later those of Hayek). At this point lines of lineage are revealed. Second, the present case may be mitigated in terms of Menger's view with regard to the French *régulation* school since it has tried to avoid these difficulties and to take Menger's critique into account. Having freed itself from the more or less orthodox Marxist influences of the 1970s, French *régulation* theory was quite successful in confronting the difficult issues of the genesis of institutions, conventions and modes of *régulation* using new tools that were more appropriate than those of nineteenth century economists. If French *régulation* theory seems more defensible than German historicism or institutionalism, it is partly due to the fact that, perhaps unknowingly, it brought methodological improvements to the contributions of American institutionalists.

American institutionalist antecedents

American economists of the late nineteenth century do not belong to the neoclassical school, despite frequent claims to the contrary; the tradition of 'The American Economic Association' is institutionalist. It is influenced by German institutionalists (Baslé, 1993) and post-Dewey American pragmatist philosophy. It should be mentioned that the American institutionalists also studied areas explored in Europe by Austrian economists such as Menger (criticising the German economists) and that some of the Austrians were also led to praxeology. Von Mises pointed out that in the methodological dispute between the Austrian economists and the Prussian historical school, just as in the debate between J.B. Clark and the American institutionalists, the stakes are far greater than simply determining the most fruitful procedure to adopt. The quarrel in fact concerns whether the economic science is absolute or relative as it is transformed into a science of rational choices or sociology.

In our view, the American institutionalists constitute a beneficial, albeit unacknowledged, antecedent of *régulation* theory. In the course of a century, they produced many promising methodological advances. To cite just one example: Veblen had already distanced himself from historicism by claiming that history alone is not sufficient and that, faced with such complexity, it is important to construct a true theory (Veblen, 1901). At the same time he tried to give an account of the dynamics of market economies and capitalisation and was unwilling to accept marginalism and the conditions of static general equilibrium. The concept of capital as the expectation of future development is entirely modern (prospectivism).

More generally, Veblen preferred the Evolutionary methodology which many are adopting today for studying areas other than technical change (Veblen, 1898). But Veblen believed too strongly in the social mastery of technological change by engineers alone (Baslé *et al.*, 1994) and he was too ready to place his bets on a rapid decline of the business enterprise (even though in doing so he discovered the modern theory of imperfect competition). His purely critical position may be explained by the fact that he remained caught in a holistic methodology with no concessions to methodological individualism. Some recourse to methodological individualism might have enabled him to think through the genesis of new institutions and the origins of institutional reform. Thus Veblen laid himself open to Popperian criticism and to the principle that one should not neglect the analysis of individual interactions and the logic of inter-individual contexts which explain social movements.

However, Veblen opened the way for the institutionalist critique of the theory that later became standard. He was followed by many American economists who, in our view, were veritable pioneers in the renewal of systematic and institutionalist analysis. Paradoxically, they were totally unacknowledged by French regulationists, who were initially influenced by post-Marxism and structuralism. Commons (1862–1945), for example, was entirely correct to reintroduce the primacy of economic analysis of property rights. He acts as a precursor by analysing modern capitalism as a system of claims and debts transferred in bargaining transactions, wage relations or acceptance of state obligations (Commons, 1924, 1934). According to him transactions exceed the atomised, individual level and are a collective concern requiring either a holistic point of view or an institutionalist perspective (Commons, 1951). Although he remains unacknowledged, Commons thus opened the way for French institutionalism and to conventionalists in general in the study of regulation, the negotiated norm and wage relations in particular (Commons *et al.*, 1910; Commons, 1913). Unfortunately, many aspects of his work are still unknown today, particularly his theory of the artificial selection of developing institutions. Mitchell (1875–1948), who was a student of Veblen and Dewey, added a passion for quantitative economics to the institutionalist movement by founding the National Bureau of Economic Research. Ayres (1891–1972) followed Veblen's approach and supplemented it with his interest in the processes of acculturation and technological apprenticeships which led to the institutional changes demanded by the widespread adoption of 'the industrial way of life' and 'reasonable society' (Ayres, 1944).

The monetary institution, an example of an American institutionalist antecedent

This brief historical review demonstrates that, although they were unaware of it, the American institutionalists prepared the way for French *régulation* theory. They are the source of the method, themes and later innovations of the French *régulation* school. They anticipated future developments in the new microeconomics, in the field of industrial economics, labour economics and the economics of public collective action. A good example of this sort of 'institutionalist' antecedent is that of monetary institutions and policies. Roscher, who took a long time to adopt the idea of the 'relative significance of money', kept to the explanation of relative prices (Barkai, 1989). But Knies was already more of a conventionalist and closer to the idea of endogenous money. The translation of Wicksell's work on *Interest and Prices*, followed by that of Hawtrey (1919, *Currency and Credit*, including a chapter entitled 'Credit without money') influenced what later became the debt economy movement. Veblen was interested in capital as the monetary value of property rights devolved to future accumulation projects. Mitchell (a student of Veblen and Laughlin, the liberal institutionalist from Chicago) wrote the famous history of the greenbacks (1903) and offered a perspective on the theory in terms of the facts of the business monetary cycle (where money is neither 'real' nor insignificant) (Hirsch, 1970). For Mitchell, who was a critical economist of the theoretical schema of the quantitative theory of money, money plays the role of a fundamental dual mediator: it is a convention at the same time as it is legal and sanctioned. Its quality is therefore as important as its quantity. Commons conceived of a system of credits and debts in which the quantity of money is only a result (endogenous money) codified by 'sovereignty'. This is therefore a credit economy with a monetisation of debt (Maucourant, 1994) anticipating both post-Keynesian and regulationist developments.

Thus when Michel Aglietta and André Orléan made 'a long journey through the recent monetary history of the United States' (Aglietta and Orléan, 1982) they found themselves back at the ambivalence of money previously described by Veblen and Commons. The considerable progress made by Aglietta and Orléan resulted from two major advances. First, they went beyond a substantial concept of value in favour of research into the negotiation, violence, pacification and socialisation of value. Second, they abandoned a solely structuralist conception of money, in other words, they recognised that the monetary unit is more than a system structured like a language and that it is not enough to simply study the rules of operation of the monetary system and the effect of these rules on behaviour.

The quantitative theory of money emphasised material aspects: agents want to hold a given stock of monetary assets. The theory of the 'monetary circuit' emphasises other aspects: money is the vehicle of circulation as a whole. For institutionalists like Commons, what is logically most important is the evolution of the stock system of credits and debts, since the risk system is guaranteed at the political level. The primary phenomenon is not exchange by means of the monetary unit of account and monetary payment, rather it is a willingness to take debts that are simply a recognition of the debts of others, in a bargaining transaction that is ultimately arbitrated, mediatised or socialised by the political authorities (the government and monetary authorities) (Maucourant, 1993). Aglietta and Orléan proposed a monetary theory that included the contradictory duality of economies of debt and financial markets, drawing unknowingly on formulations which were found not only in post-Marxism, but also in American institutionalism.

While German institutionalists adopted methods that were often considered questionable and confused, and their role as antecedent of the French *régulation* school is debatable, American institutionalists were responsible for more promising advances that can in many ways be considered antecedents of the French *régulation* school, which is generally institutionalist and systematic. Without really focusing on its antecedents, French *régulation* theory has come up against its own difficulties in addition to the pitfalls encountered by previous institutionalist movements. Initially it was hindered by the mix of different genres and spent much time in macroeconomic and post-Marxist discussions of accumulation–distribution theories. At first therefore it was unable to avoid the recurrent criticism of confusing history, theory and normative and applied economics. But this book shows clearly the creative energy of the research to which it gave rise. It is our view that this creative energy might be enhanced by a return to institutionalist sources. These sources demonstrate how, over the course of a century, the question of the genesis and evolution of institutions, the difficulties of systematic and dynamic analysis, methodological problems and support from quantitative economics have been permanent elements in debates which are of wider relevance than French *régulation* theory.

4   *Régulation* and Marx

Henri Nadel

The crisis of 'Marxisms' and *régulation*

Régulation has now reached its full age of majority; over twenty-five years have passed since its first studies were published. It is therefore timely to provide an historical review of the ideological and political landscape, the terms of the theoretical debate and an understanding of the relations between *régulation* theory and Marx and the various forms of Marxism.

In the early 1970s neoclassical theory was relatively inconspicuous in France. However, economics and the human sciences were greatly influenced by an analytical and critical return to Marx's original texts. Marxist *involvement* is specific to the French context owing to the historical alliance of politically committed intellectuals to the French Communist Party. The return to Marx is also steeped in the structuralist movement.

The crisis in Marxism, which has reached its peak today, began to emerge in the early 1980s. In France this crisis was, at first, essentially political. It had a rapid effect on ideology and the field of theoretical research. But the extension of the crisis to theory was also fundamentally political rather than scientific. A tradition of dogmatic reference (forcing reality to fit predetermined formulas by means of a 'Marxist' science), the collapse of the Soviet system and the mishaps of French 'socialism' were the main reasons for the rejection of Marxism. This defeat in the theoretical domain is all the more paradoxical given that the Marxian theory (we draw a distinction between Marxian theory and Marxist statements as they are institutionalised or interpreted) of the crisis in capitalism is indisputably superior to the neoclassical approach.

Within this context, *régulation* theory succeeded in freeing itself from a dogmatic relationship with Marxism while developing a research programme that is clearly linked with the Marxian project. This intellectual emancipation had a profound impact on methodology and still influences the work of *régulation* theory today.

Within the constraints of the present contribution, this point will be illustrated through an examination of how *régulation* theory has dealt with three key moments in Marx's programme: the questions of value and money; accumulation and crisis; institutions and the state.

Value, price and money

While the issue is extremely complex, schematically one might consider with Polyani that there are two theories of value which have formed a deep, original division within 'economic science' since its origin: a 'substantive theory' and a 'subjectivist theory'.

The substantive theory founds the origin of value in work, while in the subjectivist theory it is founded on utility. In the first case the price is an indication or sign of the labour accounted in the commodity. According to the second approach, price indicates the utility that the seeker recognises in the materiality of the object sold or on offer. Needless to say, these two approaches are irreconcilable.

A theory of value plays a central role in almost any economic theory: it is a prerequisite for establishing the formal conditions of market exchange and the mode of measurement of value through prices. Marx's *Capital* opens with an analysis of commodities and exchange; having established that the circulation of value alone does not explain the formation of surplus value and profit, Marx identifies the need for a *metamorphosis*. The relation of apparent equivalence (wage = labour) obscures a relation of exploitation (wage = labour power) and the creation of surplus value as the substance of profit. Going beyond the Ricardian expression of value in Marxian theory requires more than the formalisation of an exchange equivalent (to which neoclassical theory lays claim).

This theory of the metamorphosis of commodities and money as the phenomenal expression of value is presented in *Capital* by appeal to a method that Marx acknowledges as having derived from Hegel. The Althusserian reading of Marx rejects this method because of its idealism. Furthermore, economists are resistant to acceptance of this type of programme or methodological challenge.

At best economists try to avoid Marx's 'errors' by organising a neo-Ricardian formalist retreat, so that the question of the 'transformation' (from values to prices) has become a classic academic debate. The contribution of *régulation* theory to this debate is composed of brilliant, but scattered, suggestions.

Alain Lipietz's research (1979, 1983) is an attempt to take Marxian theses concerning the fetishising of commodities seriously in order to draw a distinction between an *esoteric* and an *exoteric* economy. These are two spaces linked by a tensor of exploitation. For Lipietz there is no possibility of withdrawal from one space to another, of a reduction of values to price. The exoteric world is that of representations that are necessarily fetishised but efficient. Lipietz's analyses often make explicit use of

Marxian categories. It should, however, be noted that in his later work Lipietz rarely returns to the question of value and prices.

Bernard Guibert (1986a) has sought to create a theory of metamorphosis through exchange, using group theory to formalise his analysis of value. However, this entirely original attempt at formalisation, which, for once, escapes from a traditional use of differential calculus in economics, did not undergo further development.

Both Lipietz and Guibert have acknowledged their explicit links with the Marxian project. Such a connection becomes problematic, however, in the work of Michel Aglietta and André Orléan (1982). Here money is understood as the first social link in a market society, and substantive analysis is renounced from the outset. Drawing inspiration from the works of R. Girard and placing violence at the origin of market society, Aglietta and Orléan propose a profound conceptual and methodological restructuring. Their essay can be read as a decisive shift in regard to the Marxian project. In particular it may be seen as abandoning 'labour value' and Marx's theory that deduces money from the development of forms of value in order to establish a 'qualitative' theory of money.

But from the authors' stated intentions one might also think that their project tries to combine a Marxist approach, freed of Ricardian accretions, with Girardian theses, thereby relating contradiction and violence in order to understand the market mode of socialisation through money. This attempt to present an organic development of forms of value can be seen alternatively as the establishment of a new link with the Marxian vision.

Apart from these two authors, most regulationist studies ignore this problem, limiting themselves to applied research, the use of current data and modelling.

As may be seen from these different research studies, in these unfinished areas of investigation and uneven programmes *régulation* theory has made an effort to establish a theoretical foundation concerned with the question of value, prices and money using Marx, but these remain disparate attempts and are ambiguous.

Accumulation and crisis

The analysis of the crisis of Fordism marks the origin and still lies at the heart of *régulation* theory research, and is organically linked with Marxian accumulation theory. Indeed, one of the first definitions of Fordism is provided by Gramsci.

In Marx, the capitalist mode of production is based on the accumulation of capital, through which surplus value is transformed into additional capital. This creates an expanding and accelerating development, which is unsustainable because of the contradiction between the revolutionising of productive forces and productivity and the principle of conserving the private redistribution of value as the mode of appropriation. Its logic is very different from that of market equilibrium and the notion of a business cycle. The reproduction of capitalism thus passes through phases of crisis, which express and resolve the contradictions caused by accumulation. Social (and therefore political) forms of this dynamic contribute to the worsening of the crisis and in varying degrees to a violent or pacific resolution of the contradictions challenging the system. The accumulation of capital is another expression of the wage–labour nexus (a *régulation* theory concept), since for Marx value is created, and the shares of surplus value and wages are determined, through the productive consumption of labour power.

The accumulation crisis reflects contradictions in the capitalist division of labour, the independence of producers and the fact that market relations do not allow the adjustment of productive capacities according to needs. In Marx the tendency of the rate of profit to decline is seen as an inevitable consequence of the nature of the capitalist mode of accumulation. The forces that counteract this tendency cannot eliminate it altogether. When the crisis erupts it resolves itself through the destruction of different forms of capital – commodities, productive and financial capital – and the bases of accumulation are then reconstituted.

At this point in the Marxian explanation of crisis, differences arise about its nature and significance. What should be done about the crisis?

For many years the labour movement expected capitalist contradictions which manifest themselves in the crisis to lead to a 'revolutionary catastrophe' and the emergence of a new social form of production. From one crisis to the next the conditions for a transition to socialism would come into place. The final stage would involve the concentration of capitalist power in the hands of the state, and this collective appropriation (nationalisation) would suffice to cause the ripe fruit of socialism to fall to the organised wage-earning class.

Régulation theory does not address this debate, owing to its hypothesis that history is a process without a subject. This historical indeterminism has been criticised. The very idea of *régulation* was said to conflict with the notion of crisis (in a narrow interpretation) and the term *régulation* was associated with constant cybernetic readjustment, a guaranteed 'self-regulation'.

The analysis of Taylorism and Fordism, the nature of inflation, long-term wage formation, the stages of capitalist *régulation* and the configurations of the wage–labour nexus are key themes in the analysis of crisis and *régulation*. Reference to Marx (if not to Marxism) is clear if implicit but very often even explicit. This is particularly the case in 'sectional' analysis of accumulation regimes and the means of differentiation between extensive accumulation (a regime of absolute surplus value) and intensive accumulation (relative surplus value) (Aglietta, 1976; Billaudot, 1976; Bertrand, 1983).

On this point *régulation* theory agrees with Marx as to the importance of specifying in the historical context structural (or institutional) forms which may produce mutually compatible accumulation regimes and wage norms. Thus, while *régulation* theory may be said to break with Marxist eschatology, it does develop the institutional dimension of the Marxian project.

For Marx the institutional dimension is essential and the dynamic of capitalism cannot be reduced to the operation of a purely economic mechanism. If social classes are formed by their place in production, their conflicts will express themselves in the economic sphere. To oppose a decrease in profit rates, Marx wrote, is to obtain by force, through means of domination in the political realm – not by respecting the laws of exchange – a reduction in wages and an increase in labour intensity (Nadel, 1994a). The conflict between capital and labour then finds its full extra-economic and institutional manifestation. In order for accumulation to start again, it is necessary not only to destroy capital but also to impose new social and wage conditions on labour power.

Claiming to account for the regulating of the mode of production, social relations and institutional forms, and considering its field as the reproduction of the economic system as a whole, *régulation* theory is simultaneously holistic and institutionalist. Its relation to Marx is emphasised in this aspect as well. Unlike the earlier theme discussed above, in this area *régulation* theory has made essential contributions that present a fruitful reinvigoration of the Marxian approach.

Institutions and economics

Essentially, the classical economic theory criticised by Marx views economics as a science which seeks to establish laws for combining production, exchange and consumption relations based on 'natural' behaviour patterns.

To this day, neoclassical economic theory ignores not only the historical aspect of economic laws, but also the fact that the very substance of economic relations is social – in other words, composed of socially instituted forms. These categories refer to the materiality challenging the shallow psychology of the 'rational', maximising individual or codified and formalised 'game' behaviour. Institutions are rejected as outside the field of economics or, worse still, as fundamentally disrupting the 'time and space' of the expectations of rational 'agents'. The nature and genesis of institutional forms are not explained, nor can mainstream theory, or any theory that maintains a strictly individualist postulate, explain it. At best, standard theory provides *ad hoc* interpretations that are often poor and reductive.

The Marxian method is the antithesis of this approach. Already in the first pages of *Capital* a commodity is presented as one of the most complex non-material elements, and its 'use value' is distinguished from the technical nature of the supporting object of the commodity, which itself is a 'social element'.

Social relations and institutional forms are given; social individuals do not choose them, nor do states impose them. History is therefore society's 'invention'; social individuals present their ever conflicting links with production and distribution within institutional forms.

Régulation theory shares this approach. Institutional forms structure the realm of production, exchanges, money, distribution and consumption. To say that these aspects are institutionalised is not, however, to imply that they are natural or voluntarily the result of social and economic activity. Societies that result from the economy of capital are not simply contingent forms of social organisation. Social forms are institutionalised by the action of individuals working through complex and unpredictable attempts between different interest groups, and are ultimately imposed/accepted as compromises. Some of these institutional forms structure the perspectives of the social actors, are codified and become norms, which appear to them to be irreversible. Money, the universalised standard of value and the sacred measure of wealth, becomes the ultimate fetish. It appears as an indispensable creation which itself further diversifies into more profitable forms.

The wage–labour nexus

For Marx the relationship between capital and labour is a social relation, not an individual or an inter-individual relation. It cannot be reduced to a contractual relationship between employer and employee, nor is it a simple relation of hierarchical domination. The 'beauty of wage form', the fetish of the 'price' of labour, creates an illusion of measurement and equity between a service and its remuneration.

Long-term analysis of the wage–labour nexus in the United States (Aglietta, 1976) and in France (Boyer, 1986a; Coriat, 1979; Lipietz, 1979), as well as in other countries such as Japan (Coriat, 1991; Nadel, 1994a), has revealed the central role of distribution in the capital–labour relation, the institutional mediations of this relation in the technical and social division of labour and its antagonistic, historical dimension. Despite the difficulties it has faced owing to an overly simplistic or mechanical formulation, and despite the many criticisms it has been subject to, the concept of Fordism and the Fordist wage–labour nexus provides a valuable heuristic device and plays a crucial role in the critical debate with neoclassical theory.

The state

In the projected 'economic work' which he never completed, but which he often contemplated and described, Marx intended to write a book about the state. Ever since Marxists have evidently been confronted in many ways with the question of the true nature of the state and particularly the 'socialist state'.

Initially *régulation* theory directed its efforts at a renewal of Marxian research into the state. Poulantzas inspired a representation of the state as an authority that both embodies compromise, producing cohesive institutions, and ensures their reproduction (Aglietta, 1982; Boyer, 1986a; Delorme and André, 1983). The state is not simply an instrument in the hands of the bourgeoisie. The development of tensions and social conflicts that are not expressed in a single co-ordinated strategy by the class in power leads to the notion of an 'embedded state' as the guarantor of 'institutionalised compromise' (Delorme and André, 1983). In this case the state is separated from its functions of representing class interests and establishes intermediary forms suited to institutionalising compromise among all interest groups – including the dominant classes. This type of analysis assumes that the state is composed of a set of institutions, structures in which social groups can adopt real positions of power. It is therefore no longer a matter of an entirely functional state in the hands of a homogeneous class.

This interpretation (simplified here) was criticised because it would give the state excessive autonomous ability, while also ignoring the intrinsic violence of the state as guardian of capital ownership and labour discipline.

More recently Bruno Théret (1992a) has sought to overcome the limitations of these regulationist studies by proposing that the state should be treated as a *social relation 'in itself and for itself'*. Analysis of the state requires not only consideration of its relations with the categories of the market economy but also consideration of its own development. Théret therefore went one step beyond other studies by *régulation* theorists towards a synthesis of Marx and Weber: he attempts to identify the political and economic logic of the state, presenting it as a social relation. From an historical perspective, the economy of the state, or the fiscal–financial economy of levies, can be seen as irreducible to that of a market economy. Théret then proposes the notion of a 'topological' configuration of the social in which the state is treated as *one* of the social relations. Finally, he distinguishes two modes of articulation of the modern state and the capitalist mode of *régulation*: the territorial mode and the wage mode.

Théret's regulationist theory of the state is therefore Marxian (even in its presentation of the 'cycles of the state' based on Marx's cycles of capital) while also remaining very different from the type of Marxism which views the state as a functional superstructure of the capitalist mode of production.

What is the future of the Marxist heritage?

Although *régulation* theory has not taken on the task of saving Marx, it does assume the weight of its Marxist heritage. So long as it maintains an approach that emphasises a long-term view of history, macroeconomics and institutions in addition to a critical attitude towards methodological individualism, it must assume its inheritance. For if nothing prevents one from leaving one's father's house, and even taking some of its values for the subsequent creation of imaginative hybrids, a critical reading of the original texts is always in order.

5 A summary of *régulation* theory

Robert Boyer and Yves Saillard

The principal direction and research programme of *régulation* theory are based on concepts and hypotheses that were first developed in the context of research on American capitalism (Aglietta, 1974) and French capitalism, and then gradually evolved and consolidated (Chapter 2). The purpose of this chapter is to bring together the principal alternatives adopted by *régulation* theory and to offer a brief presentation of the basic conceptual structures employed by this research. Definitions of the main concepts of *régulation* theory are provided in a glossary at the end of the book; terms included in the glossary are marked with an asterisk in the text.

Neither individualist reductionism nor structuralist invariability

Régulation theory was founded on a twofold critique, first of the notion of *homo economicus*, and second of the structuralist approach. Economics is not the juxtaposition of homogeneous market subjects endowed with a common principle of rationality interacting in a series of complete markets. Individuals occupy a series of places and positions defined with reference to social relations that vary considerably across time and place: a Roman patrician is not a courtier, an entrepreneur does not have the same objectives as his employees and an industrialist is different from a financier. In order to produce valuable and relevant results, it is important to establish a precise characterisation of the network of constraints in which agents interact and the resulting logic of their actions, for all rationality is situated. In this sense *régulation* theory is the antithesis of the new classical economics programme built on the fiction of a representative agent operating in an institutional void.

Régulation theory emphasises the limits of rational calculation in creating the relations that define the positions of agents: as soon as radical uncertainty prevails and groups of agents adopt strategic behaviour, the unintended effects and paradoxes of composition destabilise the expectations of even the most well endowed agents. Agents can orient themselves only through constraints, common references, procedures and patterns that transmit or support collective arrangements of rules, conventions and organisations (Orléan, 1994). These arrangements are not governed by pure economic logic; rather they arise from the construction and maintenance of a social bond. Furthermore, it can be demonstrated that individuals reduced to pure economic rationality would be incapable of resolving the simplest problems, for example the question of co-ordination.

In the Marxian tradition, *régulation* theory takes as its point of departure the codification of social relations that define a mode of production, namely institutional forms.* These institutional forms emerge from latent or overt conflicts originating in two sources of difficulty: first, it is no longer permissible to prolong the old order; second, in order to overcome the contradictions and disequilibria that appear, reference to an authority beyond the horizontal interactions of protagonists is implied. A caesura is then introduced between periods during which the constitution of new rules of the game is at stake and those when conflicts develop from previous compromises (Figure 5.1). Thus economics and politics, accumulation and legitimacy overlap, without, however, being reduced to one or the other.

An analysis of change

But must one therefore adhere to the hypothesis that political authority merely responds to the demands of economic systems, so that fundamentally the state results from capital? It would then have the responsibility of guaranteeing a transitional form of viability to a mode of production and would be essentially dedicated to its own disappearance by the nature of its contradictions. In fact, both theories and analyses of the state (Delorme and André, 1983; Théret, 1992a) suggest that it is a largely autonomous authority with regard to the form of the institutional compromises that it codifies. It is easy to imagine political configurations obstructing accumulation possibilities in an enduring manner, as in the French trajectories at the end of the nineteenth century or in Britain for over a century or in Argentina since the 1970s. In addition to this, there is nothing to guarantee that in the long term social forms will always emerge to reproduce the production relations of the prevailing mode of production.

The collapse of the Soviet mode of production is a reminder that the process of adapting institutional forms to the imperatives of economic systems and political legitimacy is not automatic. Attention must therefore be paid not only to constants (until now capitalism has in fact ensured its own viability) but also to changes in the form of social relations that are likely to produce major changes in political and economic structures. After all, the state based on Ford, Beveridge or Keynes's model of the Golden Age ('trente glorieuses') is hardly an exact equivalent of the watchman state of the eighteenth century!

Regulationists believe that change is as important as invariability and that both must be analysed together. It is because new forms have been discovered that capitalist relations have shown a degree of permanence and have spread to new areas. But this change is not directed by overarching laws such as the rise in productive forces or a fall in the level of profit, which are permanent and present in all capitalist societies. The purpose of the whole conceptual apparatus of institutional forms, accumulation regimes and modes of *régulation* is to overcome methodological individualism's inability to deal with the basic economic institutions of capitalism (by reducing them to forms of market exchange) and Marxist structuralism's inability to analyse change, particularly during major crises.

From social relations to five institutional forms

Régulation theory has gradually developed a set of conceptual tools whose general architecture and overall logic will be presented here.

Three levels of analysis may be distinguished according to a decreasing degree of abstraction (Boyer, 1986a). At the most abstract level, *régulation* theory analyses modes of production* and their connections. The inheritance of Marx's production relations is clear, but the correspondence between production relations and the state of productive forces is abandoned, as is the dichotomy between economic structure and the legal and political superstructure. In the capitalist mode of production* the form of production and exchange relations imposes the primacy of exchange value over use value and makes accumulation an imperative of the system. *Régulation* theory does not, however, infer from this that there is a simple, invariable relation between the capitalist mode of production and forms of accumulation.

At a second level, *régulation* theory describes the social and economic patterns that enable accumulation to occur in the long term between two structural crises.* These regular patterns as a whole are summarised by the notion of an accumulation regime.* At this level only regular patterns are observed: they correspond to phenomena formalised by the macro-economic modelling of growth inspired by Kalecki and the Cambridge economists. Identifying regular patterns does not require the exclusion of crises: the description of accumulation regimes includes their evolution and potential crises. Where neoclassical and post-Keynesian theory look for a general, invariable model, regulationists recognise a variety of accumulation regimes, according to the nature and intensity of technical change, the volume and composition of demand and workers' life style. Capitalist relations are compatible with accumulation regimes that are transformed over the long term and vary in both time and space.

A third level of analysis concerns the specific configurations of social relations for any given era or geographical location. Institutional (or structural) forms* define the origin of observed social and economic patterns.

The project of *régulation* theory is to describe these institutional forms and their arrangement, as well as analysing their permanent transformations. Institutional forms socialise the heterogeneous behaviour of economic agents, forging a passage from micro to macroeconomics. *Régulation* theory establishes a hierarchy among these institutional forms according to the mode of *régulation* in effect at the time and in the country under consideration. For the Fordism* of the post-Second World War period, credit money, an original wage–labour nexus and an oligopolistic form of competition proved to be more important than transformation of the state in the strict sense. In contrast to this period, in the 1990s the intensification of monetary constraint and the internationalisation of competition appear to precede and shape transformations in the wage–labour nexus.

The importance of 'money' as an institutional form* derives from its role as a general equivalent, a mode of connection between economic units. Many modalities in the form of monetary constraint are possible. There are as many monetary regimes as there are ways of compensating short-falls and oversupply between economic agents. This institutional form exceeds national limits, involving relations with wider areas of circulation and exchange. For *régulation* theory the overlapping of institutional forms implies the rejection of univocal explanations of economic phenomena. Thus the origin of inflation cannot be solely monetary, but nor can money be 'neutral'.

The privileged place of the wage–labour nexus* among the institutional forms identified by *régulation* theory is due to the fact that it describes the type of appropriation of surplus in the capitalist mode of production. Historical analyses and international comparisons have made it possible to distinguish several forms of the wage–labour nexus:

1 *Competitive*, when workers' consumption is not inserted in capitalist production.
2 *Taylorian*, when the organisation of work enables mass production, without this profoundly modifying the life style of employees.
3 *Fordist*, which combines the development of consumption norms and production norms.

Forms of competition* indicate how relations between producers are organised. *Régulation* theory is more specifically concerned with an analysis of the forms of competition that might bring about the transformation of accumulation regimes.

The forms of insertion into the international regime* characterise relations between the nation-state and the international forum. According to the definition of a state, it exerts political sovereignty over a precisely defined territory, so that relations between each nation state and the rest of the world are rarely the result of pure market relations but instead arise from political choices made during critical periods. The choice of a commercial regime, exchange management or openness to foreign capital are examples of the options which define the mode of insertion and thus the viability of an international regime. *Régulation* theory tries to avoid simple oppositions between an open economy and a closed economy, between national autonomy and foreign constraints by proposing intermediary notions, such as a strategic area,* to define the types of structuring of the international forum (Mistral, 1986).

An international regime* does not determine the mode of growth of a country by itself; everything depends on relationships established between that regime and the country's other institutional forms. The idea of an international regime emphasises that the many institutional arrangements governing trade, direct investment, financial flows and the organisation of exchange cannot be reduced simply to market adjustments. On this point, *régulation* theory agrees with the American school of international regimes (Krasner, 1983), and even more with international political economy (Kébabdjian, 1998, 1999; Palan, 1998). Thus it refers to a set of principles, norms, rules and decision-making procedures which assure the stability and relative coherence of the behaviour of different agents within the international economy. But of course these arrangements are frequently partial and sector-based and do not generally have the force and durability of national institutional forms, so that one would not be able to extrapolate the notion of the mode of *régulation* from the international regime.

The forms of the state* demonstrate how the organisation of public authorities is part of the economic dynamic. The complexity of compromises at the origin of public intervention excludes functionalist interpretations of the actions of the state. The configuration of the state is endowed with a good deal of autonomy in terms of codifying the monetary regime, forms of competition and the wage–labour nexus. Besides this, relations between political subjects and economic agents introduce differences in terms of taxation and access to the collective services produced or organised by the state. Thus it is important to study the differences between wage-earning societies in democratic states and others that are governed by the middle classes and/or subject to an authoritarian regime.

But analysis of the forms of articulation between the state and the economy leads to a consideration of the nature of the state in general. Once the logic of political power (the expression of the sovereignty and legitimacy authorising taxation) is clearly distinguished from the constraints of private accumulation, it is possible to establish a set of concepts to account for the complexity of the roles and configurations of the state. The notion of a fiscal and financial regime* refers to a correspondence between the legal and expenditure forms of state legitimacy through the intermediary of the tax-levying process (Théret, 1992a). The characteristic of *régulation* theory is thus not to isolate the state from the national economic system, while also excluding a simple economic determinism of the state.

The mode of *régulation:* the consequence of a group of institutional forms

Régulation theory considers that adjustments in the decisions of the many decentralised economic agents, whose rationality is limited, occurs through the conjunction of the effective procedures and behaviour of the mode of *régulation.** This term highlights the active process of adjusting disequilibria on a day-to-day basis and the partiality of the procedures codified in institutional forms. Only experience allows one to judge the viability of a mode of *régulation* after the fact. In contrast to fundamentalist neoclassical theory,* a mode of *régulation* replaces the notion of static equilibrium with an analysis of *dynamic processes* reducing the disequilibria constantly caused by accumulation. It inserts markets into a series of *institutional arrangements* that socialise both information and behaviour and restricts the rationality of agents to available information and cognitive abilities, in other words it adopts a *situated rationality*, illuminated by a dense network of institutions. Thus the possibility arises that the mode of *régulation* differs considerably, depending on the time and place, and that it is not the projection of a single model of general equilibrium, apart from the imperfections and friction introduced by national 'specificity' (Benassy *et al.*, 1979; Boyer and Yamada, 2000).

A mode of *régulation* establishes a set of procedures and individual and collective behaviour patterns which must simultaneously reproduce social relations through the conjunction of institutional forms which are historically determined and supported by the current accumulation regime. Furthermore, a mode of *régulation* ensures the compatibility of a set of decentralised decisions, without requiring agents to internalise the principles governing the overall dynamic of the system. This definition challenges the distinction between pure economics and the social aspects. The involvement of the economic sphere in a larger field avoids the indeterminacy to which pure economic logic leads. Thanks to this embeddedness (Polanyi, 1946) it is possible to overcome structural crises which would otherwise be even more devastating.

Three principles of action of institutional forms are proposed in order to analyse their role in directing individual and collective behaviour: first of all, the law, rule, regulation or any other constraint; next, compromise or negotiation; finally, the community of a system of values and representations or routine.

Armed with these basic concepts, *régulation* theory proposes to analyse modes of development*, in other words, the way in which an accumulation regime and a type of *régulation* stabilise themselves over the long term and how they enter into a period of crisis and then renew themselves (Figure 5.1).

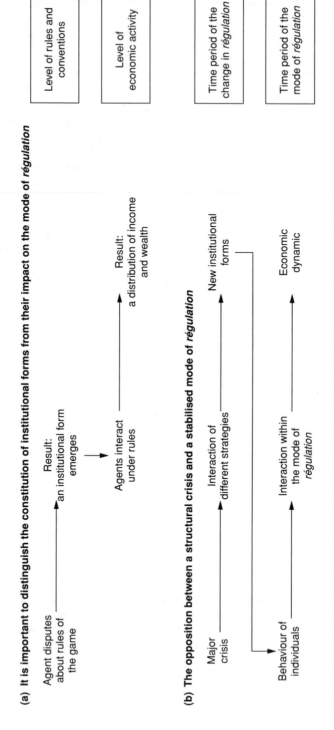

Figure 5.1 Two levels and two time scales at the origin of institutional forms and structural crises

An endogenous dynamic leading to a variety of different crises

The mode of development does not imply identical reproduction, rather it suggests inscription in historical time: unforeseen events arise, cycles follow one another, institutional forms gradually change and there emerges the possibility of evolutions so contradictory that they become explosive. These are the many different forms of crisis* which *régulation* theory identifies and for which it offers a classificatory system.

The first kind of exogenously triggered crisis* refers to shocks 'from outside', in other words, which do not originate in the mode of *régulation*, and which react only according to their specificity. While *régulation* theory accepts the possibility of crises linked with external shocks, it limits their importance and concentrates most of its attention on several other types of crisis.

Endogenous or cyclical crises* develop without any major modifications to existing institutional forms. The form and extent of these crises depend on the current mode of *régulation*, but they are its direct expression, since no institutional or economic policy change is necessary to trigger a return to recession or economic recovery. These episodes which derive from *within* the processes that determine the mode of *régulation* are described as minor crises.*

In contrast, there are periods during which the compatibility of institutional forms and the economic dynamic is no longer guaranteed. There is no automatic mechanism to govern the passage from depression to economic growth, and in general this initiates a period of tentative research for a strategy to escape the crisis, involving the reform of some or all of the previous institutional forms. In order to distinguish such crises from the crises described above, those that affect *régulation* and the accumulation regime are termed structural or major crises* (Figure 5.1). Two types of structural crisis are identified, depending on whether they originate from *régulation* or from the accumulation regime: a crisis of the mode of *régulation* and a crisis of the accumulation regime.* Indicators of this type of crisis are the inability to resume profitability and to allow the recovery of accumulation, the destruction of the social forms supporting accumulation, the dissolution of economic determinism and an increase in social and political conflicts at both the national and the international level. These signs enable real-time diagnoses of the onset of structural crises. In fact the form such crises take varies according to the accumulation regime, so that this type of classification explains why today's crisis is not a repeat of the 1929 crisis. Furthermore, it explains why even a vigorous cyclical revival (1984–9) does not signal the emergence of a new viable configuration of institutional forms.

Finally, a crisis in the dominant mode of production* is the ultimate level of crisis. This crisis, like the concept of organic crisis in Marxist theory, assumes that no new accumulation regime can emerge, even taking into account the ability of institutional forms to adapt and the long-term evolution of the economic system. During such a period, poor or catastrophic economic performance presents long-term unfavourable tendencies, while the political process of reform is blocked or counterproductive. This concept of crisis seemed very abstract or distant (the crisis of feudalism) until the collapse of the Soviet regimes provided a spectacular example (Chavance, 1989; Sapir, 1990).

A research programme

This collection of concepts and analytical tools establishes the bases of a theory that permits a gathering together of historical studies, international comparisons, macroeconomic formalisations and econometric tests (Figure 5.2). The goal is to identify some typical configurations of modes of development and their crises. A synthesis of the way the various chapters of the book contribute to this research programme is provided in Chapter 6.

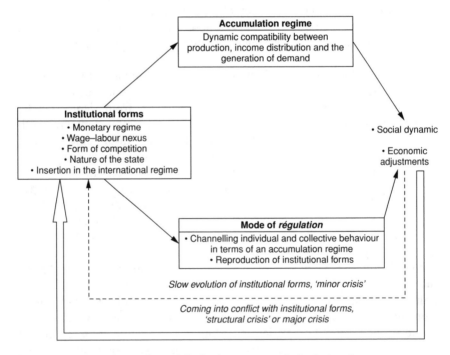

Figure 5.2 General overview of the basic concepts of *régulation* theory

6 *Régulation* theory

Stasis or confirmation of a research programme?

Robert Boyer and Yves Saillard

Concepts are worth only what they clarify or reveal. What is the ultimate contribution of the theoretical construct of *régulation* theory presented in Chapter 5 in research developments since the mid-1970s? Some people view *régulation* theory simply as a cover for historical descriptions and a 'vision' of the world of economics, with no real analytical relevance. Others, who initially supported *régulation* theory, eventually lamented the lack of innovative results, apart from the demonstration of the importance of Fordism. Still others claimed that the desire to interact with standard theory had eroded the critical and visionary virtues of *régulation* theory.

Whatever the validity of these criticisms, they reveal a misunderstanding with regard to the overarching trends and motives of regulationist research, no doubt because the specialisation and diversification of research themes have made it difficult to achieve a general overview. This chapter proposes an overall perspective by means of synthesising tables that describe the gradual evolution from initial concepts to the developments and revisions made to them. It also introduces new questions in addition to old ones which *régulation* theory must now answer. This chapter is also devised as a guide to the book to help the reader negotiate the forty chapters.

The three motives of the regulationist programme

A theory that is content simply to reiterate its basic concepts and founding insights would soon be condemned to a loss of impetus and relevance. The value of a theory is measured by the quality of the research programme that it produces. Compared with other formulations, the regulationist approach has many more reasons to continually revise its objectives, methods and even some of its basic concepts.

First and foremost, its initial formulation immediately gave rise to a number of *unresolved theoretical issues*, to which many different responses were offered. This is particularly the case with *money* (Table 6.1). If the monetary standard is no longer a commodity, the Marxist theory of value is faced with a difficult question. Regulationists sought to resolve this question initially via a distinction between an esoteric economy of value and

Table 6.1 Money

Founding research	Research developments	Current areas of interest
Money is not a commodity. *Chapters 4, 7*	Theory of the forms of money and of crises by imitation. *Chapters 4, 7*	Money subject to the arbitrage of financial markets. *Chapter 8*
Credit money alters the dynamics of accumulation. *Chapter 7*	Pseudo- and ante-validation in an exoteric economy. *Chapters 3, 7*	The return to strict monetary constraint inhibits accumulation. *Chapter 31*
Cumulative inflation is the expression of crisis in a credit money regime. *Chapter 7*	Monetary policy as the expression of creditor–debtor relations. *Chapter 7*	The monetary regime returns to the wage–labour nexus. *Chapters 9, 32*

an exoteric economy of nominal prices. Later they attempted a reconstruction of forms of value based on Girardian theory, and then focused on the theory of monetary regimes and relations with the wage–labour nexus. Likewise, relations between the stringency of monetary constraint and the possibility of intensive accumulation are central to current regulationist concerns, especially on account of the persistence of the shift in monetary policies that appeared in the mid-1980s.

The notion of a *wage–labour nexus* (Table 6.2) has given rise to theoretical debates that are all the more important since its initial basis was none other than the Marxist theory of exploitation which in the 1990s is no longer a major reference point. Today the theory centres on relations between power, wage compromise and the institutional determinants of the wage–profit distribution. In an entirely different context, when field studies wanted to use this notion it soon became apparent that it was inadequate for giving an account of the logic of agents at the level of firms and professional arenas. As a result they had recourse to other concepts: the wage relation, the employment system and social relations to work were suggested to explain differences in status and elements which led at the macroeconomic level to the regular patterns under consideration in the wage–labour nexus. Likewise, a hidden but powerful dialectic emerged between the stringency of a monetary regime and the solidity of a capital–labour compromise. Thus theoretical studies gave rise to most of the initial categories and subsequently transformed them.

A second developmental factor is specific to *régulation* theory, since *the observation of the transformations* of capitalist economies in existence since 1967–73 has invalidated some forecasts and hypotheses as well as revealing many other inadequacies. This is especially the case with *forms of competition* (Table 6.3). Prices no longer maintain their function of balancing markets for industrial products, but it is it not enough to refer

Table 6.2 The wage–labour nexus

Founding research	Research developments	Current areas of interest
The interdependence of the labour process and the mode of payment of employees. *Chapters 9, 11*	Sectoral diversity of the wage–labour nexus and the work relation. *Chapters 27, 28*	Alternatives and successors to Fordist methods. *Chapter 9*
Social and political conflicts give rise to the forms of the wage–labour nexus. *Chapter 9*	Diversity in national configurations of the wage–labour nexus: Fordist, micro-corporatist, Scandinavian, Arythmic. *Chapters 9, 30, 31, 33, 34*	Systems for the employment and training of collective agents. *Chapter 10*
Wage formation confirms these changes: early, competitive and monopolistic *régulation. Chapter 9*	Competitive forces are reintroduced but encounter tremendous inertia. *Chapters 9, 11, 31, 32*	Classification of wage systems and their evolution. *Chapter 11*
Wage benefits as the consequence of the insertion of employees in capitalism on a lifetime basis. *Chapter 12*	The principles, organisation and financing of social security insurance depend largely on the history of disputes. *Chapter 12*	The onset of crisis, the welfare state and the difficulty of reforming it. *Chapters 12, 16*
The Fordist wage compromise: an essential aspect of the post-war accumulation regime. *Chapter 30*	Reconsideration and differentiation of status The re-segmentation and disappearance of the virtuous effects of wages. *Chapters 10, 30*	The strengthening of competition re-structures the wage–labour nexus The disparity of the educational relation threatens the emergence of a new wage–labour nexus. *Chapter 10*

to the theory of administered prices either. It was necessary to establish the basis of an industrial economy on a par with Fordist theory. The destabilisation of national oligopolies through foreign competition, new technologies redefining frontiers between sectors, the appearance of overcapacity in certain branches, were factors which combined to redefine the previous regime of competition. Furthermore, these factors affected the internal organisation of firms, their relations, and even the wage–labour nexus, which was increasingly subject to the hazards of competition on the product market. The description of accumulation regimes likely to succeed Fordism presumes a careful study of competition by quality or by reaction speed to unforeseen circumstances and innovation – in other words, a development of theories of this institutional form.

Table 6.3 Forms of competition

Founding research	Research developments	Current areas of interest
Large companies and the concentration of finances signal an oligopolistic form of competition. *Chapter 13*	Oligopolistic competition is not enough to bring about a monopolistic form of *régulation.* *Chapter 13*	The internationalisation and differentiation of products: from the A firm to the J or G firm. *Chapter 27*
Administered prices (mark up applied to standard price) replace market prices. *Chapter 13*	The level of competition through prices or quality is a differentiation factor for sector and national *régulations* (e.g. France/ Germany). *Chapters 28, 32*	The role of inter-company and local relations in innovation Towards accumulation regimes that are not governed by competitive- ness. *Chapters 20, 25, 26*

Table 6.4 The international regime

Founding research	Research developments	Current areas of interest
Organised under the hegemony of the dominant economy. *Chapter 14*	A break with the post-war system and the erosion of American hegemony. *Chapter 31*	Can an international regime exist without the equivalent of a supra- national political power? *Chapters 8, 14*
The international spread of Fordism, starting with the United States from 1950. *Chapters 32, 33, 34*	The persistence of inequalities between nations is the motor of the international system. *Chapter 14*	International pressures destabilise national institutional forms. *Chapter 30*
A critique of the notion of the Third World as a periphery. *Chapter 37*	A new cartography of the international division of labour. *Chapter 35*	The emergence of new international sources of disequilibrium, such as ecological concerns, the North–South divide and the Asia–United States– Japan relation. *Chapter 29*

The transformations of the *international regime* (Table 6.4) also stimulated an increase in research combining historical and conceptual analysis.
First, the interdependence of institutional forms is analysed, since the
increasingly extravert nature of economies appears to have led to the
threshold being exceeded at which the virtuous circle of Fordism is
reversed. It is not, however, replaced by the favourable connections linked
with the rise in exports, especially since an uncertain international regime
transmits and exacerbates a series of radical uncertainties. Second, the great
difficulty in negotiating a successor to the Bretton Woods regime signals

Table 6.5 The state

Founding research	Research developments	Current areas of interest
Public expenditure as the expression of *institutionalised compromises*. *Chapter 12*	Institutionalised compromises vary in their purpose and configuration according to each country. *Chapters 12, 30*	Towards a regulationist theory of the state: combining the political system with the logic of accumulation. *Chapter 16*
Two *configurations* of relations between the state and the economy: the limited state (19th century), and the embedded state (post-1945). *Chapters 12, 15*	A reconsideration or redefinition of the limited state during the crisis in Fordism. *Chapter 12*	Classification of relations between the state and the economy: the state as relational, integrated and complex. *Chapter 15*
The state as a creditor of the wage–labour nexus. *Chapter 16*	The relative autonomy of the political. *Chapter 16*	The economy of fiscal–financial regimes. *Chapter 16*
The power and limits of economic policy: it acts as a generator of institutionalised compromises and then becomes imprisoned by these same compromises. *Chapter 17*	Styles of economic policy vary tremendously among different countries. *Chapter 12*	An economic policy *regime* corresponds to each mode of development. Consequently it is difficult for policies to stimulate emergence from a crisis. *Chapter 17*

one of the great challenges at the heart of institutional economics. How can a world order be created when no single participant is in a position to impose its solution and when no supranational political power exists? Similar difficulties are also found with regard to a co-operative wage–labour nexus, which firms and employees seem incapable of negotiating in societies where there is a long tradition of mutual mistrust.

The extension of *régulation* theory to new areas and new countries is a third, powerful impulse to revise its founding insights. The study of French capitalism emphasised the determining role of the *state* (Table 6.5) as the central impetus as well as the instrument for managing virtually all institutional forms. However, comparisons with German, British and American history show that this result is closely linked to a specifically French context. As a consequence, the diversity of institutionalised compromises requires abandoning the distinction between a limited state and an embedded state in favour of an analysis of state–economy configurations on the basis of the notion of the State as Relational, Integrated and Complex (ERIC, *l'état relationnel intégré complexe*). More fundamentally, regulationists need a general theory of the state rather than just a theory of the

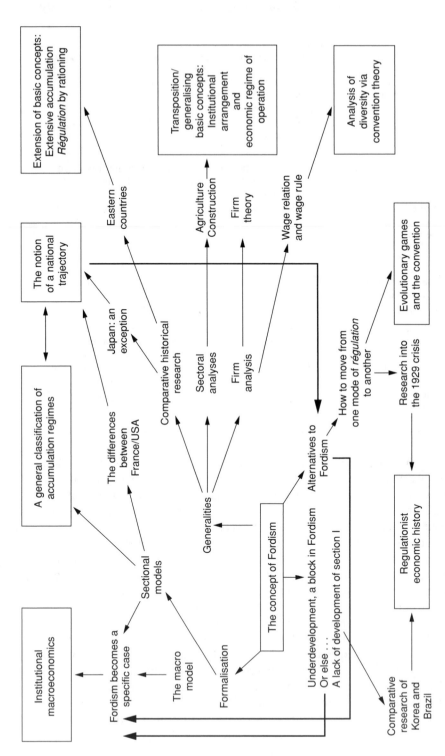

Figure 6.1 Synoptic view of developments in the concept of Fordism

state's forms. This is certainly one of the main conceptual innovations of the 1990s (Théret, 1999; Lordon, 1997a; Palombarini, 1999).

A spiral construction

Thus *régulation* theory has developed far more than is usually thought. While from the outside the galaxy situation appears to be virtually immobile, from the inside it is alive with rapid movement. The best example is surely the successive transformations of the key concept of Fordism (Figure 6.1). The use of macroeconomic modelling emphasised the conditions for viability which historical, institutional and qualitative analysis had not revealed, for example that salaries should not be indexed too high or too low in relation to productivity.

Retrospective historical analyses reveal that institutional forms other than Fordism may result in mass consumption, for example Japanese meso-corporatism (Table 6.6). In the same manner, expansion in Eastern Europe or Latin America requires the development of a range of accumulation regimes and modes of *régulation*. This implies that these concepts are expressed very differently in the 1990s compared with the original notions proposed by the founding research in the United States and France. Last but not least, unfolding in the crisis of Fordism reveals both the diversity of national trajectories and the need to develop the modes of

Table 6.6 Accumulation regimes

Founding research	Research developments	Current areas of interest
Theoretical analysis of the possibility of intensive accumulation. *Chapters 18, 19*	Statistical analysis and models in terms of productive sections. *Chapter 20*	Underdevelopment as the inadequacy of Section I. *Chapter 20*
Fordism as an intensive accumulation regime with mass consumption. *Chapters 20, 30, 31*	Maturity of Fordism in the United States, modernisation of Section II, then extraversion in France. *Chapter 20*	Case studies, international comparisons and formalising new sources of technical and organisational change. *Chapters 21, 22*
The consequence of a compromise of capital/ worker sharing of productivity benefits. *Chapter 9*	A meso-corporatist compromise may also result in mass consumption (Japan). *Chapter 34*	Classification of relations between the wage–labour nexus and the accumulation regime. *Chapters 30, 31*
. . . and of change in other institutional forms. *Chapters 9, 18, 30*	Modelling understood as the combining of a productivity regime and a demand regime. *Chapters 18, 21, 22*	Open economy, financial regime, informal sector: a generalising of accumulation regimes. *Chapters 20, 21*

Table 6.7 The mode of *régulation*

Founding research	Research development	Current areas of interest
Move from competitive *régulation* to a mono-polistic form of *régulation* after 1945:	International diversity in post-war modes of *régulation*: the examples of the United States and France are not universal. *Chapter 30*	Rhineland *régulation* compared with Anglo-Saxon *régulation*: does financial instability encourage bad forms of *régulation*? *Chapters 30, 34*
1 Credit money as legal tender. *Chapter 7*	Search for anthropological foundations of money. *Chapter 30*	The relation between credit and financial speculation. *Chapters 30, 34*
2 Wage compromise on the sharing of productivity. *Chapter 9*	Small-scale open econo-mies show institutional-isation but not Fordism. *Chapter 33*	Can a new social democratic model be reestablished at the European level? *Chapter 33*
3 Oligopolistic compet-ition on a national basis. *Chapter 13*	Eastern Europe: *régulation* by rationing. *Chapter 35*	Analysing the processes in the establishment of a market and democracy. *Chapter 36*
4 A stable international regime under the aegis of the United States. *Chapter 14*	LDCs: agriculture–industry relations and an informal market. *Chapter 37*	Accounting for differences in the Third World. (Korea is not Brazil.) *Chapter 37*
5 Embedded state: Ford/ Beveridge/Keynes. *Chapters 15, 16*		
A gradual alteration of institutional forms: in France there are three forms of *régulation* (early, competitive and monopolistic) over the course of two centuries. *Chapter 2*	A loss of coherence by monopolistic *régulation*: internationalisation, financialisation, tertiarisation and new technological wave. *Chapters 8, 14*	The absence of an inter-national regime and financial innovations destabilise most of the existing national *régulations*, including the most efficient (Japan). *Chapter 34*
A quarter century separates the change of institutional forms from the establishment of Fordism. *Chapter 2*	Twenty years of creation and destruction of institutional forms and yet still no *general* emergence from the crisis of Fordism. *Chapters 30, 32, 33*	An attempt to formalise the constitution of new *régulations*: convention theory, evolutionist theory, disequilibrium and power. *Chapters 39, 40, 41*

development likely to succeed Fordism in theoretical terms. Field studies have contributed to recognition of the diversity of organisational forms and have forced regulationists to consider the interest of evolutionary models as well as sharing research projects with conventionalists.

Thus *régulation* theory as it reaches the age of majority no longer has its original form or structure, as is shown by a retrospective presentation of the notions of *mode of régulation* (Table 6.7) and even more so by *crises* (Table 6.8). It is for the reader to decide whether this is for better or for worse.

Table 6.8 Crises

Founding research	Research developments	Current areas of interest
Distinction between a crisis *within a mode of régulation* (minor crisis) and a crisis of the mode of *régulation* (major crisis). *Chapter 5*	A classification of crises as external disturbance, expression of *régulation*, crisis of *régulation*, crisis of the mode of development or crisis of a mode of production. *Chapter 5*	Major crises are the loss of structural stability of a representative dynamic model of *régulation*. *Chapter 23*
The form of crises depends on the configurations of institutional forms. *Chapter 2*	Two confirmations: 1 the specificity of Soviet crises. 2 the variety of crises in Latin America (for example, Venezuela). *Chapters 35, 36, 37*	The notion of a major crisis can be extended to the sector level: for example to agriculture. The Soviet collapse as a crisis in the mode of production. *Chapters 28, 36*
The beginning of a crisis in American Fordism from the late 1960s. *Chapter 31*	Although they are propagated by the international regime, the chronology and nature of crises vary greatly among OECD countries. *Chapters 31, 32, 33, 34*	Formalisation of the endogenous alterations of structures leading to a major crisis: endometabolism. The outlook for accumulation regimes offering an alternative to Fordism. *Chapters 23, 31, 34*
The inflationary and non-cumulative crisis of Fordism is not a repetition of the 1929 crisis. *Chapters 7, 30*	Confirmation of the diagnosis of a structural crisis: gradual erosion of institutional forms without any viable accumulation regime, except in the United States. *Chapters 30, 32, 33*	Reasons for the inertia of institutional forms and conventions: 1 A classification of the factors of change. 2 An explanation of the duration of the present crisis. *Chapter 42*

Theorising, formalising, comparing and historicising

Nevertheless, one might well believe that greater conceptual precision and an expansion of methods and tools of analysis is generally beneficial for an understanding of a structural crisis that is far more complex than previous crises. This is the project of this work whose structure, as outlined in the introduction, is composed of six parts.

Part II presents developments in the concept of institutional forms in greater detail while offering some interpretations of the transformations at work in the major OECD economies. Its watchword is *more effective theorising*! Part III argues for the virtues of formalisation, which should not be confused with theorisation, but which can help in verifying the coherence and rigour of its basic reasoning. Furthermore, *formalising* enables the propagation of theories that are subject to this requirement. The new tools proposed should be of interest to the reader, since they concern the endogenous nature of the shift from growth to crisis, as well as the strategic aspects of structural crises.

Comparisons enable an emphasis on the general features of today's crisis in addition to its specific aspects. One of its major novelties is certainly linked with the redeployment of different institutional forms in areas that are no longer restricted to the nation state: financial markets are tending to become global, but factors favouring competition remain mainly local. Part IV proposes a variety of approaches to this as yet unresolved question. In Part V, these theoretical advances are recombined to explain the surprising inertia affecting the modifying and change of institutional forms, depending on the idiosyncrasies of each nation. Perhaps the best characterisation of *régulation* theory is its project to *historicise* economic analysis and to develop an institutional macroeconomics.

It should be recognised that while *régulation* theory provides a set of new answers, many major facts are still without sufficiently developed explanations. Part VI takes stock of similarities with other research programmes. It is therefore dedicated to specialists who subscribe to the motto 'search and search again!' Their objective is to understand changes in economies endowed with a wealth of institutions.

Part II

The five institutional forms revisited

7 Money and credit in *régulation* theory

Robert Guttmann

Neoclassical theory, the dominant paradigm in economics, treats money as a good with unique demand and supply functions. This characterisation separates money from the rest of the economy to preserve (essentially non-monetary) equilibrium conditions. Starting with Marx's *Capital* and Keynes's *General Theory*, heterodox alternatives have all understood that money is directly linked with economic activity and that its presence in production and exchange is incompatible with equilibrium. The Marxist approach (De Brunhoff, 1971, 1979) analyses money as the quintessential form of capital. Post-Keynesians (Davidson, 1978) emphasise the strategic role of money as the most liquid asset. *Régulation* theory has tried to connect these two traditions and then apply the synthesis to a systematic analysis of the monetary process in advanced capitalist economies with highly developed financial institutions and markets. This effort has given us a new look at money's role in our society.

Money as a social institution

The major contribution of *régulation* theory to monetary theory lies in its understanding of money as a social institution. Once we look at money that way, we need to ask ourselves how its defining features (its forms, the modalities of its issue, the dynamic of its circulation, the basis of its valuation) have changed over time and whether these changes have qualitatively altered the behaviour of our economic system. Regulationists approached these questions in the context of their discussion of accumulation regimes. That core concept of *régulation* theory (Boyer, 1986a) describes historically specific conditions which permit the economic system, with its current state of technological know-how and social organisation, to reproduce itself in relatively stable fashion. Such stability presumes an institutional framework capable of channelling potentially destabilising forces towards a modicum of balance. *Régulation* theory considers money a key component of any such framework and thus as one of five institutional forms defining a given accumulation regime, together with competition, the socio-technical system covering all aspects of the capital–labour relation, forms of state intervention, and arrangements governing international economic relations.

If money is to act as an institutional form, it must by definition play a major role in shaping what in *régulation* theory is termed the mode of regulation of an accumulation regime. From this perspective money is important to the extent that the modalities of its creation and circulation help determine the growth pattern of an economy. Implied here is a rather broad notion of money's endogeneity that has shaped the regulationists' thinking on the subject in two important ways.

Once money is conceptualised as endogenous in the sense that its issue is directly tied to economic activity, it obviously becomes important to clarify this linkage as precisely as possible. For this reason *régulation* theory has put a lot of emphasis on analysing the prevailing monetary standards of a given accumulation regime, focusing here in particular on the forms of money and the conditions of their issue, the organisation of their coexistence through a payment system, and their circuits of circulation. Changes in these dimensions of a monetary standard play a crucial role in the transition from one accumulation regime to another (Boyer and Coriat, 1984; Boyer, 1993).

The operation of any monetary standard is subject to specific institutional arrangements. These comprise central bank management of money creation ('monetary policy'), government regulation of the banking sector ('financial policy'), lender-of-last-resort mechanisms to contain financial crises, and rules for the transfer of funds between countries. Together these arrangements make up what regulationists call the monetary regime. Each accumulation regime has its own specific monetary regime (Guttmann, 1989). The transformation of an accumulation regime typically coincides with major reforms of the monetary regime, as happened in the case of the United States during and after the Civil War (1863–79) or in the wake of the Great Depression (1933–5).

The *régulation* theory of credit money

Regulationists built their approach to money on the post-Keynesian concept of a monetary production economy. But in contrast to the post-Keynesians (Lavoie, 1984) they use a broader notion of money's endogeneity and focus more on its institutional characteristics. These differences have enabled *régulation* theory to clarify the nature of credit money by emphasising several key features of this contemporary form of money (Guttmann, 1994; Aglietta and Orléan, 1998).

Credit money must be created and settled outside the market place, in the banking system, to operate effectively as means of payment. Its transfer into the market place occurs through a loan, and it is only when the borrower decides to spend the loan that newly issued cheques become actual money. Such cheques settle payment obligations between buyer and seller through third parties, their respective banks. Those banks in turn transfer funds ('reserves') to each other through accounts held at the central bank. This pyramid of money transfers requires a payments system, which must also be organised so as to guarantee convertibility between the different tokens of credit money. As long as the payments system runs smoothly, payment commitments arising in the circuits of exchange, production and finance are settled by a parallel circulation of funds in the banking system. It is precisely by operating the nation's payments system that a central bank has any kind of control over the money creation process by private banks. In recent years, however, a technological revolution has opened the way for new and privately run transfer and settlement mechanisms (e.g. electronic fund transfers, automated clearing houses) which compete directly with the payments services offered by the central bank.

By manipulating bank reserves in the payments system, the central bank exercises a degree of control over the ability of private banks to create new money when they loan out their excess reserves. But the central bank controls neither the willingness of banks to make loans nor the public demand for bank credit, the two other determinants of the money creation process. In that sense it is fair to say that the money supply cannot be strictly regulated by the state's monetary authorities. Instead the issue of credit money is driven by the private profit motive of banks and their customers. Since both lenders and borrowers face a trade-off between profitability and safety, the supply of private bank money tends to exhibit a pro-cyclical pattern. Private bank money is also subject to continual innovation, with much of the product development designed to escape the control tools of the central bank (e.g. borrowed bank liabilities, 'near money' deposits, Euro-currencies, 'electronic money'). These dynamic properties of private bank money tend to prevent standard policy rules, such as the 'quantity rule' of the monetarists (Friedman, 1968) or the 'price rule' of supply-siders (Miles, 1984), from working well in practice. The Keynesian prescription of low interest rates (Keynes, 1936) may prove ineffective during periods of financial instability or depressed expectations. Central banks must therefore extend their management of credit money beyond controlling bank reserves and include lender-of-last-resort interventions to contain financial crises as well as regulatory restraints to cope with innovation (Aglietta, 1991).

The linkage of money creation with bank credit has created a debt economy in which excess spending gets automatically monetised. Regulationists (Aglietta, 1976, 1980; Lipietz, 1979) have shown how this feature of credit money played a crucial role in the post-war boom by giving industry the funds needed to operate mass-production technologies, facilitating purchases of consumer durables with considerable multiplier effects (e.g. cars, homes), financing budget deficits, and transferring capital from surplus nations to deficit nations. Low interest rates helped sustain this stimulative capacity of credit money for decades.

By boosting sales volumes and making loans more accessible to cover temporary gaps in cash flow, endogenous credit money had the great advantage of increasing the spending capacity of individual agents. When the post-war boom ended in the late 1960s, this ability of credit money to relax the monetary constraint of households and firms moderated the subsequent crisis. Whereas earlier structural crises (e.g. 1873–96; 1914–39) had always ended in severe depressions, this time around we endured less brutal stagflation.

Consequences of the new monetary regime

A major contribution of *régulation* theory has been to analyse the acceleration of inflationary pressures during the 1970s as an expression of structural crisis (Boyer and Mistral, 1978; Lipietz, 1979, 1983). This approach proved much more useful than the traditional concepts of 'demand-pull' inflation or 'cost-push' inflation, since it managed to link increases in nominal price levels with the deterioration of underlying accumulation conditions in production.

Credit money played a crucial role in this linkage by providing continuous debt financing which enabled individual agents to maintain spending levels in the face of income erosion. In this way private losses, which during the regime of commodity money (the 'gold standard') had to be borne directly, could now be transferred to anyone using the national currency through an inflationary process of purely nominal accumulation gains and income redistribution (Guttmann, 1984). Such loss socialisation prevented the massive destruction of capital and asset deflation of earlier depressions, but only at the expense of a gradual devaluation of money.

While credit money thus transformed the dynamic of structural crisis, intensifying stagflation in turn had a negative feedback on the stability of that money form. As the inevitable tensions between stagnation and inflation fed through the monetary circuits, institutional arrangements regulating the issue and circulation of credit money became considerably more fragile. One problem was that inflation pushed the prices of goods and services up while at the same time reducing the value of financial assets. These opposite price movements redistributed income from creditors to debtors, a transfer made worse by central bank policies that kept interest rates lagging behind inflation rates. Debtors often added to the problem by borrowing more to maintain spending levels in the face of slowing income growth. Eventually many debtors ended up with uncomfortably large debt servicing charges whose fixed-cost nature made them vulnerable during any downturn of the economy. Inflation also created much greater uncertainty about future costs and revenues. As investors responded with shorter time horizons, speculation displaced long-term investment. *Régulation* theory has analysed this propensity to speculative activity as a key expression of structural crisis in a regime of credit money (Aglietta and Orlean,

1982; Guttmann, 1994), thus moving us beyond the post-Keynesian notion of financial instability as a mostly cyclical phenomenon (Minsky 1982; Wolfson, 1986).

These stagflation-induced contradictions in the relation between finance and industry destroyed the institutional arrangements of the post-war regime of credit money. In August 1971 the gold-backed dollar standard known as Bretton Woods collapsed amid massive speculation against the dollar, with government regulation of currency prices giving way to market-determined ('flexible') exchange rates shortly thereafter. The deregulation of credit money was taken one step further in 1979/80 when global disintermediation of funds out of traditional low-yield instruments forced central banks to abandon their traditional commitment to low interest rates.

The monetary regime in transition

The end of price regulation in the credit system, freeing first exchange rates and then interest rates from government control, changed the dynamic of the structural crisis. This movement toward market determination of currency prices and credit terms reshaped investment priorities and accelerated industrial restructuring. In that sense, volatile exchange rates and high interest rates became a new 'mode of *régulation*', comparable to the price wars and debt-deflation adjustments of the competitive accumulation regime (Guttmann, 1990).

Key to this new 'mode of *régulation*' is the effect that the deregulation of money's prices has had on the relationship between industrial capital and financial capital. By abandoning their commitment to low interest rates, governments in effect removed the pro-debtor bias of the post-war regime of credit money. To the extent that nominal interest rates could thus rise far above inflation rates, producers were forced to be far more selective in their industrial investment projects and to keep tighter control of other costs. This austerity was reinforced by flexible exchange rates, which intensified the external constraint on national economies. Any government effort at stimulative fiscal and monetary policies now ran the risk of triggering massive speculative attacks on that country's currency, followed by drastic policy reversals. The huge short-term movements in foreign exchange markets, exceeding US $1,000 billion per day, forced heavy doses of fiscal and monetary restraint even on those countries forming a currency bloc based on fixed exchange rates, as evidenced by the deflationary bias of the European Monetary System.

Those consequences of financial deregulation broke the inflationary momentum of the 1970s and accelerated the pace of industrial restructuring on a global scale. But as long as interest rates exceeded growth rates, many debtors faced the prospect of growing financial fragility. This dangerous situation extended beyond the private sector to the public sector, where the cumulative effect of historically high interest rates threatened exploding structural budget deficits, with profound consequences for the fiscal viability of the 'welfare state' created after the Second World War. That imbalance in the relation between interest rates and growth rates also encouraged short-term speculation at the expense of long-term industrial development, a troubling trend that was reinforced by increased price volatility in financial markets and by such key innovations in the credit system as derivatives.

Towards a reversal of deregulation policies

Governments will have to reverse this situation by reducing the volatility of financial markets and assuring a more balanced allocation of credit. These objectives require major changes in monetary policy and financial regulations (Guttmann, 1994). In this endeavour policy-makers will find themselves constrained by the rapidly progressing globalisation of financial capital, which assures capital flight out of countries with comparatively low interest rates and/or tough regulatory practices. As long as governments must compete with each other to attract an adequate share of increasingly mobile and global capital, they have very little room for individual initiatives to stabilise the monetary regime within their national economy. The problem of stabilising the credit system and containing the growing dominance of financial capital needs to be addressed on the international level, through multilateral initiatives of policy co-ordination and standardisation of financial regulations (Chapter 8; Aglietta and de Boissieu, 1998).

This is not to say that the future evolution of monetary regimes will be entirely global in nature. Local differentiation will still exist in the twenty-first century. Money, for so long at the core of state power, is after all an institutional form whose structural dimensions have developed on a strictly national level over centuries and tend to change only gradually. That characteristic of sluggishness is likely to persist despite the growing globalisation of financial capital and the spread of stateless money forms (e.g. Euro-currencies, European Currency Units, Special Drawing Rights).

The methodological instrumentarium of *régulation* theory is particularly well equipped to analyse the tensions between national specificities of monetary regimes and their global convergence tendencies (Aglietta and Moutot, 1993a; Boyer, 1999a). In this respect future research should concentrate on the following areas:

1   The proliferation of new money forms and their effects on monetary policy.
2   The national and international dimensions of lender-of-last-resort interventions to manage financial instability.
3   The consequences of the gradual privatisation of payments systems and securitisation of credit for the financial structure of industrialised countries.

Studying these questions will surely also open the way to new advances in monetary theory, especially concerning the structure of interest rates, the velocity of money and the role of financial markets in industrial development. Theoretical clarification of these issues is essential if policymakers are to develop the kind of policy tools and regulatory mechanisms which would give the newly emerging accumulation regime a relatively stable and well balanced monetary regime.

8 The international monetary system

Michel Aglietta

The regulating controls of the international monetary system (IMS) are the most complex of capitalist economies, and are also the most vulnerable to change. Money plays a crucial role in the economic system. It can be a source of political antagonism or a means of pacification, depending on whether monetary regulations are resisted and rejected as being unjust or inefficient, or whether they are generally accepted. The vulnerability of the international monetary system stems from the absence of an indisputable conductor in the concert of nations, since there is no supranational sovereign authority to guarantee money. After the end of the implicit monetary constitution of the gold standard that lasted for some thirty years, money was nationalised and national currencies were thus subordinated to the objectives of political authorities. International monetary control became problematic. Despite the broadmindedness of its promoters, the Bretton Woods accord that lasted for a quarter of a century eventually became a hegemonic system, legitimised by the priority of collective security against the Cold War threat. Its stability experienced devastating tensions in the late 1960s when the US government exploited its dominant position in an attempt to avoid difficult domestic decisions. Since then, disturbances in monetary relations have been caused by international upheavals (Chapter 7). These disturbances have not, however, degenerated into the conflicts of the 1930s. Financial interdependence has continued to grow with surprising energy. In the rapidly transforming world economy, we are participating in a search if not for a new monetary constitution, then at least for new multilateral co-responsibilities.

Theory: the organisation of international monetary systems

The usual method of analysing the viability of an international monetary system is to refer to Mundell's triangle (Figure 8.1). Three organising principles define the structure of an IMS. These are the degree of restriction on foreign exchange rate changes (from completely flexible exchange rates to rigorously fixed exchange systems), the degree of capital mobility

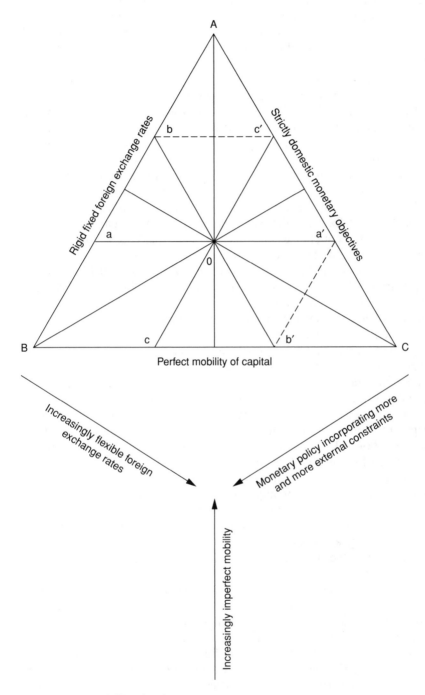

Figure 8.1 Mundell's triangle

(ranging from no mobility to perfect mobility) and the sensitivity of monetary policy objectives to external constraints (from entirely discretionary monetary policies to a common monetary policy). The combination of these criteria is represented by an equilateral triangle because they are not independent of one another. A crucial lesson of international monetary economics is the following theorem of impossibility: it is impossible to combine fixed foreign exchange rates, perfect capital mobility and independent monetary policies. However, the restriction that results from this is minimal. According to Mundell's theorem, each country is free to choose its international insertion at any point in the triangle. The IMS is simply the collection of points thus chosen by different countries.

However, this approach is not enough to determine the IMS by itself. Once government decisions have been made, the resulting more or less flexible exchange rates are assumed to be in equilibrium. The implicit postulate is therefore that the expectations of private agents are co-ordinated by government choices. Yet many actual experiences, from the giant fluctuations in the dollar between 1973 and 1987 to the foreign exchange crises in the European Monetary System (EMS) in 1992 and 1993 and the re-evaluations of the yen, indicate that the discordant objectives of governments lead to unstable foreign exchange markets. Furthermore, the hypothesis that governments choose the combination of criteria which optimises their preferences independently of choices made by other governments does not take into account the collective good character of money. The rules of the IMS extend the common services of money to international transactions. Maintaining a viable IMS therefore entails a collective advantage that governments wish to ensure because they are always acting in a context of strategic interdependence. But this implies accepting the principles of collective action based on the structural criteria described above. This results in the types of IMS represented in Figure 8.1 by three lozenges with a common apex at the centre of the triangle and with a shared apex at each of the three apexes of the triangle.

The tension for governments between preserving the common services of world money and their own national preferences for macroeconomic freedom of action is the source of a profound ambivalence in regard to money. Liquidity and financial freedom beyond all frontiers are the essential attributes of the international dynamics of capitalism. These qualities of world money depend on economies of scale and scope: the depth of foreign exchange markets, the diversity of financial instruments, the robustness of market makers and the effectiveness of prudential control. They encourage a tendency to concentrate the functions of world money in a few currencies, or even in a single key currency. This is the IMS infrastructure. But liquidity and financial freedom also depend on political determinants: market opinions on future economic policy, government rules defining the convertibility of currencies, tolerance of capital mobility and future commitments to it. These political arrangements form the IMS info-structure, on which private traders base their expectations. The assertiveness of domestic priorities within the competition between nations gives rise to a tendency to decentralise the info-structure. The IMS is therefore shaped by countervailing forces. Principles of collective action must mediate between these forces, establishing compromises to prevent currency competition from presenting a danger to the system through the effects of self-fulfilling speculative attacks.

The optimum compromise evolves over time without creating discord between two elements of a viable IMS. The two elements are the predictability of government actions for private agents, since the stability of the exchange rate depends on it, and flexibility in the adjustments that reduce, or at least limit, real economic differences between countries. Principles of collective action influence the two criteria for the system's viability through the degree of symmetry and the degree of co-responsibility. Indeed, the degree of symmetry determines the distribution of obligations related to the preservation of the common advantages of world money. When the rule of collective action is symmetrical, the obligations of national monetary authorities are similar; when it is hierarchical, these obligations differ. The country with the key currency assumes the obligation of supplying international liquidity for the whole system. The other countries assume the obligation of adjusting to a more or less rigorous rule of foreign exchange. The degree of co-responsibility determines the influence of the system over governments' decisions designed to attain their own objectives. At one extreme, countries may submit to the constituent rules of the system through automatic adjustments. At the opposite extreme, governments may try to make discretionary decisions prevail, with flexible exchange rates determining the effective division of obligations *a posteriori*. Between these two extremes, different degrees of co-responsibility are possible, more or less *ad hoc* and occasional, or more or less continuous and institutionalised. Table 8.1 illustrates a theoretical representation of some international monetary arrangements according to the regulating principles of collective action.

The table shows that there are more historical examples of the intermediary configurations. This is not simply a matter of chance. There is a trade-off between the flexibility of real exchange rate adjustments and the predictability of economic policy with respect to the degree of rigidity in the nominal exchange rate rule. For a given degree of rigidity in an exchange rate regime, the trade-off is improved if adjustments are more automatic or more hierarchical. On the other hand, it deteriorates if asymmetries of structures or shocks between countries give rise to doubts about the permanence of the foreign exchange rate regime. The tighter the exchange rate rule the more difficult real adjustments are. This relation deteriorates even more when a hierarchical system assigns adjustments to subordinate countries and automatic mechanisms concentrate the costs of adjustment on domestic economic variables. Since the rigidity of foreign

Table 8.1 Comparison of international monetary arrangements according to the principles of collective action

Sharing obligations / Govt conduct	Strong symmetry	Intermediate asymmetry	Strong hierarchy
Automatic mechanism	Ideal gold standard	Historical sterling gold standard	Mark zone
Intermediary co-responsibility	Flexible foreign exchange rates with target zones	Bretton Woods (1958–71) EMS (1983–89) Tripartite agreement (1936–39)	Bretton Woods (1947–58)
Discretion	Pure flexible foreign exchange rates	Floating foreign exchange rates with a predominant dollar (1973–85)	Floating of the Canadian/US dollar (1950–62)

exchange rate rules influences the predictability of collective actions and their ability to reduce real differences in opposite directions, the viability of the IMS is not determined solely by the rigidity of the exchange rate regime. Except in the case of very firm commitments by the monetary authorities with respect to automatic adjustments, or of a hierarchical structure with very solid foundations, extreme regimes are too unstable or too rigid. Intermediate regimes are more robust because they are better suited to smooth development. By contrast, the Bretton Woods system became too rigid because governments clung to the fixed exchange rate at a time when greater flexibility was required.

Politics: adapting the IMS to more symmetrical regulations

For the last quarter of a century, international relations have been globalised under the persistent influence of two strong tendencies: capital mobility and the emergence of new economic powers in the competitive field. With regard to capital mobility, discussed by Robert Guttmann in Chapter 7, we shall concentrate on its impact on the relation between national currencies.

Competition between currencies is a good illustration of the functional autonomy of the IMS. Despite capital mobility that opens the way to the internationalisation of currencies, and despite the chronic instability of its exchange rate, the dollar has retained its primacy. Its use in different monetary functions has developed slowly and consistently. The lack of transparency of Japanese financial markets and company business practices (billing foreign trade in dollars) have prevented the internationalisation of the yen. The international role of the Deutschmark only really took off with the financing needs created by the unification of Germany. The potential competitiveness of this currency essentially depended on political considerations: the vicissitudes in the realisation of the EMU and the success of the transition of Eastern Europe. Only the euro can become a currency as liquid as the dollar. Not only financial instability but also monetary instability would result from a strong substitutability of currencies.

This observation directs us towards the second major tendency that can transform the IMS irreversibly, beyond the constant supple adaptations linked with financial liberalisation. This tendency is the regionalisation of the world economy, under the pressure of new economic powers.

A political reconfiguration of the world is at work, reinstituting the central role of geography in economic relations (Chapter 14). If capital mobility is causing the infrastructure of the IMS to develop only very gradually, regional groupings are modifying its info-structure. The challenge of a multipolar world economy for the coherence and viability of the IMS derives from the heterogeneous aspects affected by the forces of regional attraction. Business trade, capital inflows and growth dynamics do not coincide with zones of monetary integration, except in the European Union, which is a unique case and which still has many unresolved difficulties. The world economy is not moving towards a tri-polar system, but rather towards the overlapping of poorly articulated multipolar arenas. In these multipolar arenas major continental powers (China, India, Brazil soon and Russia, when it returns to an influential position) will exert their economic weight long before they are implicated in monetary co-responsibility.

Taking into account the characteristics described above, it is possible to outline the consequences of the two major tendencies of financial liberalisation and regionalisation of the world economy for the *régulation* of the IMS.

When exchange rate rules were definitively relaxed in March 1973, American monetary policy no longer acted as an anchor for world prices. The system began to evolve towards greater symmetry in the sense that each country followed a national monetary policy tilted towards domestic preferences. Exchange rates against the dollar tended to be influenced by inflation differentials and the structure of foreign debts and assets. In the short term, because of overshooting in the dollar exchange rate caused by speculative dynamics, the governments of other important OECD countries sought to reduce these fluctuations through interventions with partially sterilised dollars. There then ensued a co-variation in the growth of the money supply in the OECD zone: depreciation of the dollar against other currencies and runaway monetary growth in the late securities, a dramatic monetary slowdown and dollar appreciation in the early

1980s. This monetary dysfunction demonstrated clearly that workable co-responsibility had not replaced the leadership of the United States despite the virtual symmetry permitted by floating foreign exchange rates. The discordance between discretionary monetary policies and the accumulation of deficits and surpluses in the balance of payments perpetuated the dilemma of the dollar standard beyond the Bretton Woods system, modifying its form of expression. Lack of international liquidity was no longer a problem. But countries suffered from the dilemma through two possible disadvantages: the loss of domestic monetary control or excessive variation in the exchange rate of their currency against the dollar. The exacerbation of this dilemma, under the effect of generalised capital mobility, culminated in the vertiginous appreciation of the dollar from the autumn of 1984 to the winter of 1985.

The distortion of foreign exchange rates eventually aroused the concern of governments, provoking a political response by the G7 in the Plaza Agreement and the Louvre Accord. These arrangements sought to put flexible exchange rates under multilateral surveillance. A triumvirate (the United States, Japan and Germany) apparently gave birth to a tri-polar system, with other OECD countries involved in privileged exchange relations with one of these currencies or a basket of them.

The minimal co-operation included implicit target zones whose central rates were secret and revisable, depending on the development of the founding members of the group. Wide and porous margins of fluctuation were tolerated. A further step was taken towards symmetry at the time of the concerted public interventions to defuse the foreign exchange crises between the dollar and the other two principal currencies. These interventions implied that each central bank must borrow or hold reserves of the currencies of its partners.

The advantage of increased symmetry in a fluctuating foreign exchange regime, at least in principle, is disconnection of the rates of interest, allowing the desynchronisation of the business cycles and creating a source of greater world economic stability. The advantage of increased co-responsibility is that it limits foreign exchange rate distortions. The tendency of the dollar to depreciate *vis-à-vis* the yen and the mark appears to have ceased since 1987. However, the development of more ambitious co-operation in the IMS (symmetry and co-responsibility) remained fragile, intermittent and not extended to domestic policies. It has not generated a collective learning. Since co-responsibility is limited to managing exchange rates without implications for domestic monetary policies, short-term exchange rates remain too volatile for G7 interventions to stabilise market expectations apart from reversing excessive movements of the dollar. Finally, G7 was created for and by large developed countries; it cannot therefore act as a macroeconomic governance system with regard to problems presented by the emergence of the new major powers.

Financial globalisation and the formation of regional groups exert greater forces than the monetary arrangements that came out of the breakdown of the Bretton Woods system. In the 1990s, financial globalisation has extended into the long-term capital market. After the spectacular consequences of capital mobility in Europe in the EMS crises, the spread of financial tensions to bond markets in the spring of 1994 was largely disconnected from the fundamentals of the economies experiencing it. The contamination of long-term capital markets by waves of speculation calls into doubt the efficiency of capital allocation, in other words, the main argument in favour of financial liberalisation. To preserve what free trade ideology considers an element in improving well-being, governments of the main OECD countries have to recognise that financial stability demands more of multilateral co-responsibility than simply managing occasional foreign exchange crises. The external effects of market expectations in the possible discordance of economic policy are becoming stronger and more unpredictable. The criteria of predictability have to be increased since the continuous flow of international investments towards emerging markets is an essential element in the formation of a truly global economy. The form in which this demand could be met will not be a dramatic advance in institutionalised co-operation. It is more reasonable to predict tacit agreement to respect international standards. The deeper significance of this development would be to depoliticise money in order to reclaim the collective advantage of a stable IMS. A more significant innovation than the creation of new international institutions or the return to fixed exchange rates is the upcoming extension of the principle of the independence of central banks. Because they are able to pursue compatible objectives with a long-term perspective, independent central banks make it possible to imagine a co-responsible use of sovereign monetary policies without explicit co-ordination. This approach could be reinforced by more frequent international consultation, judicious communication about markets so as to facilitate the co-ordination of foreign exchange rate expectations via benchmarks indicated by the authorities, more thorough prudential arrangements and energetic intervention at opportune moments.

Even if a kernel of monetary stability in the OECD zone is necessary in order to avoid the worst disorders of financial liberalisation, it is far from sufficient given the increasing commercial and financial importance of countries outside this zone, whose exchange rates are becoming increasingly important. The G7 is not an adequate forum for treating the international problems posed by relations between heterogeneous regional groups. However, if regional areas must remain open – an essential condition for improving the well-being of the world economy – it is necessary to go beyond mere trade agreements. Massive inflows of investment in so-called 'emerging' countries will make them financial centres. This implies responsibilities with regard to exchange rates that may prove to be incompatible with the deliberately non-co-operative exchange rate policies that some countries have maintained so as to maximise their comparative advantages. But if multilateral surveillance of exchange rates is to include these new capitalist countries, problems arise, since this type of surveillance can be directed only by a common development policy. So far no development policy has led to a shared, coherent approach. This is why regional groupings may provide an answer to the inability of principles of collective action to take into account too many different interests and to influence the world economy. But, at the same time, these groupings give political force to a wider range of disparate priorities. This may greatly weaken the global viability of the IMS, like its legitimacy for those who are excluded from the monetary consultations of the G7. Thus the renewal of a global monetary role for the IMF, in agreement with the aim of its founders but in a geopolitical environment that has been utterly transformed, must eventually occur. If the IMF were given a mission by its General Assembly to explore the means and criteria of multilateral surveillance of exchange rates, perhaps that would be the starting point for realistic reform of the IMS. It could open the way to a system designed to regulate a truly global economy.

9 Perspectives on the wage–labour nexus

Robert Boyer

In standard economic theory the labour market is no different from the product market. It is only a few imperfections or asymmetries that prevent the law of supply and demand from being fully applicable, and these are the flaws which policies towards flexibility must try to eliminate (OECD, 1994). John Maynard Keynes suggested that the labour market is not in fact a market since the nominal wage is the result of negotiations between wage earners and companies and the volume of employment is determined by the level of effective demand, which in turn is governed by future expectations. In orthodox Marxist theory, labour is a special commodity since it alone creates a surplus, but the value of labour power is governed by the relentless competition exercised by the army of unemployed workers.

For *régulation* theory the wage–labour nexus is defined by the complementarity of the institutions framing the employment contract and their compatibility with the current mode of *régulation*. As a result, the wage–labour nexus varies historically and geographically, with configurations that differ according to economic performance. In the 1990s there was a great transformation of the post-Second World War institutional order, which is the origin of unemployment, the financing problems of social security insurance and, more generally, difficulties in returning to strong growth in Europe (Petit, 1985, 1998a, 1999).

Exchange relations and the wage–labour nexus: a hidden dialectic

In a structuralist reading a capitalist economy is defined as the conjunction of an exchange relation and a production relation that simultaneously oppose and merge into a single system of wage earners and capitalists. The contribution of *régulation* theory is to have brought to the forefront the idea that, in spite of its contradictions, the remarkable resilience of the capitalist mode of production is a result of the *adaptation* and *transformation* of the monetary regime and competition in addition to the wage–labour nexus. The wage–labour nexus* refers to the process of socialisation of production activity under capitalism; it is what becomes the wage-earning class. A *form of wage–labour nexus* is defined by the set of legal and institutional conditions that govern the use of wage-earning labour as the workers' mode of existence. The wage-earning class has developed dramatically because the wage–labour nexus has constantly adapted itself to social conflicts and to the constraints imposed by accumulation.

As a result it has structurally complementary* relations with the two other institutional forms, which are the monetary regime (Chapter 7) and the forms of competition* (Chapter 13). If monetary constraints are stringent, as, for example, under the gold standard, the wage–labour nexus must be flexible. On the other hand, when political movements impose a codification of direct wages and benefits, an accommodating monetary regime and oligopolistic competition must validate the capital-labour compromise (Boyer, 1993). The so-called Kondratief long waves could even be interpreted as expressions of the oscillation between these two configurations.

The notion of a wage–labour nexus moves away from pure economics to place wage, productivity and employment determinants in an institutional context that reflects previous conflicts and structural crises. Following Karl Polanyi (1946), it is clear that neither money nor labour is a true commodity, since both are in fact the conditions of possibility for a market economy. The rules governing work are therefore no accident, introducing so many frictions to adjustments that are otherwise perfect. Instead they guarantee the viability of what can be called, for short, the 'labour market'. This framework of analysis has a second consequence: if money tends to be governed by principles of competition with other foreign currencies, the resulting instability also compromises the viability of the wage–labour nexus (Boyer, 1993, 1999a).

Many theoretical approaches: the regulationist hologram

The wage–labour nexus was originally part of the Marxist theory of exploitation, conforming with value theory (Chapter 4). But analysis of American capitalism over the long term (Aglietta, 1976) emphasises the extent of the changes which have taken place in consumption norms, which are supposedly invariable in traditional and even in modern Marxist analysis (Roemer, 1981). There was the race between the capitalist quest for relative surplus value thanks to increases in productivity in terms of wage goods, which lower the value of labour power and the demands of wage earners for improved living conditions. This initial contribution of *régulation* theory consists in making consumption norms endogenous, just like production norms. Their rapid and virtually synchronous development offers a precise definition of Fordism, as the articulation of a specific wage–labour nexus and accumulation regime.

Henceforth the nominal wage acquires a new status, in the field of the exoteric economy constructed on the lines of the esoteric economy governing value (Lipietz, 1983). Under certain conditions of competition and monetary creation, increases in the nominal wage may introduce transformations in the life style of workers. This is all the more the case if collective conventions codify, for example, a process of automatic revision in terms of the costs of living adjustment (COLA): the real wage then escapes the direct forces of the labour market, at least momentarily (Boyer, 1978).

It then becomes possible to define the wage-earning class apart from the Marxist theory of exploitation. Wage earners are defined as individuals who do not have access to credit and who are consequently unable to set themselves up as autonomous producers (Benetti and Cartelier, 1980; Roemer, 1981; Aglietta and Orléan, 1998). Thus, at the most fundamental level, within a capitalist economy, the wage–labour nexus and the monetary regime are closely connected. Contemporary events confirm that the revenge of creditors on debtors (Aglietta and Orléan, 1982), when extremely high interest rates weaken companies, forces or causes considerable wage concessions (Boyer, 1986b).

Even if labour has a price, its supply is not necessarily governed by pure market logic, if only because the main principle of demographic reproduction is not capitalist profit. In fact, labour is produced in the family, school and any other institution that contributes to the socialisation of individuals. Also, once the wage-earning class becomes the dominant social form, it is not surprising that during major conflicts, workers demand the principle of social security insurance, possibly collectively financed and organised. The same movement which institutionalises the formation of the direct wage establishes the bases for the conditions of the modern welfare state (Chapter 12).

The Fordist wage–labour nexus

The wage–labour nexus is one of the basic conditions for the long-term viability of Fordism, founded on the lifetime insertion of wage earners in capitalist societies. This transformation occurs all the more logically when democratic regimes prevail with a political arena capable of imposing new obligations on private accumulation (Chapter 16). As a result of this process, wage earners are partially liberated from the risks of unemployment, sickness, disability or lack of income during retirement (Saillard, 1995). These are the elements of benefits that affect the life style and that also change the dynamics of the nominal wage, which becomes less sensitive to economic cycles (Bowles and Boyer, 1995).

The growth of a wage-earning class is accompanied by an increased division of labour, evident in the dynamics of technical change (Boyer and Schmeder, 1990; Amable *et al.*, 1997) and in the stratification of wage-earner status according to specialisation, position or profession in each country (Chapter 10). In this context, struggles in classification are superimposed upon or follow class struggle. In these classification struggles every wage earner seeks to defend his or her categorical interests by securing specific advantages – even at the risk of compromising the viability of a capitalist society based essentially on wage earners (Aglietta and Brender, 1984). This Girardian interpretation has not gained a following, but nevertheless clarifies certain aspects of the crisis in the contemporary wage–labour nexus, including its extreme segmentation (Beffa *et al.*, 1999).

Finally there is another theoretical source of inspiration which is both a critique and a development of regulationist hypotheses. Convention theory sees the wage relation as the conjunction of a convention of productivity for the direct wage formation and as an unemployment convention governing social benefits (Salais and Storper, 1994). Although this approach is more individualistic than holistic, there are striking similarities: there are as many labour conventions as there are modes of production and these configurations depend on the type of market, the nature of technical change and the principles of performance evaluation (ibid.: 73–88). Modes of co-ordination are an important determinant in performance, resulting from previous interactions between agents. Is this not the equivalent, at a microeconomic level, of the wage–labour nexus and the accumulation regime dialectic?

Thus, while these different approaches may not be entirely coherent, they are at least less contradictory than a cavalier view might suggest.

An institutional analysis of wages: the impossibility of a pure wage theory

This construct has received a dual critique. For some, the wage–labour nexus is no more than a basic theory of the nominal wage (De Brunhoff, 1982), while others accuse regulationists of not having produced a general wage theory (Reynaud, 1994a). Both of these viewpoints misinterpret the regulationist project, whose goal is to provide an institutionalist, and therefore historical, theory of wages.

First, the wage–labour nexus is defined by the coherence of labour organisation and a payment principle. This means that in order for wage formulas to be viable they must take into account specific control problems characterising each major period in the history of labour, as well as considering the various sector configurations (Coriat, 1982, 1990). Empirical studies undertaken at a company level (Chapter 11) confirm this fundamental Marxist intuition, adopted by both American radicals and regulationists.

Second, wage theory is immersed in a wider analysis of employment contracts and wage relations, which may give the false impression that a general theory is lacking. But would it be preferable to adopt an entirely normative theory, such as the Walrasian labour market, or a partial theory which reduces the richness of wage relations to a single determinant, as in the case of the skilful, imperialistic modern microeconomic theories (Cahuc, 1993)? Surely not, both for theoretical reasons, since the wage–labour nexus cannot be understood apart from its founding institutions, and for empirical reasons, given that the predictive value and interpretative capacity of a pure wage theory are poor.

In fact, the history of labour shows the variability and effect of institutions governing labour in wage formation (Boyer, 1978). Regulationist research has collated many institutional analyses and econometric tests (Boyer, 1991; Mazier *et al.*, 1993; Boyer *et al.*, 1994; Boyer and Yamada, 2000) which support a double proposition. First of all, a pure wage theory is impossible; second, and most important, the configuration of the wage–labour nexus has a determining impact on the dynamics of productivity and wages. Institutions introduce more than frictions in regard to the fiction of a pure market functioning: they constitute different modes of *régulation* (Howell, 1992: 1–30) changing over the course of time (Boyer, 1988b).

But these demonstrations may be contested since they confirm only after the fact (*ex post*) that there is a correspondence between legal and institutional evolution and radical changes in wage formation. In addition, the regulationist programme has taken a new direction by establishing the bases of a connection between microeconomic behaviour and the macroeconomic patterns generated by institutions to intervene in an explicit manner (Bowles and Boyer, 1990b, 1995). Starting with the same group of companies and wage earners, it is possible to show analytically how any change in their relations (perfect competition, collusion of companies with or without a union, which is or is not centralised, etc.) affects the equilibrium average wage and its determinants, and consequently also unemployment, once this labour analysis is placed within a general macroeconomic model.

From a strict theoretical point of view therefore, wages are conditioned by the institutions framing the wage–labour nexus, and this result confirms the previous conclusions of long-term historical studies and international comparisons.

The wage–labour nexus and wage relations: micro–macro connections

The vocation and relevant domain of the concept of a wage–labour nexus are principally macroeconomic. The notion of wage relations corresponds to the projection of this concept to a level and categories that are meaningful for actors (Chapter 11). Likewise, if one wishes to emphasise the creation of rules governing a professional domain, the notion of an employment system* offers interesting perspectives that are similar to labour sociology research in terms of society-wide effects (Chapter 10). Finally, if one considers the creation and reproduction of professional status, the skill–labour nexus provides a precise description of relations between the organisation of the educational and training system on the one hand and the social and technical division of labour on the other (Boyer and Caroli, 1993).

The wage–labour nexus has therefore given rise to a network of connected concepts. Nevertheless, the question of relations between these levels of analysis is as important as ever. In the 1970s the implicit hypothesis was that the Fordist wage–labour nexus was *homogeneous*. This hypothesis was based on the observation of the spread of scientific management methods to a series of industrial and service branches such as banking, insurance and even fast food. This hypothesis was very useful in establishing a micro–macro connection that ultimately merely reproduced the usefulness and limits of the representative agent of standard theory.

Later it became useful to presume the coexistence of a *competitive wage–labour nexus*, influenced by relatively rapid adjustments to employment and a great exposure of wage earners to the economic cycle, and a *Fordist wage relation*, in which employment is relatively stable and wages are contracted over the long term. This made it possible, first, to interpret aggregate wage relations (Boyer, 1991) as the consequence of the varying importance of these two modes of wage relations, depending on the country, and second, to rediscover the intuition of radical theories of segmentation (Piore, 1982). This was all the more important since the long crisis in Fordism resulted in the gradual reinsertion of competitive principles into 'labour markets' (Chapter 31 for the United States, and Chapter 32 for France).

Recent research has shown that beyond *coexistence*, the two wage relations can be *complementary*. In Japan, for example, competition for access to employment in large companies and the internal aspects of a wage-earning career are strongly affected by unequal status in comparison with smaller firms (Ebizuka *et al.*, 1997). Likewise, the organisation of social security insurance has a retroactive effect on the formation of direct wages (Saillard, 1995). Thus the viability of a configuration of the wage–labour nexus presumes an adequate connection between direct wages and benefits, including unemployment benefit (Bowles and Boyer, 1990b).

Finally, beyond any direct transfer of the Fordist wage–labour nexus, the application of the regulationist approach to an analysis of the *diversity* of work organisation at the sector (Chapter 27) or firm (Chapter 11) level may provide a classification for wage relations. Depending on the type of work organisation, the nature of uncertainty on product markets, the intensity of technical change and, naturally, the connection with the accumulation regime, it is possible to identify a few typical configurations.

Thus, in spite of appearances, the findings of regulationists (Du Tertre, 1989) and conventionalists (Salais and Storper, 1994) are mutually reinforcing. A new and important challenge then emerges: to establish an original pathway connecting the micro with the macro and vice versa, without using the notion of a representative agent or a purely statistical theory of aggregation. It is a weakness of both of these institutionalist approaches to have not yet developed a fully satisfying connection. On this point the research agenda of conventionalists and regulationists is the same.

10 The wage–labour nexus and the employment system

Hugues Bertrand

From an economic macro to a social macro: the wage–labour nexus

The concept of a wage–labour nexus has been extremely successful. This success is due perhaps more to its broad, synthesising and overarching nature than to its specific content. According to Robert Boyer's definition (1986a: 49, trans. 1990: 38), the wage–labour nexus refers to 'the type of means of production; the social and technical division of labour; the ways in which workers are attracted and retained by the firm; the direct and indirect determinants of wage income; and lastly, the workers' way of life'. The concept of a wage–labour nexus has a Marxian filiation in as much as it considers the wage-earning class as a political subject whose mode of social construction, exchange relations and submission to or conflicts with other social agents play a determining role in overall economic functioning. It also originates from macroeconomic modelling and an interpretation of key equations, particularly for wages and productivity.

This interpretation leads to a dual research agenda. First of all in the context of the social space of 'institutional forms' which explain these relations by acting as a common thread or social basis; second, the search for intermediary categories, which differs from the individualist psychology of neoclassical approaches. It opens up a vast area of research into the economic construction of the social dimension through 'institutions' and collective 'agents'. In parallel with this, an economic perspective on agents and their relationships leads to an analysis of economic content: their role in the development of exchange elements can be rendered into universal equivalence, and hence construed and reduced to economic objects.

There is therefore an effort to widen the economic field to include social aspect, along with a simultaneous reduction of the social arena to its economic functions. In its most basic economic form, the 'Fordist' wage–labour nexus is understood as an exchange of social purchasing power for anticipated productivity gains. In various explanations, attempts have been made to analyse the founding social matrix, in other words, the way in which social groupings have been formed historically and have then created, through opposition and conflict or tentative compromises, the equivalent classes of economists and the norms of sociologists. The analysis of new post-Fordist 'wage formulas', understood as the emergence of new rules of development for wage earners, is a good example of this tentative search for formulas constructed as new rules of equivalence (Chapter 11). It should, however, be noted that the circumstances for developing these rules within a company, and their consequences, are emphasised over conditions and places of possible social validation.

In its reduced economic form – in other words, in its condensed form as a 'wage formula' – the wage–labour nexus is a fundamental element in regulating the economy as a whole, which, through its incorporation in a model, tends to render it endogenous by confirming its economic validity. In order for a wage–labour nexus to 'succeed' a dual validation combining reproduction in both the economic and the social fields is required. In other words, this approach involves not only making 'social forms' economically endogenous, but also rendering an economic model socially endogenous.

However, this dual dependence is not the end of the story. First of all, the institutional forms supporting the wage–labour nexus provide economic agents with the necessary exogenous markers to aid in the formation of expectations and in decision making. Second, the macroeconomic impact of a wage–labour nexus is an expression of its economic success or failure more than its concrete social modes of functioning or development, which are made explicit by the underlying employment system.

Employment systems and the construction of collective agents

To help understand the wage–labour nexus, its terms must be clarified. An 'employment system' is simply an explanation of the wage–labour nexus in terms of the construction of social agents and their relationships within the social arena. In macroeconomic terms, the employment system is the exogenous aspect of the wage–labour nexus that develops two specific elements: the organisation and division of labour in connection with the 'employment relation', and retaining and mobility systems. The determinants of wage income will not be dealt with here, since they are discussed in Chapter 11; the formation of benefit income is also a separate area of investigation (Saillard, 1995). Research into employment systems inevitably leads to the displacement and, to some extent, to the inversion of traditional questions.

The central question is the move from the individual to the collective, and the way in which intermediary collective agents are construed, not as 'representative agents', but as social mediators constitutive of enduring and progressively institutionalised social and professional identities. Furthermore, the initial emphasis on the result of these collective mediations (such as a dominant 'wage formula') is displaced by the manner in which common rules are developed and transformed through the interaction of collective agents. This is the condition for moving from intriguing retrospective explanations (a criticism often levelled against *régulation* theory) to analysing likely outcomes.

Gradual advances in the research programme have naturally led to the analysis of systems of industrial relations. These were analysed initially on the basis of results and then through the construction of collective agents according to two principal lines of enquiry. The first was directed towards the construction of employment and the employment relation, that is, the matrix in the production of professional groups and social agents. The other was more concerned with the creation and administering of identities and collective representations, going back as far as education systems.

Industrial relations and *régulation* vary according to country

The analysis of industrial relations systems plays a major role in the wage–labour nexus. For *régulationists,* the founding work in this field was that of Jean-Marc Grando *et al.* (1980), which compared modes of union organisation, levels, areas and the content of conflicts and negotiations in Great Britain, Germany and Italy. The authors sought to demonstrate the link between these 'institutional forms', the concrete aspects of the 'wage–labour nexus' and overall economic functioning.

Essentially, British trade unionism was found to be incompatible with a true Fordist wage–labour nexus. This was because British trade unionism impeded the ability to reorganise work processes and blocked the exchange relation (the Fordist 'social compromise' of wages in return for productivity achieved) by forcing companies to apply strict and narrow codes for the use of every labour force category.

On the other hand, after the war Germany instituted a system of industrial relations that was clearly based on a type of Fordist wage formation. By neatly separating the branch level at which wages, categories and the collective timetable are determined and discussed, and the level at which the company manages daily work relations (recruitment, labour cutbacks, training or timetables), the Germans invented their own style of institutions within an organic Fordist model. This model involved a formal dissociation between the places of wage formation and those of production organisation. Connections between these two aspects were made at the branch level through a confrontation of the wage earners' branch unions (for wages) and company federations (for productivity). This model ensured a general distribution of wage increases (or a retrospective redistribution of productivity gains) throughout the branch, thereby resolving two problems. The first was the need to spread wage norms in order for the model to work (on a macroeconomic level); the second concerned co-ordinated management (by employers and unions) of the social conditions of competition, with the branch acting as the locus for responding to this as and when required.

These approaches have great advantages. First, they offer a pedagogical advantage through the concrete demonstration of the link between methods of constituting agents (trade unions or branch unions, for example), the social area for managing conflicts and compromises, and the methods of global economic *régulation*, even if the link is not always perfectly controlled.

Furthermore, they made it possible to establish a new, productive synthesis of approaches based on areas of qualification and professional mobility, since they attempted to describe and analyse the interaction of social agents at the level of professional groups, as well as their methods of organisation and action. However, these syntheses still required greater precision, for, although branches play a decisive role in the creation and management of professional arenas and their corresponding groups in Germany, they are not the only bodies involved. Branches do not play the same role in France as they do in Germany in terms of the definition and development of professional arenas and groups. It is necessary to return to work organisation and the concrete methods of work force management in order to understand the nature of areas of effective mobility and thereby to identify how professional identities and groups are created. The way in which branch institutions function in Germany allows one to understand, for example, why, particularly in the system of dual apprenticeship, this tends to homogenise the work force, its representations and areas of qualification. In France the branch plays this role far less because professional groups are constructed differently (Bertrand, 1990).

The regulationist research agenda was thus faced with two new sets of questions. It needed to understand the origin of the large and persistent gaps between professional areas, groups and relations according to country (Boyer, 1998b). It also became involved in the development of a conceptual framework suited to conceiving modifications to these structures and representations (Lordon, 1994a, c, 1997a).

From a societal effect to the theory of conventions

This research agenda overlaps with sociological research interested in identifying a 'societal effect', particularly the research of LEST. In this context Jean-Jacques Silvestre (1990) lists three closely related areas of research: the identification of agents and their construction, areas of action and, finally, the generating of rules. The concept of a 'professional arena' is the cornerstone of this approach; these authors define it as 'an overlapping and stable system of identities and changes that do not destroy these identities'. Professional arenas act as areas of separation in as much as they constitute distinct professional identities. It is tempting to establish a link with theories of labour market segmentation, even though the starting points are very different. In the first case, the construction of professional identities and in the second the differentiated modes of labour market operation contrast a rule-governed segment with one that is governed by market mechanisms via a central dichotomy. The rule-governed segment is more suitable for governing qualities and qualitative apprenticeships.

But it is not enough merely to recognise the existence of different systems of rules and collective agents; it is also necessary to understand their origins. This is the main objective of 'convention' theories.

In the view of Olivier Favereau (1994a), while the regulationist approach emphasises the results of collective agents' negotiations (cf. the concept of 'institutionalised compromise') above all, conventionalists are primarily interested in the methods of constructing procedural rationality in an uncertain universe. As the collective agent *par excellence*, unions are perceived less as producers of results than as producers of the rules framing effective work relations. The importance attributed to the production of rules and organisational apprenticeship processes enables a better understanding of frameworks for collective action, but it does not raise questions about the construction of agents or the move from the individual to the collective (Reynaud, 1995). Perhaps on account of the obsession with rules and the fabrication of the framework of action, research into the 'models of an equitable social bond' ignores two concepts that are necessary in the construction of this passage: the concept of collective identification, and, second, constraint or a relationship of force, which may lead to imposed relations without an agreement. There are many ways of understanding how collective agents are formed and disassembled.

What are the successors to Fordism?

Neo-Taylorism, neo-Fordism, post-Fordism, Toyotism, Ohnism and Sonyism are among the many terms invented to describe newly emerging forms of work organisation. Several leading ideas shared by many authors emerge from this terminological jungle.

The first idea relates to the increasingly complex nature of productive organisations linked with the extension of markets and their heightened volatility and changeability. Hence the frequently emphasised ineffectiveness of the Taylorian mode of organisation, and the need for new modes of organisation and involvement, new forms of co-ordination which will be more supple and complex (Lichtenberger, 1993). The role of individuals and collective work bodies has been redefined from prescribed work to 'conscience' work, from obedience to responsibility. There has been a move from simple functional organisation to supple and decentralised organisations allowing quality control. This may be seen, for example, in the shift from the vertically co-ordinated planning A firm to Masahiko Aoki's (1988) horizontally co-ordinated and adaptable J firm. It is also shown by a move from a qualified and stable organisation to Philippe

Zarifian's (1994) concept of a qualifying and developing organisation in which the company is redefined as a site of a complex organisational apprenticeship.

The second idea deals with the redistribution of economic power implied by these transformations. The accompanying decentralisation creates an increase in individual and collective operational autonomy, and hence in the characteristic power margins. This change encourages the aspirations of those who see in it the emergence of a new worker with strong and increasing professional and relational abilities, communicating, analysing, taking initiatives and decisions, developing projects – in short, the new autonomous and responsible emblematic figure of a post-Taylorian worker. Without denying this change, others qualify it in the context of increased segmentation of the labour market, seeing it as a well established beginning for a new division of labour. From this viewpoint designers are no longer separated from those executing their idea through the specification and a formal production work schedule. Instead the difference lies in the power of a general strategic level and production line managers. These organisers apparently benefit from greater autonomy, but it is limited and controlled by strong constraints in terms of results (reorganisation into profit centres, results based evaluation, quality management) (Boyer and Durand, 1997). The claim is that this heralds the birth of a new economic division of labour between production units, profit centres and companies with a specialised professional vocation, and large companies or groups with an important financial role, plying a 'trade' as strategic assembler and reassembler. This trend is shown in the cutbacks made by large companies and the rapid displacement of employment towards independent or supervised small and medium-size firms (Appay, 1992; Lichtenberger, 1993).

These new forms of work organisation have a great effect on employment relations. During the Fordist period employment relations tended to be uniform, while today they tend to diversify into forms adapted to many different situations. The employment relation is gradually spreading over a large continuous spectrum, extending from wage contracts to trade contracts. But the method of managing the wage contract (the evaluation of results) tends to be quite similar to a trade contract (from a means contract to a results contract) while the content of trade contracts increasingly includes the co-ordination of means.

In this more complex, changing and uncertain production universe, individuals find themselves simultaneously overly constrained in the short term and underdetermined in the long term. They are overly constrained in the short term because of employers' higher expectations and greater professional demands, as well as by the co-ordinating constraints to which they are subject and which they must manage. They are underdetermined in the long term owing to the absence of visibility, great uncertainty over company development, the work collective, their position, profession and potential areas of development. This time reduction, together with an explosion in individual professional orientation, may partly explain the weakening of earlier collective agents, through a lack of clear identification processes and great difficulties in the emergence of new agents, places and content able to produce new rules and collective meaning. This is occurring during a period when there is a strong need for them.

The importance of the educational relation

An understanding of national differences requires a return to the education system, which is the other matrix in the constitution of professional arenas and identities. Its essential role in the formation of professional identities and categories is recognised, particularly through the identification of points of entry to the production system, and hence in relations to the labour market. These points of entry vary tremendously according to individual countries and education systems and contribute in an essential manner to constructing professional identities and divisions (Bertrand, 1990; Boyer and Caroli, 1993). The dual German system is frequently compared with Latin systems. The openness of the German apprenticeship system, through which most young Germans pass, not only offers a better articulation of the needs of companies and the professional preparation of recruits, but also plays an essential role in the homogenisation of the social body and opening up of professional markets.

In contrast, points of entry are more distinct and hierarchical in Latin countries, producing strong divisions that are then maintained by the closure, which may be extreme, of the professional categories that are thereby produced. The relative weakness of professional markets in these countries, due as much to the nature of the initial general training as to the later functioning of internal markets, limits the flexibility which ease of circulation among companies would encourage (Bertrand, 1990; Annandale and Bertrand, 1990).

In short, the study of employment systems includes three closely linked central areas of research. First, the study of the rules and conventions governing the employment relation; second, a survey of the social framework producing these rules, or more precisely collective agents, their mode of constitution, organisation and interaction; and finally consideration of common social representations as the basis for constructing this framework. Research into the wage–labour nexus focuses on the macroeconomic impact of these rules, in other words, the implicit macroeconomic function of a mode of operation made explicit by the employment system.

11 Diversity and rules in wage determination

Bénédicte Reynaud

As a theory of long-term dynamics seeking to develop an institutional macroeconomics *régulation* theory has paid particular attention to the institutional forms which constitute accumulation regimes, i.e. money, competition and the 'wage–labour nexus'. In this perspective *régulation* theorists have studied the levels of the average wage and its development, observed over a long period, in order to identify the laws of wage formation (United States: Aglietta, 1976; France: CEPREMAP-CORDES, 1978; Boyer, 1978). This research came to the conclusion that the principles of wage determination (in terms of both level and development) are influenced by history: they depend on configurations of the wage–labour nexus and hence, ultimately, on different corresponding modes of *régulation*.

Wage theory is thus a by-product of the theory and wage–labour nexus of the mode of *régulation*. In presenting this thesis, regulationists simultaneously reject the thesis that wages are a market variable. Nevertheless, the mechanisms by which institutions and organisations contribute to wage determination are still not well understood.

Two limits to *régulation* theory

First, the diversity of rules in wage determination does not fit well with a holistic theory. There is only one way to reconcile this type of methodology with the fact that companies adopt different rules, and this is to show that the companies' strategies, and consequently the choice of rules in wage formation, are solely dependent on the effort to increase surplus value. Michel Aglietta began with this approach (1976: chapter 4), viewing the piece-based wage of the Taylorian era as a derivative form of the time wage.

Second, development of a theory of rule diversity is all the more difficult if rules are viewed as arrangements that are unambiguously applied (Reynaud, 1997). This outlook derives from research into the emergence and dissemination of technology in order to analyse social rules (Boyer and Orléan, 1991, 1994). But it also excludes one of the possible explanations of diversity, that is, the role of interpretation at the point when rules are instituted. Yet some research has emphasised the need to link rule interpretation and application (Livet, 1994; Livet and Reynaud, 1997; Reynaud, 1992, 1994a, 1995).

Finally, two levels of analysis should be distinguished. The microeconomic level refers to a particular form of work organisation, company style and the rules in wage determination which are directly dependent on it, for instance job-based salary. The other level of analysis is macroeconomic, from which the rules acting in wage determination are derived retrospectively, for instance the so-called Fordist system in the case of the Fordist accumulation regime. If these two levels are distinguished from one another, rules in wage determination observed at a microeconomic level can be used as indicators of potential changes at the macroeconomic level, and in this lies the question of the future of Fordist wage systems.

Different rules, but common principles, in wage determination

Acknowledgement of the institutional diversity of wages should have encouraged regulationists not only to show that the historical succession of laws of wage determination is a by-product of the wage–labour nexus of the mode of *régulation* of the same period, but also to consider the opposite relation. Given that the application and interpretation of rules in wage determination is a process that leads to the formation of individual wages, and eventually an average wage, is it possible to identify a single practical and logical principle of formation for the average wage through an analysis of these rules?

Since the wage–labour nexus is a macroeconomic concept, the use of the expression 'wage–labour nexus' at the micro level is a misinterpretation caused by a confusion of levels of analysis. Admittedly, it has been used incorrectly in previous texts (Reynaud, 1990, 1992), in attempts to account for a diversity of wage relations which, ultimately, are no more than local expressions (of the industry, company, etc.) of the same wage–labour nexus.

What law in wage determination does the diversity of rules in wage fixing correspond to? To find an answer based on empirical studies instead of pure speculation, we have adopted the hypothesis that it is possible to construct a representation of the wage–labour nexus based on the distribution of wage relations at the firm level. From this perspective, twenty-one variables were extracted from the 1986 Survey of Wage Structures by the Institut national de la statistique et des études économiques (INSEE), the French national institute of statistics and economic surveys. This identified indicators such as: the link with institutions (connection with a collective agreement or company accord), industry, company size, work organisation, characteristics of the labour force employed and the type of benefits (measured by the sick pay scheme). The use of a variance analysis model makes it possible to estimate specific effects and, other things being equal, the different elements of the wage–labour nexus, through the twenty-one variables for each rule in wage determination.

According to these econometric results, variables related to control at the workplace are the most significant element of the wage–labour nexus when a rule in wage determination is adopted. Indeed, a form of work control corresponds to each rule in wage determination. The control relates to three functions: task guidance, work evaluation and the motivation and disciplining of employees (Edwards, 1979). The diversity of payment rules relates to a single law of wage determination: as a means of encouraging work (the 'carrot'), wages depend on forms of work control.

Four rules in wage determination

The first rule, *a monthly salary with no bonus* reflects 'a simple form of control' (Edwards, 1979). This wage system embraced 13.8 per cent of the work force in 1986; it is common in small companies (under 50 employees) with virtually no involvement in collective agreements, in declining industries (often, for example, in the leather industry). The policy is based on the desire to reduce wage costs. The labour force is not regarded as an investment. Indeed, the company is not concerned about keeping its employees by offering bonuses or insurance cover more generous than the law requires. Apart from the principle of monthly payment, which has been compulsory since 1978 in any case, the absence of formal rules leaves room for personal relations between employer and employees. In this situation the head of a company is responsible for evaluating and monitoring work, which requires both authority and charisma. Rules are informal, allowing for paternalist management of the labour force.

The second rule, *a monthly salary with a bonus equal to less than a 'thirteenth month'* (30.9 per cent of workers in 1986), is one form of simple control. Institutional connections are restricted to taking company-level agreements as a reference in determining wage changes. The labour force is far more qualified and companies are larger. Borrowing the terminology of Luc Boltanski and Laurent Thévenot (1987, 1991), these two types of management present a 'domestic' company model.

The third rule, *a monthly salary with an individual or collective bonus incentive wage*, reflects Taylorian or Fordist 'technical control'. The individual incentive wage (6.4 per cent of workers in 1986) is one of the vestiges of Taylorism that is still applied in labour-intensive industries such as footwear and clothing. A collective incentive wage (5.9 per cent of workers in 1986) characterises Fordist 'continuous process' industries. These rules are typical of 'technical control' based on the technical structure and organisation of company production. Indeed, in both cases machines set for a planned quantity of work exercise power, rather than supervisors. Wages depend on position and the individual or collective quantity produced. Individual incentive bonuses reflect a Taylorian company model, while collective incentive bonuses reflect a Fordist company model, based on team-based organisation. Work encouragement and employee surveillance, the third function of monitoring, is guaranteed by a system of negative incentives that are based largely on the threat of dismissal.

The last rule, *a monthly salary with an annual bonus higher than a thirteenth month* (37.4 per cent of workers in 1986) reflects 'bureaucratic control'. This is typical of a mode of long-term organisation that encourages employees to remain with the company (thirteenth month, seniority bonus and attractive insurance cover). It is found in companies with close ties to the institutional system, in 'statutory' industries such as gas, water and urban heating (in France), or in industries of typically intensive accumulation, such as the automobile industry, applied to specialised workers and qualified workers of high seniority. This rule of payment is linked with 'bureaucratic control'. It is the model of the 'statutory' company in which favourable agreements for employees protect them from outside competition. Wages, which are dependent on formal rules, act as job-based salaries rather than individual remuneration.

From the company to the industry

In the light of these results, the company appears as the principal architect of rules in wage determination, and the industry is seen as one of its collaborative tools.

The size of companies, team-based organisation and the industry are three important explanatory factors in the adoption of different rules in wage determination. The larger the company the more favourable rules of wage determination are to the employee. Furthermore, collective incentive bonuses are used in establishments organised in three shifts. Finally, the industry appears both as an area where macroeconomic restrictions appear and as an essential means of co-ordinating economic activities. Bearing in mind the history of companies and the professional relationships they have established, the industry expresses the force of tradition; it acts as a vehicle for shared values, the repository of collective knowledge. These results confirm what common sense suggests in addition to evaluations of earlier data (Reynaud, 1986).

Thus unlike the macroeconomic and holistic approach of *régulation* theory that views wages as a by-product of the wage–labour nexus, we have suggested an opposite relation whereby wages are defined by rules in wage formation whose diversity reflects a common company logic. This shared logic is the search for a constantly active controlling of work processes.

Two major types of rules

The institutional dimension of wages emphasised by *régulation* theory can be clarified with reference to its productive parallels with the 'conventionalist' theory of wages (Favereau, 1993a; Reynaud, 1994a) according to which wages are not only a price, but also the result of rule interpretation. The central hypothesis is as follows: the establishment of a rule has a different impact on the accumulation regime, depending on whether it acts as a 'point of reference' or an 'interpretative rule' (Livet and Reynaud, 1997). This distinction is based on an alternative conception of rules whereby, instead of dictating behaviour, a rule acts as a context for action, requiring interpretation. The majority of conventionalists share this approach.

The *rule as a point of reference*, or 'rule 1', is defined with reference to thresholds, indicators, ratios, etc. Its interpretation, which consists of choosing an indicator from an existing whole, is focused on these salient points through an evaluation of the statistical robustness or accuracy of the various competing indicators. This requires minimal interpretation. This is the case in the rule of indexing wages to prices, which specifies several types of price indices (usually taken from INSEE and the Confédération générale du travail, of CGT, a major French trade union). The application of the indexing rule requires a choice of one of these indices.

In contrast, *the interpretative rule*, known as 'rule 2', refers to an area of interpretation (e.g. 'wages depend on work intensity'). A supposedly central prototype or model often indicates the area of possibilities. Its interpretation is first a matter of defining the field of possibilities, in other words, of finding a principle of coherence that enables a comparison of the rule subject to interpretation with those which are already in effect, so as to make a decision. Since the 1958 French edict which 'prohibits the indexing of wages to prices' is a negative rule, its application requires an exploration of a new field of possibilities.

Profound transformation or tinkering with Fordism?

The Fordist regime is in crisis. Since 1982–3 the policy of most European countries has been to de-index wages from the cost of living. This is a direct attack on one of the pillars of Fordism. The new systems are no longer the optimistic wagers on the future (expected increases in productivity) of Fordist logic or the industrial world's certainties about the future; instead they reflect real individual or collective results. Wage development depends on local, rather than national, economic conditions, and this is enhanced by the shift of wage negotiation from branches to companies (cf. the 1982 Auroux laws on the obligation to negotiate wages and a company ranking system). Finally, the arrangements of the 1986 edict and the 1990 law on employee incentive profit-related schemes make it possible to subject part payment to results. Companies are becoming less hesitant about reducing wage levels in exchange for promises of employment security.

The results of a survey (Appendix 11.1) show that in the 1990s companies chose to modify rules of wage development (either individually or on the wage bill) rather than alter the method of determining wage levels. This reflects uncertainty about employees, making a part of wage income dependent on actual results. It is confirmed by a 1998 study (Beffa *et al.*, 1999).

New rules in wage development are *interpretative rules* that are a sign of a real transformation of Fordism in the development of the average wage. First, this is the case in the indexing of wages according to government expectations of inflation levels. Likewise, taking previous results and the market into account is an expression, in terms of rules, of the interpretations put by companies on the prohibition of indexing on the basis of past inflation. It is also the case with individual increases that require interpretation, even when they are strongly codified. Companies believe that there are two advantages to acting in this way: it limits work reorganisation to technological imperatives and therefore does not question the concept and content of a job.

In contrast, other rules that are not very new are *reference points*. The criterion for determining the base-level wage is always position, whether it is defined through collective agreements or on a system of job classification drawn up by consultancy firms. This is a far cry from the employment flexibility permitted by the voluntary imprecision of employee job descriptions found in Japan. Masahiko Aoki (1988, 1990, 1991) emphasises the 'fluid and ambiguous' nature of work roles. 'But since the boundaries between positions are fluid and definitions of roles remain quite ambiguous there has been a tendency to establish them on the basis of employee ability and experience, interpreted in the widest sense' (1991: 61). The restriction of general increases to non-executives is the only significant rule that has been subject to a minor modification, the suppression of one option among many. The setting of wage levels according to work roles corresponds exactly to Fordist work organisation.

It appears that this is the reason why current transformations amount to tinkering with Fordism rather than *a priori* radical change. This does not mean, however, that the changes are ultimately unimportant (Beffa *et al.*, 1999). But why stop at 'tinkering' when we know the regime is in crisis? Is it easier to change interpretative rules than the rules formulated as points of reference? In contributing to a theory of regime changes, it would be interesting to develop an approach based on rules and their inertia. Evolutionist games could be used (Boyer and Orléan, 1991, 1992, 1994), and the findings of experimental surveys (Samuelson and Zeckhauser, 1988), which have much to contribute but remain an untapped resource, could be incorporated.

Appendix 11.1 The transformation of wage rules: France in the 1990s

A study of the wage policies of the largest companies, which had 'bureaucratic control' at least prior to the crisis of Fordism (Reynaud and Najman, 1992), enabled an analysis of ideal-type wage systems to decide whether or not they are signs (manifestations and/or causes) of profound transformations in the Fordist wage regime. The systems, presented in Table 11.1, are always characterised by three types of rules:

1   A rule for the development of the company wage bill, which may depend on the state's expected rate of inflation at a constant rate (M1); company and/or market results (M2); the expected rate of inflation and previous results (M3); the expected rate of inflation, previous results and the market (M5).
2   A rule for the wage level: types of classification ranking depending on whether or not it refers to position.
3   Development rules for individual wages (a general increase, an individual increase, etc.).

In the 'civic environment' individuals count only in as much as they are part of the collective. They are subject to the general will. Solidarity is an essential characteristic of this world. For example, the application of the development rule of the wage bill according to the government's expectations of the rate of inflation results from this principle.

The 'industrial environment' is characterised by the search for efficiency, performance and productivity. It is characterised by forecasting possibilities and projections for the future. The division of a company into positions, with well defined descriptions, matches this logic.

In the 'market environment' action is initiated by desire. Rather than being stimulating, competition between individuals degenerates into rivalry. Prices are the most important mode of evaluation.

Table 11.1 Wage systems in the 1990s

Type		Wage system
1	'Industrial civic'	M1 + salary according to job + general increase for all employees
2	'Co-operative industrial'	M3 + salary according to job + collective flexibility + general increase for all employees
3	'Defensive industrial'	M2 + salary according to job + general increase for non-executives
4	'Market' for executives	M5 + starting salary according to qualifications + career salary depending on the 'market' + individual increase

12 The welfare state and institutional compromises

From origins to contemporary crisis

Christine André

In recent years throughout Europe there have been increasingly frequent debates and reforms attempting to deal with the 'crisis of the welfare state'. To understand how and why the welfare state, considered one of the essential foundations of the period of the Golden Age ('trente glorieuses'), and developed thanks to economic growth, is being reconsidered today, it is necessary to examine its origins.

A methodological difficulty: which concept of the welfare state?

Currently there are several different concepts of the welfare state. In a strict sense the welfare state is understood to ensure the social insurance protection of individuals and groups. In this case it is associated with social security and welfare, or with social policy, a term with variable meaning according to country. On a broader interpretation the welfare state includes all public intervention on behalf of groups or individuals. This includes education policies, employment policy, industrial relations and housing. Finally, in an extreme view, the welfare state is confused with a Keynesian interventionist state.

The second of these interpretations seems closest to the *régulation* approach. Research into relations between the state and the economy in France over the long term (Delorme and André, 1983) has in fact indicated periods of regularity for each of the five 'institutional forms' of *régulation* (Boyer, 1986a). In this conception, the welfare state is equated with public intervention through its relation to the 'wage–labour nexus', which refers as much to the method by which direct wages and benefits are formed as to the use of wage income, the organisation of the labour market, etc. (Chapter 9). Empirical studies have confirmed the interdependence and complementarity* of various aspects of the welfare state. However, there is no real divide between this and state intervention related to the other four institutional forms (Delorme and André, 1983; Théret, 1992b, 1997, 1999; Chapter 16).

Long-term analysis of public intervention in France has led to the conclusion that since the early nineteenth century there have been two successive configurations, characterised by the relation of the state to the economy. The first developed on the basis of the rules that came out of the Revolution, and lasted until the First World War. This is the notion of a 'limited' state that relates to an economy that is seen as an autonomous realm. The Second World War marked the change to a state 'embedded' in the economic sphere. In France this involved truly taking on responsibility due to two major innovations: the institutionalising of benefits and the concept of co-ordinating monetary administration and general economic policy under the aegis of public authorities. The welfare state is most closely associated with the embedded state configuration.

International comparisons have shown that since the early nineteenth century this successive order of configurations has been valid, in addition to indicating great national specificity within these configurations (André and Delorme, 1982).

The role of institutionalised compromises in the development of the welfare state

Out of the three underlying logics of state activity (Delorme, 1991; Chapter 15), both legitimacy and co-ordination are essentially dependent on the social realm, while today sovereignty is only a slight concern, even though the issue of public order had a fairly important role in the nineteenth century.

Like co-management in Germany, social security insurance and education have played the most important roles among the various aspects of the welfare state in legitimising the state by giving rise to the formation of institutionalised compromises* (Delorme and André, 1983). What is the definition of an institutionalised compromise? Institutionalised compromises result from situations of tension and conflict between socio-economic groups over a long period, at the conclusion of which a form of organisation is established, creating rules, rights and obligations for those involved. Institutionalised compromises act as frameworks in relation to which the population and groups involved adapt their behaviour and strategies; their founding principles remain unchanged over the long term. These types of arrangements prove to be particularly resistant to change and exert a decisive influence over public interventions. Given their importance, the formation of institutionalised compromises will be emphasised in this brief historical description of the development of the welfare state.

The origins of the welfare state

Even though 'social' measures were adopted well before the nineteenth century in some countries (e.g. Britain), it was then that the state began to establish the foundations of social insurance, organising and establishing central control over education, developing legislation for workers' labour and encouraging housing. Public intervention in the social arena originated mainly in the tensions caused by two factors: those linked with the question of the nation state and those resulting from industrialisation and the growth of the wage-earning class.

While previously 'social issues' were primarily a matter for aid groups and charity, organised at the local level or by the Church, the insecurity of workers' lives, in a context of weakened traditional solidarity, provoked many calls for greater security guarantees in the event of loss of wages due to accident, illness or retirement (Donzelot, 1984; Rosanvallon, 1981). Expression of these claims was facilitated by the creation of workers' organisations and by the state's recognition of them. In order to retain the work force in industries where work was particularly arduous and had a high turnover rate (mines, railways), some companies established insurance funds. Mutual benefit societies were also organised by unions or corporations, but only for the most well-off section of the population. Furthermore, in France government bond acted as a form of insurance for the middle classes. But this context, shared by all the countries under consideration here, presented marked national differences in the importance of pre-established arrangements, pre-existing state organisations, the characteristics of the participating agents, the movement of influential ideas, representation (Merrien, 1990) and the selection of problems thought to require state intervention.

Germany's pioneering role in creating social insurance is well known. Bismarck's government's need for legitimisation led to the instituting of a set of guarantees intended to distract the working class from the influence of socialist ideas, since opposition arose essentially from this category of workers. The presence of a strong government made it possible to impose these laws on both employers and unions, along with simultaneous repression of the unions. The social insurance instituted at the time involved obligations linked to the work contract, and its administration was left to insured individuals and their employers so as to respect recognised traditions of self-protection within co-operatives, as well as local autonomy. In this way an institutionalised compromise was established. Unlike France, the legitimating of the nation state did not occur through education since there was already a very extensive education system as a result of Prussian influence.

In France the greatest challenge for the state at the end of the nineteenth century was the legitimisation of the Third Republic. Opposition among the population was widespread and was not associated particularly with workers, who were relatively less numerous and less well organised than in Germany. The institution, during the 1880s, of secular, free and compulsory primary education through a central organisation sought to spread republican ideas among the population and to combat the influence of the Church. Thus on this occasion the institutionalised compromise concerned education (Delorme and André, 1983). On the other hand, social insurance was instituted through union pressure and an increase in strikes, after it had already been introduced in Germany. Furthermore, it benefited only a limited group within the population and offered only limited coverage (Hatzfeld, 1971).

Unlike these two countries, Britain did not experience a politically motivated reappraised of the role of the state. The unions were only slightly open to political influences and the socialist movement developed slowly. The tradition of 'government at a distance' led to few public interventions and to the favouring of individual solutions. In this context, the setting up of an insurance system took place relatively late. It was only in the early twentieth century that the formation of the Labour Party by the unions, the carrying out of surveys by experts and civil servants, the influence of the Fabians, the positions of a section of the employers and the example of Germany led to a re-appraisal of the role of the state. The important law of 1911 took account of existing interests by authorising the already highly developed mutual benefit societies and insurance companies to administer insurance systems. But the move from an aid-based method to an insurance system took place on the basis of benefits calculated to cover only a bare minimum and so only partly challenged established traditions. As in France, insurance systems did not involve an institutionalised compromise, nor was there an institutionalised compromise in the education sector, where the increase in state control took place gradually.

The inter-war period gave rise to a degree of improvement in the coverage of the population by the insurance systems of these three countries, although their approaches were very different (André and Delorme, 1982).

The break caused by the Second World War

The Second World War marks a shift to the new configuration of an 'embedded' state. The institutionalisation of what was referred to as 'indirect wages' or 'benefits' implied a radical change (Saillard, 1995). The specificity of social, economic and political contexts and previous social arrangements, the various degrees of influence of Keynesian theory (Hall, 1989) and Beveridge's ideas, resulted in the adoption of different social security systems, even though reforms everywhere aimed at improved benefits and wider coverage (Flora, 1986). It should also be mentioned that public interventions targeting professional relations, the labour market and housing also underwent new developments.

In France the Liberation brought together exceptional conditions: co-operation among all government political parties, the creation or reconstituting of union organisations and large-scale industrial action, the weakened position of employers, the influence of the National Resistance Council programme, ideas developed by 'progressives' during the 1930s, and the Beveridge report. As a result of this general situation, a total reorganisation and extension of social insurance according to new principles took place in the 1945 edicts that created a social security system. This then acted as a new institutionalised compromise (Delorme and André, 1983). The typically French emphasis given to supervision by a central state can also be seen in the forms of organisation adopted and the initiatives establishing contributions and benefits as a matter for the public authorities, even though the administration of funds was entrusted to insured individuals and employers.

In Britain, unlike the First World War, the Second World War gave rise to a strong sentiment of national solidarity, creating a favourable climate for extending the insurance system. Rejection of the policies of the pre-war period, a new recognition of the need for state intervention to manage the constraints of scarcity, social unrest, the Labour Party's rise to power in 1945 and the impact of the Beveridge report facilitated the adoption of reforms that constituted an institutionalised compromise. Social insurance was extended to the general population and the move to a system of national health care financed by taxes was seen as linked with a dramatic transformation of relations between state and society. These measures now affected the public at large. However, even though the social insurance system was to be administered by the state, liberalism remained, as can be seen by the low level of benefits granted, which left a great deal of room for supplementary private coverage.

In terms of social insurance in Germany continuity prevailed and the late nineteenth century institutionalised compromise remained essentially unchallenged. On the other hand, the characteristics of an institutionalised compromise were to be found in a new area, namely in co-management or co-determination, which extended forms of worker participation which had appeared temporarily during the Weimar republic. As a result of strike threats in the core sectors (coal, iron, steel), in 1951 employees obtained joint representation on the supervisory boards of companies in these sectors. The law was later extended, but with less employee representation. The workers' councils whose initial form had been legalised in 1920 were reintroduced in 1952. The councils enabled employees to participate in the social and economic administration of companies. They established a principle which has since been the core of labour relations and is a major source of social cohesion.

The differences between these national social security systems that were originally based on individual principles have subsequently been mitigated. Today they all combine aid and insurance to cover virtually the entire population.

It was above all thanks to the introduction of social security after the war that expenditure patterns governing all the public sector emerged. Several elements should be taken into account in explaining this phenomenon: demography, the growth of the wage-earning class, continual improvements in legal coverage, increased responsibility for pension plans, accompanied by developments in acquired rights, the growth of the health sector and, later, the development of unemployment compensation. From the end of the 1970s this uninterrupted and sustained increase in expenditure became problematic.

The crisis of the welfare state

Today the globalisation and increasing internationalisation of economies have had the effect of severely limiting the possible range of state action. However, workforce management is still a matter for the territorial state. Up to now, therefore, the welfare state has remained a national phenomenon.

The slowdown in economic growth, particularly in recent years, has had the effect of increasing financial pressure on public budgets. Given the specific dynamics of social expenditure while revenue has experienced only a slight increase, particularly owing to unemployment, much attention has been paid to budgetary matters. Furthermore, the anticipated ageing of the population in the early twenty-first century has led to fears of increasing difficulties. The crisis of the welfare state referred to so often nowadays is therefore first and foremost a financial crisis.

But criticism of the welfare state also questions its efficiency and the supposedly excessive cost which social security imposes on companies, thereby impairing their ability to be competitive. These are all areas of current controversy (Pfaller *et al.*, 1990). Another critical current reproaches the welfare state for its inability to solve the problems of impoverishment and to avoid social exclusion, showing that social security systems are not well suited to dealing with atypical work and unemployment. Finally, a crisis of the legitimacy of the state could develop if challenges concerning the efficiency of public intervention and the weakening of social cohesion were to increase.

The difficulties the welfare state encountered in responding to these tensions are partly increased by the rigidities of institutionalised compromises. The arrangements corresponding to these compromises are linked with specific problems created by a given historical context. Subsequent historical developments have led to a disjunction between the arrangements and new areas of tension. It is only recently that reforms directly challenging institutional compromises could be instituted. The only institutional compromise to remain unchanged is German co-management. One may wonder whether its relatively late institutionalisation and the fact that, unlike other institutional compromises, its legal codification relates essentially to a process rather than to any 'substantial' content, have contributed to its preservation.

A redeployment of social intervention at the supranational, national and regional levels may be expected. It seems that the administration of responsibilities at a European level will remain limited for a long time yet, given differences in the labour market, the variety of national arrangements and the difficulty of harmonising them, as well as the absence of strong, widely recognised participants able to lead European initiatives in this field. The scope of the Social Chapter that has already been adopted, except by Great Britain, is still essentially restricted to the free movement of workers, equal treatment of men and women and questions regarding health and safety in the workplace. Social administration will therefore remain territorial in the medium term, although the balance of national, regional and local responsibilities may alter.

The second kind of transformation to be expected is connected with a shift of the tensions to which the welfare state is supposed to respond. The main challenges are now related to employment, particularly since the rise in unemployment has been accompanied by impoverishment and social exclusion, thus also putting social cohesion at risk, since, particularly in Germany and France, social security systems are still based largely on work. The problem of training is also recognised as being of great importance. In Germany the difficulties are intensified by unification. Traditional social policies cannot resolve all the problems caused by a sustained high level of unemployment and by transformations in work organisation and forms of employment. The general tendency to transfer social security to a professional or individual level runs the risk of aggravating the inequalities between different categories of the population and straining social cohesion, in a situation in which the potential for family solidarity has been reduced. This could result in a two-layer system, with the relief of poverty being considered the responsibility of the state, while a rapidly increasing demand for services by the middle classes may lead to a variety of solutions. However, private responses to social security issues can act only as a supplement and not as a substitute for the welfare state. Another possibility would be not the withdrawal of the state but instead a renewal of its methods and areas of intervention, in order to maintain a strong sense of solidarity. Given the uncertainty over future economic prospects, emphasis could be placed on the institutionalisation of procedures, for instance new forms and levels of negotiation, rather than a fixation on the 'substantial' content of public intervention. Germany is further advanced than either France or Great Britain in this respect. The question is, will a new institutionalised compromise, based on this approach, and capable of giving the state greater legitimacy, be found in the future?

13 Forms of competition

Michel Hollard

Analysis of the 'forms of competition' often plays a decisive role in identifying different periods of economic development or in comparing different economic systems. Forms of competition may be identified by several aspects that include production unit size, company size, relations between companies involved in different stages of the production process, the role of the market and organisation of co-ordination procedures, relations between finance and industry, buyer and seller relations in markets, the type of objects exchanged in markets and the ratios of physical goods to services. It is necessary to prioritise these various aspects and to situate competition within a general theory.

For *régulation* theory forms of competition are some of the structural (or institutional) forms which indicate patterns in an accumulation regime. Competition 'describes how units of accumulation relate to each other' (Boyer, 1986a: 48, trans. 1990: 37). Starting with the question 'How are relations organised among a set of centres of accumulation which *a priori* make decisions independently of each other?' Robert Boyer points out that

> the concept of the form of competition makes it possible to respond to this question, distinguishing various polar cases. Competitive* mechanisms are at work when the fate of privately produced goods is determined by a confrontation in the market *after* production. Monopoly* reigns when certain rules of socialisation prevail *before* production through the maintenance of a social demand whose quantity and composition are largely geared to supply.
>
> (Boyer, 1986a, trans. 1990: 39)

The role of transformations in competitive forms during the change from one accumulation regime to another is initially presented as open to debate. This distinguishes it from a linear historical view of capitalism in which the concentration and centralisation of capital are the essential tendency. It recognises that forms of competition cannot be analysed separately from the other two institutional forms, namely the co-ordination of agents within monetary constraints and the appropriation of the surplus connected with the wage–labour nexus.

What role does the concept of forms of competition play in regulationist research? Its principal role is the claim that in a 'monopolistic' form of company profit is not determined in a residual manner through the difference between market price and production costs. Instead the market price is influenced, if not determined, by the search for a mark-up calculated *prior* to the sale of the product and which is added to production costs.

The theoretical status of prices in the model used by Robert Boyer and Jacques Mistral (1981) emphasises their *implicit* mode of determination. This approach involves a direct examination of the determinants of profit and other returns by the same procedure employed for factors in wage formation. It is a matter of clarifying the prior determinants in the movement of profit, given that the level subsequently attained depends on the group of factors introduced, for example, by demand, salaries, etc. The model explains the logic behind an *offering price* that does not take specific *demand* factors directly into account. This logic is similar to the determination of production prices in Marx's theory. (The main difference from Marx's theory is the endogenous nature of sector based *nominal* salaries.) Money becomes a permissive condition in the development of inflationary processes. Since investment is an expenditure of capital that must be *financed* and then *valorised*, any increase in investment tends to be inflationary as soon as incompatibilities emerge between the development of total production and maintenance of the previous profit rate.

The choice of this model for determining nominal prices for the period 1968–73 is justified by the rapid redeployment of sectors, the accelerated transformation of work processes and the increasing overlap of industrial and banking capital. The necessary criteria for monopolistic pricing are therefore met: a profit rate is applied to all advanced capital and mark-up rates are fairly insensitive to variations in the growth rate.

In general, *régulation* involves the contrasting of monopoly and competition, although it is clearly connected with the move to concentrate and centralise capital. International comparisons reveal a hierarchy which conforms to expectations: 'The United States and Germany are best able to safeguard their profits during a crisis owing to a "malleable labour force" as well as the high level of capital concentration and centralisation.'

This analysis is similar to those of Joan Robinson, N. Kaldor and M. Kalecki, which explain the formation of profits and prices through capital accumulation. For Kalecki, the price of commodities can be deduced from production costs by applying a mark-up according to the degree of monopoly. 'Capitalists earn what they spend,' he claims. For Joan Robinson, prices are fixed at a level that allows for the necessary profit rate to satisfy investment decisions. The logic behind this argument is clear. Before product valorisation on the market can take place, the concentration and centralisation of capital imply co-ordination between companies.

This coherence enables them to transfer differences between production and distributed returns to the agents as a whole, via inflation.

The opposition between 'monopoly' and 'competition' is less relevant now, for both theoretical and historical reasons.

The question of relations between price determination and forms of competition relates particularly to interpretations of company behaviour. Our understanding has been dramatically altered by research undertaken in situations of disequilibrium and in the interaction between agents and their expectations. For example, it is possible that two contracting parties who have signed a contract committing them both for a given period may change from a competitive situation to a situation of bilateral monopoly.

Furthermore, descriptions of the development of competitive forms between companies cannot be reduced to an opposition between monopoly and competition.

Forms of competition and price determination

Gérard Duménil and Dominique Lévy (1993) have provided a synthesis of the classical theory of competition and prices. This is of interest because of the many overlaps between classical and neo-Keynesian approaches to price determination and distribution. According to this approach, the *prior* determination of prices in terms of the desired rate of profit is dependent more on the interpretation of the functioning of competition than on its form. It is more closely related to a way of posing the question of competition in general than to specific hypotheses about existing forms of competition (Cartelier, 1990: 202–62). This concept of competition is different from the theory of general equilibrium in that it includes the behaviour of agents reacting to the disequilibria of an earlier period. Thus the starting point of the analysis is a 'microeconomics of disequilibrium'. Equilibrium, towards which the system may or may not converge, depending on the situation, acts as a fixed point in a recurrent relation. The behaviour of agents in this microeconomics of disequilibria is presented in the following manner.

1 Capital accumulation results from two types of agents: *centres of capital allocation*, which displace capital from one activity to another, and *companies*, which make decisions about investment, production and prices.
2 These agents behave according to a *reaction to disequilibrium,* in terms of the profitability of activities, stocks of finished products and the rate of capital utilisation.
3 Money is created by decentralised monetary authorities that take the rate of inflation and the rate of capital into account when deciding whether to grant companies credit.

The behaviour of agents is then adjusted on the basis of disequilibria observed afterwards rather than according to the rules of optimisation determined by previously anticipated variables.

This analysis enables the construction of classifications from *parameters of sensitivity*. These include sensitivity to capital movement in profit differentials, to stock prices, to the production capacity utilisation rate at the rates of previous periods, to the capital utilisation rate in stocks and to investment at the rate of capital utilisation. As a result of the existence of several possible areas of convergence, the parameters influence both stability and the level of equilibrium. It is therefore possible to simulate conditions of stable homothetic growth alongside very unstable levels of growth.

The criteria of stability at the margin in production employed by Robert Boyer and Jacques Mistral and the parameters of sensitivity which Gérard Duménil and Dominique Lévy have described are evidently similar. But in the case of parameters of sensitivity the concept of forms of competition that is central to comparisons of the two polar forms of monopoly and competition is no longer explicitly present in the analysis. Instead there is an emphasis on familiar variables of industrial economy, including, first and foremost, the mobility of capital between different activities.

The contrast between static analyses, centred on the existence of equilibrium (for instance, in a bilateral monopoly) and analyses based on dynamic approaches and procedural rationales is also present in industrial economics (Arena, 1991). One of the questions at the centre of the debate is the issue of price formation. The recognition that most companies employ the notion of full cost to establish prices has long since introduced the problem of the relation between these practices and microeconomic theory. The 'Oxford school' (initiated by Hall and Hitch's 1939 observations and then, from 1950, continued in the work of Andrews and Brunner) was characterised by its analysis in terms of full costs (Mongin, 1992). Should one therefore deduce that marginal calculus is irrelevant? Should one make a connection between market forms and price determination practices? Is it simply a matter of the difference between short and long periods? Many of these questions remain unanswered.

Discussions about the rationales behind company decisions show that explanations in terms of monopoly are not the only ones to suggest that company selling prices are relatively independent of quantities sold. Classical theory has therefore been able to make use of analyses in terms of procedural rationality to explain price practices aligned with full costs, a notion analogous to Marx's production prices and Joan Robinson's normal prices. This perspective implies further analysis in terms of *régulation* in order to understand potential modifications of company behaviour. The number of companies sharing the same market is an insufficient explanatory variable; it is also necessary to explain the adjustment processes pursued by agents.

A theoretical analysis is therefore necessary (Chapter 18) in order to provide a better definition of the relative parameters for describing the transformations of competitive forms. The parameters of sensitivity discussed here relate to the general behaviour of companies when faced with environmental transformations. In this case, forms of competition refer first and foremost to relations between companies.

Changes in the forms of competition

Analysis of forms of competition usually emphasises the structure of markets, which are described in terms of the number of agents involved in supply and demand (Stackelberg, 1934). But the definition of a market also relates to other aspects. In what follows we focus on three of the most important aspects: relations of competition and co-operation among companies, the object of competition and geographical aspects of competition.

The first two aspects are closely linked. Market competition is commonly described through three of the features (linked with service) of the product on sale: *price, delivery time* and *quality.* This tripartite description of competition is not new, but what is new is that industrial companies, particularly in Europe and America, have been confronted with Japanese competition that focuses on non-price ('non-cost') aspects of competition. This change led to major transformations in company organisation so as to control production costs and bring new products to the market as soon as possible, delivering them to the client in due time. The implications of this change affect more than the international division of labour: as questions of quality and delivery time become increasingly important in relation to price in the competition between producers, prices are increasingly stabilised (Taddéi and Coriat, 1993).

The development by companies of techniques to create products that correspond to a certain cost bracket is not in contradiction with this idea. In fact it is a matter of calculating a price *beforehand* by taking the desired mark-up rate into account. On the other hand, the status of use value and technology in relation to competition has been dramatically modified. These can no longer be considered as exogenous (as they still are in the classical theory of competition). The strategic areas in which the competitive advantage of companies is at play are changing. The production line is no longer the sole consideration; the activities of design and research are also strategic now, both in terms of operating costs and in the time span of new product development. Co-ordination of the various activities involved in the design, development, manufacture and marketing of a product is more important now (shown by the development of 'industrial engineering'). Such co-ordination involves a group of companies and occasionally public research centres that are connected with one another, at least during the manufacture of the product. Competition in terms of the ability to design new products and to master technology involves groups of companies co-ordinated by leading companies, rather than independent firms (Chanaron and Ruffieux, 1994). It also concerns services, whose development is very important in this shift in forms of competition (De Bandt and Petit, 1993; De Bandt and Gadrey, 1994).

The fact that competition has taken on a global dimension obviously modifies the analysis of competitive forms. Besides the question of the competitiveness of national companies (Aglietta and Boyer, 1982), it raises the problem of the role of foreign exchange restrictions in competition. There are many *a priori* structural reasons to explain the unequal adaptation of countries to international monetary instability. The model proposed by Aglietta *et al.* (1980) shows some of the most important relations. This model is based on a system of normal prices with two sectors, an international sector (where price acts as a constraint) and a domestic sector (where price is determined by production cost plus a mark-up based on a specified allocation of returns). It also includes five structural parameters: the rate of productivity increase, the importance of different sectors in the economy, the wage–price relation, the homogeneity of wages in different sectors and the mark-up rates applied to production costs. This sort of model shows that an increase in foreign exchange rates leads to a decrease in export profits, pressure to increase domestic costs and competitive difficulties. The way in which these connections interact depends on the structural parameters of the different countries: the ability of a country to impose its prices and profits on an international scale, and the control a country holds over its domestic market. It is interesting to note that in this case countries, rather than companies, are described as 'price takers' or 'price makers', and, furthermore, that this anticipated the concept of 'global performance' employed ten years later in the text of the eleventh French national plan (Gandois, 1993).

The complexity of competitive forms

The concept of competitive form has undergone considerable development during recent years. This is the obvious conclusion to be drawn from a consideration of theories and events.

For *régulation* theory an essential question concerns the integration of the observation of structural transformations, particularly those identified in relations between companies, with the general analysis of accumulation regimes. While the problem of the potential stability of a medium-term regime is the central question (Chapters 18 and 19), today it is no longer possible to limit oneself to the difference between competition and monopoly. To analyse forms of competition, we must therefore take into account not only the number of contenders in the various markets, but also the adjustment processes employed at different stages of production. The analysis of competitive forms must include forms of production organisation (relations within and between companies), market forms (rules of operation), management rules, the objects of competition (services, goods or information) and the co-ordination between companies and the financial system. It is then possible to examine the conditions for the establishment of a stable regime. While the initial conception of *régulation* theory appears to have overestimated the ability of centres of capital accumulation to co-ordinate themselves *ex ante*, subsequent research shows that this is no longer the case. It remains, however, to integrate these results within an overall analysis.

14 International regimes

Jean-François Vidal

As an institutionalist macroeconomics, the concepts and formulations of *régulation* theory often privilege the nation state, so that most of the research that it has inspired concerns the dynamics of nations. The aim of this chapter is to present the paths by which the regulationist method can be applied to an analysis of international dynamics.

Three approaches to international *régulation*

In the approach developed by Gérard de Bernis (1987) and Rolande Borelly (1990), later referred to as 'the Grenoble *régulation* school', the funda-mental entity is the productive system, rather than the nation state. The productive system is defined as a multinational group of closely integrated productive activities. The British Empire (not the British economy) is an excellent example of an earlier productive system. The productive system is a space, as defined by François Perroux, made up of a home country and affiliated countries, in which the process of capital accumulation develops. *Régulation* is a set of adjustments and institutions which operate as counter-tendencies to a lowering of the profit rate, ensuring the circu-lation of capital between branches and reproducing the hegemony of the home country. It is characterised, among other things, by unified mone-tary circulation, with the currencies of affiliated countries acting as multiples or sub-multiples of the home country's currency. This is often accompanied by a mechanism for centralising currencies, which thus avoids or diminishes difficulties in the balance of payments between countries within the same productive system. From this perspective, regionalisation mechanisms override both national and global dynamics.

International monetary regimes have been analysed in particular by 'the Parisian *régulation* school', especially Michel Aglietta (1986a); the reader is referred to his contribution in the present volume (Chapter 8), as well as to that of Robert Guttmann (Chapter 7). Jacques Mistral (1986) has proposed a grid of analysis for stability and change in international economic relations. Unlike the Grenoble school, this analysis focuses on nation states and competitive relations between industrialised countries.

Each nation has productive resources and related *régulations* that reflect attitudes towards technological change and which ensure arbitration to resolve conflicts linked with competition and income distribution. International relations develop from the initiatives of private agents and in response to the structural differences between countries. They reproduce these differences while integrating them at a national level. The international regime transforms this tension into a growth system, by developing complementarity between nations and by limiting differences between nations to tolerable variations, thereby also restricting destructive competition.

The nature of the international regime is particularly linked with the dynamics of the dominant economy. This economy is characterised by its great potential for technological and social innovation. It offers opportunities for growth to other countries while simultaneously imposing constraints on them. The competitiveness of a national economy is founded on its ability to transform its domestic relations so as to adapt to international norms. This involves the ability to engage in sectors with increasing returns and in markets that are growing rapidly, while simultaneously managing a domestic market.

International *régulation* translates the principles of the international regime into norms and institutions which direct the decisions of private agents and which determine the rules for state intervention. The principal forms of international *régulation* are trade and financial networks, multinational firms, the international monetary system and trade agreements.

The 'American school of international regimes', which refers to research collected by Stephen Krasner (1983) and published in the journal *International Organisation*, analyses mainly the development of international economic institutions in the broad sense and can be described as *internationalist institutionalism*. For the American theory of international regimes, an international regime is a set of principles, norms, rules and decision-making processes which ensure the stability and coherence of behaviour by the different international actors, and which are instituted in order to avoid expensive conflicts. According to this approach, the notion of an international regime can be applied to a specific sector (such as oil) or may have a wider field of applicability, as in the GATT agreements. It may be made explicit through official agreements, or it may be the result of informal practices. The strength or weakness of a regime is reflected by how frequently norms are fully respected.

The different meanings given to the concept of an international regime in the three approaches referred to above is a consequence of the theoretical hypotheses of the different authors. It also derives from the fact that the international economy is so multi-faceted that it is very difficult to interpret it within an overall framework.

Is the *régulation* and international economy approach an adequate method?

In order to transpose the *régulation* method to the international economy in a legitimate fashion it is necessary to show that international exchanges follow stable trends and developments over sufficiently long periods, that international relations are framed by coherent institutions which are respected, and that international fluctuations are contained by stabilising adjustment processes.

With the aid of research synthesising the history of the international economy, particularly the work of A.G. Kenwood and A.L. Lougheed (1971), it is possible to focus on two periods characterised by relatively stable and coherent tendencies.

The first is the two or three decades preceding the First World War. In terms of volume and value, the expansion of trade in manufactured products and of that in raw materials were equivalent; raw materials represented a stable proportion at about 60 per cent of world trade; most trade took place between industrialised countries and primarily exporting countries. During this period, north-western Europe, the cradle of industrialisation, experienced moderate growth, while new countries, which were the rich, primarily exporting countries (the United States, Argentina and Australia), benefited from a rapid increase in exports. Meanwhile Italy, Russia and Japan experienced strong industrial growth. The new powers issued massive bond loans on the London and Paris markets, using them mainly to finance the extension of transport networks. The tendencies of world trade were mainly connected with extensive geographical expansion.

The second period to which this method can be applied without serious difficulties is the 1950s and 1960s. This period was characterised by a far more rapid increase in trade in manufactured products than in raw materials. The role of trade between industrialised countries increased rapidly, the market share of the developing countries (except the oil-producing countries) decreased and trade in similar products between similar, neighbouring countries developed far faster than trade between different countries. It was thus possible to realise increasingly high returns and to find large markets for standardised products. Direct international investment by American firms was the main form of international movements of capital. These developments correspond to the spread of intensive accumulation from the United States to Europe and Japan, which were gradually moving towards the level of American productivity thanks to a rapid overhaul of their production systems and ways of life.

Were stable and coherent international institutions set up? Close analysis shows that it is difficult to speak of 'regimes' (Palan, 1998; Kébabdjian, 1999) framing international relations, even during periods of stability, as some significant examples have shown.

It is difficult to give a precise definition of the trade regime for the years 1890–1913, since practices varied greatly from one country to another, as demonstrated in the in-depth analysis of Paul Bairoch (1989). From 1840 to 1850 Great Britain, the champion of free trade, launched a kind of 'unilateral disarmament' but nevertheless retained customs duties on tropical products and alcohol. Following Germany, which raised its tariffs unilaterally in 1879, from 1880 to 1890 Western European countries adopted increasingly protectionist policies. Tariffs also varied tremendously from one product to another. The United States and Russia imposed prohibitive tariffs equivalent on average to 40 per cent on imports. The most that can be argued is that continental Western European countries applied average rates of customs duties, and that these were moderated by trade agreements.

The institutional framework of the 1950s and 1960s was perhaps less coherent than theoretical analyses might lead one to believe. The free trade regime that was gradually instituted included many exceptions. Thus one of the major principles, stated in the first GATT agreement, was non-discrimination and 'most favoured nation' status, though in fact preferential agreements multiplied over the next three decades – for example, the European common market, multi-fibre arrangements, export restriction agreements and the Lomé accords. Many products were excluded from free trade for a long time; it is true, however, that the Uruguay round later abolished many of these exceptions.

The 'Bretton Woods monetary regime', understood in the strong sense, did not last very long. The principles of the 1944 agreement could only really be applied as of 1958 when the European currencies became convertible; the first attacks on the dollar occurred in 1961, and in 1968 the instituting of the double gold market limited the convertibility of the dollar. However, the principle of fixed but adjustable exchange rates was applied from 1949 to 1971. International regimes are often a combination of haughtily affirmed principles and vague and flexible rules of application. As a striking example one might cite a regime with exchange rates which are in principle fixed but with a total margin of fluctuation of 30 per cent. One of the reasons for this is that sovereignty is still an international principle.

Were international fluctuations limited by stabilising adjustment processes? During periods of stability, adjustments limited the extent of international fluctuations by lessening the processes of transmitting economic conditions between countries, and especially the impact of the cycles of the dominant economy on the rest of the world.

During the decades preceding the 1914–18 war there were three principal mechanisms limiting international fluctuations:

1   The major role of agriculture in production and global trade, which weakened international multiplier effects.
2   The difference between the development of the United Kingdom's domestic and foreign investment flows, or the 'Atlantic cycle', which

limited the impact of the British economy on the rest of the world, and which contributed to equilibrium in the balance of payments, through the adjustment of the capital balance with the current balance. In the short term (but not the long term) international prices fluctuated only slightly.

The limited fluctuation of prices is difficult to explain. It can be seen partly as a result of the rapid development of the transport network, which regulated the world supply of staple commodities, and partly as due to belief in the stability of nominal prices that was linked with the gold standard and generated expectations which had a stabilising effect. On the other hand, great international mobility of capital guaranteed the connection of monetary markets so that interest rates varied synchronously in many countries. The rise in interest rates, which was inevitable in a system where the money supply had to be proportionate to gold reserves in the medium term, could trigger a financial crisis, particularly in new or semi-industrialised countries that were accumulating foreign debt in order to finance their development.

During the 1950s and 1960s many mechanisms limited the international transmission of local economic conditions. Monopolistic *régulation*, with its automatic stabilising properties linked with the welfare state and to a fixed wage bill, restricted fluctuations in demand, and consequently imports from the great powers, as well as variations in the prices of manufactured products. Short-term capital movements were partly controlled, and rates of interest were often regulated, so that connections between monetary markets were slight. Contrary to what is often claimed, it appears that the issuing of international liquidity in dollars was regulated by spontaneous mechanisms that ensured a partial adjustment of the American balance of payments. In fact an expansion movement in the United States led to a deterioration in the trade balance. However, the increase in domestic profits and interest rates reduced the outflow of capital, so that variation in the balance of liquidity was attenuated; during periods of recession symmetrical effects often came into play (Vidal, 1989).

The rise and fall of international *régulations*

The American perspective on international regimes, which analyses the emergence of international institutions in particular, proposes several theoretical interpretations.

The theory of hegemonic stability attributes the establishment and dissipation of international regimes to the rise and fall of a dominant power. For example, the collapse of the liberal order and the 1929 crisis were consequences of the decline of British power (Kindleberger, 1986), while the new international order instituted between 1944 and 1947 was connected with the activities of the United States, whose relative weakening led to disturbances again in the 1970s. But the means of action of hege-monic powers vary and thus contribute greatly to determining the character of a regime. The colonial system is based on coercion, although asym-metries between industrialised countries cannot be based on force in a stable manner (Snidal, 1985). The hegemonic power must therefore nego-tiate and make at least some concessions. A good example is the negotiations pursued by the United States first of all with the United Kingdom and then with other European countries between 1942 and 1948 (Gardner, 1980). The first GATT agreements were largely reflective of American interests, but the United States had to set an example by agreeing to higher tariff concessions than those offered by its partners.

The theory of hegemonic power has one essential weakness: the nature of the international regime cannot be determined solely on the basis of the nature of the dominant economy. The international regime instituted at the end of the Second World War moved away from traditional liberalism, since it recognised the importance of social equilibrium, especially full employment. The Bretton Woods accords authorised devaluation and encouraged signatory countries to apply foreign exchange controls (which is surprising in retrospect) in order to avoid deficits in the balance of payments and the flight of capital being re-absorbed by deflation. These arrangements, which were requested in particular by the British delega-tion, were accepted by the Americans, since generally they reflected developments in economic doctrine among the industrialised nations (Gardner, 1980).

A negotiated order is based on voluntary agreements. It probably implies a limited number of partners, for the complexity and cost of negotiations grow disproportionally with the number of participants. However, the mechanism of the GATT agreement shows that negotiations can be concluded between two or three major powers and the results imposed on smaller countries in return for a few concessions. Changes in power rela-tions between countries and the spread of economic doctrines are no doubt the essential factors in the development of international institutions. From a long-term point of view it is possible that the development of the European Union may be explained partly by the supremacy of the mark in addition to the increasing influence of liberal ideas.

The spontaneous order favoured by Hayek is probably quite common in international relations. It appears that the main international institutions at the end of the nineteenth century were the result of spontaneous conver-gence rather than hegemony or negotiation. Thus clearly the United Kingdom had no interest in reinforcing protectionism, but it was unable to avoid it.

There is no convincing evidence that the gold standard was imposed by the United Kingdom. Before 1871 very few countries made use of this monetary regime, but during the 1870s most of the countries of Western Europe adopted it. The members of the Latin Union were obliged to abandon bimetallism essentially because of the steep decline in the value of money and Germany's decision to adopt the gold standard, which amplified the mechanisms of Gresham's law. Becoming aware of the relative weakening of their country in comparison with Western Europe, Russian governments adopted an industrialisation programme based on the construction of infrastructure networks. To obtain international finance, they decided to stabilise the rouble in relation to gold. Thus in its concern to ensure credibility in the eyes of private capital lenders, Russia was led to adherence to the gold standard, although previously it had frequently employed a compulsory exchange rate.

How therefore should the concept of international *régulation* be understood? It is largely the result of the interaction of national *régulations*, brought together by the exchange of goods and capital, mainly through private decisions. The evolution of national *régulations* is based partly on domestic factors, especially major crises, but also on constraints imposed by the country's international insertion (Palan, 1998; Kébabdjian, 1999).

Many examples suggest that international movements of capital have major effects on national monetary and financial *régulations* (Aglietta, 1995; Aglietta and De Boissieu, 1998). Besides the instance of the spread of the gold standard, one could mention the role played by the increased mobility of capital in the move to flexible foreign exchange rates during the 1970s and in the deregulation of financial systems during the 1980s. These transformations modified the methods and efficiency of monetary and financial policies quite dramatically, and probably contributed to the rapid deterioration of balances during the 1980s, which were then forced to undergo readjustment during the 1990–3 recession.

The effect of the exchange of commodities on work relations is more ambiguous. It appears that even if exchange is based on specialisation in the traditional sense, marked differences will remain in workforce management methods (Wallerstein, 1980, 1984). Indeed, each country is bound to a specific range of products and sectors, whose technical characteristics, growth and productivity potential and markets are very specific, so that in order to remain competitive each country moves towards particular work relations. On the other hand, if the exchanges are between branches, with different countries producing similar goods, it is possible that those wishing to make exchanges will be obliged to conform with the most effective. However, there is a great deal of inertia in work relations, for they are strongly 'embedded' in non-trade-based relations, so that this type of development can be difficult to achieve, as can be seen by the differences among European countries even in the 1990s.

The difficulty of analysing international *régulation* is that it must always define several relevant levels (region, nation or world) acting simultaneously. The effects of internationalisation are ambiguous: it produces homogeneity while also reproducing or amplifying differences between the national and regional levels.

15 The state as relational, integrated and complex

L'état relationnel intégré complexe (ERIC)

Robert Delorme

Research on the state from a regulationist perspective has developed in several directions since the 1980s, to which we cannot do justice in the present context, but illustrations of which are found in several of the chapters of this book.

The state may be seen in terms of three types of problematic: the foundations of theory, theory itself and economic policy. There is a logical hierarchy in descending order from the foundations of theory to theory and then to economic policy. Each level is dependent on the previous level. In the context of the present volume we shall focus on theory, emphasising a particular theoretical category and the concept of the state that underlies it. The theoretical category is the mode of relation between the state and the economy (*mode de relation entre l'état et l'économie,* MREE) and the state is conceived as relational, integrated and complex (*l'état relationnel intégré complexe,* ERIC). These two concepts have gradually emerged from our research into relations between the state and the economy.

Contrary to custom, we have chosen to print the French word for state (*l'Etat*) with a small letter rather than a capital. The French habit of capitalising 'state' has somewhat obscure origins. Is it a question of magnifying the 'State'? If such is the case this ethnocentric heritage must be abandoned once the states with which we are concerned are no longer confined to the unique cases of France and countries that were influenced by French legal culture. Is it a matter of singularising a general concept, in a manner logically similar to that of 'society'? In that case, why not follow the common practice of using a small s for society? Otherwise it would make sense to use a capital letter for both terms. Finally, there is an even stronger reason for using a small letter. This reason emerges from the argument developed below, which presents the state as a singular category bound up in a multi-faceted logic along with other categories with a similar logical status. In this respect even the position of this chapter, in a part of the book on the institutional forms of *régulation* theory, illustrates a frequently referred to dimension of the state: the state is both an institutional form and other things, and it is precisely to these 'other things' that we shall return. One task of theoretical reflection on the state from a regulationist perspective consists in defining and re-examining these 'other things'.

The ubiquity and plural nature of the state impede the desire to grasp this complex labyrinth in a unified pattern from the start. Reflections on the state and a pure theory, which is more or less speculative and cobbled together, may claim to overcome this obstacle. But these exercises are in a different field from the theoretical research that requires empirical validation of its claims as a constant form of discipline. In this field the best referee is international comparison. International comparisons provide a good antidote to ethnocentric extrapolations based on national cases and to facile, non-qualified and unrestricted use of the many stereotypes commonly associated with the state (welfare, police, interventionist, liberal, etc.). This is not to criticise these images in themselves, only to point out that they are frequently extrapolated and insufficiently mastered. Theoretical research into the state combined with empirical investigation makes a virtue of prudence, requires tenacity, and above all learns to remain modest, abandoning scientism and impatience.

Our project is to contextualise and to offer a unified representation of the heterogeneous relations between the state and the economy. The reason for emphasising these aspects is consideration of the importance of a vantage point and perspective chosen from many possible points of view. This is the objective of the first section. We shall then present the MREE (mode of relation between the state and the economy) and ERIC (the state as relational integrated and complex).

Relations between the state and the economy as an object of study

The proposed approach is economic; the difficulty of this approach is that the perspectives of sociology, political science and law are no less relevant *a priori*. It can even be argued that reflection on the state is rather cramped within academic definitions of disciplines and areas of knowledge. Other regulationist research on the state confirms this (Jessop, 1990b; Bertramsen *et al.*, 1991), sometimes in an overtly interdisciplinary perspective (Théret, 1992a, 1999). This diversity indicates a key element, which is the question of point of view. We accept that theories of the state, like all objects of study, depend first and foremost on observing a theorist's project and that no project is illegitimate *a priori*. This investigative freedom is compensated for by the obligation to demonstrate the appropriateness of a given theory to a proposed project. Hence the importance of explicating the project, point of view, point of attack, problem to be resolved and effectiveness of the theory – in other words, the degree to which it responds to the problem.

Our *project* is the place and role of the state in economics. 'In economics' involves two levels. First, the field of social activity of the production, distribution and use of the material conditions of existence. Second, discourse and knowledge about this field of activity. The *point of view* adopted here is the state–economy relation. The *point of attack* is bipartite: historical and international comparison. The *problem to resolve* is the *contextualisation* of this relation and a *unified manner* of comprehending the co-ordination of these homogeneous and heterogeneous aspects. The notion of the mode of relation between the state and the economy offers a solution to this problem. For the sake of clarity in what follows, it is necessary to distinguish what is derived from reflections about the state from theory and research strategy. Reflections on the state can adapt to a principally deductive, descendant, top-down perspective which is programmatic and open to speculation, while a theoretical representation is far more restricted. It must be supplied with a form of explanation or representation of reality, which is explicitly subject to a test of validity. In the present context we have adopted the theoretical position. It provides us with the concept of veritable 'conditions of contract' which defines the problem to resolve as well as the conditions of its resolution. This chapter should therefore be read in relation to this particular, significant point of view.

The state is understood as the set of institutions with the prerogatives of public power via the central state, local administration and social security organisations. In the conception of *régulation* theory these are viewed as the processes by which a degree of order remains in a socio-economic system which is under unavoidable tension (Delorme, 1991). Although it recognises the existence of deliberate actions intended to adjust the activities of many agents, the approach we have adopted rejects the reduction of observable processes to a sole result of conscious and intentional regulating mechanisms. Economic adjustment is considered as the temporary consequence of a collection of local, heterogeneous decisions. This perspective starts with the tendency to disorder, compensated by 'a degree of order' which alternates with the prevalence of disorder during periods of structural crisis. It should be noted that it therefore concerns crises affecting the areas of regularity that characterised the previous order, rather than the principles of organisation defining the system.

The mode of relation between the state and the economy (MREE)

The concept of a MREE expresses the reciprocal presence of the state and the economy within one another. The term 'presence' is used purposely because it is more neutral than 'intervention' which connotes a deliberately corrective action imposed on the economy by the state.

The MREE results from a double historical and international comparative investigation. In historical terms, research in France and other countries has revealed the discontinuous, sporadic nature of long-term movements of the state and the economy. Since the Second World War the *embedded* state has been dominant, subsequent to the *limited* state that prevailed before the First World War. The two World Wars precipitated the move to a new configuration of the state–economy relation. The idea that appears to best express this modified relation is the notion of the involvement of the state, whose economic aspects are social security and new monetary and financial implications.

International comparisons enable a refinement of this concept and lead to the concept of the MREE as a unified representation of the place and role of the state, allowing the presentation of similarities and differences between countries through an interpretative grid.

The concept of mode, rather than form, for the relation between the state and the economy indicates the presence of strong patterns of regularity creating the system, referring to a context which is defined historically (the embedded state) and geographically (the embedded German, French, etc., states) (André and Delorme, 1989). Historical research and international comparisons have enabled a gradual identification of several aspects of the place and role of the state in the economy, whose intersection forms a table that symbolises the MREE.

Four places for the state

The place of the state requires a fourfold distinction, in a descending hierarchy from the highest level of society as a whole to the most immediate level of its actors. The first level is the state as a societal principle according to the historical distinction between state and civil society. The progressive development of the modern state occurred simultaneously in England and France in the eighteenth century. This was the model that later spread throughout the world (Delorme, 1991). Essentially this level defines the social game. At the second level the rules of the game become apparent. This is the level of a common framework and the five institutional forms.

As an institution of this type, the state involves several phenomena:

1   The development of the law and its means of control (the justice system, police).
2   The production and codifying of other rules of the game-institutions.
3   The rules of operation of the legislative and executive powers; centralisation–decentralisation; the administrative state – the authoritarian state – the legal state; the structuring of the territory.
4   The rules of financing and taxation.
5   The rules of relations with other states.

The third level is where the game is played out, to extend the image. It involves forms of action and interaction. It consists of markets, hierarchies, associations, alliances and different networks. Their relative weight and interrelations are unlikely to be similar from one economy to the next. The state appears in these hierarchies as a public hierarchy alongside the private hierarchies of companies. It also appears in relations with other forms of interaction.

Finally, at a fourth level, the state is an actor. This is the case in the domestic, internal order. Choices and decisions are made and based on its behalf. It may prove to be in competition with other actors (public companies, public and private education systems). It is also an actor in the international order. In this field it is the first actor, with each state supported by the recognition and legitimisation granted to it by other states.

Three roles for the state

What is the underlying logic in the daily operation of institutions and the state as actor? A general answer that is occasionally given is reproduction through perpetual taxation, limited by the need for the commodity field to reproduce (Théret, 1992a). Our point of view leads to a distinction between three types of logic for state actions: co-ordination, legitimisation and the power of constraint linked with sovereignty.

Co-ordination is a common notion in economics. Co-ordinating institutions are often seen as what are referred to here as institutions of action–interaction. It is a matter of co-ordination within a common framework.

With legitimisation we are touching on a less shared, more public notion. It is necessary to distinguish two possible meanings. In the first sense, legitimisation characterises the degree to which a situation is rendered just or acceptable even if it has co-ordination failures (unemployment, inequalities). Public action of a social nature, information about public action in general and its presentation, particularly in the media, illustrate this role. This is the narrow meaning that remains focused on instrumental aspects. In a wider sense, legitimisation refers to the creation of a set of norms and values that influence the representation of the reality available to actors. The perceptions of actors, the references of public policies, the processes for access to power are aspects of this social construction of reality that the state does not have a monopoly over, but in which it is the key place for playing out the stakes, acting as an essential arena. A comparative study of the development of public social insurance in Europe demonstrates the importance, in understanding national differences, of the way in which facts are selected and interpreted prior to the way in which problems are resolved.

The third role of the state is finally the one that is no doubt commented on the least often. This is the exercise of sovereignty: 'no higher power'. But this is not absolute. European integration offers a contemporary example of the way in which areas of sovereignty of member states have slipped towards a new entity under construction, the European 'state'. But this is still a matter dealt with exclusively by states. Economic theory does

Table 15.1 The mode of relation between the state and the economy

| Place of the state | The role of the state | | |
	A Co-ordination	B Legitimation	C Coercion
I Societal principle			
II Institutional form constituting the common framework	Mode of relation between the state and the economy (MREE)		
III Form of interaction			
IV Actor			

not leave much room for the two aspects of legitimisation and sovereignty, which are concerned with the formation and exercising of power, either through consent or in the mode of forced implementation. However, historical examples and comparisons demonstrate what impoverishment and technical and positivist misinterpretations are produced by concentrating solely on the co-ordination aspect.

Table 15.1 summarises this argument. The mode of relation between the state and the economy can be defined as the intersection of the place and role of the state in the table. It constitutes the matrix from which variations in history and between countries can be identified. International comparisons could be used to fill in the spaces in the table. The task is undoubtedly daunting, but there seems to be no other way to identify enduring similarities and differences between countries. The comparison between France and Germany, begun some time ago, is an example of this (André and Delorme, 1989; Delorme, 1991). To limit it to a realistic framework, until now it has mainly concerned comparisons of the common framework (II) and co-ordination (A). This is simply a first step towards the necessary description of contexts, illustrated by MREE, within which the presence of the state is exercised and economic policy is formed.

A key issue must also be made explicit in this context. In Table 15.1 the state does not have an exclusive role. The state is the principle, form and actor in relation to three roles, along with other principles, forms and actors. These notions interact through substitution and complementing, and this varies over time and in different places. In a simple sense, then, the state is an institution and actor among other institutions and actors in the socio-economic game, being therefore both unique and similar to others. This is not to trivialise the state, only to mention that it has nevertheless been brought down to earth. Hence the emphasis on a small letter, rather than a capital letter, for 'state' at the beginning of this chapter.

Those readers who find this minimising gesture sacrilegious can only be reminded that the goal of this clarification exercise is not to present the popular image of the immediate French perception of the state. Instead we wish to share the lessons which emerge from a systematic international comparison.

There are differences from one country to another, but it is not enough simply to say so; it is necessary to incorporate the differences in a structured representation. The mode of relation between the state and the economy seeks to answer this need. It gives a precise content to the notion of context and to the idea that the characterisation of the context, which gives meaning and intelligibility to the observation of differences between countries, is a preliminary stage in a comparative study of economic policies.

The state as relational, integrated and complex (ERIC)

The concept of the state that emerges is that of a relational, integrated and complex state. The state is relational in that it is perceived not as a substance defining an intrinsic essence by disjunction, but rather through a conjunction of phenomena indicating strong patterns. It is integrated in the sense that nowhere is there a duality between the state seen only as structure in contrast to a state seen only as actor. All in all, we are faced with the ubiquity and multiple nature of the state, and the theory accounts for this. In that sense the state is certainly a complex category, which suggests that the market economy be perceived more as a composite than in terms of a state–market coupling.

Cell III A of Table 15.1 provides an illustration. For example, in terms of institutional forms of interaction, the state appears as one form among others, in this case h_2, in the crossing of place III with the role of co-ordination A. The configuration A of co-ordinating forms of interaction can then be formulated in the following manner (Delorme, 1991):

$$A = (m, h_1, mh_1, h_2, a)$$

where m is external markets (stock exchange), h_1 is private internal markets, hierarchies or private organisations (companies), mh_1 competitive markets between private organisations, h_2 hierarchies or public organisations, and a is other forms, including the networks and connections between institutions (family, clans, alliances, partnerships, etc).

From the perspective of co-ordination, then, the economy can no longer be reduced to a state–market coupling, since a composite conception asserts itself. It is complex because the respective places of the elements vary with time and different places. Only empirical investigation can provide the content of this composite, and international comparisons remain the most operative judges. It is therefore possible to envisage the heroic effort required to retain a perception of explanations of dynamics either in terms of the failure of the market or in terms of a failure of the state.

16 The state, public finance and *régulation*

Bruno Théret

From the point of view of orthodox political economy the period of the Golden Age ('trente glorieuses') is paradoxical, since it was characterised by a combination of strong growth in commodity production together with high levels of taxation and public spending. In France during this period the rate of long-term growth of gross domestic product (GDP) more than doubled its mean value of the previous hundred years. The level of public spending associated with GDP also more than doubled (from a maximum of 15 per cent before the First World War to more than 40 per cent in the 1960s and 1970s). Active public finance is thus not necessarily an obstacle to strong economic growth.

For both factual and theoretical reasons, however, it would be wrong to infer that the secret of economic growth lies in forceful financial intervention by the state. First of all, a correlation is not proof of causality; two phenomena that entertain causal relations with the same third phenomenon may be correlated without determining each other. In the case of the relation between public spending and growth, domestic transformations caused by an extension of the wage–labour nexus to the majority of the population appear to be this type of third term.

Furthermore, the indicators usually employed to assess the role of the contemporary state in the economy overestimate the size of public finances in comparison with commodity production. This overestimation increases as indicator levels increase, therefore also causing overestimation of the growth and differences among countries of this size. Owing to the feature of democratic regimes whereby the tax system is self-financing, subjecting the public sector to the same tax law as the private sector (public spending thus becomes productive of tax resources), private resources that deviate from direct use by the tax system are generally less than those accounted for in it (Théret and Uri, 1987, 1991a, b; Théret, 1992a).

Finally, as seen first in the 1930s and then in the 1980s, a high level of public spending can just as well be accompanied by slow growth as by a strong growth rate.

Theoretically, to postulate a mechanical, ahistorical relation between growth and high levels of public spending is to make a return to the

functionalism of orthodox economic theories which claim that state intervention can be logically derived from the economy or its model. Once it
is a matter of analysing relations between the economy and *the state as
it really exists,* these relations are viewed not as functional but as the
product of mutual adaptation involving the invention of appropriate regulating institutional forms. Furthermore, the life of these institutions appears
to be limited to a period during which their individual and collective,
combined and cumulative effects create the historical conditions of their
own deviation, followed by a *régulation* crisis. This formulation of the
problem is one of the original and distinctive aspects of the regulationist
approach, which always avoids making the state the necessary and sole or
central regulator of a commodity economy. Instead the state is considered
one structural form of the mode of *régulation* among others (Théret, 1990).

However, for a long time regulationists 'forgot' to analyse the form of
the 'state' according to their epistemology. The concepts of 'institutionalised compromise' and 'wage benefits' that were initially proposed (Chapter
12) are mainly economic, and are used to account for the forms of public–
private interactions, rather than political *régulation* itself. Only in the
1990s was a collection of studies concerned with political *régulation* published (Bertramsen *et al.*, 1991; Boismenu and Drache, 1990; Delorme,
1991; Jessop, 1990; Théret, 1990b, 1991a, 1992a, 1994a, 1999; Palombarini, 1999). These studies all explore the economic implications of an
autonomous political sphere, viewing the state as both *an active party
in the economy* (via public finances and money) and as *constitutive of the
environment of the commodity economy* (through the interaction of public
policies).

The fact that the connection between extensive fiscal activity by the state
and economic growth is reversible indicates that the state can hold back
the development of capitalism just as much as it can encourage it. To take
this into account, we can posit an *a priori* hypothesis that *the state, capitalism and the family refer to different practical spheres, each with its own
historical laws of development.* This hypothesis is both historically and
theoretically founded. Historical research supports the view that the
economic and the domestic realms appear as autonomous spheres through
a process of separation from an overarching political sphere. Theoretically,
this differentiation leads to a definition of these spheres as follows. The
economic sphere is a social space in which social domination is motivated
by the capitalist logic of the endogenous accumulation of material posses-
sions and the monetary titles that represent these goods. The political
sphere, on the other hand, is a space in which domination is an end in
itself, where the economy may be instrumental, oriented to the accumulation of power over others and the legal titles that represent such power.
Finally, the domestic sphere is an autonomous space where the population
is produced and reproduced as a 'natural' resource that is exploited in the
other spheres once a separation in the contradictory logic of the state and

capitalism is established. To analyse the relation between one type of state and a type of capitalist growth is, from this perspective, to clarify the historical laws corresponding to each sphere and the system of monetary, legal and ideological mediations that enable these heterogeneous spheres of practices to coexist.

The economy of the political, its organic circuit and fiscal and financial regimes

In order to be autonomous, the different spheres of social practices must be endowed with their own economic system for obtaining the material resources necessary for their functioning. To examine the financial development of the state in this manner therefore calls for an analysis of the 'fiscal' economy of taxing which is without a direct counterpart. This economy is managed by agents who are looking for the means for a 'final', non-utilitarian expense, intended to support the reproduction of the state's power. The fact that the economy is politically oriented in this manner does not prevent it from having its own rationale, its own professionals and a specific institutional and organisational consistency. Furthermore, the fact that it endures through different economic contexts is an indication that it experiences long-term endogenous processes of reproduction and that its dynamic is partly self-regulated. A regulationist approach to the state must therefore attempt to clarify this dynamic within the political sphere – in other words, to find the system of political constraints that gives public finances a rate of development or that may lead to crisis.

The Marxian model of the cycle of capital that inspired the concept of an accumulation regime also suggests a distinction between three major forms of the state that are linked together in the cycle of its functional metamorphoses:

1   Purely political forms of sovereignty.
2   Forms of legitimacy.
3   Tax forms.

These three functional forms are convertible in what can be termed the *organic circuit of the state*. In demonstrating how, in a given historical situation, this organic circuit effectively creates a 'cycle', authorising some financial growth of the state and the development of political power, a *fiscal regime* is established, along with the mode of *régulation* of the corresponding political sphere (Théret, 1992a). A fiscal regime ensures a functional correspondence between legal and expenditure forms of the state's legitimacy through the intermediary of the tax levying process.

Because the description of political *régulation* at the first level is purely economic and primarily descriptive, it does not clarify the origin of the form of the fiscal regime, nor how or why a crisis might arise. For this, a second level of functional interdependence within the political sphere must be taken into account. This is the level of relations that expresses the dependence of the fiscal regime on the political regime (in its classic meaning), in other words the equivalent of the relation between the accumulation and property rights regimes in the economic sphere. Hence the need to analyse the way in which at some time the sovereign state (governed by a political regime) creates forms of legitimacy, consolidates the legal state, shapes the tax state through its mediation, and structures its expenditure.

Hybrid spaces, modes of social *régulation* and fiscal metamorphoses of capital

A third level of interdependence must also be taken into account, since the nature of the state also depends on its economic, social and international environment. Even if restricted to an examination of relations between the political and economic spheres at the national level, it is clear that this type of interdependence cannot be viewed as the fruit of functional, direct interactions. Indeed, it appears that, owing to their contradictions, the logics of economic and political reproduction can communicate and 'compromise' only through the mediation of a set of monetary, legal and ideological constructs which, as a historically circumscribed whole, constitute a *hybrid space* situated in between the different spheres. The domestic sphere is also situated in this hybrid space, since the reproducing population is a resource for both the political (power of force) and the economic (work force) spheres. If this hybrid space is endowed with coherence, the set of procedures and institutions (including institutionalised compromises and wage benefits) of which it is constituted forms the kernel of the mode of social *régulation*. This mode of social *régulation* ensures the social bond by shaping political and economic *régulations*, as well as the fiscal regime and the regime of capital accumulation.

We can illustrate this point first with the relation between an accumulation regime and a fiscal regime. First, this is a monetary relation, since a currency is a common means of payment and a unit of account that enables public finances to connect directly to the commodity economy. But the relation between the two regimes is also legal and ideological, since forms of taxation and the assignment of public outlays depend on the *philosophical conception* of citizenship, as well as the nature and extension of rights to income redistribution which are *legally recognised*. Finally, monetary relations between public finances and growth depend on two interdependent elements: the assignment of public spending and the role vested in private finance in relations between the state and the productive economy.

The economic nature of taxation depends on the assignment of public outlays: if spending is purely political (military, ostentatious display, etc.), then tax simply levies a surplus, if not the value itself (thus destroying the bases of simple reproduction). If spending finances infrastructures whose utility is not only linked with the military and administration but is also productive (transport systems, communication networks, improving the quality of the work force, etc.) public financial intermediation is a social-isation of capital advances and represents the *fiscal metamorphoses of capital* (Théret, 1993a). The state then participates directly in the accu-mulation regime on specific terms: the assignment's structure of public spending must always correspond to a fiscal completion of the organic circuit of the state.

Moreover the level of financial constraint on the monetary regime and, through its mediation, on the accumulation regime as well as on the fiscal regime depends on the place of private finance in the overall economic system. If private finance is directly connected with public finances, it will have a major role in political *régulation*. Loans will be the privileged instrument for funding a self-maintained budget deficit, since the cost of loans will play a central role in the fiscal regime (Théret, 1991b, 1992a, 1993b, 1995). But if private finance does not succeed in imposing itself as the necessary intermediary for relations between the state and a produc-tive economy, the power structure between creditors and debtors may swing in favour of debtors, allowing monetary financing of both capital accumulation and the state budget. Financial constraint on the monetary regime is weakened in favour of a social constraint, and the monetary *régu-lation* no longer depends on a finance-based anchoring of the national currency on a value standard outside the social system (either a material standard or a foreign currency). Instead it is directly dependent on an internal institutionalised compromise (for instance, an income policy) between the tenants of the three spheres: the administration, employers and employees.

From a virtuous configuration of Fordism and the welfare state to its crisis

A virtuous configuration linking high levels of public finance with growth is obtained if the marginalisation of private finance in the sphere of public finances is twinned with fiscal metamorphoses of capital favourable to both capital accumulation and development in the political sphere. This was the case during the Golden Age ('trente glorieuses'), when Fordism and the welfare state were mutually reinforcing.

The rights acknowledged to a person in the political sphere form a *public debt* in his or her regard. This is the other side of the state's duty to protect; it is the foundation of the legitimacy of the state's monopolisation of phys-ical force. Whether it is financial or social, in a general sense the 'public debt' is the revised central legal form of state legitimacy, institutionalised in official 'books' where people are named and their position or 'status' in the political sphere is registered (Bourdieu, 1995). This includes the accompanying 'securities' and titles unlocking rights to the fiscal resources (census list, peerage, debt registers, the cadastral register, the register of births, deaths and marriages, the index of welfare recipients, academic qualifications, etc.) (Théret, 1992b, 1994a, 1995). From this perspective the question of the welfare state concerns the specifically wage-based content of the public debt. In a liberal state political citizenship is restricted and social citizenship does not exist, since state protection is reserved exclusively for society's managers (civil servants, those in 'high finance', the landlords and state's *rentiers*, trader-bankers). But in the welfare state the state's obligation to protect is extended to all wage earners, and is subsequently widened to include the general population.

When a true labour market develops, the public debt takes on the universal form of social security and a public right to training for all. The service of this debt is made up of all the spending which, along with private spending, enables the maintenance or improvement of the 'life capital' of the population, and thereby its capacity for lifetime employment and the market value of the labour force. Once the value of the 'life capital' distributed to individuals as counterpart to the public debt to them, through expenditure dedicated to life protection and composed of a collective investment in health, education, etc., is recognised on the labour market, it is an element in the value of the work force. While public investments are the source of productivity increases, for wage earners they can be reflected in an increase in the reservation wage and wage differentials based on the different official 'statuses' by which they are recognised, according to their ability to appropriate public resources to themselves. In return, this market validation of public spending is the source of an endogenous growth dynamic for the welfare state since it is self-financed. Its extended reproduction is ensured by the increase in public revenue generated through its effects on production and the wage bill. This is the virtuous cycle that explains how, during the Fordist period, strong economic growth was allied with a high level of public spending and taxation.

Just as the political *régulation* of liberal states was destabilised by the tendency for real interest rates to fall, causing them to reach a crisis point when the power structure between creditors and debtors was reversed, the welfare state is in a crisis when its self-financing circuit is challenged and the value of 'life capital' that it produces is no longer considered equal to its cost in the economic sphere. Hence the return to a competitive *régulation* of the labour market in the 1980s, which tended to make public investment a write-off from an economic point of view, and the restoring of a nearly fixed monetary regime. This led to an increasing public financial debt in competition with social debt, reflecting a profound crisis in the welfare state through the crisis in the regime of capital accumulation. But this strong return of private finance in the state and this loss of efficiency in the fiscal metamorphoses of capital occur in an entirely different context from the one that enabled the 'limited' liberal state to stabilise itself on these premises (Delorme and André, 1983). Also, it is less the actual type of welfare state associated with the wage norms of socialisation that is in crisis than the national space in which the welfare state has been deployed until now (Théret, 1994c, 1997).

17 *Régulation* theory and economic policy

Frédéric Lordon

Régulation theory undoubtedly has a contradictory relation to economic policy (Lordon, 1997a, 1999): regulationists are eager to take part in debates on economic policy and to 'propose projects', yet theoretically it is clear that the inaugural act of *régulation* theory was precisely the exclusion of economic policy. This creates an obvious contradiction and is one of the great difficulties with reintegrating the issue of economic policy into a theoretical corpus that was not created with economic policy in mind. The contradiction is all the more awkward because, given the extent of the recession of the early 1990s and the obstacles to a transition to a hypothetical post-Fordism, the need for economic policy has rarely been more urgent. Moreover, it is unfortunate that the original analyses of crisis proposed by *régulation* theory have not also produced definite principles of action.

From criticism of the 'voluntarist illusion' to the primacy of a historical dynamic

The historical perspective adopted by *régulation* theory reflects an intention to view short-term change (including economic policy) in an appropriate perspective by also having due regard for deep-rooted, long-term trends. After thirty years of triumphant Keynesianism this is no easy task, but the crisis of the Fordist regime provided an occasion for a review. *Régulation* theory also seeks to show that emergence from a crisis has no more to do with a better balance of the policy mix than the growth that preceded it resulted from supposedly enlightened conduct of economic policy. Countering the claims of economists who, armed with an IS–LM model, want to attribute the prosperity of the Golden Age ('trente glorieuses') to the effectiveness of their economic policy, *régulation* theory demonstrates how the long growth phase was the product of a unique structural configuration, created and instituted in the long term. It suggests instead that the intense accumulation of the 1950s and 1960s should be attributed to a process of historical evolution and a series of institutional changes that brought the economy to the regime that regulationists call Fordism. Growth is viewed as the effect of a conjunction of a number of deep-rooted mechanisms (technical progress, demand creation, etc.) supported by specific historically based institutional forms, rather than as the fruit of skilful stimulation by economic policy. Acceptance of this thesis, which is so different from the received idea of a godlike directing of growth through public intervention, requires a theoretical and rhetorical strategy that includes strong depreciation of economic policy. Criticism of the 'voluntarist illusion' (the expression is from Delorme and André, 1983) thus involves proving the 'anecdotal' or superficial nature of economic policy in respect of the long-term dynamic forces that are principally responsible for shaping growth trajectories.

This general intent to devalue economic policy can also be seen in the limited role it plays in a regulationist view of the historical dynamic of capitalist economies, in which, more or less, phases of 'regime' economy alternate with episodes of crisis.

'Regime' economies reflect the structuralist aspects of regulation theory. Mature and stable institutions reduce the diversity of agents via channelling and grouping, thereby predetermining their behaviour. Within this set of structures, economic policy is but one institutional form among others, functioning according to its own self-adjusting mechanisms in accordance with its role in the general arrangement of the mode of *régulation*. In the general context of 'structural predetermination', economic policy is directed mainly by compromises imposed on it or the institutional forms to which it is related (monetary constraint, the wage–labour nexus, etc.). In these conditions, economic policy generally lacks autonomy.

Episodes of crisis are no more conducive to restoring the sovereignty of economic policy, but obviously for very different reasons. While structures challenged by a crisis may have less of an impact, thereby apparently recreating a space for economic policy, this is only to confront it with the disorder of restructuring and the search for institutions. In that case it is not excessive predetermination but indeterminacy that paralyses economic policy, which, when faced with effervescent innovation and an elusive social dynamic, is incapable of providing the general leadership needed to emerge from the crisis. 'Enslaved' by the weight of structures 'during a regime' and disoriented by crises, there is no doubt that a regulationist perspective leaves little room for economic policy.

Four regulationist positions in regard to economic policy

The exclusion of economic policy takes different forms according to the theoretical approach, which is generally sceptical, despite individual heterogeneity. The position of regulationists in respect of economic policy can be reduced schematically to four main arguments.

The first position is that economic policy is directed by institutional compromises. This view, which can be described as 'radical Poulantzasian' (Lordon, 1994c), is the centre of gravity for *régulation* theory in regard to economic policy. According to this view, economic policy is less an act of sovereignty than the result of the 'automatic' functioning of institutionalised compromises over which it has very little control. This can be seen in budgetary policy, where the deficit is presented as 'an algebraic reflection of the costs and benefits of partial and diverse *régulation* procedures' (Théret, 1990) or as 'the result of non-arbitrated conflicts rather than the voluntary means of intervention by the state' (Aglietta, 1986a). So too with the 'hostage' monetary policy (Aglietta and Orléan, 1982) of social groups with conflicting interests, or those which are still sufficiently steered by the inflationary compromises of the wage–labour nexus to earn the label 'labour standard' regime (Boyer, 1993). Deprived of all autonomy in this conception, economic policy acts as the centre of gravity for institutionalised compromises.

However marginal it is within the regulationist corpus as a whole, the Girardian breakaway, as found in 'The Violence of Money' (Aglietta and Orléan, 1982), provides the most radical critique of economic policy. Since no one is immune to imitative violence when involved in the affairs of the world, all maxims for action reflect rivalries and are ontologically polluted by private interest. The discourse of political economy does not avoid this partisan fate. An 'objective' discourse capable of perfect exteriority – in other words, able to rid itself of all partisan commitments and keep contagious rage at a distance – can be viewed only as a total renunciation of the will to act on the world and an abstention from offering any directives. Thus if any economic discourse does attain 'truth' and 'objectivity', the most certain way of identifying it is through the marked absence of any indication of economic policy!

At the risk of partially contradicting the previous statement, it should be recognised that not all regulationists share this pessimism in respect of economic policy. Lipietz is probably the author most representative of 'resistance' to pessimism. His approach is to plunge directly into the arena of recommendations or 'programmes', demonstrating that economic policy is not a problem in itself (Lipietz, 1984a, 1985, 1993b, 1998, 1999). The question of whether it is possible is either not discussed or receives an implicit, immediately affirmative response. Evidently such confidence does not imply that the definition of economic policy is simple, or that it is enough to follow the same paths as 1960s Keynesianism. First, in making his recommendations Lipietz is very aware of a regulationist analysis of crisis and emphasises the 'structural' aspect of actions to be taken. Second, he is careful to include many recommendations for 'effective institutions', emphasising in particular the 'socio-political engineering' that must support this type of economic policy. The ability to identify and 'organise' a 'good' hegemonic bloc, that is, a set of social and political forces supportive of the central authority, which it can use as intermediaries for its actions, implies that directing social dynamics is an original and important aspect of this conception of economic policy.

Finally, there is a fourth position (Boyer, 1986a, 1999a) involving a synthesis of contradictory tendencies, and implicitly favouring the minority optimism of Lipietz: 'according to this conception of the forms of state intervention, neither strict predetermination nor complete autonomy is the rule' (Boyer, 1986a, 53, trans. 1990: 42). However cursory, once the relative autonomy of state action is acknowledged, this formulation reopens a limited but real space for a partially sovereign economic policy.

Inserting economic policy in *régulation* theory

The area examined by this chapter does not allow an explanation of the principles involved in a regulationist theory of economic policy. Simply pointing out that it starts from the theoretical foundation of the relative autonomy of the state should suffice to indicate the extent of the work to be done! In this context, therefore, the reader is referred to Théret's extensive analyses (1990, 1992a), which provide many theoretical and historical elements in addition to numerous and varied suggestions (Lordon, 1994c, 1997a, 1999; Palombarini, 1997, 1999; Boyer, 1999a).

It is, however, possible to outline some of the categories through which economic policy can be included in the regulationist theoretical apparatus while respecting two of its founding principles. These two principles are the periodising of the historical dynamics of capitalism and the identification of the institutional configurations that characterise each era (Lordon, 1994c).

First, the emphasis on the transience of accumulation regimes suggests a distinction between two forms of economic policy. The first form, called 'the economic policy of a regime', is part of the mode of *régulation*. Here economic policy appears as a supplementary form of co-ordination at the macro level, alongside 'traditional' institutional forms (the wage–labour nexus, forms of competition, etc.) which it supplements and reinforces. Thus the economic policy of a regime works *within* the structure, which it receives as a given and quasi-invariable aspect of an economy 'in a regime'.

But – and this is specific to *régulation* theory – economic policy may also be confronted with a growth regime's crisis. State intervention then takes the form of an 'economic policy of regime transition', and in this case the uniqueness of the state as institution is reasserted (Théret, 1990; Lordon, 1994c). As an institution alongside other institutions the state is also seen as a superior institution, since it is endowed with a limited but real power to transform other institutions. To explicitly envisage the possibility of an economic policy of regime transition thus requires regulationists to acknowledge fully the topological ambivalence of the state (Théret, 1992a; Lordon, 1994c). Being both interior and exterior, the state is an arrangement that works *within* the mode of *régulation* (see the famous 'forms of the state', Boyer, 1986a) as well as an external support mechanism through which it is possible to act *on* the mode of *régulation*.

Even if the historical uniqueness of major crises makes it difficult to establish a general theory of the politics of regime transition, according to the second founding principle referred to above, it is nevertheless possible to view the construction of the economic policy of a regime as an institutional form.

From this point of view, one might propose a consideration of the form of the 'regime of economic policy' based on the following elements:

1   *The forms of intervention* include all the instruments employed by the economic policy of a regime: the budget, money, foreign exchange, incomes policy, etc.

2   *The institutional framework of intervention* clarifies the type of organisation or agency in charge of the conception and/or conduct of economic policy. Is it a national, international or supranational agency? Is it governmental or extra-governmental, a committee of 'experts', and are they in contact with university circles or not? The definition of the institutional form of economic policy also involves examination of the structure of the state apparatus, detailing the distribution of power, the authorities creating doctrines or holding legitimacy, the way in which even administrative organisation leads to biases in developing economic policy, etc.

3   *The conditions of validation by private agents* emphasise the importance of interaction between the implicit or explicit representations involved in economic policy and those of the recipient private agents. Bearing in mind Aglietta and Orléan's warnings (1982), it is important to recognise the morphogenetic impact of imitative contagion, that is, the ability of polarised private opinions to create macro-behaviour, through collective election and self-validation. This is liable to cause the failure of an economic policy that contradicts their 'vision of the world' too strongly. An example is the particularly bitter 'conflict of representation' in the early 1990s between a policy of competitive disinflation and the polarisation of agents' opinions in the demand for a lowering of interest rates. In this instance, whether or not the agent's opinions are well founded is not the issue. While such adverse polarisation of agents' opinions of the real economy is unusual and characteristic only of periods of profound crisis, it has become a permanent element in economic policy through the monitoring of economic policies by international financial markets. In terms of the 'conditions of validation by private agents' the explosion of financial markets in the 1980s is evidence of a fundamental change in the regime of economic policy.

4   Finally, an element *of interface with the mode of régulation* can supplement the definition of the economic policy regime by detailing the way in which this institutional form interacts with its counterparts in the mode of *régulation*. Essentially it is a matter of specifying the

relation of economic policy to the institutional compromises incorporated in the other forms of the mode of *régulation*. An initial
classification (Lordon, 1994a) presents many configurations, far more
than the unique 'Poulantzasian' type of predetermination of state intervention via the automatic functioning of compromises; this corresponds
to a 'dominant' regulationist position. Apart from this instance of
'predetermination', economic policy can also be exercised independently, without affecting institutional compromises, even facilitating
the exercising or clearing of some of their consequences, but it may
also find itself obstructed by resistance originating in them, or may
lead to their dismantling.

Elements of a regulationist discourse on economic policy

Regulationist discourse on economic policy distinguishes itself by taking
many temporal frameworks into account, with special emphasis on long-
term dynamics and 'structural effects', as well as the presence and
transience of institutional forms.

In terms of the first aspect, concerning the structure, long-term and
economic policy of a regime, *régulation* theory already provides a number
of warnings based on its theoretical framework.

1   The first condition for the effective economic policy of a regime
    depends on the quality of the 'structure' (the accumulation regime)
    upon which it is exercised. Stable macroeconomic patterns in the econ-
    omy of a regime ensure not only the quality of their comprehension
    and instrumentation by economic policy, but also the 'homogeneity'
    and predictability of agents' reactions in response to economic policy
    initiatives. In contrast, an accumulation regime undergoing change is
    indicative of the weakening of an institution's ability to form groups,
    a rise in heterogeneity and thus confusion or the break-up of macro-
    patterns, making it far more difficult to direct economic policy.
2   *The search for an 'optimal' economic policy is probably illusory.* The
    intensity and sign of the influence of a measure of economic policy
    depend essentially on the structure to which it is applied. Aglietta *et
    al.*, (1981) have demonstrated how the same exchange policy can
    produce radically different effects, depending on its place within the
    international division of labour and the competitive position of the
    productive apparatus subject to the policy.
3   *'Short-term' policy also has long-term effects.* Regulationists have
    already warned that, in terms of the short/medium-term effects of
    competitive policies of disinflation in restoring profits, it is necessary
    to consider supplementary obstacles encountered on the way to a 'post-
    Fordist co-operative' model. Centred on controlling costs, competitive
    disinflation extends a 'logic' of competitive prices, the very logic found

in the abandoned Fordist model, making the advent of a 'logic' of structural competition and its organisational forms more difficult.

Employing the construction of the previous section in a more direct manner, it may therefore be suggested that the regulationist vision of the 1970s open crisis should be supplemented by suggesting that the exhaustion of a growth regime coincides with a crisis in an economic policy regime. Initially this crisis appears paradoxical since it is simultaneously endogenous and separate. It is endogenous because the difficulties of the Keynesian regime of economic policy inevitably deviate from the crisis of Fordism that provided some of the conditions that made it possible. But it is also separate since the loss of effectiveness of the economic policy of a regime is largely related to a group of relatively independent factors at the 'heart' of Fordist growth, for example the technological paradigm or forms of the wage–labour nexus, etc. Indeed, it is not possible to overlook phenomena such as the increasing contradiction between the internationalisation of trade and the persistent conduct of economic policy through national agencies (in which the institutional framework of the regime policy is questioned). Nor should we overlook the drastic modifications in the conditions of validation by private agents correlating to the emergence of financial markets. These are all elements that ultimately owe little to the main characteristics of Fordism (Chapters 8 and 14).

While it does enable an orderly rereading of the past, the conceptual framework outlined above may also (and this would be a sign of its productivity) provide support for a prospective attempt to discern the elements of a future 'post-Keynesian' regime of economic policy.

In terms of future prospects, beyond the horizon of the policy of a regime, the 'greatest concern' for regulationists in respect of economic policy is the question of defining a regime transition policy. *Régulation* theory appears to have passed through three stages in regard to this question. After the paradoxical Hayekism of its early days (i.e. it is impossible to grasp the transition that results only from a 'spontaneous' tinkering of social groups aided by great 'redistributions' of history such as war, catastrophes, etc.) an acceptable post-Fordism model was identified (Taddei and Coriat, 1993; Boyer and Durand, 1998). The third stage now on the agenda is a question that will no doubt occupy regulationists for some time to come: how do we move into a post-Fordism era?

Part III

Macroeconomic dynamics and structural change

18 Institutional forms and macroeconomics

Bernard Billaudot

Traditionally, studies of macroeconomic dynamics have been interested in the quantitative aspects of the overall economic development of a country (e.g. growth, inflation, unemployment, productivity, consumption *per capita*); regulationists do not question this definition of the field. However, their conception of the macroeconomic dynamic – not as the displacement of general equilibrium (including the Keynesian sense of the term) but as a *historic process* – leads them to a pluralist viewpoint. Going beyond the only local theory of the Fordist accumulation regime, the first generation of research by the Paris school produced the following general proposition.

The macroeconomic dynamic is not subject to a general law; the laws of a country at any given time depend on the existing institutions. If, over the course of a historical period, the forms of these institutions harden, the system of forms creates a set of partial *régulations* whose elements are generally stabilised (time periods for adjustment, levels of indexation, etc.); this causes a specific macroeconomic dynamic. Over the long-term perspective in which structural change is observed, regular patterns are to be recognised: it is an accumulation regime or a long-term growth regime. This regime can be considered the result of a dynamic creation of consistency between a mode of *régulation* and a mode of development. It involves giving these two concepts an empirical meaning that is somewhat different from the usual *régulation* theory definitions. In this context the 'mode of *régulation*' refers to the routine way in which the set of decentralised decisions made by individual and collective agents (or actors) is adjusted reciprocally. The 'mode of development' refers more specifically to the connection between a way of obtaining an improvement in hourly labour productivity (at the macroeconomic level) and a way of using this improvement to change the living conditions of the population.

For reasons that are endogenous to the basic conditions of the regime, its exhaustion is necessary. This leads to a period of crisis,* marked by a strong alteration of previous patterns or their entire dissolution. A change in institutional forms is at work.

The research considered here tests the correctness of this proposition in the light of the facts. Limiting itself to developments observed in the main industrial countries, the research identified two regimes:

1   From 1850 to 1913 a regime of cyclical growth with recurrent peri-odic crises linked with a competitive mode of *régulation* and a mainly extensive mode of development (weak growth in productivity and the power of wage consumption).
2   From 1945 to 1970 a regime of almost continuous growth linked with a monopolist/Fordist mode of *régulation* and with a mode of devel-opment that connected production and mass consumption intensively (strong parallel growth in capital intensity, labour productivity and the purchasing power of wage incomes, without decreasing hours worked).

Furthermore, research into countries at the limits of the strategic area of the dominant growth regime has produced a widening of the classification of accumulation regimes (Chapter 20).

This research had an additional object: to deduce the macroeconomic dynamic implied by institutional forms through the use of models. This is indispensable in going from partial *régulation*, where each is reflected in a relation of the model, to overall *régulation*. However, it has been subjected to many criticisms. Some critics (Mingat *et al.*, 1985) claim that the two periods/objects of the analysis are not clearly distinguished. Others (Cartelier and de Vroey, 1989) consider that the only theory constructed is of the Fordist regime, with the reference model provided by Hugues Bertrand (1983). Have subsequent analyses with this secondary purpose managed to supersede these limits? Have they brought about a refinement or revision of the general proposition described above? The chapters of Part III answer these questions.

Chapters 18 and 19 are restricted to studies dealing with the short and medium-term macroeconomic dynamic within the analytical framework of an isolated economy (only institutional forms operating within the nation state are taken into account) in terms of linear modelling.

The first model described is that of Robert Boyer (1988b). This is a *medium-term* model. The second is the one Bernard Billaudot (1994a) constructed to supplement some of the gaps in the earlier model. Billaudot deals explicitly with agent reactions in the *short term* (including in terms of price), so that it is able to generate changes in the medium term and thus deal with the stability and instability of this type of development. Unlike Bertrand's model, which is a sectional model specifically relevant to Fordism, these two models are global and general.

The construction method of the two models will be considered, meas-uring the continuity and developments that characterise the move from one to the other, as well as the limits retained. The results yielded by these models are presented below.

Constructing a general regulationist model

The construction of a theoretical rather than an econometric macroeconomic model reflects a pre-set figure. This figure is specified by a frame of analysis, establishing the causal relations of the overall variables (GDP volume, general price level, etc.) found in this framework, starting from hypotheses formulated in terms of the behaviour of elementary agents and the rules governing their relations. In an equilibrium approach, this behaviour derives from an individualist *a priori* rationality at the different levels (e.g. production levels). The model constructed is first and foremost a model of equilibrium: the temporal dynamic is studied by displacing the equilibrium obtained using comparative statistics. The only problem the realisation of this pre-set figure then presents is the aggregation, which prompts the common subterfuge of employing a representative agent.

In an approach based on *régulation* theory different problems are encountered. Once behaviour is derived from *a posteriori* rationality, it affects reactions intended to modify an existing state of affairs, so that causal relations are only relative to changes in overall variables. This is a simplification, but, on the other hand, behaviour and rules change along with institutions. In every institutional system, macroeconomic patterns have consequences for the formation of microeconomic routines (or modes of management). Since this often results in crowd phenomena (reciprocal imitation), the subterfuge of the representative agent is no longer appropriate. How are these problems interpreted and resolved in the models considered here?

Historical alterations in institutional forms

By definition, all macroeconomic causal relations link changes in a variable with current or previous levels and with changes in other explanatory variables. The regulationist hypothesis is that any given system of institutional forms has a corresponding set of individual relations, whose parameters (coefficients or elasticities, autonomous impulses) are stable in the medium term. How then can the historical variability of institutional forms be integrated in a single model that is general, even though it is restricted to the past?

The solution adopted is to gather together in one causal relation various specifications, each of which is derived from a particular mode of *régulation* and translated into explanatory variables. In Robert Boyer's model, this principle leads to the conclusion that the parameters in the relation constructed in this way are variable elements in historical time. In Bernard

Billaudot's model, two directly opposite specifications, with explanatory variables and given parameters, are considered initially: one corresponds to the competitive mode and the other to the Fordist mode. These are then combined to obtain a general relation. The expression of this combination provides another type of parameter, which is historically variable (e.g. the level of collective procedures for wage bargaining). In terms of the overall model, these additional parameters are aspects of the forms of organisation of the economy.

Institutional forms, rules and behaviour

As we have seen above, the purpose of the model is not to generate new institutional forms. It is simply to 'produce' the macroeconomic dynamic that results from a given system. The question is how to formalise the way in which institutions function. Three acknowledged principles of action are (1) collective and coercive laws, rules and regulations; (2) compromise, following negotiations between private agents or groups about the official conventions governing mutual engagements; (3) custom (a common value system, shared representations) or a tacit behavioural convention (Boyer, 1986a: 55–6, trans. 1990: 44–5).

In the first generation of research macroeconomic relations were derived directly from this type of system of rules and conventions; the microeconomic behaviour path is rather unclear, and was not in any case formalised. Robert Boyer's model is still based on direct derivation, but the analysis justifying the specification(s) retained is no longer based on a holistic method, and this change is mentioned quite regularly. In Bernard Billaudot's model the first partial attempts to formalise the model are found, especially with respect to the policy of acquisitions and scrapping of fixed equipment in the large Taylorian company (cf. Fordist specifications). The hypothesis put forward is that agents conform to prevailing rules and conventions in so far as they lead to developments considered satisfactory at their level. The model constructed only enables a study of the implications of this conformity.

Macroeconomic patterns and microeconomic routines

To some extent direct derivation 'eliminates' the problem posed by system effects, such as those presumed in the formation of management routines by agents (company, household, bank, etc.). Not that these effects can then be ignored, but they are not formalised as such. This is the case even in the field limited by the object of the model: it is not a matter of establishing a theory of the hardening of routines, or a theory of their alteration, when developments are no longer deemed satisfactory. In fact, they are taken into account through the presence of explanatory variables in all or some of the causal relations. For example, past changes in final consumption in relation to the development of investment, within the Fordist context. If we adopt the Keynesian norm of expectation (i.e. future events will develop as they have in the past, unless there are specific reasons to expect a change), the role of macroeconomic patterns is to create a future forecast for agents, supporting such observation with statistical data. Consequently, according to the hypothesis that this type of predictive convention exists at the level of each professional sector, in the example given previous changes in demand reflect an anticipated role of demand in the medium term. The fact that only changes in final consumption are taken into account is derived from an aggregate logic (branch/sector/global) without crowd phenomena.

Aggregate and crowd phenomena

Crowd phenomena are similar to system effects: they are taken into account more or less explicitly at the point in the analysis underlying direct derivation. The solutions adopted often depend on individual cases. If the field of technical change is left aside (cf. the causal relation in the evolution of productivity, a topic discussed later in Part III), processes of reciprocal imitation are mainly at work in terms of prices and wages, whatever the institutional context. If we limit ourselves to the formation of the general evolution of nominal wages in a Fordist context, the problem posed relates to the presence of decentralised levels of the collective negotiation of wage increases. Following Boyer and Mistral (1978), the solution is to postulate the existence of a *leader sector*, to which other sectors adjust.

In this field, as in previous areas, a theoretical approach is adopted. But it does not involve retaining specifications inferred from an econometric scanning and then attempting to justify them. Certainly, deductive analysis still lacks rigour. Many intermediary analyses could replace direct derivation. These imply reference to formal tools other than those employed to establish a microeconomic foundation for macroeconomics, without excluding game theory. They require the criteria of 'satisficing' of the various agents to be specified. Nevertheless, the models studied have already produced interesting results in regard to the stylised facts requiring explanation.

19 Short- and medium-term macroeconomic dynamics

Bernard Billaudot

This chapter presents and compares two models. Robert Boyer (1988b) offers a *medium-term* model, whose horizon is defined theoretically as the time of overall *régulation*, that is, the period at the end of which the set of reciprocal adjustments between the various economic agents is exhausted. It is possible to produce *regimes* with this time horizon. By definition, a medium-term regime involves a dynamic in which each macroeconomic variable evolves at a constant rate over the selected time period. In this instance, the model's variables are these constant rates, but this does not imply that the dynamic is in equilibrium in the common sense of the term. In terms of a general model *many* regimes are produced (Chapter 18).

Bernard Billaudot (1994a) discusses a *short-term* model: the causal relations derive from short-term macroeconomic variables. While the medium term refers to the closure of overall *régulation*, a short-term horizon relates to its origins in terms of the accumulation of fixed capital, that is, the reaction time shown in this field. This is the time that elapses before gross acquisitions or scrapping of permanent equipment are influenced by the recent state of the installed capacity utilisation rate. By definition, changes in this capacity are therefore exogenous in the short term. Viewed thus this horizon differs from a cyclical horizon which, in the short term, refers to the time period of adjustment of production scheduled in response to demand.

By taking short-term reactions into account and dealing explicitly with changes in nominal wages and prices, this model leads to new results and a reappraisal of some of the results of the previous model. The present chapter concerns the short-term dynamic and a reconsideration of the nature and validity of the various medium-term regimes encountered in the process.

A medium-term regime: intersection of a productivity regime and a demand regime

The model is resolved so as to produce two reduced equations initially. The first links the evolution of productivity with the growth rate of production, recognising the way in which growth ultimately controls productivity in the medium term: this is a *productivity regime.* The second links the evolution in the volume of global demand with improvements in productivity, acknowledging the way in which demand is ultimately impelled by productivity, through the effect of productivity on real distributed income: this is a *demand regime.* Since production adapts to demand, all medium-term regimes result from the intersection of these two partial regimes (Appendix 19.1).

Base parameters are known to vary according to institutional forms. When the fields of variation of these parameters are examined, the model produces very diverse intersecting configurations. Four configurations are highlighted, corresponding to the historical periods of the nineteenth century, the 1920s and 1930s, the 1960s and the 1970s and 1980s (see Lordon, 1991, for a more detailed presentation).

Some regimes are described as stable. This term simply implies that the intersecting configuration is not explosive: if advances in productivity differ from equilibrium value, there is a convergence towards this value (this is the case in the configuration represented in Appendix 19.1). Other regimes are unstable: there is no convergence towards the point of equilibrium as defined formally by the intersection of the productivity regime and the demand regime.

The active parameters in the shift from stability to instability as defined in the present context are principally the degree of indexation of real wages to productivity, the extent of dynamic returns to scale (elasticity of the medium term from productivity to growth in the basic order) and the impact of past profits in investment formation. However, this shift cannot be attributed to either factor, since each regime is characterised by a system of parameters. The conjecture that the viability of each institutional form is not individually constitutive, but relies instead on the system in which it is inscribed, is thus confirmed if not proved.

A second model involving short-term dynamics: existence and stability

According to the definition of the short-term horizon given above, evolution by volume of fixed investment is exogenous to this horizon for all institutional frameworks (Appendix 19.2).

The main results in this time frame concern the differences between the dynamics of competitive *régulation* and Fordist *régulation.* These differences arise in the move from collective procedures for wage bargaining to an absence of short-term adjustment of employment in effective production and an endogenous evolution of the money supply (increased deposits in ordinary banks). Consequently the possibility of crisis conditions, that is, the explosive dynamic in a short-term horizon, due to great elasticity in the average wage in employment, disappears. The nominal increase in salaries also has the status of a second impetus, exogenous to short-term growth, supplementing the evolution by volume of fixed investment; the dynamic multiplier of this factor is clearly reduced. Finally, all the depressive effects in the structural improvement of labour productivity are removed when accumulation is already intensive in the short term, as in the transitional inter-war period.

In any given institutional context (reflected in a system of parameters of the second type as defined in Chapter 18) the model presents the conditions required for a medium-term regime (at least) to exist. This regime is defined as the progression that occurs through regular development. In every instance these conditions are defined by the institutional context under consideration. They affect the parameters that express the elements of *régulation* within this framework.

Comparison with Robert Boyer's model suggests that what is called the condition of *stability* of a regime in his model is one of the conditions of the *existence* of the regime in the second model. Thus for all the medium-term regimes produced with the first model, those classified as 'unstable' are regimes without economic existence, even though they are defined mathematically. (They correspond to a progression through infinity.)

This leads to the following reappraisal. The criteria of existence and the criteria of stability must be clearly distinguished: a medium-term regime is not economically possible (or viable) unless its existence is confirmed and unless it presents stable progression.

Two results: the conditions for full employment and the origin of evolution of the real wage

As a consequence of the causal patterns, one example among others of progression in a regime is that the utilisation rate of the installed capacity remains stable, owing to existing orders. The growth rate determined by demand is then equal to the growth rate allowed by net accumulation. If this second growth rate is unique, only one regime can exist. Such uniqueness is achieved when the output rate is exogenous in the medium term. This is the case in competitive *régulation*, even after the predominance of large firms, given that a forecasting horizon for demand in the medium term was not established for large firms. From this point on, the unique medium-term regime cannot lead to changes in employment adapted to changes in the available active population, even if those changes are partly endogenous.

When a Fordist regime is established, the output rate becomes *endogenous* to the demand regime. This creates a spectrum of regimes. In one regime, full employment is ensured permanently. The flexibility of the output rate, rather than technical choices (Solow) or the wage/profit division (Kaldor and Robinson) would then be capable of ensuring the conditions of the golden age.

It is worth mentioning that this result was obtained by employing Michel Aglietta's hypothesis (1974) that 'scrappings are structurally incorporated in the formation of new capital assets' in large firms. This analysis therefore differs from Hugues Bertrand's analysis (1983), which is limited to a combination of two extreme solutions. Either there are 'dominant' firms, with the dynamic of full employment achieved by adjusting developments in wage purchasing power (the Cambridge solution), or else firms are 'dominated', with the rate of substitution between indirect and direct work acting as the variable of constraint (the neoclassical solution).

There is one point where the difference between regulationist analysis and different 'growth theories' is established: far from being a natural consequence, progression in the real wage with productivity results from the establishment of a new wage–labour nexus. We have already seen that in Robert Boyer's model this hypothesis is reflected directly through a causal relation in changes in the real wage, a relation in which the elasticity of the real wage with productivity acts as an institutional parameter. This 'coefficient of the division of productivity gains', which does not exist in competitive *régulation*, increases so long as wage formation 'results from a capital–labour compromise that codifies this division'.

In the second model, this type of relation is obtained as a reduced equation, through partial resolution, on condition that there is progress in a regime. Elasticity is then expressed as a function of all or part of the institutional parameters in the basic relations. Analysis of this function leads to an initial observation: such elasticity varies from zero (competitive *régulation*) to one (Fordist *régulation*). In this sense the regulationist hypothesis, as adopted by Robert Boyer, is confirmed, except in the case of a level higher than one. But a second observation leads to its reappraisal. In the general model the level of elasticity does not depend primarily on *the extent of collective procedures for wage bargaining*. The parameters, which link sales prices with manufacturing costs, play a determining role. This is the impact of large (anonymous) firms and the degree of extension of financing through debt by means of financial institutions. The hypothesis is that the Fordist context is characterised by a large impact and a high level. This level is such that all firms must attain an operating return norm, as far as possible. In this case, the norm expresses the *financial conventions* formed at the level of the banking system (in the broad sense) by reference to the level of its real refinancing interest rates. (This is the variable of action in the monetary policy of a debt economy.) In these conditions, large firms are no longer limited in their offering price policy by the fact that other firms are not subject to the norm. This ensures stability in the effective rate of return of all firms in a medium-term regime, even if this rate is at a permanently lower level than the fixed norm (in the framework of a regime of creeping inflation, at a constant real rate of interest). Apart from this type of context, the policy is only partially effective; the overall rate of return is not stable in a regime and the elasticity of real wages in relation to productivity is less than unity.

In any case, the overall conclusion is that the progression towards more competitive *régulation*, including the replacement of a debt economy by a financing economy, leads to a dissociation between the purchasing power of wages and the level of global productivity.

From the instability of competitive *régulation* to the stability of Fordist *régulation*

We now turn to the most important result, namely that the shift from competitive *régulation* to Fordist *régulation* is accompanied by a shift from *instability* to *stability*. The criterion of stability here is the absence of the 'knife edge'. The application of this principle does not present any difficulties. Any progress in a regime produced by the model whose existence is confirmed is such that the autonomous impulses of fixed investment and final consumption are endogenous to the regime; they have well defined, constant levels. A regime will therefore be stable when, following a transitory shock affecting one of these impulses, countervailing forces sufficient to bring back the effective progression to the regime initiated by this shock appear. In practice, the complexity of the model requires the use of numerical simulation.

In competitive *régulation* the only regime that exists is unstable. This is mainly owing to the fact that investment depends both on the recent level of the utilisation rate and on past profit, with profits being pushed up by an acceleration of the growth in volume, through the positive effect of growth on inflation. So long as not all the elements of the Fordist institutional system have yet been established this instability remains.

On the other hand, when these elements are in place, the regime of full employment, whose existence is thereby ensured, is stable. A determining element in this shift is the fact that investment is no longer sensitive to the recent installed capacity utilisation rate, owing to the 'predictability of demand'. Likewise with the existence of increasing returns in the short term, which causes a shift from a positive to a negative effect of growth on inflation. Thus the spontaneous development of the economy in medium-term progress involves oscillation around this regime. The effectiveness of a counter-cyclical economic policy, through the real interest rate and the autonomous element of final consumption, depends on this stability. Far from being able to create it, it allows only a limiting of the amplitude of oscillations. However, the continuity in wage increases is the main guarantee against strong deviations from the trend. This result confirms the conjecture that the transformation of the wage–labour nexus has a determining role, even if it turns out that the swing from instability to stability cannot be attributed to any particular institutional change.

This also supports the conclusion that the obscuring of the predictability of demand in the medium term, introducing a degree of flexibility for employment in the short term by changing the dominant productive model and alterations in general salary increases, are all elements that contribute to instability.

These appear to have been the conditions of *régulation* since the break in 1974. Of course, these results established in an isolated economy cannot be transposed to any particular national economy, whose growth is dictated by changes in its international environment. Nevertheless, it is possible to apply them to the overall dynamic of economies in 'an initial analysis', with the confusing of the predictability of demand in the medium term then being related to the international extension of the market of large firms.

What improvement?

In terms of the stylised facts that a model of the macroeconomic dynamic tries to explain, the necessary improvements concern the ability to 'produce' a cyclical evolution according to institutional forms. This still relates to analysis in an isolated economy, even if some international processes are obviously at work, as was particularly the case in the 1990s. It implies a need to develop the analysis in the cyclical horizon along with improved integration of financial operations in terms of the stock and flow of debts (Aglietta, 1993; Boyer, 1999a) and credits. A study of the formation of the savings rate of households is therefore needed. This is one of the *structural* variables, whose average level is considered a given in a medium-term analysis whose development partly dictates the long-term rate of accumulation. This implies freeing the *family* from the blind spot where it has remained with the regulationists, with the exception of Bernard Guibert (1986a). The challenge is to reconsider the variety of the cardinal institutional forms of the capitalist market economy at the level of a particular political socialisation. It is then a matter of identifying the institutions that give rights to the principal agents in this form of economy (firm, family and state) and those that enable their co-ordination, i.e. money, the wage–labour nexus and the market, understood as the relation between firms in their common quest for customers, employees and capital (Billaudot, 1996).

Appendix 19.1 A medium-term model (Boyer)

We note $\dot{Y}$, the growth rate in a production regime (GDP volume), $\dot{PR}$, the growth rate for the visible productivity of work (GDP volume per job) and $\dot{D}$, the growth rate of the overall final demand (consumption plus gross fixed investment). After linearisation, the first stage in resolving the model produces:

$$\dot{PR} = a\dot{Y} + b \qquad \text{(I) (productivity regime)}$$

$$\dot{D} = c\dot{PR} + d \qquad \text{(II) (demand regime)}$$

Since $\dot{Y} = \dot{D}$, ultimately we have the following medium-term regime:

$$\dot{Y}_r = \frac{bc + d}{1 - ac} \quad \text{with} \quad \dot{PR}_r = \frac{ad + b}{1 - ac}$$

Each reduced parameter (a, b, c, d) is expressed in terms of the parameters of the base relations. The terms b and d are exogenous impulses synthesising the impulses of these relations.

And, in graphic terms (the example of the 1960s), Figure 19.1.

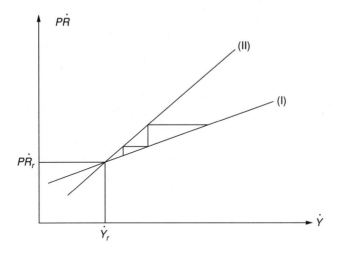

Figure 19.1 Growth as a consequence of a productivity regime and a demand regime

Appendix 19.2 A short-term model (Billaudot): simplified version omitting social security benefits

Average nominal wage (after linearisation):

$$\dot{w} = v(\lambda w \dot{p} - 1 + \beta o) + (1 - v)l(\dot{N} - \dot{L}F)$$

where N is employment, LF ordinary labour supply (short-term) and v the extent of collective bargaining for wage increases.

General level of prices (after linearisation):

$$\dot{p} = \mu'\Theta(\dot{w} - \dot{P}R) + \mu'(1 - \Theta)(\dot{p}o - \dot{e}) + \lambda_p(\dot{Y} - \dot{Y}^p)$$

where $po = yr(1 - q)/(r\cdot 1 - 1)$, $m' = m/(1 - m + mq)$ $l'_p = l_p(1 - m)/(1 - m + mq)$; Y is the volume of effective GDP, Y^p the volume of potential GDP, PR labour productivity (Y/N), e the productivity of capital, ρ the operating rate of return, r the interest rate, q a risk premium depending on financial convention, Θ the share of wages in GDP, μ the degree of monopolisation of the market in goods and services (or the degree of clientelism of markets), y the impact of financial intermediation in company financing.

Employment

$$\dot{N} = d\,\dot{N}a + (1 - d)(\dot{Y} - \dot{P}R^p)$$

where PR^p is the potential productivity of labour, $\dot{N}a$ change resulting from previous maladjustment of effective employment to employment normally justified by effective production, d the degree of job security in the short term.

Fixed investment

$$\dot{I} = \varphi\dot{I}(2) + (1 - \varphi)\dot{I}(1)$$

where

$$\dot{I}(1) = f + \Sigma m_1 \,\dot{R}\dot{E}BE_{-1} + \lambda 1(Y/Y^p - 1)$$

$$\dot{I}(2) = f + \Sigma v_1 \,\dot{C}_{-1} + m\,[\rho - (r + \Theta)] - 1$$

where REBE is the purchasing power of the gross operating surplus, C final consumption and φ the impact of large firms (with a forecasting convention of demand).

Final consumption

$$\dot{C} = c(\dot{RW} + \dot{N}) + z\dot{Y} + g$$

where RW is the purchasing power of the average wage.

Labour productivity

$$\dot{PR} = \dot{Y} - \dot{N}$$

$$\dot{PR^p} = a + d\dot{Y}^r$$

where $\dot{Y}^r$ is medium-term change in volume of GDP.

20 Accumulation regimes

Michel Juillard

Régulation theory is based on the idea that institutional arrangements influence the growth trajectory of an economy. The projection of this relation in a purely macroeconomic field is described as an accumulation regime. In this sense, the accumulation regime provides the schema or growth model of a national economy in a particular era.

This concept owes much to Marx's reproduction schemas and to the debates they inspired. Indeed, the approach ascribes as much importance to the conditions of production (productivity, return) as to the conditions of sale (clearance) of commodities. Although the reproduction of the system is always evident *a posteriori*, since the system continues, its requirements still present specific constraints on the possibilities of growth. Above all, while reproduction is never entirely impossible from a solely economic point of view, its scale may vary enormously.

The relationship between technical change and income distribution

At the heart of the concept of an accumulation regime there is the relation between technical progress and income distribution. This relation presents several questions. First in terms of the motors of technical progress: many authors have tried to identify the effects of innovation, mechanisation or, more generally, the capitalistic intensity of production, and returns to scale. It is immediately apparent that these different aspects of technical progress depend partly on the institutional arrangements governing growth and are partly endogenous to the mode of growth itself.

Suffice it to say that innovations were not produced in the same way by the brilliant, individual inventors of the nineteenth century as they are by internal company R&D departments, which are subject to the imperative of returns, in the second half of the twentieth century. Furthermore, the growth of capital *per capita* is evidently largely a function of the distribution of income and the prevailing rate of accumulation in the economy.

Returns to scale, which are more elusive, are also largely dependent on institutional arrangements and their historical development. At the overall aggregate level of an economy, returns to scale are to be sought not only in firms extending their operations but also at the level of the system as a whole, in market development, transport and communication networks, concentrating on large urban centres (Chapters 21 and 22).

Technical progress involves the growth of product *per capita* and the appearance of new products. The accumulation dynamic is determined mainly by the way in which the supplementary product is distributed between labour and capital. Here again we find many different sources of influence. Of course, there is the effect of return on future investment; there are also the many different demands created by the different types of income and their consequence for the growth dynamic, in other words whether or not any virtuous circles exist.

In more general terms, the accumulation dynamic is considerably modified by the mode of reproduction of the labour force. So long as workers have strong ties with the countryside, their reproduction mainly escapes capitalist relations. From the end of the nineteenth century (somewhat earlier in the United States and later in Europe) workers depended increasingly on the market for their reproduction. This insertion of the reproduction of the labour force in the accumulation schema modifies its properties dramatically: consumption by wage earners becomes an important market.

Of course, if, as in the standard neoclassical model of growth, savings and accumulation are independent from the distribution of income between wages and profits, since the saving propensity of households does not depend on the origin of income, these effects do not exist. Likewise, it might be considered that in the medium term Say's law works well and that no problems arise in clearing the commodities produced. However, the questions raised by the accumulation regime do not concern static equilibrium in the medium term, they affect only the type of dynamic it produces (Chapters 18 and 19).

Extensive and intensive accumulation

Accumulation regimes exist in two different situations: they may be either predominantly extensive or predominantly intensive. Extensive accumulation relates to the capitalist development that conquers new branches and new markets, spreading its production relations to new spheres of economic activity, without altering conditions of production and the efficiency of labour or capital in any significant manner.

In contrast to this, in a regime of intensive accumulation, conditions of production are systematically transformed with a view to increasing the productivity of labour. New investments primarily take the form of an increase in the capital stock per worker.

This is obviously a logical distinction more than a type of historical identification, since it is common knowledge that an intrinsic characteristic of capitalism is the transformation of the conditions of production.

The industrial revolution effectively inaugurated a new historical period marked by the tendency of capital *per capita* to rise and a more or less steady growth in the apparent productivity of labour. In contrast, for the last twenty years the United States has experienced growth in the form of extensive job creation and only a slight growth in productivity – in fact in some years there has been none – suggesting renewed importance of the extensive dimension of growth. This differed from the European and Japanese economies over the same period.

Although it is difficult and reductive to classify sub-periods of capitalism directly according to predominantly extensive or intensive periods, the conditions of production of technical change have altered dramatically over time, the rate of innovation has varied, and these changes can be identified in different labour productivity growth rate trends according to period and country. This phenomenon is more evident in France, for example, than in the United States, where the growth rate of the apparent productivity of labour was in fact quite stable until the rupture of the late 1960s (Baslé *et al.*, 1999).

Fordism

Researchers have shown the greatest interest in the post-war accumulation regime. They sought to understand this remarkable period through the speed of its growth and its slight cyclical fluctuations. In reference to Gramsci's description of the situation of the American proletariat, this accumulation regime is termed Fordism.*

The post-war period is remarkable partly owing to the growth in productivity and the profound quantitative and qualitative changes that occurred in the life styles of wage earners. Studies of Fordism have stressed two virtuous circles. The first is based on the growth of the real wage in proportion to the apparent productivity of labour. This indexing of the real wage to productivity generates steady growth in the demand for consumption goods, guarantees the stability of such demand and allows the development of mass-production industry for these products. In turn, this expansion allows systematic use of returns to scale and the stability of demand allows optimal planning for investment. Productivity gains obtained in this manner are again shared with workers and a cumulative process is initiated.

The constancy of the wage share is obviously a corollary to the constancy of the profit share, which allows the self-financing of expansion investments, but rationalisation investment too. These also generate growth in the apparent productivity of labour through increased mechanisation, hence the growth in profits; this is the second virtuous cycle. In order for this process to be durable over the long term, the apparent productivity of capital must remain constant. In the event that it diminishes, growth in profits is less rapid than growth in capital stock which, ultimately, weighs on the return on capital measured for example by the profit rate.

Analysis in productive sections

As ideal growth types the accumulation regimes presented above imply a constraint on long-term reproduction equivalent to growth balanced between the fundamental determinants of technical progress, demand and the distribution of income. The study of accumulation regimes also revealed other types of regimes, which can be described as transitional regimes, since they describe periods of intense transformation of the economic system of a country and do not reflect the constraints of balanced growth. Hugues Bertrand's study of France (1978, 1983) provides the best example of this.

The problem posed by the evolution of the productive system and the living conditions of the wage-earning class quite naturally suggest a reference to the division of the productive system previously used by Marx in the reproduction schemas.

The originality of this division derives from the fact that productive activities are grouped according to the final macroeconomic destination of production, rather than by branches or sectors. With the help of an input–output table, it is possible to reaggregate the part of the productive system that contributes directly or indirectly to the production of goods and services for consumption, investment and export. This is an abstract division, since a single capital or company can belong partially to many sections. Such is the case, for example, with the production of motor cars, which are simultaneously consumption goods, investment goods and exports, depending on the buyer.

The establishment of accountancy based on productive sections provides the descriptions in terms of jobs, productivity, the investment rate or capitalistic intensity for each section.

The advantage of this type of approach for describing an accumulation regime that is interested in the links between modifications of the production system and the overall macroeconomic relation is clear.

In his analysis of France from 1950 to 1974 Hugues Bertrand presented the active role played by the mechanisation of the consumption goods section. This acted as an outlet for growth in the relative weight of the investment goods section, in addition to enabling the development of mass consumption (Appendix 20.1).

This was undoubtedly a transitional regime in so far as, in the very long term, the capitalistic weighting of production would have ultimately weighed heavily on the return on capital. Historically, however, this was not the contradiction that caused the 1970s crisis, rather it was due to a new factor: the internationalisation of the French economy. With the increased importance of foreign trade, wages appear increasingly as production costs, rather than as one of the elements in the effective demand for production. The bases of the earlier compromise cracked and it was not possible to establish a lasting new equilibrium.

In contrast, an analysis of productive sections in the United States

(Juillard, 1993) from 1948 to 1980 shows their evolution to have been in step to a much greater degree. Unlike France, there is therefore no asymmetrical dynamic between sections to act as a motor of accumulation. It can be inferred that at the end of the Second World War the American economy had already reached a level of maturity in its mode of accumulation. This reinforces the idea that analysis of productive sections is a special instrument in the study of economies in transitional phases and implies a modification of the relation between large macroeconomic functions (Appendix 20.2).

The crisis of Fordism

The slowdown in labour productivity in the late 1960s, which played a fundamental role in the development of the American economy in the following two decades, appeared to affect all productive sections in the same way. It is therefore necessary to seek its origins elsewhere than in the intersectional dynamic. Although the explanations commonly advanced are always very partial, they refer to aggregate phenomena, for instance exhaustion the scope for productivity gains in the Fordism technological paradigm, stronger resistance to the mode of labour organisation in large-scale mass-production industry and saturation of the needs that can be satisfied by mass production.

The differing evolution of employment in the United States and in Europe during the 1980s and 1990s is a good example of the use of the concept of an accumulation regime. In the United States employment growth was accompanied by a dramatic slowdown in productivity gains and stagnation, sometimes even regression, in real wages. In Europe, by contrast, the growth of employment, traditionally weaker than in the United States, practically stopped, while mechanisation and productivity gains continued to show definite if slow progress.

It is clear that the two growth modes have a profoundly different internal logic. Likewise, these growth modes have sufficient coherence to remain dominant over extensive periods, despite the serious problems involved: the extension of poverty and the number of wage earners living below the poverty line in the United States; mass unemployment and the re-emergence of poverty and social exclusion in Europe.

Beyond the simple accounting equivalence, which claims that at the same production growth rate a slower growth in labour productivity is accompanied by a higher employment growth rate, original mechanisms can be distinguished which reinforce basic tendencies. In the United States, for example, stagnation of the real wage *per capita* contributed to an increase in the rate of participation of women in the labour force, in so far as this allowed a degree of growth in real household incomes. In turn, this development favours the increase of the labour force and attenuates the risks of social tension inherent in the stagnation of real individual wages.

Finally, the Fordist regime gave way to largely extensive accumulation, still centred on mass consumption but differentiated by income disparities.

A tool for analysing underdevelopment

The description above shows that Fordism is only one accumulation regime among a great variety defined by the combination of at least three factors. First of all, the nature of technical change in the extent to which it may affect productive sectors differentially. Next, the level of contribution of wage income to the dynamic of the means of consumption section, with possible variants depending on whether inequalities remain stable or participate in the completion of accumulation. Finally, the degree of extraversion of the economy is a factor that is measured through the construction of an export section, whose revenue serves to finance the two other productive sections. As described in Chapter 33, the accumulation regime of small open economies is original in this respect (Biesmans, 1988; Cassiers, 1989).

In terms of formalisations, it is necessary to examine the conditions under which an accumulation regime can be established and what factors the rhythms of medium to long-term growth depend on. Some initial results were obtained in a study of Italian and Taiwanese growth (Bertoldi, 1989).

A series of empirical studies have already demonstrated that these criteria can provide an account of the diversity of accumulation regimes for some newly industrialised countries. The opening of the sectional model and the description of the export section present an interesting image of growth in Korea (Lanzarotti, 1986, 1992), but also reveal differences in regard to Brazilian growth. In Brazil the inequality of income distribution plays a determining role in the accumulation regime, since consumption is supplied primarily by the middle classes (Cartier-Bresson and Kopp, 1981), rather than by an industrial wage-earning class prefiguring a Fordist regime (Coriat and Saboia, 1987). A long-term study in Mexico demonstrated the relations between an internal blockage of productivity sources and extraversion (Aboites, 1985).

In this regard, it would be interesting to undertake a systematic comparison of the application of sectional models to developing countries, since this is undoubtedly a possible method of overcoming the limits encountered in the 1990s by the classification suggested by Latin American regulationists (Ominami, 1986).

It would also be useful to apply the exercise to older industrialised countries, since these two exercises together would enable the definition of a rigorous, synthesising and virtually exhaustive temporal and geographical analysis of accumulation regimes (Bertrand *et al.*, 1982). Furthermore, this would be a better way of revealing the constraints weighing on accumulation regimes that could potentially succeed Fordism, the list of which has been extended during the 1990s (Aglietta, 1998; Petit, 1998a; Baslé *et al.*, 1999; Boyer, 1999a, d).

Appendix 20.1 Growth and crisis in France: an interpretation in terms of an accumulation regime

From the 1950s, the establishment of Fordism was reflected in the modernisation of the consumption goods section, under the impetus of a new wage–labour nexus (Figure 20.1).

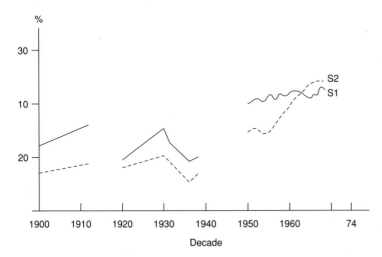

Figure 20.1 The labour composition of section 2 meets that of section 1. Labour composition = indirect labour/direct labour (%)

The double origin of the crisis (Figure 20.2): at the maturation of the modernisation of section 2, there is an increasing extraversion of accumulation.

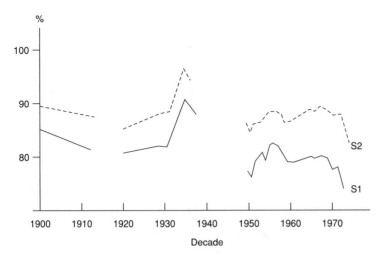

Figure 20.2 The rate of coverage of the domestic market falls rapidly after 1967
Source: Bertrand *et al.* (1982)

Appendix 20.2 Due to precocious Fordism, the American trajectory is different

In contrast to France, a parallel evolution of capital *per capita* can be observed in both sections (Figure 20.3).

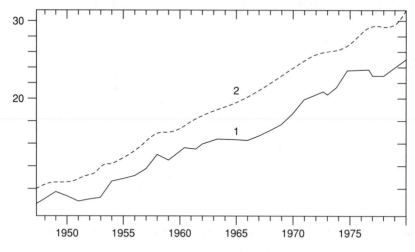

Figure 20.3 Evolution of capital *per capita* in section 1 and section 2

Consequently, until the mid-1960s, the growth of section 2 is virtually parallel to the growth of section 1 (Figure 20.4).

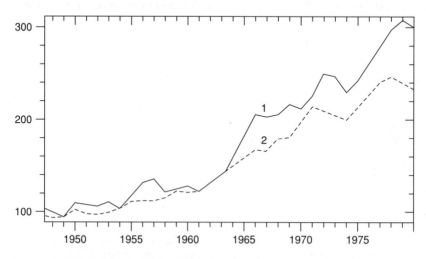

Figure 20.4 Volume of added value in both sections
Source: Juillard (1993)

21 *Régulation* theory and technical change

Bruno Amable

Technical change plays a major role in *régulation* theory's macroeconomic formalisations because of its role in long term economic development and because the connections between technology, the organisation of production and other institutional forms are the bases of a growth regime.

The place of technical change in *régulation* theory

Régulation theory has been interested in the endogenous factors of technical change from very early on, while for a long time the traditional medium/long term macroeconomic approach limited itself to an exogenous determination. This is not the only unique feature of regulationist treatment of technical change. *Régulation* theory rejects technological determinism, where the economy would merely adapt to changes in technology. It is necessary to consider both organisational forms and institutions that are not just the result of technological change.

An important concept is the 'coherence' or appropriateness of a set of institutional forms to technology. In general such coherence is confirmed only after the fact. The manifestation of a loss of coherence is crisis, when the compatibility between institutional forms and an accumulation regime is lost.

The analysis of technical change is not an end in itself for *régulation* theory. Even if some studies have examined it 'in its own right', the objective has been primarily to connect it with other elements in the mode of *régulation*. Technical change is integrated within an overall representation of the productive system, since the coherence or compatibility of a given 'technical system' and a set of institutional forms are essential to the definition of a growth regime.

The technical supports of a mode of production should not be confused with its economic and social aspects. Fordist *régulation* combines mass production with the generalised application of scientific methods of the organisation of production and mass consumption. In itself, the Fordist assembly line cannot claim to constitute the mode of *régulation* any more than 'lean production' or flexible workshops define post-Fordism.

Obviously, the Fordist period of growth cannot be reduced to Taylorism, since there was also a need for a new social compromise concerning the distribution of productivity gains, which allowed simultaneous growth in production and demand. This compromise was supported in particular by a set of institutional forms (Keynesian economic policy, the indexation of salaries, monopolistic competition, etc.).

On the other hand, technical change cannot be governed by a need for systematic coherence to be integrated by each individual agent. In general, major innovations are not stimulated by a response to a macroeconomic problem. The concordance established between production and demand in a given set of institutional forms is an uneven process, the consequence of adjustments to partial, and sometimes contradictory, rationales.

Different modes of *régulation* are associated with different accumulation regimes, with each one attributing a particular role to science and technology. These ideas are represented in the simple macroeconomic model presented in Part III, which can be considered as the basic reference for regulationist macroeconomic modelling. *Régulation* theory research has always had an applied aspect. For example, the observation of trends in productivity at the macroeconomic level made it possible to identify periods of fast or slow growth (CEPREMAP-CORDES, 1977; Baslé *et al.*, 1999). Since then other studies have given empirical support to regulationist models.

Endogenous technical change from a regulationist perspective

Endogenous technical change is an important part of formalising growth regimes in regulationist models: 'in order to translate the simultaneous determination of production and consumption norms into mathematical terms, it is necessary to have a model in which technical progress is largely endogenous and real wages are sensitive to differences in the configuration of the wage relation' (Boyer, 1986a: 104; trans. 1990: 91). In the Kaldorian tradition, regulationists have emphasised the role played by dynamic economies of scale, the links between the macroeconomic division of labour and the extent of the market, and the macroeconomic effects of training (Boyer and Schmeder, 1990). It is mainly the Kaldor–Verdoorn law that stipulates that productivity growth depends on the growth of production, which was taken up again and explicitly reintroduced in models or derived from less reduced formulations. Many empirical and theoretical studies have been undertaken with a view to isolating the characteristics of productivity regimes and their compatibility with the mode of formation of demand.

Endogenous Kaldorian technical change gathers together the effects of training and technical progress incorporated in the installations and should be inserted in a cumulative conception of growth. A more extensive division of labour enables not only greater specialisation in the work force (the 'Adam Smith' effect) but also the increased specialisation in industries and the use of specific installations of plant and equipment to increase productivity. The increasing returns linked with the division of labour then affect an entire sector, if not the whole economy. It is the fact that growth is characterised by increasing differentiation in production inputs, rather than being simply quantitative, which explains the importance of *dynamic* economies of scale. It should be noted that these economies are not limited to Fordist production methods. Boyer and Schmeder (1990) refer to an 'Aokian' division of labour, which abandons extreme professional specialisation in favour of flexible qualifications and polyvalence. This type of organisation of production has considerable effects in terms of training, which is a foundation of dynamic economies of scale. Increasing returns to scale are not therefore exclusively a characteristic of Fordism.

Formal representations

The most synthetic representations of regulationist macroeconomic modelling of endogenous technical change are those of Boyer (1988b). There are two versions, a 'closed' version and an 'open' version, of a model in which production is determined by demand and where endogenous technical change plays an important role in the definition of the growth regime.

The closed economic model can be summarised by six equations (Boyer, 1988b and Chapter 19). The evolution of productivity is determined in an endogenous manner by linking a Kaldor–Verdoorn effect of dynamic economies of scale with a Kaldorian law of technical progress (1981) in which productivity gains depend on investment and the use of new equipment

$$\frac{\dot{\pi}}{\pi} = a + b\frac{\dot{I}}{I} + d\frac{\dot{Q}}{Q} \tag{1}$$

where π is productivity, Q is added value and I is investment. Investment is determined by a Keynesian pseudo-accelerator and by profits. The presence of the investment term raises an interpretative difficulty. If there is an attempt to include the effect of new generations of equipment in productivity, in a manner analogous to the Kaldor and Mirlees (1962) formulation, then it gives a medium term formulation for productivity gains, since the long term rate of technical progress depends on improvements in the productivity of equipment. From a long term perspective, the investment variable in the productivity equation may represent the effects of learning related to equipment, rather than a simple effect of technical progress introduced through new generations of equipment, unless some more sophisticated interactions between investment and the generation of technical progress are taken into account.

Wage formation is an important aspect of the mode of *régulation*. The formalisation adopted, which is the distribution of productivity gains, reflects a Fordist compromise. Different specifications could be adopted, introducing unemployment and greater or lesser flexibility in the labour market. The solution of the model links a 'productivity regime', i.e. an endogenous determination of the rate of technical progress:

$$\frac{\dot{\pi}}{\pi} = A + B + \frac{\dot{Q}}{Q} \tag{2}$$

with a 'demand regime', i.e. an endogenous determination of the growth rate of the economy depending on the rate of technical progress:

$$\frac{\dot{Q}}{Q} = C + D \frac{\dot{\pi}}{\pi} \tag{3}$$

The productivity regime is shown in the reduced form of a Kaldor-Verdoorn law. It not only includes the technical determinants of investment; the formation of demand and the determining factors of investment also play a role. As a corollary, changes in the parameters of the productivity regime could have technological origins, or they could result from modifications in demand or investment. The productivity regime may therefore take several forms:

1   A classical productivity regime which links very low returns to scale, or none at all, to the determining of investment by profits and a competitive determination of wages.
2   A Fordist productivity regime in which returns of scale are large, investment is determined by demand and wages evolve according to productivity gains.

In either case it is possible to obtain an increasing or decreasing relation between productivity and growth depending on the values of the parameters. The demand regime, which assembles the elements of the model that formalise the distribution of productivity gains, may also take several forms (classical, Fordist or hybrid). Endogenous determining factors of growth in demand and productivity define the economy's mode of growth. Two questions then arise regarding the rate of growth and the stability of the growth regime (Boyer, 1988b; Lordon, 1991).

The open economy model adds a determination of the growth rate of exports $(\dot{X})$ depending on price competitiveness (with the nominal wage, $\dot{W}$) and the growth of the world economy relative to the closed economy model equations. It also adds imports $(\dot{M})$ depending on the growth of investment $(\dot{I})$ and consumption $(\dot{C})$ (Bertoldi, 1989; Boyer, 1994a).

$$\frac{\dot{X}}{X} = \alpha + \beta \left[\left(\frac{\dot{W^*}}{W^*} - \pi^* \right) - \left(\frac{\dot{W}}{W} - \pi \right) + \frac{\dot{e}}{e} \right] + \omega \frac{\dot{Q^*}}{Q} \tag{4}$$

$$\frac{\dot{M}}{M} = m_1 \frac{I}{Q} \frac{\dot{I}}{I} + m_2 \frac{C}{Q} \frac{\dot{C}}{C} \tag{5}$$

where e is the exchange rate and * represents the variables of the rest of the world. Obviously it is possible to modify the specifications of these two functions in foreign trade.

Formally, taking foreign trade into account does not change anything fundamental in the reduced form of the model that can once again be expressed in productivity regimes and demand regimes which are analogous to those of the closed economy. However, this does enhance the interpretation. Growth regimes led by exports can be represented; Boyer (1994a) presents four of these. They are differentiated according to the greater or lesser sensitivity of exports to price competitiveness and of wages to labour market disequilibria. The coherence of the labour market (and hence the mode of determining wages) and the competitiveness of the country determine the growth regime of an open economy. Depending on the specific instance, an increase in the activity of the rest of the world may or may not lead to a rise in production or productivity.

Another type of formalisation concerns the possibilities of differentiating national growth trajectories together with different forms of competitiveness (Amable, 1993a). Technical change has a dual form. On the one hand there is the Kaldor–Verdoorn law linking growth and the productivity gains which make lower prices possible. On the other hand, the quality of the products exported depends on training in production. The cumulative mechanism of growth and technical change in an open economy thus involves the two channels of price and non-price competitiveness. It is then possible to exhibit different growth trajectories depending on the parameters of a country's competitiveness.

Applied research

Owing to the role of the Kaldor–Verdoorn law in the cumulative growth model, many empirical estimates have been made. In explanations of crisis and the fall in productivity gains, a structural modification of the productivity regime in terms of the breaking down of this law is often emphasised. Indeed, Boyer and Ralle (1986) identified a break of this type in a pooled estimation. Before 1973 the Kaldor–Verdoorn relation was fairly well estimated, with a coefficient of roughly 0.6. After 1973 the quality of the estimation and the value of the coefficient decreased (Boyer and Petit, 1991). Amable (1989) confirms these results, but the breaks do not appear in time-series estimations. The question is whether the weakening of the

Kaldor–Verdoorn law has 'technical' origins, for example, as with the weakening of economies of scale due to the exhaustion of Fordism, or whether the entire model of cumulative growth is affected, since the productivity regime is a reduced form combining all the other determining factors. To answer this question it is necessary to take a macroeconomic cycle into account.

Boyer and Petit (1981) considered a simple growth model of industry for six European countries over the period 1960–76. The model includes four equations, determining the rate of investment as well as the growth rates of employment, value added and exports. Technical change appears in two ways. An endogenous determination of productivity gains is deduced from employment and value added equations. Thus the Kaldor–Verdoorn law is not explicit, but is deduced from the two equations. Second, two variables representing innovation (the percentage of process innovation in total innovation and the ratio of R&D expenditures to GDP) are included in the equations for employment, investment and exports. This model therefore allows the calculation of the long term effects of R&D expenditures, although this aspect of technical change remains exogenous.

An analogous exercise for eight OECD countries is presented in Amable and Boyer (1992) with the emphasis on growth and international competitiveness. The determining factor of technical change, which is endogenous this time, in the form of a patent variable, instead of R&D expenses, makes it possible to connect growth, investment, foreign trade and innovation. The model shows the possibility for national cumulative growth trajectories linked with endogenous technical change.

A recent contribution (Pini, 1994) tests a growth model for nine OECD countries over the period 1960–90. The model involves ten equations and is very similar to Boyer's (1988b) open version model. It is thus possible to deduce demand and productivity regimes as reduced forms, and to test their stability during various sub-periods. Estimates reveal that throughout the entire period the demand regime was principally Keynesian, but with a significant classical influence. It also appears that behaviour differs depending on the sub-periods and groups of countries considered. Compared with other countries, EU nations are characterised by a smaller B coefficient (equation 2 above) in a productivity regime. There are notable differences between the two groups of countries in the indirect effects of investment on employment. Furthermore, the Keynesian element of investment is more noticeable in EU countries. But above all the modulation of demand and productivity regimes from one sub-period to another calls for attention. Indeed, the slowdown of growth after 1976 is shown by a modification of both the productivity regime (B decreases from 0.97 to 0.36) and the demand regime (in other words, equation 3 above: D falls from 0.71 to 0.51). The factors responsible for these changes are, among others, the greater (negative) influence of investment on employment after 1976 and an increase in the growth effect (the pseudo-accelerator) in the investment equation. The combination of these two mechanisms gives a more moderate growth in employment. At the same time, the demand regime becomes more 'classical', with an increased role for profits in investment and a more competitive determination of wages.

Some macroeconomic studies of technical change and growth differ somewhat from the basic equations of Boyer's (1988b) model, in order to study the process of growth over a wider sample than the large developed economies. Amable (1993b) presents a growth and catching up model for a sample of developed and developing countries. Technical change, represented as a patent variable, is determined in an endogenous manner. Different national growth trajectories are also revealed, separating countries in which cumulative growth enables the catching up of those that are maintained in a vicious circle of weak growth. The 1990s renewed this analysis and provoked an extension of it when the possibility appeared of a connection between analyses of national systems of innovation (Nelson, 1993) and the characterisation of modes of *régulation* (Amable *et al.*, 1997).

22 From cumulative growth to *régulation* theory

Pascal Petit

The aim of *régulation* theory is to develop an economic approach that reflects the historical and institutional conditions that determine how the dynamics of production and demand in an economy interact. To attain this objective, *régulation* theory employs two major concepts: the accumulation regime and the mode of *régulation*. The danger is that the regulationist approach is reduced to a combination of accumulation regimes and modes of *régulation*, with one bearing economic weight and the other institutional and historical determinants.

However, many regulationist studies have avoided this pitfall by employing the scheme of cumulative causation, which furnishes a general reference framework and a matrix for specific models.

A very general dynamic scheme

Essentially, the principle of cumulative causation stipulates that in an economy market changes govern developments in productivity gains and that in return the use of these gains governs the demand and market dynamics. The cumulative causation scheme explains this retroactive effect between creating and using productivity gains by linking a set of cause and effect relations in a circular fashion. Productivity gains may be obtained from five different sources: (1) creating economies of scale; (2) improvements in the division of labour among firms; (3) acquisition of new, more efficient plant and equipment installations; (4) training schemes; (5) innovations increasing the quality of products and thus the satisfaction they afford.

The formation of demand through these various elements (consumption and investment, be it national or foreign) depends on the way in which productivity gains are distributed among those involved, i.e. wage earners, holders of productive capital, financiers, the state. The interdependence of these dynamics that generate gains or form elements of demand cannot be reduced to price effects. For example, the forms of labour organisation that contribute to achieving productivity gains are linked with methods of wage formation which themselves contribute to the development of certain types of markets that are more or less suited to taking advantage of the production organisation schemes.

The principle of cumulative causation is thus to identify, within the creation/distributing circuit of productivity gains for each growth regime, the intensity of retroactive effects between methods of production organisation and demand formation. These retroactive effects vary in their stability and extent. In a growth regime the structure of hazards (which are subject to probabilities, in contrast to situations of radical uncertainty encountered during crises) characterises the *short term*. The extent of retroactive effects determines the degree of intensity of accumulation in the *medium or long term* horizon which *régulation* theory focuses on.

The scheme of cumulative growth applies to the analysis of both intensive and extensive growth regimes. The endogenous dynamic that these retroactive effects exhibit may result from increasing returns to scale as a positive factor in the economic system under consideration.

The history of the concept of cumulative causation can also be read as a gradual explanation of the origins and conditions of development of this endogenous dynamic.

A long history

Adam Smith's famous law stipulates that the division of labour depends on market size. Young (1928) was the first to suggest that in a dynamic framework the reverse of Smith's law may be true. He suggested that extension of the market depends in return on the division of labour dynamic, if accompanying innovative behaviour is taken into account in terms of products and processes.

Kaldor's explanation (1970, 1972, 1981) of the scheme of cumulative causation is based on the expression of the dynamic of structural and technical change to emphasise dynamic returns to scale. (He borrows terminology from Myrdal, who used it in a different context, for the catching up of developing countries.) Kaldor avoids confusing Young's scheme with a reformulation of Say's law of markets (according to which supply creates its own demand). He refers to the Keynesian debate on multiplier effects and reiterates the need for a cumulative growth scheme to depend on an autonomous demand element. In developed countries in the 1970s this stimulating effect on growth was attributed mainly to industrial exports (a type of growth referred to as export-led), but this autonomous stimulation of demand can also come from investment projects or from a voluntarist wage policy. In the same perspective he adopted in analysing the conditions of a macroeconomic circuit, Kaldor stresses the complex intermediation, both financial and commercial, that contributes to the development of markets. In the process of demand formation the tertiary sector plays a special role, which is very influenced by national experience in terms of organisation, and is considered linked globally with industrial activities by the first approaches to the scheme of cumulative causation.

The analyses in fact tend to concentrate on the specification and calibrating of dynamic returns to scale (Chapter 21), starting from the linear relation between the growth of production and productivity proposed by Verdoorn. Many neo-Keynesian economic studies assessed these dynamic returns to scale (*JPKE*, 1985). Cornwall (1977) offers one of the few developments that try to establish an overall understanding of the cumulative causation scheme.

Regulationist studies employing this 'cumulative' perspective have maintained a global approach to the cumulative causation scheme from the start. In other words, this approach was adopted not only in the explanation of the foundations of dynamic returns to scale through what have been called productivity regimes, but also in the bases of demand formation (Boyer and Petit, 1981, 1984).

An extensive series of regulationist studies have developed the analysis of productivity regimes in particular. They have made use of institutional analyses of demand regimes only in terms of wage formation (see Bowles and Boyer, 1990a, b; 1995) and more rarely in the structuring of markets, making a distinction between sectors exposed to international competition and sheltered sectors (Aglietta *et al.*, 1981). In order to understand these developments more thoroughly, it is useful to distinguish between two different uses of the cumulative causation scheme in regulationist analysis of accumulation regimes.

From a pedagogic tool to a regulationist model

The primary role of the cumulative causation scheme is pedagogical and rhetorical. It enables the presentation of the main themes of an approach connecting temporal interactive processes based on the key institutional questions of a given historical period in a logical manner. It is thus possible to measure a set of interactions between productivity and demand regimes on a macroeconomic scale.

Expressed in its most reduced form by two linear functions for productivity and production growth rates, this scheme lends itself quite well to the calibration of simple assessments supplying initial elasticity sizes. With these it is possible to periodise and describe the national trajectories of growth regimes (Boyer, 1988b). These linear forms reduce the dynamic properties of the trajectories dramatically (Chapter 19), simply identifying fields in which retroactive effects are too great and therefore destabilising growth through the explosion or implosion of rates within areas of possible elasticity. The introduction of non-linear dynamics into these simple expressions of productivity or demand regimes makes it possible to add more complex stability problems to the scheme and to introduce differences between long and short dynamics. This is an original illustration of the regulationist problematic through the relationship between cyclical and structural crises (Chapter 23).

The second role of the scheme is to act as a matrix for a more developed model. The challenge then is to find formalisations of accumulation regimes that offer an earlier specification of the mechanisms of creating and distributing productivity gains by accounting for key institutional elements.

Models used in assessments present quite classical techniques. But the values of the estimated parameters define the periodising of various growth regimes and the characteristics of national trajectories, whether these refer to productivity regimes (intensity of gains, link with R&D activities, etc.) or demand regimes (laws of wage formation, price sensitivity of demand, profit behaviour). Further analyses may be found on Taiwan (Bertoldi, 1989), the United States (Boyer and Juillard, 1992), Canada (Boismenu *et al.*, 1994) and Japan (Uemura, 1992; Ebizuka *et al.*, 1997). Other models with a comparative analysis perspective are more restricted in order to reveal a common growth scheme and a few differentiation factors for a group of developed economies (Amable, 1993b; Amable and Boyer, 1992; Petit and Tahar, 1989). One might have expected to find more non-classical indicators in the formalisations, reflecting institutional dimensions, as in the cost of job loss in the model especially adapted to the United States by the radical American school (Bowles *et al.*, 1983). This remark applies less to analyses of productivity regimes (Amable, 1993a; Chapter 20), where forms of innovation and the effects of learning and imitation between countries are taken into account, than to analyses of demand regimes. In addition to the specific questions of the determination of labour and capital remuneration in each country, questions also arise about the reorganisation of markets, such as the internationalisation of fixed capital and development of intermediation and the role of financial capital. This is certainly an important area of research (Boyer and Petit, 1991). Regulationist studies have already analysed many aspects of the structural forms in question, particularly in terms of international relations (Mistral, 1986; Aglietta, 1986a; Baslé *et al.*, 1999). In fact the paradigmatic dimension of the cumulative causation scheme contributes to maintaining more synthesised and relevant formulations.

A tool for analysing structural change

The advantages of developing the scheme of cumulative causation in a regulationist perspective appear to be as follows:

1 It explains the central forms of organisation and motivation at the origin of productivity gains.
2 It explains the main types of arrangements in the distribution of these gains and the way in which conflicts of interest are, or are not, settled.

3   It emphasises the mutually supportive nature that the forms of organ-
     isation and types of arrangements can maintain (recognising that not
     everything is interactive and that some institutional frameworks belong
     to a general context of period and country).

This formulation is very general, but it makes it possible to place any relation in a 'retroactive' macroeconomic scheme and to calibrate the impact
more or less, thereby selecting the most relevant relations in terms of the
overall dynamic.

The type of scheme is in fact largely imposed by the need to take into
account major contemporary structural modifications such as the internationalisation of economies, the development of tertiary activities and
changes in the technology. By way of example, one might consider how
these structural changes are a part of the cumulative scheme and the refor-
mulations they imply.

The internationalisation of economies therefore has two aspects. In terms
of productive systems, internationalisation shows the working of dynamic
returns to scale at the global level that had already been emphasised at the
national level. This occurs not only through the internationalisation of trade,
a phenomenon that is already well integrated in the analysis, but also
through the internationalisation of fixed capital and a corresponding mobility of financial capital that is more difficult to take into account. In terms
of the distribution of these gains, there are many questions: globalisation
gives a greater strategic role to financial capitals and to intermediation on
an international scale, to the detriment of the remuneration of local factors,
other things being equal. The shape of this new factor is still fluctuating.

The development of tertiary activities is doubly linked with the internationalisation of the production systems discussed here. Relocation and
'deindustrialisation', which emphasise a tertiary specialisation of activities, are motivated by the search for dynamic returns to scale at the world
level. But these transformations go together with a rearrangement of
competitive relations (marked by the increased importance of non-price
competition) that favours the development of intermediation activities. The
continuous development of a household service sector is added to these
two growth factors in business services. In contemporary developed
economies, this causes two-thirds of employment to be concentrated in the
tertiary sector. This development leads to a profound transformation in
productivity and demand regimes. The slowdown effects on the productivity dynamic are similar to those described by Baumol in his two-sectors
model. But the effects on demand regimes, both in the reorganisation of
forms of competition and in the modification of aspects of the wage/profit
division, are more difficult to grasp because they are still being generated
(Petit, 1994a, 1998a; Petit and Soete, 1999).

Taking the systematic character of current technical change into account
complements an understanding of the previous structural modifications in

some senses. In fact internationalisation and the development of the tertiary sector have been heavily influenced by the development of information technology, which, through its ability to be used at all stages of economic activity, has led to a new technical system. This structure favours complementary or competitive network phenomena that are decisive factors both in creating and in distributing productivity gains. To keep track of these changes a good description of the laws of diffusion via these networks is required (Antonelli *et al.*, 1992). This provides a better understanding of the behaviour of agents in a universe that is more open to competition, even though it is a form of competition that is less governed by prices.

We can therefore see how the approach, through the three structural changes mentioned above, involves a reconsideration of formulations of the cumulative causation scheme and the introduction of new determining factors. These determining factors include dynamic returns to scale, the intermediation structuring demand formation and relations between different types of capital.

The challenge is still to introduce these types of innovative shifts, without rendering too complex the schematisation in which the logic of cumulative causation must remain globally accessible in order to be used in debates on economic policy.

It is also useful to recall that the coherence and effectiveness of this cumulative scheme involve some limitations. The emphasis on the relation between creating productivity gains and demand formation tends to relegate the problems of depreciating capital, and thus profit, to secondary importance (Gordon, 1991). Likewise, the temporal horizon of feedback effects between productivity and demand regimes favours a medium-term perspective (Skott, 1991) to the detriment of taking into account the relation between cyclical and structural movements (Chapter 18).

Apart from these limitations, the cumulative scheme is a conceptual framework that is particularly well suited to articulating the formulation of accumulation regimes within a context that explains the prominence of certain institutional forms in a particular historical period.

23 Formalising regulationist dynamics and crises

Frédéric Lordon

What is a regulationist growth model? If *régulation* theory is to assert a strong identity, recognising the 'standards' of the discipline and the role played by formalisation, it must answer this type of question clearly. Some commentators have argued that *régulation* theory fails precisely through its inability to formalise its main perceptions (Cartelier and De Vroey, 1989), that it produces well crafted Marxist or Keynesian models which are not, however, specifically 'regulationist' (Duménil and Lévy, 1993).

There are two ways for a model to 'merit' the term 'regulationist'. It may be regulationist in a 'positive' sense, in other words, by formalising a 'history' or scenario taken from the regulationist corpus. Examples of this are found in the models of Bertrand (1983), Boyer (1988b) and Amable (1992) (Chapters 18 and 19). But there is also a more 'methodological' manner of constructing a regulationist model, which emphasises the ability to incorporate the major insights into *régulation* theory's speciality, that is, the historical dynamic of the capitalist economies, by providing them with appropriate formal representation. Independently from the 'stylised histories' on which they started work, these general dynamic principles are a major part of regulationist identity. Owing to their rich complexity, they present a real challenge to formalisation.

Dynamic principles based on the regulationist classification of crises

While neoclassical approaches to growth, even those reworked to include the theory of endogenous growth (Lordon, 1991), still infinitely create dynamics, propelled by an invariable set of trans-historic mechanisms, *régulation* theory emphasises the periodisation of long dynamics in capitalist economies and the need to distinguish various growth regimes involved in their 'life cycle'. Thus 'structural' invariance prevails only in a stabilised growth regime, described through a set of original and historically dated macro-patterns.

Nevertheless, there is nothing to guarantee that perfectly steady growth patterns will prevail in this type of regime. On the contrary, the process of capital accumulation constantly generates disequilibria and maladjustment. But their clearing, like their generation, takes place in an essentially endogenous manner, without challenging the overall structure of the mode of *régulation*. *Régulation* theory describes this type of temporary disequilibrium, which gives growth trajectories their fluctuating form, as a 'minor crisis'.

But – and this is the central feature of the 'long-term view' suggested by regulationists – beyond the fluctuations of minor crises, a growth regime is itself transitory. The reproduction that it appears to give rise to in the mature phase is only apparent and imperfect. Indeed, true to a Marxist dialectical intuition, growth regimes are constantly affected by endogenous structural change. Thus the very operation of a growth regime structure creates the forces and tendencies of its transformation. The 'torsion' or endogenous drift of one or several of its main 'elements' may challenge the systematic coherence that previously provided the viability of the growth regime, bringing it to a point of rupture that initiates a 'major crisis' episode (Boyer, 1986a).

The dynamic principles of *régulation* are thus arranged on the basis of the classification of crises, including those that are responsible for the regulationist growth model's distinctive 'methodological' identity. Developments in methods of non-linear analysis, structured by different types of mathematical instability, provide tools that are particularly well suited to employing these types of dynamic principles and provide an illustration of the dichotomy between a 'minor crisis within a regime' and a 'major crisis and regime change'.

Fluctuations and 'minor crises': dynamic instability

In heterodox approaches to the economic dynamic the modelling of endogenous fluctuations is a constant. *Régulation* theory is naturally part of this current, sharing the emphasis on the intrinsic instability of growth trajectories. Without underestimating the effects of exogenous shocks, the concept of a minor crisis emphasises the fact that the original disequilibria and the fluctuations to which they give rise are endogenous.

It is notoriously impossible to derive these types of endogenous cycle dynamics from a linear framework because, as shown by the difficulties encountered by Harrod, all dynamic instability in an endogenous cycle is immediately global, degenerating into collapse or infinite explosion. The use of a non-linear model makes it possible to break the identity relationship between local and global, so that local instability of the stationary state does not prevent attracting forces from predominating at greater distances, thus ensuring the containment of the dynamic in a limited area around equilibrium. This is the essence of the Poincaré–Bendixson theorem (Hale and Koçak, 1991), where repelling tendencies at a short distance from a locally unstable stationary state compromise with more distant attracting tendencies, causing endogenous fluctuations. A very 'theoretical' stylised illustration of this dynamic mechanism is the example of a variant on the Goodwin model (Goodwin, 1967) in which endogenous technical progress is introduced in the form of a Kaldor–Verdoorn law (Lordon, 1994b). When the destabilising effects of increasing returns of the productivity regime are sufficiently powerful, growth becomes explosive if not contained by non-linear 'side effects', for instance the Phillips effect near full employment or the collapse of investment when the wage share reaches extreme values near 0 or 1. At a distance these side effects 'bring the economy back' to equilibrium. The conjunction of these opposing dynamic tendencies takes the form of the endogenous fluctuations that create the 'intrinsic' irregularity of the growth pattern.

Nevertheless, the endogenous cycles that make it possible to generate dynamic local instability in a non-linear framework, via the Poincaré–Bendixson theorem and the Hopf theorem (Lorenz, 1989), do not provide a completely satisfactory representation of economic irregularity. Indeed, these cycles are periodic and present an image of growth fluctuations that is still too 'regular'. However, it is not clear that in order to attain this type of 'disordered' fluctuation it is necessary to use models with exogenous stochastic shocks. Indeed, using determinist chaos, the non-linear dynamic has developed tools that make it possible to generate considerable dynamic irregularity. Initially introduced to economic dynamics through unimodal endomorphisms of the interval (Benhabib, 1992; Lordon, 1994a), determinist chaos suffered greatly from the narrow specifications of unidimensional logistical forms. The formalisations of chaos in continuous time, which require a dimension equivalent to at least three, allow for greater theoretical content. Of these formalisations, the 'route towards chaos' (Newhouse et al., 1978; Bergé et al., 1984) has the additional advantage of being general and relatively simple to implement. This facilitates explanation of a dynamic of equilibrium that exhibits aperiodic fluctuations and presents the now commonly recognised phenomenon of sensitivity to initial conditions.

Thus the model of periodic cyclical growth described above can be transformed into a chaotic growth model (Lordon, 1993a, 1994b). It is simply a matter of viewing the oscillator previously obtained as representative of a sector, creating a tri-sector model, and then considering the disturbance of the torus T3 obtained through inter-sector combinations, for example through the common participation of sectors in a single labour market or through external technological events.

Taking advantage of the possibilities created by situations of dynamic local instability, the non-linear dynamic thus provides an appropriate representation of irregularities that result from the disequilibria and endogenous upsets that *régulation* theory has described as 'minor crises'. However, the major contribution of the regulationist dynamic is the endogenous 'warping' processes of growth regimes and the 'major crisis' episodes to which they give rise.

Rupture, bifurcation and 'major crises': structural instability

Models of these episodes of major crisis are made possible through an entirely different type of formal tool for a non-linear dynamic, one which involves another form of instability: structural instability.

By identifying the 'structure' of the economy as the set of macro-economic patterns that form the growth regime of a given era, it can be given formal representation through the mathematical structure of an associated model, in other words the functional form f of a general dynamic system $\dot{x} = f(x)$, where $x \in R^n$ represents the state variables that characterise the conjuncture. In simpler terms, for an invariable functional form f it is possible to link the structure with the data of parameters λ of a dynamic system in the following equation:

$$\dot{x} = f(x; \lambda), x \in R^n, \lambda \in R^p \tag{1}$$

'Conjuncture' and 'structure' thus refer to different, specific mathematical entities, variables for the first and parameters for the second, while a process of structural change can be represented in simple terms as a modification of the parametric configuration $\lambda = (\lambda_1, \dots \lambda_p) \rightarrow (\lambda'_1, \dots \lambda'_p)$.

In a non-linear framework, the differentiated variety of stationary states of a system such as equation 1 may allow for singular points whose projection on to the space of the parameters defines points of bifurcation λ_k. At each of these points of bifurcation a situation of structural instability prevails (Hirsch and Smale, 1974; Thom, 1972) where the slightest modification of the parametric configuration is enough to alter the dynamic phase 'profoundly'. This means that when the structure of the growth regime experiences a transformation that causes it to cross one of these 'critical' points, the growth trajectory is altered qualitatively. The alteration may take the form of a collapse from 'high' growth to 'low' growth, or a sudden destabilisation, as seen when a smooth and regular path starts to fluctuate or even become chaotic. In this bifurcation phenomenon a brutal dynamic accident occurs that acts as a manifestation of a 'major crisis' because it relates directly to a transformation in the underlying economic structure, that is, the growth regime.

Formalising endometabolism: structural change and endogenous 'major crises'

Developing the possibilities of structural instability and rendering the dynamic phenomenology associated with 'major crisis' episodes from bifurcation is just the first stage. Indeed, in order to represent the regulationist insight completely, a means of formalising *endogenous* processes of structural change is needed. This type of change, given the distinctive term endometabolism* (Lordon, 1993a), where structural deformations are gradually generated from a repetition of the conjuncture over a long period, is especially resistant to formalisation. To model the process by which it is the very functioning of the structure that alters the structure involves *identifying* and *forming a connection* between two dynamics that occur in very different time scales. Indeed, it is not enough to make structural sizes endogenous by asserting:

$$\dot{x} = f(x; \lambda) \tag{2}$$

$$\dot{\lambda} = g(x) \tag{3}$$

Certainly equation 2 expresses the endogenous nature of changes in structural sizes (parameter λ) in relation to the short-term dynamic (state variables of x). But on the other hand it completely misconstrues the distinction of the specific temporality of these two dynamics by conferring on it temporal constants *of the same size*.

Thus it is not immediately, but rather via a long-term effect, that short-term repetition eventually warps the structure. A special formal tool is needed to express this difference–connection of different time scales. The tool is provided by so-called slow/fast dynamic systems, as used initially in the theory of relaxation oscillations (Grasman, 1987), and was later termed the 'adiabatic approximation' in 'synergetic' approaches (Haken, 1983) (for several economic applications see also Zhang, 1991). Structural variables made endogenous are written thus:

$$\dot{x} = f(x; \lambda) \tag{4}$$

$$\dot{\lambda} = \varepsilon g(x) \text{ with } 0 < \varepsilon \ll 1 \tag{5}$$

The 'small' parameter ε then guarantees that, despite the fact that structural change is endogenous, the structure can be considered quasi-invariable *within the temporal horizon of the cycle*, thereby representing the fact that the connection between the short term and the structure is only a long-term effect.

Many 'endometabolic' scenarios

Linking non-linear models with bifurcation and with slow/fast dynamic systems enables the formalisation of the changes that lead to endogenous 'major crises'. *Régulation* theory evidently involves many scenarios that deserve this type of formal treatment:

1   *The long-term dynamic in the endogenous growth of the wage-earning class and distribution crises.* It is therefore possible to derive a stylised scenario from the crisis of the 1930s. Starting with an initial pre-Fordist regime where company demand was formed mainly outside the wage-earning class, success in growth led endogenously to a long growth movement in the wage-earning class and to the increasing importance of wage earners' consumption in the solvency of final demand. Beyond a certain level this endogenous and progressive rise in the power of consumption in final demand may contradict the remaining competitive mechanisms of wage formation whose excessive 'fluidity' threatens market stability.

2   *A 'Fordist' prolongation of series and endogenous extraversion.* A similar chain effect provides a partial scenario in the crisis of Fordism. The Fordist 'logic of productivity' brings about a long endogenous movement of extraversion as the domestic market becomes saturated and no longer allows the prolongation of the series. This progressive opening of the economy, which was present even in the dynamic of the Fordist regime, 'imports' a logic of competitiveness that may contradict a monopolistic wage *régulation* adapted to supporting wage consumption in a context of self-centred growth.

3   *The exhaustion of the Fordist productivity regime.* A modification of Goodwin's model, similar to the one referred to above, that supplies a 'rapid dynamic' block in which a non-linear Kaldor–Verdoorn law (synthetically expressing the productivity regime) can give rise to many states of equilibrium through which 'catastrophic' bifurcation occurs. A 'long dynamic' block can then be joined to it, formalising a scenario of the endogenous exhaustion of the Fordist productivity regime through an increase in differentiation. In the long term the success of growth gives rise to saturation in the norm of Fordist consumption and to an endogenous rise in the preference for variety (Boyer, 1986b). This long evolution, contradicting a productive apparatus whose logic of productivity rests on the prolongation of homogeneous series, gradually causes a shift in the Kaldor–Verdoorn productivity relation until a point of bifurcation is crossed endogenously and the economy falls dramatically from a high to a low growth pattern (Lordon, 1993b, 1997b). This series of events, which is obviously very partial and stylised, allows a formalisation of the process of genesis and the endogenous triggering mechanisms of the Fordist 'major crisis'.

Concerning the proper use of a non-linear dynamic by *régulation* theory

The tools of the non-linear dynamic are clearly not the sole property of *régulation* theory. Nevertheless, *régulation* theory has an obvious interest in using them, so long as they are appropriate for the representation of its essential dynamic principles.

Formalisations of dynamic instability make it possible to model a succession of minor crises. By causing endogenous fluctuations *within a given parametric configuration*, in other words, in economic terms of the given state of the structure, formalisations express the fact that these minor crises occur *within an invariable mode of régulation* without upsetting it.

In contrast, bifurcation models present situations of structural instability that correspond formally to *dynamic regime transitions*. This characteristic obviously suggests that they be used to represent the major crises that mark *changes in accumulation regimes*. Finally, the tool of slow/fast dynamic systems provides a means of giving formal representation to the endometabolic processes that give rise to this type of transition.

Of course, the importance of these formal tools and the 'need' for them should not be exaggerated. It is not a question of falling under the tyranny of the non-linear dynamic and slow/fast systems. *Régulation* theory has much to say and formalise that can do very well without this type of formal framework. The very nature of the sort of endogenous, determinist and long term structural change discussed in this context is enough to show that the formalisms of endometabolism are related exclusively to the dynamic of *entering* a major crisis. Entirely different tools would be required to undertake a formalisation of the 'recomposition' processes through which new institutional forms emerge. Furthermore, moving in this direction, there is a field which regulationists have every interest in exploring so as to complete the formal repertoire which enables them to grasp the historic dynamic of capitalist economies.

Part IV
New spaces of *régulation*

24 Globalisation, localisation and sector-based specialisation

What is the future of national *régulation*?

Yves Saillard

The development of international relations, an emphasis on specificity in activity sectors, regions or local territories and considerable institutional progress in the construction of Europe are areas of investigation that meet in a single question. Does the concept of 'overall economic *régulation*', defined essentially at a national level, still have any meaning (Palan, 1998)? Even in a subtle form, this question calls for a clarification of the connections between different levels of *régulation*. What level of analysis is relevant to *régulation* theory's research programme? It is no surprise that research into these themes is highly innovative, actively suggesting significant conceptual revisions. The debates, which have *a priori* a destabilising effect on *régulation* theory, also offer an area for it to assert its individuality and demonstrate dynamism.

Contesting national *régulation*: a multi-faceted question

The 'natural' level of analysis for macroeconomics and *régulation* theory is the nation as defined by a sovereign authority. But, methodologically, regulationist analyses tend to play down the economic role of the state (Chapter 15) and to endow the political sphere with relative autonomy (Chapter 16). They also contribute a new perspective on the role of the state in macroeconomic interactions.

Since the first 'regulationist' studies, relations between national, international and regional spaces have been under examination (Lipietz, 1974, 1977). *Régulation* theory started on a basis of structuralist-Marxist hypotheses and alternative critical analyses (the 'productive system' of the 'Grenoble school', the description of space provided by François Perroux, the nature of the environment that promotes innovations, the industrial district, etc., Chapter 25). Since then it has evolved towards a conception that tries to integrate an appreciation of relative regional and local autonomy, the influence of international institutions and their role in overall economic *régulation*, and the maintenance of national elements.

A parallel revision occurred in applications of the theory at the sectoral level. Although regulationist approaches have occasionally given in to the simplification of the Fordist model, the heterogeneity of sectors was acknowledged from the start (CEPREMAP-CORDES, 1977; Mazier *et al.*, 1993). But the diversity of sectors was functionally integrated in *régulation*, either through the distinction between consumption and investment goods sectors, or through a hierarchy that reflected the role of leading sectors. Other studies have contributed an examination of the importance of sectors (Reynaud, 1992; Chapter 27). However, these studies were all based on a macroeconomic perspective. They adapted *régulation* theory to a 'semi-functionalism' with regard to sectors. The renewed interest in sector-based *régulation* is due primarily to the development of studies that start at a sector level and then consider how it relates to the macroeconomic context. Viewed as a whole, these studies converge towards a shared methodology.

A method of analysis

The methodological choices involved in an analysis of sectors that range from local to international regimes are obscured by imprecise vocabulary. The most questionable term is undoubtedly the 'intermediate level'. Between what terms are territories, sectors and regions 'intermediary'? This description can only be the result of analysis. Methodologically, reference to an intermediary level invites confusion: economic analysis of territories, sectors and regions cannot be reduced to the abstractions of micro and macroeconomics. On the other hand, this approach must provide a critical understanding of these levels of analysis.

The questions posed by sector specificity (particularly Bartoli and Boulet, 1990) to *régulation* theory have prompted methodological suggestions (Boyer, 1990b) that have been frequently applied. This method defines four requirements that have been partially adapted to local analysis, following the suggestion of Jean-Pierre Gilly and Bernard Pecqueur (Chapter 26).

1   Clarify the origins of the unit of the level of analysis selected. Sectors, territories or international institutions are not intermediary levels that require description. Meso-economic analysis should indicate how they are socially and historically constructed. The definition of the unit of analysis also involves the identification of collective actors (producers, consumers, associations, unions, etc.). No doubt the most complex aspect is the definition of relevant territories and spaces, since it must be based on geographical proximity and political organisation in addition to economic and institutional criteria.
2   Describe the institutions that enable the unit of analysis to function. This involves a description of institutional rules that are coherent at the level of the sphere of analysis, the production of norms by institutions and the way in which they direct or constrain the behaviour of

collective actors. These institutions define a mode of interaction between actors. They reflect transformations observed in the long term.

3   Indicate how the sphere of activity under analysis is a part of macro-economic interdependences and what its place is in the accumulation regime. It is then possible to define 'operating economic regimes'. In each case relations between the overall mode of development and the unit of analysis should be empirically defined, as they will vary over time.

4   Identify the places of an institutional and economic dynamic that founds reciprocal transformations of the unit under analysis and the overall economic system. From this point of view, institutions and forms of organisation are important. They contribute to a definition of cyclical adjustments as well as long term dynamics.

The chapters in Part IV follow this general method.

Gilles Allaire and Amédée Mollard discuss the agricultural sector (Chapter 28) and Christian du Tertre discusses the building and public works and the service sectors (Chapter 27). Allaire and Mollard show how the agricultural sector was established and justifies this level of analysis. Sector-based *régulation* is then described through the interactions and connections between the agricultural sector and the whole economy, which affects each of the institutional forms, and the place of agriculture in the accumulation regime. The connection between sector-based and overall *régulations* shows that the period of Fordist growth was highly dependent on the agricultural sector. It was also involved in other developments such as the internationalisation of trade (as were territories).

Institutional rules are assigned to sectors through the concept of an insti-tutional arrangement* (Du Tertre, following Bartoli and Boulet; Chapter 27) and the local institutional forms of the territory (Chapter 26). In the analysis of international regimes, 'multilateral co-responsibility' and levels of infrastructure and info-structure also imply a clarification of these rules for international monetary systems (Chapter 8).

The macroeconomic inclusion of spheres of analysis brings to light some particularities. But the sector level is also the only level that allows suffi-cient precision for certain types of analysis (Chapter 28). Sector-based analysis therefore has its own special character, clarifying logics and char-acteristics that cannot be grasped at the macroeconomic level.

Open questions

However, the general methodology that is applicable to the meso-economy leaves some questions unanswered. The first is, to what level one must go in order to explain the coherence of an infra-macroeconomic unit of analysis, unless it is assumed that the answer is to be derived from historical and social analysis, which seems somewhat excessive. The sector (or space) is also constructed through the analyst's choices: is the building and public works 'sector' socially and historically constructed? Might it not be necessary to isolate public works, for example? Christian du Tertre (Chapter 27) emphasises the heterogeneity of the service sector and the advantage of defining more precise identification criteria than those currently employed (company and household services, business or non-business).

This question is illustrated by the case of agriculture. Gilles Allaire and Amédée Mollard (Chapter 28) analyse *régulations* at the product level (wine, poultry farming, vegetables, etc.). At this local level the main aim of the analysis is to explain 'the social definition of an accumulation base'. Enormous diversity in configurations is possible and obviously it is more complicated to trace them back to macroeconomics. On the other hand, this type of 'micro-institutional' approach broadens the analysis of micro-patterns, the advance of crisis and potential elements of change.

This option is favoured by Pierre Bartoli and Daniel Boulet (1990), who demonstrate the advantage of distinguishing two sub-sectors in wine production (wines with the guaranteed quality label, *appellation contrôlée*, and those with a common label, *appellation courante*) and show what this 'micro-institutional' analysis makes possible. This is particularly the case with the insertion of various institutional arrangements into international regimes (for example, the diverse effects of EU directives). A further method involves research into typical configurations without looking for a map 'on a scale of 1 to 1' for modes of *régulation* at the sector level (Boyer, 1993: 88). The advantage of this method is linked with synthesising studies that gather and compare sector results, as well as the construction of classifications. Meso-economics defines a major methodological object by allowing a quasi-experimental analysis of regulationist themes, starting from a 'fractal reduction of the general economy' (to use Robert Boyer's 1993 expression in the context of the agricultural economy), with the general theory not yet complete.

A second series of questions is more conceptually based. Is it possible to transpose concepts that have been created for the analysis of national *régulations* to a different level? The question is asked explicitly for the first time in the context of accounting for the characteristics of the unit of analysis.

In an agricultural context Anne Lacroix and Amédée Mollard (1994) have suggested replacing the concept of the wage–labour nexus with that of work social relation. This is due to the extent of self-employment, as well as the role of the family patrimony, the type of resources involved and the specific mode of capital development.

Likewise, the social relation of a particular service must be taken into account. In a manner that traverses all sectors and takes into account the elements of competitiveness excluding price that emerge from differences between work processes Christian du Tertre has used a concept of 'productive configuration' (Chapter 27). But the issue is not simply a matter of specificity, it also concerns conceptual coherence. Pierre Bartoli and Daniel Boulet's schemas indicate connections between institutional forms and institutional arrangements and also between accumulation regimes and economic regimes of operation. These schemas do not exhaust the interdependences at work in sector trajectories. Regulationist ecology also encourages an explanation of the constraint of social–environmental relations (Chapter 29 in regard to development models and sector-based energy surveys). The economic dynamic is also reflected in ecological reproduction (Lacroix and Mollard, 1993). But this very general connection can be derived only from individual empirical case studies.

The same question appears regarding the wage–labour nexus, which cannot be 'sector-based', since it can only be the local expression of the macroeconomic wage–labour nexus (Chapter 11). These questions focus on the aptness of the concept of a 'mode of *régulation* at the sector level'. The chapters of this book offer a significant advance in the conceptualisation of this aspect by regulationist research.

What *régulations*?

Does an analysis of intermediate or global levels make it possible to demonstrate alternative '*régulations*' to national *régulation*?

Is it even possible to talk about 'international' *régulation*? Both Jean François Vidal and Michel Aglietta, who study the development of international monetary regimes, are somewhat sceptical, unless the term *régulation* is to lose all its analytical content. The organisation of international trade does not satisfy the criteria of duration, legitimacy and stabilising adjustments, even to the point where the concept of 'international regime' should not be interpreted too strictly (Chapter 14). What is important is that these observations relate to long periods of stability and not to crises. The same conclusions cause Lipietz to prefer concepts of weak *régulation* or configuration to the concept of a regime. Finally, developments in the organisation of international monetary systems show that national sovereignty is still active, and that there is nothing comparable at the international level.

Is the construction of Europe the beginning of a supranational mode of *régulation*? National modes of *régulation* have already been gradually but profoundly altered. However, in the case of Europe, EU intervention has placed severe constraints on old *régulations*, and has led to damaging short-term adjustments rather than creating sufficiently powerful institutional forms at the European level to compensate for the loss of autonomy by nation states (Mazier, 1995). The connection of national and European levels should therefore aim for reciprocal reinforcement. Thus it is necessary to abandon a simple opposition between national sovereignty and multinational authority (Boyer, 1998a, 1999d). From a methodological viewpoint this research shows the potential use of the term 'international *régulation*': it is a method of analysis that requires simultaneous recognition of national, transnational and plurinational levels, and a demonstration of how they interact, as indicated by Jean François Vidal. On the other hand, the use of the concept of 'international *régulation*' as an empirical result is inappropriate. In their discussions of the connection of these levels with the overall macroeconomic system Christain du Tertre (at the sector level) and Jean-Pierre Gilly and Bernard Pecqueur (at the local level) reach similar methodological conclusions. Alain Lipietz emphasises the fragility of the forms of *régulation* from ecological contradictions (Chapter 29), which no doubt results from the fact that in international negotiations institutionalised compromises are still in process.

Christian du Tertre considers it preferable to refer to a sector 'dynamic' than to a sector '*régulation*'. All that corresponds to the sector level is an 'incomplete *régulation*' that makes sense only in relation to overall economic *régulation*.

The particular status of local institutions with regard to institutional forms led Jean-Pierre Gilly and Bernard Pecqueur (Chapter 26) to propose the elements of a detailed classification of crisis levels. This extends from the routine behaviour of local actors and the absence of crisis to major crises that imply a transformation of local institutional arrangements which may or may not have an impact on the institutional forms of overall economic *régulation*.

The common conclusion that emerges is therefore that national *régulation* is perhaps under debate, but it has no serious rival. The challenge is not really that of the relevant level of analysis, but rather a more definite conceptual understanding of *régulation* theory.

The space of *régulation*: a motor of progress?

Georges Benko and Alain Lipietz (Chapter 25) recall the role played by the analysis of space in the emergence of concepts such as competitive and monopolistic modes of *régulation*. More generally, the connection between different levels of *régulation* is a place of conceptual challenge and innovation.

Many concepts have been 'imported' from other approaches or have provided inspiration: Perroux's growth poles, the district, the mode of governance and the territory as innovative environment.

Other chapters suggest important alterations of basic concepts, such as those made regarding the 'labour social relation' and the 'productive configuration'. Jean-Pierre Gilly and Bernard Pecqueur describe 'local productive systems' and seek clarification of a 'territorial' institutional form. They emphasise the 'spatial horizon in capital development' (to which they attribute a function similar to the temporal horizon), which was already part of Alain Lipietz's initial research.

In short, this is an area of innovation. It asks questions that go to the heart of reflections on *régulation* theory such as how and by what means are institutions transformed, how do they move from micro-patterns to macro-patterns and how do their crises occur?

25 From the *régulation* of space to the space of *régulation*

Georges Benko and Alain Lipietz

Spatial metaphors have provided *régulation* theory with a seemingly inexhaustible reservoir of images. One might expect this, given that the theory studies changes in modes of *régulation* and accumulation regimes over time and that these changes are viewed as 'synchronies' that can be represented spatially (cycles, stationary regimes). It was therefore entirely natural that reflections on the structuring of human geographical space formed a major part of the early work. These definitions of space subsequently became fields of application for a more mature approach, as seen in the emergence or reproduction of innovating territories or forms of industrial organisation and in relations between local and all-encompassing spaces.

Early research

In an early study of urban land rent that was still strongly influenced by structuralism (and even Althusser), Lipietz (1974) identified a particular spatial regime, the Economic and Social Division of Space. This enquiry examined the mechanisms by which space was reproduced or transformed as a result of private initiatives by property developers. He presented the role of land prices and urban planning institutions, stressing (especially in Lipietz, 1975) two modes of *régulation* in the production of urban space. These were *competitive* and *monopolistic régulation*, depending on whether the developer or public agency was subject to, or in charge of, organising modifications of the division of space caused by these initiatives. This terminology was adopted once several modes of *régulation* had been identified in a report (CEPREMAP-CORDES, 1977). In turn, examination of land prices, their active role and divergence from the Marxist 'theory of value', underlined the difference between an 'esoteric' level (structures) and an 'exoteric' level (behaviour) (Lipietz, 1983, 1984b).

In analogous manner, Lipietz (1977) considered the coexistence of several types of regions within national space as a spatial deployment of the technological paradigm and the Fordist accumulation regime in *branch circuits*. However, this structuralist perspective was already qualified by the relative autonomy of regions, introducing the issue of interregional *régulation* and the active role of regions in their potential insertion in an 'interregional division of labour'. Transposed to an international scale, once the regulationist approach was fully developed, this dualism was emphasised by Lipietz (1985). In contrast to the structuralist perspective of dependence theories of the international division of labour, which viewed the characteristics of a region or country as dependent on its place in an all-encompassing space, there was an emphasis on the fragility of 'international configurations' and the difficulties involved in their *régulation*, particularly with respect to the autonomy of spaces within them (in this instance, nation states).

In the same vein, Aydalot (1984, 1986a) wished to foreground the self-production of local territories, thereby bringing up the vast question of local *régulation*.

Territories: from industrial organisation to governance

Following the insights of Aydalot and GREMI, which were not initially concerned with *régulation,* from the late 1970s there was a revival in research focusing on territorial analyses of innovation and of economic and social organisation. It was claimed that the success and growth of industrial regions were essentially due to internal dynamics. This perspective breaks with both global structuralism (which no doubt accounts for the *decline* of regions, Massey and Meegan, 1982) and with Rostow's theory of 'stages of development'.

Schematically, several main research categories can be identified. First, research associated with the concept of an *industrial district*, involving three typical instances: technological agglomerations (e.g. Silicon Valley), small-scale or small- and medium-size firms (the Third Italy), and financiers and services (major cities). This research was based on Alfred Marshall's early insights, reinterpreted through *transaction costs* theory or evolutionist theories of technical change. These analyses tend to privilege trading relations between firms, but new research influenced by regulationists examined alternative forms of co-ordination between firms, the types of capital–labour relations dominating territories and local development policies directed by the elite.

Research into industrial districts was initially done in Italy. Working on the 'Third Italy' and emphasising the socially endogenous character of development (the '*social construction of the market*'), Beccatini (1992), Bagnasco and Trigilia (1993) and Sebastiano Brusco analysed the industrial organisation of these regions. They revealed a combination of competition–emulation–co-operation in a system of highly specialised small- and medium-size firms. The mode of *régulation* and the technological paradigm of this productive environment enabled the reintroduction of an earlier concept, the 'industrial district', described by Alfred Marshall in 1900. The term was used to refer to co-ordination, through the market and through reciprocity based on geographical proximity, of a social division of labour (*vertical disintegration*) among small firms specialising in a segment of the production process.

Piore and Sabel (1984) interpreted the success of industrial districts as an individual example that was indicative of a more general tendency. Making reference to the *régulation* approach, they suggested that rigidly structured *Fordist mass production* would be succeeded by a regime based on *flexible specialisation*, whose spatial form would be the *district*, just as the branch circuit had been the spatial form for the deployment of Fordism. This *new industrial bifurcation* involved a full recognition of the professionalism of the work force as well as decentralised innovation and co-ordination (through the market and reciprocity) between firms. These two characteristics were seen as creating the social *atmosphere* of an industrial district.

In parallel, and in response to these various influences, research was done in France into 'localised industrial systems' (Courlet and Pecqueur, 1991, 1992) and into the territorial aspect of industrialisation and innovation (Gilly and Grossetti, 1993; Dupuy and Gilly, 1993).

At the same time the Californian school of economic geography, represented principally by Allen J. Scott, Michael Storper and Richard Walker, who were impressed by the growth of California and particularly Los Angeles, reached similar conclusions on a slightly different basis. They studied the *metropolis* or *megalopolis*, where they later identified a patchwork of districts. However, although they were familiar with the regulationist approach, whose terminology they employed, they based their work mainly on neo-Marxist and neoclassical analyses (Coase, 1937; Williamson, 1975) of the division of labour dynamic and agglomeration externalities.

This established the 'Coase–Williamson–Scott paradigm' which claimed that industrial organisation arbitrates between the firm's internal organisation costs and transaction costs between firms. An agglomeration of firms in the same location obviously minimises transaction costs. Once the increasing importance of economies of scope shows a preference for flexible productive systems by concentrating on large firms that are favourable to economies of scale, the Fordist spatial systems (integrated vertically) are replaced by agglomerations of firms seeking minimal transaction costs (Capellin, 1988).

Storper and Walker (1989) suggested a model of emergence for growth poles that were created virtually *ex nihilo* in California. A. Scott (1988a, b, 1993) developed his analysis of contemporary production systems so as to include a social division of labour, transactions between actors in a production space, different types of relation systems, a Marshall atmosphere along with institutions and the role of political or quasi-political agencies, etc.

Economists, geographers and sociologists studied a specific form of district termed the *technopole*. This spatial form is created by a deliberate industrial policy (Japan, Germany, France) or as the first site in the move towards flexible accumulation (Orange County, Silicon Valley, etc.) (Benko, 1991; Scott 1993; Castells and Hall, 1994).

Thus from the smallest Italian district to global megalopoles, the new technological paradigm of 'flexible specialisation' inspired not only the return of factories and offices to urban zones, but also a revival in the quantitative growth of metropolises, the spatial form that eventually emerged out of the crisis of Fordism. The future hierarchy of towns and global urban regions was the result of the internal strategy of these districts or groups of districts.

Intersecting with reflections on districts and evolutionist approaches to the spread of technical change, another approach viewed territories as 'innovative environments'. The European team of GREMI developed this possibility in particular. They analysed the external conditions necessary for the creation of companies and the adoption of innovation, taking the position that companies do not pre-exist local environments, but rather that they are fostered by them (Aydalot, 1986b). They sought to theorise the different forms of interdependence that are woven together in a territory and that intervene in technological development, thereby incorporating extremely varied elements. These studies tie in with research done in the field of industrial organisation theory, as well as analyses of industrial districts (Maillat and Perrin, 1992). They increasingly tended towards an evolutionist perspective that offered new approaches to the emergence and spread of innovation, while the evolutionists themselves took the opposite direction, stressing the 'environment' and thus territories that were favourable to innovation (Dosi and Salvatore, 1992).

In response to this research that theorises a canonical form of 'post-Fordism' by borrowing elements from the regulationist approach, Leborgne and Lipietz (1988) attempted a restructuring through a more systematic application. They added two further essays to their initial proposal (Leborgne and Lipietz, 1991, 1992) emphasising the following points.

1   Not all territories move towards a 'flexible' wage agreement. Some do, but others show a preference for negotiating the involvement of wage earners and their qualification, and this conflicts with a high degree of flexibility.
2   The 'vertical disintegration' tendency of production processes is common, but there are very different forms of co-operation and hierarchy among firms.
3   Territories with the most flexible capital–labour relations often demonstrate quite 'brutal' trade relations between firms, while those where

'loyalty' between capital and labour prevails often become involved in forms of inter-firm partnership.

4   These different forms of territorial development (which prompt a comparison with the different types of local productive systems proposed by geographers) reflect the 'defensive' or 'offensive' strategies of their elite.

Thus it is clear that French regulationists have remained sceptical about the uniqueness of 'post-Fordism', *flexible accumulation* and its spatial translation, i.e. the district. On the other hand, Belgian economists and geographers working with the same methodology propose a more unified view of the post-Fordist era (Moulaert and Swyngedouw, 1988, 1992).

Lebourgne and Lipietz's remarks on the variety of forms of inter-company relationships make considerable qualifications to the 'Marshall district' model, which is regulated by a combination of trade relations and an 'atmosphere' of reciprocity. Economists, geographers and engineers later studied the forms of organisation of relations between production units and their spatial deployment more closely, given that the hierarchical form of the branch circuit and the solely market-based form of the 'Coase–Williamson–Scott' district were but two extreme, caricatured forms.

The spatial dimension of a form of *régulation* of relations between productive units is termed a 'network' and the mode of *régulation* of these relations is referred to as 'governance'. This generally involves a combination of different forms, including hierarchy, subcontracting, partnerships, 'atmosphere' and public or parapublic agencies. Storper and Harrison (1992) present many different modes of governance.* The engineer Pierre Veltz (1990, 1992) studied the systems of large companies and the territorial hierarchies of production. The logic of externalisation does not necessarily imply a return of the market. Hierarchy-based organisation is transformed into a network organisation, based on notions of partnership, contractual relations, flexibility, and co-operation between firms. The same terms also appear in analyses of districts and environments.

As we have seen, Storper and Harrison (1992) introduced the notion of governance into spatial analysis as a form of inter-company organisation that goes beyond business relations. This is a complex theorisation derived from wider reflections in the fields of industrial organisation, the social division of labour, institutions and conventions, and possible localities. This concept can also be extended to any system of territorial human relations (Chapter 26).

Salais and Storper (1994) analyse the possible methods of economic co-ordination between people, products, conventions, basic areas of action and the forms of uncertainty facing economic actors. The 'possible worlds' of production considered in this way are then compared with real worlds, through empirical regional studies. Salais and Storper have constructed national economic identities for several countries using this same method.

Thus a general understanding of the concept of governance* emerges, referring to all the modes of *régulation* between pure market and pure politics (of the nation state) – in other words, what Gramsci called 'civil society'. This is a reminder to acknowledge *régulation* theory's debt to Italy in general.

Local and global

As we have said, regulationists confronted the question of the connection between local and global spaces very early on. It even served as a paradigm for the nodal area of research of the regulationist approach, i.e. the relation between individuals and society.

Once the individuation of regional and *a fortiori* national territories is recognised as seen above (because of the role of 'governance' and *a fortiori* the state) the question of the *régulation* of their reciprocal relations arises. Mistral (1986) distanced himself immediately from the two common hypotheses, which are homogenisation/optimisation through the market and the instituting of hierarchies through the authorities. He recognised a map of the international division of labour but, unlike structuralists and dependence theorists, he emphasised the problem of the insertion of national formations within the strategic area of the dominant model. The only forms of *régulation* between these individualities, separated by the osmotic walls of national frontiers, are networks and transnational firms, monetary power relations and the rules of adjustment.

Working closely on the question of North–South relations, where a true division of labour within unique Fordist production processes tended to establish itself, Lipietz (1985, 1986, 1990, 1993a) took the same direction. There is a 'world economy', but it is not a causal force, and multinational firms are not the originators of the 'new international division of labour'. Instead, this division should be seen as a configuration, a weakly regulated encounter between national trajectories, some of which are heavily dependent on the global context (hence the terms 'primitive Taylorism', 'peripheral Fordism', etc.).

This concept of a vague regime (*configuration*) and weak *régulation* coincides with the standpoint of 'international regime' specialists such as Krasner (1982), Kéohane (1982) and, more generally, the Cornell school and the journal *International Organization* (Chapter 14). But it also created the possibility of 'neo-structuralist' reform, based on resistance to a view of territories as monads exchanging products, even if they were innovative districts.

The debate raged among geographers, sociologists and regional economists between two versions of the regulationist heritage. The first version emphasised local structure, while the second emphasised global constraints, commenting ironically on the 'mythical geography of flexible accumulation' (Amin and Robins, 1992) and emphasising the weight of oligopolies (Martinelli and Schoenberger, 1992) and the predominant megapolises (Veltz, 1992). Various collections of essays mark stages in this debate (Storper and Scott, 1992; Benko and Dunford, 1991) and a French synthesis (Benko and Lipietz, 1992, 1999).

It should, however, be acknowledged that this local/global debate disguises the inability of regulationists to identify the characteristics of 'post-Fordism'. The great impact of the hypothesis of *flexible specialisation* in the area of regulationist influence in the English-speaking world (see, for example, the journal *Society and Space*) has often caused confusion by taking Mistral's hypothesis concerning the stronger or weaker insertion of territories within a *unique* strategic area too literally. The doubts of French theorists (Boyer, 1992d; Leborgne and Lipietz, 1992) about the uniqueness of post-Fordism stimulated a new analysis by raising the possibility of the coexistence of very different local models within a single global area.

Conclusion and areas of research

As we have seen, for now the productiveness of the regulationist approach to space leaves more questions unanswered than it provides answers to, especially since 'space' is by nature an interdisciplinary field.

'Local *régulation*' and the concept of governance must be developed (Chapter 26). The issue of the interlocking of spaces then arises. Between the resurgence of the local as a condition of competition and social *régulation*, and globalisation as the space of the economy or even culture, the regulationist approach provides a profoundly renewed conception of international relations. A few explicitly regulationist texts (Lipietz, 1992b, 1993a; Leborgne and Lipietz, 1990) have dealt with questions such as the influence of international modes of *régulation* on a selection of technological paradigms, the macroeconomics of continental agreements (EEC, ALENA) and the possibility of different development models coexisting in the same free trade area. These considerations coincide with 'neo-structuralist' developments (Palan and Gills, 1994; Palan, 1998) reflected in the launch of the *Review of International Political Economy*.

Finally, there is a comparison to be drawn with Anglo-American sociological (or even aesthetic) analyses of space, inspired by Giddens's (1984) 'structuration theory' and the debate on 'structure versus agency' that goes right to the heart of the *régulation* problematic. Another connection is established by Harvey's (1989) audacious comparison of 'post-Fordism' and 'postmodernity' in architecture and urbanism. The work of Gregory and Urry (1985), for example, marks a stage in this link that bridges the French regulationist approach and *'radical'* Anglo-American geography (the journal *Antipode*) or even feminist work, which confronts the double question of the spatial deployments of gender relations and the social (and hence local) construction of gender (MacDowell, 1993).

26 The local dimension of *régulation*

Jean-Pierre Gilly and
Bernard Pecqueur

Analysis of local development involves very similar methodological and theoretical issues to those that arise in sector-based research (Chapter 27), since both examine the relation between partial and global *régulation*.

The territorial approach that examines the regular patterns that make up intermediary economic forms is considered here to be a relevant but incomplete level of analysis. We do not define a territory simply as a demarcated resource space. For us a territory involves 'the mode of establishment of a group in a natural environment which institutes and secures the conditions of communication – language and collective learning – in the organisation of activity localities' (Perrin, 1992).

Defining a territory

Of the approaches identified and described by Georges Benko and Alain Lipietz (Chapter 25), those based on the concept of governance* provide the basis of a clearer understanding of how a territory is founded institutionally. However, this concept requires further clarification and its field of analysis must be expanded.

The concept of governance includes several interpretations with different meanings and objectives. Writings on governance are essentially concerned with the theory of the firm and its mode of co-ordination, especially organisational forms that are not based on either the market or hierarchy (Williamson, 1985; Aoki, 1986). Storper and Harrison (1992) expanded the concept to include different types of productive systems, taking into account groups of firms in specific spatial contexts. Campbell *et al.*, (1991) define governance as the totality of institutional arrangements, rules and rule-making agents who co-ordinate and regulate transactions within and beyond the frontiers of an industry. The concept of governance, which was originally created for sector-based analyses, could be transposed with a view to understanding territorial dynamics, just as Parri (1993) did with Marshall's industrial districts. Parri demonstrated how infranational spaces are increasingly structured by public institutions at the local and regional level.

However, governance cannot be reduced merely to a transposition of the concept of *régulation* to a smaller scale. It is perhaps excessive to refer to it as covering 'all forms of *régulation* that are not commercial or state-based: it is civil society minus the market ... plus ... local political society' (Benko and Lipietz, 1992).

In our interpretation, the governance of a territory describes a structure composed of different actors and institutions at a given moment, offering an understanding of the rules and routines that lend a place its distinctive character compared with other places and with the overall national productive system. To deal with the dynamic of a territory's *régulation* it is also necessary to appreciate the strategies of actors, the local ability of the territory to adapt to the exogenous logic of branches and the effects of learning. In other words, it is a matter not only of having information about the structures of governance, but also of examining the foundation of their cohesion and long term success or failure (Corolleur, 1994).

The concept of 'institutional thickness' suggested by Amin and Thrift (1993) could supplement the concept of governance, introducing a qualitative view of the institutional combination described by the mode of governance. Both the number and the diversity of institutions are judged, along with the degree of interaction between them and the power structure (stabilised at the time of observation) on which the interaction and the group of actors' sense of belonging to a common company are based.

Territories foster conflict and opposition through their production processes, but neither governance nor institutional thickness can account for these conflicts. An analysis of configurations of the wage–labour nexus within territories is therefore necessary. It is possible to show how the local wage–labour nexus is simultaneously dependent on and autonomous from the global level. Dependence can be measured through the recognition by local actors of laws and regulations established at the global level as well as through the action of professional associations and unions that are organised by sectors rather than territories. Autonomy can be observed through the processes of developing customs and unwritten rules for employers and employees in a local branch within a zone and the way in which relatively stable local compromises are established. Raveyre and Saglio (1984) demonstrated this with the example of the plastics processing plant located in Oyonnax, as did Dunford (1988), who discussed Grenoble and Scotland, and Gilly (1987), who studied Toulouse.

To conclude, a territory can be defined institutionally and local forms of *régulation* can be approached by three complementary aspects: the type of governance, the degree of density of institutions and an evaluation of the conflicts and compromises made through the wage–labour nexus. However, the local configuration of the mode of *régulation* is incomplete (lack of proper accumulation regime, totally exogenous monetary constraint, influence of the state level, etc.) and local *régulation* can therefore only ever be partial *régulation*.

Local productive systems

The concept of an actor (individual or organisation) is not the first object of analysis for *régulation* theory, which is fundamentally a macroeconomic theory. However, only consideration of actors' behaviour provides an understanding of the mode of operation and dynamic of productive systems and their modes of *régulation*. In the words of Alain Lipietz, it is a matter of introducing 'into a world of structures without agents the ferment of instability and change that represent the possibility of the deviance of individuals and social sub-groups without, however, collapsing into a world of agents without structures' (1988).

Beyond individual actors, the mode of co-ordination of many actors must be conceptualised. This is the case when it is organised through an intermediary structure of collective learning generating a specific collective dynamic made up of a group of companies, production subsidiaries, a network of co-operation between firms, local innovation systems, etc.

This is the focus of meso-analysis, whose aim is to identify and examine organised productive sub-sets (meso-systems). Today this approach has been reinforced by neo-institutional theory and the convention school, in so far as the meso-system is composed of processes of socialisation permitted by rules that form a shifting point of interaction between individual behaviour and global institutional forms. During stable phases in a productive system's mode of *régulation* the meso-system acts as a 'place' of legibility, intelligibility and dissemination of the productive and institutional principles of this mode of *régulation*. During phases of crisis it acts as a 'place of emergence of new patterns'.

A meso-system is an organisational form which is generally national or transnational (networks of co-operation, groups of companies, etc.). When structured in a restricted geographical space, it is called a local productive system. This is an organisational form in which a process of collective learning develops *through an effect of proximity* (Dupuy and Gilly, 1994). This involves a process of co-ordinating activities as well as a process of co-ordinating behaviour. For a territory to exist, there must be an overlap, which will always be partial, between geographical proximity, organisational proximity (linked with technical-productive complementarity) (Rallet, 1991) and institutional proximity (linked with the collective cognitive behaviour of searching for solutions to production problems). Institutional proximity (Kirat, 1993), which ensures the social cohesion of local productive systems, is based on a logic of collective actions founded on conventions and the local institutions that are created, adapted and shared by actors. In this respect, Salais and Storper's work (1994) is an innovative attempt to understand the economic identity of France by linking the production of conventions to the global development of *régulations.*

The overlapping of different conventions, characterised by their density and institutional 'thickness', defines the concept of *local régulation* once a territory is able to identify a predominant overall convention that enables the non-predictable adaptations demanded by the industrial dynamic in an uncertain environmental context. This is only a temporary definition. It would be helpful to identify local institutional forms, since they participate in the process of capital accumulation. This approach is similar to Christian du Tertre's (Chapter 27) when he defines the relations between the overall economic system and sector levels via a dual connection: accumulation regime–operating regime and institutional forms–institutional arrangements.

Conventions and institutions at the local level may be either formal (territorial authorities, professional organisations, etc.) or informal (rules of the game tacitly adopted by local actors). If they are informal, they play an essential role in processes of collective learning and the setting up of the co-operative relations that cement local productive systems and, particularly, the processes of territorial innovation (Gaffard, 1990; Planque, 1991). Geographical proximity favours connections between organisations whose purposes, spatial references and strategic temporalities differ (firms and research centres, for example). It also accelerates the spread of knowledge and know-how among territorial protagonists (this is especially the case in local systems of innovation when technologies have not yet been codified and formalised), in addition to facilitating the creation of value systems and collective representations based on reciprocity.

Positioned between global institutional principles and local conventions, territories can therefore be viewed as the centre of local–global relations *for some configurations*.

Local and global *régulations*

As a localised process of collective learning, the territorial approach allows the introduction of the question of the dynamic of intermediary (and global) structures. Conventions governing the behaviour of actors (especially the wage–labour nexus) are never definitive: they are social compromises that can be partially revised and that introduce an element of play into the rigidity of *régulations* (Friedberg, 1993).

To understand how local *régulations* participate in or resist the global *régulation* of an economic system and how an economic system influences or is influenced by local *régulations*, two situations should be distinguished:

1   A situation in which actors adopt routine behaviour and where territories show enduring patterns in their organisation and connection with the global productive system. In this instance, territorial *régulations* and the overall mode of *régulation* support each other.
2   A situation in which actors adopt deviant behaviour that is outside existing local conventions. Two cases may then arise.
    (a) It might signify a 'local crisis' that can be resolved within the framework of the prevailing mode of *régulation*. The local *régu-*

lation conventions are sufficiently efficient to reduce behavioural differences among actors and to maintain or collectively transform the local socio-economic trajectory. For example, the shift from mechanical technology to quartz technology in the watch industry in the Jura in Switzerland (Maillat *et al.*, 1993).

(b) Or else a 'major crisis' occurs when existing local *régulation* is unable to channel the deviant behaviour of actors. In these conditions territories explode or reform according to a new local socio-economic trajectory. The Lacq Basin is an example of this type of reconversion zone (Daynac and Dupuy, 1991).

In the second alternative, contradictions between a territory's dynamic and that of its environment create a 'major crisis'. An interesting case occurs when the institutional and technical-economic innovations established in a territory require the explosion of the institutional and productive forms of the global economic system in order to develop. But obviously not all local institutional innovation is intended to spread and transform the prevailing accumulation regime and mode of *régulation*.

The main issue is to find the local determinants of the radical transformations of an economic system and its accumulation regime.

Analysis in terms of industrial districts encourages an interpretation of the local level as the privileged level of innovation and emergence from transformations in an accumulation regime.

Before the regions of Lyon in France and Birmingham in Great Britain became heavy industry zones they were industrial districts. A mass of small units that usually worked in small-scale crafts created a tradition of know-how on the basis of intense circulation of information about new trades (weaving, light engineering, steelwork, etc.). The heavy industry that later became Taylorian was not generated spontaneously. Originally productivity gains were obtained through proximity effects and through a dissemination of know-how that created a pool of professionals. It was only later that the development of the activity was pursued through a process of concentration in large establishments that played on economies of scale and intensified division of labour within establishments.

But the accumulation regime of the global economic system also modifies the local productive system. It is especially the large industrial and financial groups, 'the real actors and creators of the world economy' (Amin and Robins, 1992), that act as vectors of the tension between the local and global, and as the source of the industrial and institutional dynamic. Furthermore, the global dimension, which is far more worldwide than national today, refers to multinational spaces such as Europe. The autonomy of local spaces is in danger of being even more reduced by it (Amin and Thrift, 1993).

However, globalisation cannot be interpreted as a simple linear process of making behaviour and spaces uniform. On the contrary, it implies more complex adjustment strategies and the emergence of specificity at the territorial level. In periods of structural change, competition between territories is combined with competition between firms. In particular, this means that the external features produced in a territory are not only the generic and static availability of an endowment of abundant and cheap elements, but also a specific, dynamic interactive skill involving activities, abilities and know-how.

Finally, one may put forward the hypothesis that, in the contemporary period, the processes of territorial relocating of production provide some analytical keys to understanding current changes. In this case, the organisation of actors' strategies at a territorial level are only temporary but necessary forms at a precise moment in the recomposition of global *régulations* (Pecqueur, 1989).

Measuring the local

The 'natural' space for validating *régulation* theory is national space. The globalisation phenomenon (Chapter 14) borne essentially by the large industrial and financial groups, and analysis of the local dimension of *régulation* present the same question as *régulation* theory making the spatial variability of economic processes endogenous.

From this perspective, and following the work of Julla (1991), regulationist methodology could be expanded in two directions:

1   The accumulation regime could involve macroeconomic spatial regularity alongside its temporal horizon, through the introduction of a spatial horizon of capital development, on the basis of which a principle of spatial management of actors' strategies (particularly globalisation) would be identified.
2   The overall institutional configuration for steering the accumulation regime could be enriched with a 'supplementary' institutional form: territorial organisation. This would emerge from the overall administrative relations of *régulation* theory's five institutional forms, and more particularly the state policy of regional territorial development. Territorial organisation would regulate the macroeconomic space of the accumulation regime.

This conception would contribute to an analysis of the relations between economic space (accumulation) and institutional territory (of *régulation*). These relations are obviously contradictory. The intensification of international competition between firms reinforces historical competition between nations as well as revealing infranational competition, which is extended among large regions as well as among more modest rural cantons. They no longer play solely on the availability of 'cheap' or abundant elements, but instead focus on the specific resources constructed by actors, sometimes at the end of a very long process. The infranational landscape of the major industrialised countries is undergoing massive changes and reveals strong alterations in the spatial hierarchy of the accumulation regime.

Regional territorial development, understood as the set of procedures and institutional arrangements that contribute to producing territorial organisation, therefore appears to be a relevant tool of analysis for local conditions in the recomposition of an accumulation regime. Beyond the role of an analytical grid for connections between the local and the global, territorial development must be seen as a concrete instrument of action and a challenge within a perspective of enduring local development and social solidarity.

27 Sector-based dimensions of *régulation* and the wage–labour nexus

Christian du Tertre

Régulation theory is primarily a macroeconomic theory. However, a small group of researchers who make direct reference to this theory have undertaken meso-economic analyses with a large sector-based component. They have studied two areas. The first area of investigation involves a demonstration of sector-based *régulations*, which require an explanation of the relations established between these *régulations* and the *régulation* of the overall level. The second area concerns differences in the capital–labour relation, involving a clarification of the tremendously diverse labour organisations and modes of labour force management in a context where the Fordist wage–labour nexus predominates.

Defining a sector

Regulationists have viewed the sector as a relevant level of analysis not on the basis of the Walrasian concept of product homogeneity, but from the complex social construction of a historically identifiable productive sphere. Particular use value productions, made on the basis of specific technology, are linked with processes of structuring for economic purposes that materialise through *ad hoc* institutions in which professional interests are represented through the co-ordination procedures of productive units (Boyer, 1990b). Sectors correspond therefore to spheres of activity that involve particular institutional arrangements* (Bartoli and Boulet, 1990) and can be defined on the following bases:

1   A labour social relation based on the instituting of a precise productive configuration.
2   The confrontation of individual capitals in a framework of organised competition.
3   International regulations that frame the sector's dynamic within the international regime.

This historical, social and economic concept has given rise to surveys and debates on the divisions to be drawn between different productive activities. This is especially the case with the petrochemical sector (du Tertre, 1989) and with agriculture. It applies to agriculture as a whole (Lacroix and Mollard, 1994) or at a less aggregate level, and even extends to the distinction between the sectors of *appellation contrôlée* and common wine (Bartoli and Boulet, 1989, 1990; Chapter 28). Divisions in the service sector have not yet been formalised. The differences between traded/non-traded services and household/business services (Petit, 1985) are elements of the analysis of forms of competition, but are not enough to define them precisely. There are also other contributions that use non-regulationist approaches, such as Bell's (1973) historical approach, which is derived from an analysis of changes in demand and is influenced by Engel's law. Despite its interesting aspects, this approach is somewhat cut off from institutional and labour social relation dynamics. The difficulties in identifying divisions within the service sector are perhaps due to the fact that the activities are in the process of deregulation/restructuring or structuring. This is also the case with activities that involve intangible elements (du Tertre, 1994a).

Non-Fordist sector-based dynamics

Throughout the growth period, the 'non-Fordist' construction sector experienced very strong capital returns together with weak labour productivity. The transfer of productivity gains, from the most dynamic manufacturing sectors to the construction sector, can be explained only by the heavy demand for this sector and by its central role in spreading Fordist consumption and production norms, thereby supporting the establishment of an intensive accumulation regime (Campinos-Dubernet, 1984).

Since 1970, given the slowdown in state and company demand, the most active element has been household demand. The slowdown in the growth of purchasing power, along with its decrease and instability for many social categories, has caused a vulnerable, fluctuating sector dynamic. Despite a restructuring of the industrial fabric of the construction sector and despite the appearance of new rationalisation strategies for productive activity that have greatly modified organisational and labour arrangements, productivity gains have remained weaker than in other sectors. This sector is unable to create a growth in demand in an endogenous manner via a lowering of housing prices, even when the potential household demand is twice as high as solvent demand. These difficulties derive from aspects of the forms of competition and wage–labour nexus, as well as from the increasing sophistication of building technology.

As a product, construction is subject to regular developments that reflect increasing demand for quality by companies, households or the state. Companies are looking for more flexibility in the use of space, requiring new wiring systems to support modern communication systems, etc. Households and local or regional authorities are making new demands in terms of the quality of the living environment and additional services in habitat norms (e.g. home automation and urban services).

The transformation of forms of competition within the overall macro-economic dynamic, the constraints of company flexibility and the rise in service activities have transformed the socio-technical characteristics of the construction sector as well as affecting product costs. But, in return, the sector's ability to meet new types of demand has become a require-ment for post-Fordist industrial activity, growth in the service sector and spatial modifications to the locality of emerging activities. This prompts the question of new institutional interventions as a new dialectical move-ment between the macroeconomic dynamic and the sector dynamic develops (du Tertre, 1994b).

The characteristics of the *agricultural* dynamic will not be discussed here, since this sphere of activity is analysed in Chapter 28.

Other studies have clarified the role of the service sector as a whole within the macroeconomic dynamic (Petit, 1985) and the relations that connect it with industry (de Bandt and Petit, 1993). These studies reveal the extent of the displacement of activities and the creation of new jobs since the early 1960s. International comparisons (Petit, 1994a) have contributed analytical elements to their impact on the growth rate. This raises the question of the new functionality of some types of service within a new accumulation regime.

The development of the service sector involves a sector-based speci-ficity that invites the introduction of new institutional *régulations*. In respect of this, four points can be highlighted (du Tertre, 1994a).

1 Many services, particularly intangible services, have been influenced by the development of a 'service relation' such that an activity is created and frequently pursued in collaboration with the client. The extent of this phenomenon leads to the problem of establishing new institutions in charge of the *régulation* of service relations and the social determination of norms for product quality (Gadrey, 1990, 1992). Furthermore, studies by INSEE have demonstrated that diffi-culties encountered in the stabilisation of quality norms are at the root of the increase in relative prices for some services.

2 It is all the more important to recognise this institutional intervention into quality, since the service sector has special forms of relation to innovation–productivity–employment. These forms account for a rela-tively weaker decrease in jobs compared with industry, and a relatively stronger extension of markets. This is due not to a simple delay in the productivity effect on employment, but to characteristics of the life cycle of this type of product, which is an inversion of the life cycle of manufactured products. The effect of capital/labour substitution is less than in industry (Petit, 1990) and is recompensed primarily by a quality effect.

3   Most services are produced at the time they are consumed. Thus their
     spread to households and companies depends not only on changes in
     relative prices, but also on a reduction and reorganisation of hours
     worked. This factor, whose impact on employment has been the subject
     of many industry surveys (Cette and Taddei, 1992), ought to be studied
     in societal terms (Boulin, 1993a, b). Distribution of productivity gains
     no longer occurs simply through the growth of profits and purchasing
     power; it now also includes a reduction in hours worked. The division
     of productivity gains creates new 'institutionalised compromises'.
     Consequently the reduction and rearrangement of work time are viewed
     not as part of labour distribution, but as part of a fundamental change
     that must sustain the demand for intangible services. Just as the 'high
     wage' policy (Coriat, 1979) was an essential element of Fordist *régu-*
     lation, the reduction and reorganisation of work time is an essential
     condition for new consumption and production norms to develop.
4   Finally, research has analysed the difficulties involved in transforming
     observable social needs into social demand in the context of contem-
     porary, conflict-based changes in urban life. The 'solidaristic economy'
     (*économie solidaire*, Laville, 1993) or the knowledge industries
     (*quaternaire*, or fourth sector) are an area of activity that enables appar-
     ently local needs from the 'domestic' sphere to emerge and develop
     into an integrated social demand within the dynamic of the overall
     economy. The extent of institutional support that this area of activity
     receives affects the exclusion or integration of associated activities
     within the accumulation regime and their contribution to the process
     of job creation.

Essential challenges are created by the rise in service activities that not
only affect the dynamism of these sectors, but also have an impact on the
rate and form of economic growth.

Sector dynamics and macroeconomic *régulation*

As a whole, sector analysis has brought up the issue of clarifying a precise
formulation for the link between sector dynamics and macroeconomic *régu-*
lation. But this objective seems to be the result of progress in the debates
among researchers who lay claim to *régulation* theory (Boyer, 1990b).
Several studies present a rationale that relates specifically to sectors and to an
original institutional arrangement at the sector level.* The focus on meso-
economic questions can then be viewed as occurring through a *synthesis*
(Boyer, 1990b) of two types of concern: a demonstration of sector specificity
and its relation to an overall rationale. This is based on four main principles.

1   Initially sector dynamics are influenced by sector-based aspects of the
     labour social relation, the organisation of competition and the history

of institutional arrangements. It is thus a matter of recognising the foundations of sector heterogeneity which form part of the productive dynamic.

2   But the overall macroeconomic system also has an influence. It creates constraints and opportunities that depend on the place of the sector within the accumulation regime. The sector dynamic is thus dependent on the semi-functionality of the sector.

3   Given substitution effects that are always possible at the level of productive combinations (through technical change or the use of foreign producers) and the different histories of institutional arrangements, some activities flounder while others prosper. Restructuring and regrouping thus occur within the macroeconomic arrangement.

4   In turn, these transformations may influence the dynamic of the overall macroeconomic arrangement.

Following Bartoli and Boulet (1989, 1990), referred to by Boyer (1990b), it is possible to schematise the connection of macroeconomic and sector

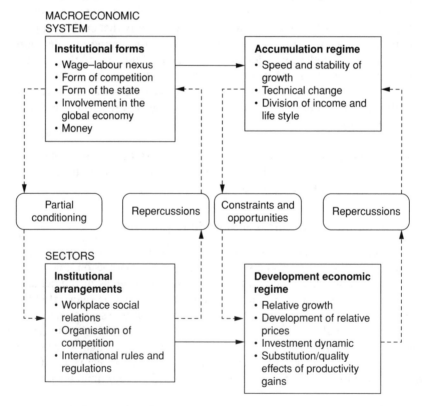

Figure 27.1 Macroeconomic and sectoral structure
Source: adapted from Boyer (1990: 69)

levels. If there is no *régulation*, in the strong sense of the term, other than at the macroeconomic level, it is nevertheless possible to identify a 'sector dynamic' or an operating economic regime* (Bartoli and Boulet, 1989) with specific characteristics and a history. This operating economic regime is structured in the following manner.

1   'Institutional forms' at the macro level affect institutional arrangements* at the sector level. But sector changes can also contribute to alterations in some institutional forms.
2   The characteristics of the accumulation regime create constraints and opportunities for the operating economic regime* (at the sector level), but in return this may affect developments or changes in the accumulation regime. This influence on the overall dynamic can be greater or lesser, depending on the degree of maturity and fragility of the accumulation regime.

To conclude, the contribution of sector-based *régulation* research is based essentially on its ability to provide a detailed account of real changes in various productive activities during growth periods as well as at the beginning of a crisis. It also suggests a frame of reference for what is involved in emerging from a crisis, reflected by restructuring and reorganisation at the sector level. The development of research into non-Fordist sectors and especially the service sector should enhance the potential contribution of *régulation* theory.

Differentiation of work processes and productivity determinants

Following A. Sohn-Rethel (1977), referred to by B. Coriat (1980) and B. Kundig (1984) in France, an initial distinction was made between industries that act on the form of products and those that act on their state and chemical composition. The first are affected by hours worked and the completion rate of production sequences, while the second are influenced by the quality of physical-chemical operations, which affects the quantity and quality of products. These initial suggestions permit the identification of sectors that are primarily dependent on rate and hours worked (form industries) and those that are linked to the overall return on production equipment (process industries). In these instances, productivity gains are obtained on the basis of the same quantity of work, capital and intermediary consumption thanks to improvements in the quality of physical intervention and organisation.

A second distinction is then introduced for form industries, between those that produce in series and those that produce single units on site. Serial production is subject to the constraints of the *direct intensity of labour*, in other words the rate of directly operational elementary tasks, while site production involves the *intensity related to labour* (du Tertre, 1988). In this instance, the rate and quality of the production sequence depend on the quality of control tasks that are intrinsically linked with operational tasks.

This approach, using the economics of time, led researchers to define the *socio-technical characteristics* of work processes and their connections with different rationales obtaining for internal economies. A distinction in terms of equipment is made between tools, machine tools and machinery in identifying the impact of their properties on productivity. A detailed analysis of the quality of work required is undertaken in order to establish distinctions between direct operational tasks and control tasks, as well as between prescription and control arrangements instituted by a hierarchy. In process industries, the existence of a marked difference between prescribed work and actual work produces strong collective labour autonomy. This involves the interplay of tacit qualifications, a collective dimension and recognition by the company hierarchy. Finally, organisational arrangements are examined to reveal their degree of autonomy in relation to technology. While in serial industries balancing techniques enable the conception of production scheduling based on the definition of work posts whose duties are individualised and optimised, in other situations these techniques cannot be used and organisation enjoys a great deal of freedom. Given the specific constraints of variability and the spatial aspects of the activity, this is particularly the case with building.

These analyses reveal three different types of work processes: serial, site and process (Coriat, 1979, 1980; Campinos-Dubernet, 1984; du Tertre, 1988, 1989), with preferred levels of internal economies. Subsequent research developments defined the analysis of productivity determinants for changes in forms of competition and sought to go beyond the very concept of a work process.

Other research (Hollard and Margirier, 1986; du Tertre, 1989; Coriat, 1990, 1991; du Tertre, Santilli, 1992) worked hard to define the set of productivity determinants by clarifying their connection with the overall economic cycle and new constraints on flexibility, quality and time periods (Chapter 13).

Returns to scale are defined in relation either to serial volume or the degree of variety in products made with the same production equipment. The mechanisms of *economies of scale* (lowering the unit cost of commodities through the volume production of a specific product) and *economies of flexibility* (lowering the unit cost through the versatility of equipment) have variable impacts, depending on the characteristics of work processes and sector dynamics. Serial industries, such as continuous process industries, are very open to economies of scale. However, transformations in the rate and form of growth that appeared after the two oil shocks are symptomatic of a relative exhaustion of the driving role provided by these economies. The modification of forms of competition reveals new constraints on variability in these sectors, causing an increase in the power of variety economies, described here as economies of flexibility. The dynamic of site industries is relatively unfamiliar with economies of scale and far more sensitive to the effects of flexibility economies. This results in considerable site autonomy with respect to centralised management by companies, through the importance of organisational flexibility in the building sector.

The processes of integrating productive activity reduce the cycles of capital development and the size of liabilities. A distinction must therefore be drawn between processes of *static integration* that make production sequences more compact through mechanisation, and processes of *dynamic integration*, which develop production in 'hidden time' through new technologies and the circulation of information in 'real time'.

Concerning the concept of the work process

The research undertaken on a sector basis led to a bypassing of the concept of work process because of two limitations. The first is the fact that work, technology and organisation are understood to be structured around a single tension that is created by the governing rationale of internal economies. The analysis thus concentrates on the workshop or site as the central place of development. But research shows that productive arrangements are also subject to the tensions of competition exclusive of cost. The structuring of work, technology and organisation may therefore also depend on questions of quality and innovation time periods, reflected in the increasingly important role of the *functional arrangement* of companies and its *coherence* with regard to the directly productive arrangement. The work activity is thus understood through the concept of *productive configuration* (du Tertre, 1992) which widens the field of analysis to include co-operative and conflicting relations between productive and functional arrangements.

This conceptual development is also implied by research into the service sector. The concept of the work process is not very effective at grasping the productive aspects of service activities. This difficulty is due to the specificity of the *service relation* between providers and recipients and the impossibility of defining reliable tools for measuring productivity gains (Gadrey, 1990, 1992). Thus a *social service relation* must be integrated into the analysis (du Tertre, 1994a; Gadrey, 1994).

The second limitation of the concept of the work process is due to its focus on the wage-earning class. Research into agriculture (Lacroix and Mollard, 1988, 1994) has shown that agricultural activity is based on processes of capital development that involve not only the fixed capital, circulating capital and direct work that define the work process, but also land, natural resources and living resources. Furthermore, this research has highlighted the importance of self-employment, in a family context, and the way in which work relations are structured around family relations. In this way patrimonial and land interests are linked to the capital/labour relation. Overall the results of this research led to the concept of a *labour social relation* being proposed. In addition to extending the approach beyond the wage-earning class, this concept takes into account the different ways in which work activity is connected not only with technology, but also with living resources and with 'land space'.

Analysis of different work processes was therefore one way by which it was possible to construct an understanding of the diversity of work situations (using new conceptual developments), and researchers soon accepted the need to replace work within the sector dynamic of capital development.

The sector dimension of the 'wage–labour nexus' or the 'labour social relation'

The expression 'Fordist wage–labour nexus' is sometimes used at two different levels of analysis which, if they are not clearly distinguished, can lead to serious confusion. On the one hand, this concept refers to the wage–labour nexus that appears in an intensive accumulation regime. It sanctions a certain place for work within society, which is consonant with the dynamic of other institutional forms. On the other hand, the expression is sometimes wrongly restricted to organisational forms of work and labour force management in serial sectors, whose archetype is the automobile. Even if *régulation* theory retained the first definition when making macroeconomic claims, it should be recognised that confusion appeared in as much as the automobile played a central role in France in the post-war period (Veltz, 1983). Now, even if the industrial dynamic that prevailed in this sector could function as a model for many companies in spheres of activity that are not related to assembly, production arrangements and styles of labour management were still very diverse (du Tertre, 1989).

At the sector level the wage–labour nexus refers to:

1   A type of production configuration (techniques used, form of labour organisation, the quality of work required).
2   An institutional arrangement (branch conventions in classifications; forms of mobilisation of the labour force; specific training arrangements).
3   Conditions for the creation of direct income.

Beyond the description of sector-based wage–labour nexuses and the classifications to which they give rise, research has sought to resituate work analysis in the long term development of the place of sectors within the overall macroeconomic dynamic. Their functionality in an intensive accumulation regime and in the ensuing crisis creates a system of constraints and opportunities that influences the dynamic of their development and the forms of the wage–labour nexus. Examples of this are Campinos-Dubernet

(1984) for the construction sector; Allaire (1988) and Lacroix and Mollard (1994) for agriculture; du Tertre (1989) for a comparison of the automobile, construction and petrochemical sector; and Petit (1985) for the service sector. The constraints on development defined from the relative extension of markets and transformations in the forms of competition, different changes in relative prices, the influence of the evolution of capitalistic intensity and the concentration of capital, form a set of specific constraints on work organisation and labour force management.

Thus for example, during the growth period du Tertre (1989) concludes that the automobile sector is a stable but blocked sector in terms of the labour force; the construction sector has a shift-based work force, with little possibility of promotion; and that the petrochemical sector has a stable work force with strong promotion possibilities.

By taking into account the constraints linked with the characteristics of production configurations and the differentiated functionality of sectors in the accumulation regime, a synchronous analysis of the different forms of work, resituated in a historical dimension, can be developed.

Even if the Fordist wage–labour nexus was the driving force during the period of growth, affecting all productive activities, work retained a meso-economic specificity. This was clearly marked by aspects of the work process or production configurations and by the place of the different spheres of production in the macroeconomic dynamic.

Analysis of these specific aspects is all the more important today when the Fordist wage–labour nexus has been destabilised and the place and role of different sectors are changing. The establishment of a new wage–labour nexus at the emergence from a crisis borrows some aspects of the different work social relations, depending on the new position of sectors in the overall dynamic. The challenge for research consists of suggesting hypotheses and arguments about the way in which some of these characteristics will play a major role in a new overall *régulation.* A detailed analysis of services and other non-Fordist spheres of activity, such as the construction sector and agriculture, should produce many new theoretical and empirical advances.

28 Sector-based *régulation*

The case of agriculture

Gilles Allaire and Amédée Mollard

Transformations in farming and the food industry, which converged with and complemented Fordism, led to a call for regulationist schemas. The resulting research involved very varied sector configurations. Some research adopted an extended perspective that included the entire food industry sector (Néfussi, 1987). This had the advantage of accounting for the close relations that developed between agriculture and the agricultural and food processing industries during the Fordist period. Other researchers defined a far more restricted field of application, such as milk (Gouin *et al.*, 1985) or wine (Bartoli and Boulet, 1990). This enabled more in-depth analysis, but also favoured conditions of exchange over those of production. This disadvantage is avoided by authors who study agriculture under its current definition (in terms of national accounts), such as Kenney *et al.* (1988) and Debailleul (1990) for the United States and Allaire (1988) and Laurent (1992) for France. This choice is justifiable so long as it is demonstrated that this sector has been historically and socially constructed.

An agricultural sector?

French agriculture has shown a very strong economic and institutional consistency whose gradual creation since the mid-nineteenth century can be described as follows.

1   Most farms are similar in terms of the technical, economic and social organisation of production (cf. the concept of 'productive configuration' in Chapter 27). Whatever farms produce, their labour always involves the soil, natural resources and living matter. The spatial context almost always has an important role in the process and organisation of production, which is generally based on self-employment by family members, with very little wage labour. An implicit or explicit objective is often the creation of an inheritance to be transmitted to future generations. All production has common characteristics in terms of the procedures of initial training, know-how and the technical skills required for managing biological processes.

2   Agriculture is defined and created as a key space of competition
    between producers on the product markets, while capital is fairly
    immobile. Competition is reflected in frequent changes in production
    due to soil and climatic constraints, revealing considerable intra-
    agricultural mobility, which is accentuated by the interplay of European
    competition, the integration of farms by food processing industries and
    the organisation of each subsector. This mobility is not widely recog-
    nised, since it is hidden by the apparent stability of farms.
    Consequently, this space of intra-agricultural competition is the only
    level of economic observation that is stable in the long term, with land
    structures providing the cement of this stability.

3   Finally, most of the agricultural institutions affecting the two previous
    areas, and structuring the behaviour of agents, are the result of secular
    historical developments. (Barral, 1968; Gervais *et al.*, 1976; Postel-
    Vinay, 1991). Unions and the agricultural profession (credit, mutual
    insurance systems and co-operation) were created as of 1884. In 1881
    Gambetta appointed a specific Minister, in his words a true 'Minister
    of the Interior for peasants'. Then, in 1924, Chambers of Agriculture
    were set up. From the end of the nineteenth century there was a gradual
    unification of agricultural markets (transport, customs duties, foreign
    trade). This was followed by the organisation of public support for
    agricultural markets after the 1930s crisis, then a general system in
    the 1950s which was reinforced by the Common Agricultural Policy
    of the 1960s. There was a system of co-management by the state and
    representative professional agricultural organisations in order to direct
    the modernisation of production structures. This was accompanied by
    a special social security system (*Budget Annexe des Prestations
    Sociales Agricoles*, or BAP-SA, a supplementary budget of social bene-
    fits for farming) and a national policy on property ownership and
    agricultural structures (the country code). It should also be mentioned
    that many resources, from land restructuring to genetic material, have
    a collective basis.

These institutional characteristics are entirely coherent, confirming the
hypothesis that agriculture does have a sector configuration.

Sector-based *régulation* of productivist agriculture has been possible
owing to two major elements.

1   The technical, economic and social organisation of production directed
    entirely towards a rapid and intensive industrialisation of agriculture.
    Despite some obviously unique features, it shares some characteristics
    with Fordism at this level (Boyer and Durand, 1997).

2   Forms of competition and the organisation of agricultural markets
    through a policy of permanent public support.

Agriculture in global *régulation*

Economic growth does not create a dynamic demand for food products, since people must be fed whether they are working in the fields, factories or offices. There is a limit on food spending (Engel's law). The main source of agricultural growth during the Fordist period was a 'quality' effect involving two elements: the service provided by regularly distributed products from the food processing industries and an increase in the proportion of meat and dairy products in the diet. An endogenous growth dynamic was created by the intensification of grain production, which found a market in animal feed. This technological paradigm, which emerged in the United States during the inter-war period (Berlan and Rosier, 1986), is a key aspect of the growth regime. Likewise, the decrease in agricultural assets is a consequence of agriculture's growth, and not a result of an unfavourable international insertion. The vigour of general growth absorbs the social effects of agrarian changes. This regime is now exhausted and the main mass-production sectors depend on market changes at the global level.

The productivist dynamic, which is based on the spread of standardised technology, was supported by the general growth regime in so far as inflation facilitated the adjustment of markets through innovations while simultaneously reducing the fear of debt. But the construction of a world of industrial agricultural and food processing involves a profound transformation in behaviour, supported by institutional arrangements and public incentive policies. These 'institutionalised compromises' that characterised the New Deal in the United States and the '1960s model of development' in France (Allaire, 1988) were established through national agreements.

The major structural aspects of productivist agriculture and the global economy between 1945 and 1975 can be seen more clearly during the time when the agricultural crisis permanently altered this sector's profile and economic insertion. This *ex post* examination reveals many interactions between the global level and sector dynamics. Three important aspects can be pointed out in the case of France.

1   The keystone is the productivist compromise of the 1960s between the state and the agricultural profession (the Debré and Pisani laws) as an extension of the Treaty of Rome (article 39). This agreement, which was reached in a context of frequent, intense demonstrations by farmers, is like the great wage negotiations and the Fordist institutionalised compromise of sharing productivity gains (Delorme, 1984; Debailleul, 1990). Wage negotiations were part of the 'virtuous circle of productivism' (Lacroix and Mollard, 1993), just as the institutional compromise reflected the 'virtuous circle of Fordism' (Boyer and Mistral, 1990).

2   This productivist compromise perpetuated the principle of public, state support for markets (inaugurated in 1936 with the Wheat Office) and established an innovative policy for production structures. On the one hand, agriculture committed itself to contributing to global economic growth by industrialising, becoming competitive and exporting, as well as accepting the agricultural exodus. On the other hand, the state recognised the right of agriculture to share in the resulting productivity gains and to obtain income parity with other professional categories. From a different perspective, agriculture was assisted to invest and benefit from dynamic economies of scale created thus (Chapter 21; Allaire, 1994). The agricultural budget reflected these general objectives in financial terms, and, under neo-corporatist control, public financing for the sector expanded (Bourdon, 1990).

3   There is a *dialectical relationship between agriculture and the Fordist wage–labour nexus*. Agriculture contributes to the construction of this relationship while becoming increasingly subject to its norms, even though its social work forms differ.

The contribution of productivist agriculture to the formation of the wage–labour nexus occurred through two principal channels (Mounier, 1992). First the supply of a work force to industry (agricultural exodus) and second the development of mass consumption of food ('a car in every garage and a chicken in every pot', F.D. Roosevelt). Alongside the construction and public works, energy or automobile sectors, agriculture therefore played a strategic role in the emergence of a model of standardised consumption. A double structure for agriculture and the global economy was created. Fordist growth gave dynamic impetus to the demand for new food products and therefore to agricultural production. In return, productivity gains in the sphere of agriculture and food processing (which public investment contributed to through research and training) allowed a reduction in the cost of food products and a decrease in their share of household budgets, from more than 30 per cent in 1960 to 18 per cent in 1990.

At the same time, aspects of the wage–labour nexus increasingly influenced the agricultural work relation and it became subject to Fordist norms. Examples of this are: consumption norms for housing, household equipment, transport and communications; a move towards social security and retirement funds for wage earners; and a convergence of life styles with the norms of wage earners in terms of holidays and leisure time, even though there was still a long way to go (Lacroix and Mollard, 1988). The work process was also affected by Fordist production norms: labour intensification, specialisation and deskilling of tasks, standard techniques and, more generally, a heteronomous work process (Lacroix and Mollard, 1994). In short, during this period the Fordist wage–labour nexus had a considerable influence on the productivist work relation in economic terms, and destabilised legal elements that were a part of the long historical tradition of the peasant's status as founded on property. Contemporary tendencies break with this development through the increasing importance of management choices for farms.

Finally, agriculture played a supportive role in developing the intensive Fordist accumulation regime by contributing in a significant manner to the major balances of the overall economy and the inter-industrial dynamic in a national framework.

This insertion of agriculture into the industrial dynamic led to a muddying of the exchange matrix with upstream and downstream industries. For upstream industries, farmers expanded purchases from the chemical industry for agricultural mechanisation, building and animal feed. Downstream, the proportion of farm products transformed by the agricultural and food processing industries developed rapidly (more than 80 per cent in the 1980s), and the share of farm products has fallen dramatically in terms of the value of food products (less than 50 per cent).

This change has created a dependence relationship. The dynamic of industrialisation from above has been the vector of a technical-economic model of production whose creation has largely eluded farmers. Even if the rise in co-operatives in the 1960s was an innovative attempt by the agricultural profession to master downstream markets, the internationalisation of the agricultural and food processing industries and trade soon showed the great economic dependence of farmers.

The need for a micro-institutional analysis of the farming sector

Despite the coherent aspects mentioned above, the agricultural sector shows great diversity in terms of modes of organisation and production. There is therefore a danger of describing the whole of the agricultural sector with excessive generalisation. Analyses of productivism often refer to dairy production, where a quasi-Fordist wage–labour nexus reigned from 1975 to 1985, which had the following objectives: simplified production, standardisation of equipment and genetic material, centralised negotiation for 'milk pay' and fewer and larger accumulation centres (specialised production pools). Another line of analysis, referring to poultry farming or processed fruit and vegetables, reveals the role of large firms and a selection by the market that was more decisive. This was accompanied by a less centralised organisation of markets, but with a *régulation* of relations between actors ('contract economy') in them. The diversity, however, is also geographical. Different social, national or local configurations provide different means of modernisation, and varying models for the organisation of farm and food production.

Given this diversity, analyses of relations between the sector dynamic of agriculture and overall economic *régulation* requires the identification of the levels at which strong consistency between modes of production and institutional arrangements exists, thus clarifying mechanisms of *régulation*.

P. Bartoli and D. Boulet (1990) demonstrated a link between institutional arrangements* and operating economic regimes.* Arrangements develop over long periods and lead to relatively autonomous subsidiary trajectories. The case they considered, wine growing, is all the more interesting since this activity is based on specialised production zones. The social construction of mass wine-growing *régulation* (in terms of wine status), from 1907 to 1935, involved a productive wine-growing regional system (Languedoc) supported by an inter-class alliance. The markets and social spaces concerned are not regional, but this regional wine-growing bloc was a major collective actor in the *régulation* of the activity (monitoring plantations and volumes through public programmes of negotiated withdrawal). The lowering of prices in the 1970s reflected a move from a national organisation dominated by the Languedoc to European organisation. The effectiveness of the regional corporatist bloc was rapidly eroded (Bartoli, 1990), preparing for the explosion of local production systems (Touzard, 1995) and a long transition of local production systems towards 'quality' agriculture. The structural nature of the crisis was revealed by a change in the position of regional wine growing in intra-sector competition. Alternative diversification strategies developed, but encountered the obstacle of sector arrangements. The structural crisis was a crisis of the quality convention governing the production of table wines. The transformation of the market led to a gradual and problematic change in the rules for determining prices (a move from proportion of alcohol per hectolitre to a system based on differentiation by quality).

In a more general sense, European market regulations ('Community market organisations') imply a definition of quality to which actors of the subsidiary must adapt (Heintz, 1992, for the case of wheat). Depending on the economic cycle, the quality produced is adjusted according to this norm. But the margins for manoeuvre are limited by irreversible public and private investment. When a qualitative transformation intervenes in supply and demand, a consequent adaptation of regulatory arrangements does not occur immediately. The rationales of producers and users then become autonomous. During the 1980s, and prior to the 1990 reforms, the transformation of institutional arrangements took place in stages, via an institutional learning process sanctioned by previous failures. Market logic exerts pressure on quality definitions and leads to a restructuring of inter-professional arrangements. The emergence of policies of contractual quality challenged the principle of normalisation brought about by the centralised management of the market. With the reform of the Common Agricultural Policy in 1992 the institutional crisis was hastened, sanctioning the relative failure of the structural adaptation phase of the 1980s.

In poultry farming, a commercial crisis in industrialised production arose rapidly during 1963 and was resolved by concentration. But a 'civic' response was also formulated, protecting small-scale networks through reference to quality via a label defined by decree. However, labelled production only took off in about 1975, with the organisational forms adapted to the industrial sector (Sylvander, 1994). However, the organisational experience of labelling allowed companies that were faced with a demand for variety to pursue segmentation using the new references to distinguish quality.

Convention theory* and contract theory were called on to analyse forms of competition in the farming and food sub-sectors, particularly those with a contractual economy. In fact many products are related to an 'economy of quality' (Karpik, 1989) in the sense that, even when the farming contract has been signed, some uncertainty remains about the quality of the product to be delivered and its production costs. Take, for example, the production of processed vegetables. E. Valceschini (1993) described the 'interprofessional arrangement' that has existed since 1961 as a combination of civic co-ordination (definition of the product fixed by public rulings, examples of negotiation and forms of representation of a legislative and regulatory nature) and industrial co-ordination (normalisation and instrumentation of decisions linked with the execution of the contract). He describes the 'interprofessional contract', from the level of agreements negotiated by collective actors in the arrangement, as an 'incomplete' contract. At this level, authority and trust are no longer enough to complete a contract. Three 'completing' factors are suggested: relatively stable growth, an inflationary context, and the mechanisms of the Common Agricultural Policy. This is none other than an agricultural version of Fordism, although Valceschini does not say as much.

These examples share some general features. Whether the institutional forms of the sector are old or new, a convergence of dynamics is identifiable during the Golden Age ('trente glorieuses'), either in the intensification of production or in professional organisation. The sector trajectory is nevertheless dependent on its territorial insertion in production, competition and negotiation spaces. The cases outlined suggest the existence of several levels of governance. An agricultural production sector is an institutional space in which regulating arrangements are established with a view to defining an area of competition. The organisational forms of collective actors reflect arrangements in the sector. The question for *régulation* is to understand the mechanisms that stabilise or destabilise this framework by considering different time horizons.

Today, in most agricultural production sectors, there is a move towards commercial operators rather than production areas, supported by changes in European regulations. The relation between the market and norms is changing (Thévenot, 1994). But crises have arisen in the different cycles of sectors, depending on their area of specialisation, concentration, regional diversity and institutional frameworks. In the sectors described, the events of a crisis differ according to the space provided for new market logics by institutional forms and according to the support given to new organisational forms. The modes of *régulation* of sectors are transformed in many different ways.

The general crisis of growth dynamics challenges the most firmly established arrangements for sector *régulation.* A crisis in institutionalised compromises arises across agricultural activities, while each intra-sector crisis has a structural role, and market logics challenge product definition. The management principles of production systems are at issue. During the agricultural growth trajectory, professional forms relayed quasi-integration through the spread of new technology. The extension of structural crises or quality crises in sectors results in professional crises or a crisis in institutionalised compromises (Allaire, 1994).

Régulation crisis and Common Agricultural Policy

Gradually since the 1970s public rules for sectors have been integrated into the European context, whether in structural policies or in policies for the different markets. Certain products have had a guaranteed price, as in the case of grains, wine and milk. The level of prices determined in these sub-sectors has had an indirect effect on the prices of substitution products. Contrary to a pro-market point of view that considers this an obstacle to the spread of innovation, such (relative) control over income was a necessary condition for the creation of expectations. In dynamics, expectations create quality conventions in sector arrangements.

A ten-year transition period was needed before the Agricultural Policy was transformed radically (in 1992) into a policy of supply control along with compensatory subsidies. During an initial period, an adjustment of sector policies made it possible to maintain an intensive logic. Later arrangements for cyclical regulating were added (various forms of storage), as well as rationing arrangements (freezing land, dairy quotas, tearing up vines). Again, a crisis in *régulation* occurred. A *régulation* crisis emerges with the cycle of crises demanding general institutionalised compromises (particularly at the level of incomes policy); this was the case from the mid-1970s until the end of the 1980s. The national context was still important in analysis of the events in the 1980s crisis. But the establishment of the European Common Market, followed by the creation of the World Trade Organisation (the Casablanca agreements), gave the European level the upper hand again.

The reform of the Common Agricultural Policy promotes a trade logic that destabilises sector arrangements, but includes new concerns on the basis of which new institutional arrangements are emerging. The reform opened up the possibility of a coupling of direct subsidies, in proportion to volume produced, with the production of externalities that correspond to new objectives for the environment and territorial arrangements. This coupling requires new regulatory arrangements with a clear territorial element. Thus the restructuring of the Common Agricultural Policy, which is intended to promote the play of the market, also encourages the interplay of territories.

29 Regulationist political ecology or environmental economics?

Alain Lipietz

The relation between a *régulation* approach and an environmental approach involves a strange paradox. Several economists known for their contribution to regulationist thought are equally well known for their involvement in ecological movements, parties, clubs and foundations. Conversely, when ecologists want to found their actions in economic analysis, they usually rely on the regulationist analysis of the 'productivist' Fordist model. Yet until the late 1980s regulationists had hardly contributed at all to an 'economy of the environment'. The critique of Fordism included only a few denunciations of its attacks on nature, as if the 'ecologist citizen' was speaking out among economists inspired by this type of analysis (Clerc *et al.*, 1983; Lipietz, 1985; Beaud, 1989).

Yet in the 1990s regulationist and conventionalist approaches have been active in at least two areas: the economy of the environment *per se,* and debates on the UN Conference on the Environment and Development and the geopolitics of global ecology.

The paradox of Green ecologists

The main reason for the relative lack of interest on the part of ecologist regulationists in an economy of the environment is that generally they are political ecologists, not environmentalists. They view human ecology as the relation between humans, the environment and human activities, on the basis of an 'already given' environment which is transformed (Lipietz, 1993b, 1999). Initially therefore they are interested in the way in which the social relations of production and consumption model the environment. From the outset they believe that 'the constructed context is the main form of the living framework of capitalism' (Lipietz, 1974) and that urban ecology and the *régulation* of urban forms (or, later, the town–country relation) therefore exhaust most of the topic 'the environment and Fordism*'. In short, the initial uninterest of regulationists (even ecologists) in the economy of the environment is similar to their initial lack of interest in the economy of technical change. Technology, like the environment, is an artificial production in which social relations materialise. Furthermore, this marginalisation of Nature and the Machine conforms to an originally Althusserian distrust of the 'naturalisation of productive forces'. Just as regulationists do not recognise technological determinism, so they refuse to acknowledge an institutionalised compromise* with Nature. Institutionalised compromises exist only between humans and the technological and societal paradigms that unify or set them in opposition to one another, thus affecting the evolution of techniques, nature, living things, landscapes and the rights of future generations.

A second reason is the fact that the primary object of study for the *régulation* approach is essentially the industrial model of Fordism. It is difficult to claim that Fordism entered a crisis because of the relation between society and the environment. Ecologist regulationists have occasionally criticised the effects of Fordism on the environment, but when looking for a way out of the crisis of Fordism they focused on its origins (the crisis of the wage–labour nexus and a lack of international *régulation*), particularly in the context of the failure of the left in France. They are more concerned with the social living conditions that need to be established (employment, housing, etc.) than with defending the environment as such, especially since they are all influenced by the earlier success of an industrialist model, even if its faults have been criticised.

It was only when they examined the Third World (Lipietz, 1985; Beaud, 1989) that regulationists, and those inspired by them (particularly Michel Beaud in his 'Vezelay Appeal'), began to consider the society/environment relation as a real constraint in the choice of 'post-crisis' models. This was especially the case in the late 1980s when the magnitude of global ecological crises became clear. In a conclusion to the international survey for the World Institute of Economic Development Research on capital/labour relations at the dawn of the twenty-first century, Lipietz (1991) emphasised that, from an ecological perspective, models 'implying negotiation' by wage earners are more favourable than models that depend on labour force flexibility. You (1994) also emphasised the disastrous consequences of Korean-style 'authoritarian developmentalism'.

From an ecological point of view, the new development models are preferable because they promote the autonomy of individuals in implementing production forces, and social interaction within companies through income and job redistribution. Once the negotiation of the capital/labour compromise relates to a reduction in work time rather than the growth of material consumption, it becomes extremely favourable to the environment. The ecological orientation of some regulationists is probably most clearly expressed here, in the choice of a development model where 'abstaining from polluting' is chosen over those that seek to direct growth to minimise pollution or to repair its effects. Thus in sector studies of energy, it is a matter of reducing consumption before encouraging less dangerous forms of production (Lipietz and Radane, 1993).

Régulation of space

However, two branches of the regulationist school could not avoid dealing directly with the issue of the environment, including the 'natural' environment: spatial and agricultural studies.

Early research on urban ground rent (Lipietz, 1974) showed the way in which, in instances where human economic activity essentially creates its environment, variations in land prices (different ground rent according to locality; intensive rents due to investment) are directly related to 'environmental value'. This guarantees a *régulation* of the allocation of space, even in the absence of a regulating urban agent who may be indispensable under some conditions. As a form of *régulation*, land prices play an important role in the economy of water, where a regulating agent is indispensable for 'internalising external effects'.

For agricultural specialists, the object and product of labour meet at the crossroads of human activity and the biosphere. In his thesis on agriculture in the United States, Guy Debailleul (1990) encountered 'Nature' in the two major crises that frame Fordism. The first was in the 1930s, with the formation of 'dust bowls' (an erosion crisis). Roosevelt's powerful forms of *régulation*, regulating agricultural revenue and leaving fragile land fallow, lasted until the 1980s, when the enormous American surplus collapsed. Debailleul demonstrates that there were two origins to this crisis. First, the mode of *régulation*, i.e. the inability of national regulatory institutions to take control of farming, which was increasingly oriented towards exporting. Second, a strictly 'ecological' origin in the dramatic rise in legal obstacles instituted by public authorities to the use of chemical inputs near water courses that were increasingly being polluted by intensive farming. Catherine Laurent's thesis (1992), which examined the unexpected failure to free up farming in France, follows the regulationist programme in the 'farming–society–environment' relation exactly. It moves from the crisis and reform of the Common Agricultural Policy to the appearance of ferns and eagles in freed pastures, through the end of the hegemony of professional agriculture over the use of rural space and the utilisation of non-profitable land using non-standard forms of production.

Anne Lacroix and Amédée Mollard's assessment (1993) of the absence of the environment in the regulationist corpus should therefore be at least slightly nuanced. This diagnosis does, however, depend on an extension of the concept of the environment, particularly in its relation to ecology. These authors are correct when they identify three major advantages of the regulationist approach:

1   The environment presumes an economy oriented by ethics and public decisions.
2   The environment presumes an economic dynamic founded on social reproduction and included within ecological reproduction.
3   The environment presumes a long- or very long-term economy.

New research developments

Among conventionalists, whose stance is similar to that of regulationists and who adopt several of their concepts, a new approach to the economy of the environment is now developing. The economy of the environment must deal with the specific problem of the relations of different elements within a given environment. The *régulation* of relations 'between equals' (as opposed to the asymmetrical dominant/dominated relations of the wage–labour nexus) is precisely the area investigated by the conventionalist approach. The *régulation* of this type of relation already involves either the market or politics; Lipietz (1992a, 1993b, 1999) clearly argues that political *régulation* is not necessarily 'statutory' but (as Tariq Banuri, 1992, reminds us) it may take the form of face-to-face community-based negotiation.

The contributions of Godard (1992a) and Hourcade (1993) mainly served to advance the conventionalist–regulationist approach of the economy of the environment under fairly specific conditions.

First of all, the forms of *régulation* affecting ecological contradictions are still at an early stage. Often there is no agreement on objectives (the regime to be obtained) or legitimate forms of *régulation*. This is therefore a *controversial* rather than a *stable* universe, in which the initiatives of today may be invalidated tomorrow by changes in ideas and regulations (contestable legitimacy). The regulationist–conventionalist approach can be useful for compromises that are in the process of institutionalisation, as well as in cases of persistent differences. This is because it can reveal the relationship between instruments that could be implemented (quota markets, eco-taxes, norms, prohibitions, moving from the market to the rule) and the results to be expected from the regime that emerges. Of course, in all cases (even in market creation) the initiative of the political authority must have adequate sovereignty available. In the context of this '*ex ante* conventionalism' there has been a reinterpretation of the debates on the institutionalisation of potential future compromises in controversial systems, and the precepts of 'limited rationality'. This suggests a precautionary principle, time gains in learning and 'no regret' strategies.

This rationalist intellectual framework laid the groundwork for the Rio conference and international negotiations on the greenhouse effect (Godard, 1992b; Hourcade and Baron, 1992). However, they revealed such conflicts of interest, such asymmetries of power and such differences over objectives and values that they justified a return to analyses in terms of contradictions (particularly North–South) rather than conventions or co-ordinating rules. It was in this spirit that some economists and geographers (regulationists and Anglo-Saxon 'radicals') understood negotiations over global ecological conflicts (in the context of international research co-ordinated by UNESCO and WIDER) (Lipietz, 1992a; Bhaskar and Glyn, 1994). In so doing they joined the neo-structuralist agenda of international relations (Campos de Mello, 1992).

Even if there was agreement on the environmental consequences of a given accumulation regime, it is important to note that different social and national structures assess in different ways the likely costs to their futures of the various regime options. This is in addition to assessing the implementation costs of the corresponding mode of *régulation*. Furthermore, in each social formation, there may be differences between the interests of the various social groups (potential victims of ecological crises) and the interests of an elite involved in negotiations. Thus while negotiations on the greenhouse effect ought to have opposed the *laissez-faire* strategy of a 'guilty' North to the precautionary strategy of a 'victimised' South, the reality is in fact far more complex. Between the two extremes represented by the United States and Bangladesh (whose negotiators conform roughly to this schema), there are the Newly Industrialised Countries that have highly productivist elites. There are also highly advanced industrial countries that chose a co-operative strategy of capital/labour at the end of the crisis of Fordism. These countries have both the technological means and the hegemonic ambition to suggest that the rest of the world should adopt a strategy of collective precaution in the light of climatic dangers.

Thus in the geostrategic field of the global ecology (Lipietzy, 1999) some results of research into the wage–labour nexus reappeared. But it is clear that the result of a search for an institutionalised compromise that is interclassist, international and intergenerational will be far more complex than a simple nationally based capital/labour 'New Deal'!

Part V
National trajectories

30 From canonical Fordism to different modes of development

Robert Boyer

Since the crisis that started in the 1960s, what has become of Fordism and the monopolistic mode of *régulation*? Has a new development model emerged? Are countries moving towards similar configurations of institutional forms in response to an unprecedented degree of internationalisation? It is time to bring together the threads woven by the preceding analyses around these central questions. While Part II analysed the five institutional forms separately, each of the following chapters analyses an individual country. The hypothesis is that the nation state is still a relevant unit of analysis, even when a high level of internationalisation is destabilising many of the institutional compromises of each country.

Internationalisation and the relevance of the nation state

The authors of these chapters make use of the analytical tools presented for identifying the macroeconomic dynamic and structural change (Part III) in an eclectic and inevitably partial manner. A single motive underlies the questions, basic concepts and methods. A common diagnosis refers to the *structural crisis* that hit the United States from 1967 to the 1990s, and Japan after 1991, when the financial bubble burst. It also considers the collapse of the Swedish model in the early 1990s. However, the conclusions reached point to the specificity of each national trajectory.*

These analyses refer to more general reflections on strategies for recovering from a crisis and examining possible successors to Fordism. In parallel to this, the extraversion of national economies for the last twenty-five years also presents some serious difficulties for the reconstruction of national institutional forms. Is it true that international financial markets are increasingly governing the monetary regimes of individual countries? Is competition affecting increasingly large geographical areas? These are obviously some of the main themes of Part IV. These analyses allow an updating and revision of some of the initial formulations of *régulation* theory.

From institutional forms to accumulation regimes: the concept of Fordism revisited

The diffusion of *régulation* theory has been affected by a damaging misunderstanding caused by confusion between one of its main conclusions and the question and methods on which it is based. It is true that the exceptional growth of the Golden Age was due to the implementation of an intensive accumulation regime based on mass consumption. This change was one consequence among others of a labour–capital compromise based on a *qui pro quo*: acceptance of Fordist production methods in return for productivity gain sharing.

But that is not all there is to say about this theory, since, contrary to the persistent claims of some authors (De Vroey, 1984; Cartelier and De Vroey, 1989), other accumulation regimes preceded Fordism and others will therefore follow. Furthermore, refinement of the method and the many lessons of events in the crisis between 1971 and 2000 have led to a superseding of the somewhat monolithic concept of Fordism. Initially, various qualifiers were attached to the label of Fordism: in Germany it was flexible, in Italy delayed, in Great Britain obstructed, while in Sweden it was social democrat and in France it was state-based, etc. (Boyer, 1986b). As a result of more serious analytical difficulties, many other descriptions were proposed for developing countries. If the claim is that Fordism is the cardinal accumulation regime against which all others must be assessed, this approach is rightly open to criticism.

Fordism can therefore be defined far more precisely as an accumulation regime that combines three characteristics.

1   First, a system of *work organisation* which, starting from Taylorism, pushes still further for the division of labour into separate tasks, the mechanisation of production processes and a complete separation between conception and production. The assembly line is the emblem of this form of industrial engineering, and tends to create a mimetic effect in many other sectors. This is the first element of an intensive accumulation regime, in other words a regime that is founded on the search for and attainment of continuous growth in productivity.

2   However, assembly lines alone cannot create a Fordist growth mode. It is also necessary for employees to obtain an *institutionalised share of productivity gains*, in a manner other than through the effects of labour shortages that appear when accumulation becomes too dynamic. The American collective bargaining agreements of the 1960s and the French policy of 'sharing the dividends of progress' are examples of long-term contracts codifying wage income. The combination of these two characteristics defines the Fordist wage–labour nexus.

3   But this combination alone is not enough, since it must be linked with compatible institutional forms, whether it occurs under oligopolistic competition or in a monetary regime based on credit. Furthermore, an

essential characteristic is that the process of adjusting production and demand occurs primarily *within a single country*; at least the lack of competitiveness must not obstruct the synchronisation of production and consumption norms within a national territory. In other words, intensive accumulation is governed by internal consumption and is inward-looking.

A strict application of these three criteria implies that Fordist growth existed up to 1967 in the United States (Juillard, 1993) and 1974 in France (Bertrand, 1983). This can be shown using a macroeconomic model designed to ensure that the associated path of development is stable. The model is more or less complete, depending on whether it integrates only the core of the accumulation regime (Chapters 18 and 19) or whether it claims to incorporate the monetary regime and external forms of competition (Aglietta *et al.*, 1980). This is because economies are always open but are constrained by the international dynamic differently.

Classifying accumulation regimes

On the other hand, each exception to the three criteria above provides a basis for *alternative accumulation regimes*.

1   Once the *work process* ceases to obey all the criteria that define Fordism, it may initiate a new model. This could involve older forms such as Taylorism, which is still seen in some branches (Chapter 11), or it might be a more or less ambitious superseding of the limits of Fordism (Boyer and Durand, 1997). This is the case, for example, in the polyvalence and professionalism of German workers, who are atypical with regard to the Fordist wage relation. Toyotism might also be interpreted as the expression of a new conception of industrial organisation (Coriat, 1991, 1994a). The assumption of a new type of accumulation regime is reinforced by a wage compromise that is not Fordist at all (Chapter 34).
2   This is the second exception, then, which explains significant differences from American Fordism. It is in fact quite rare for the wage–labour nexus to incorporate an explicit and codified sharing of expected productivity gains. Either wage-earner organisations do not exist or they are too weak, or else the compromise involves stability of employment (and/or the maintenance of full employment) and career prospects rather than salary. The first configuration is found in many developing countries where the informal sector introduces considerable competitive pressures (Chapter 37). The second relates to the micro- or meso-corporatism of large Japanese companies or to the Swedish economy prior to 1989. In these two countries economic activity has a large impact on wage formation (Boyer, 1991).

For example, looking at dramatic falls of the real wage, as in Brazil or Mexico, it is highly improbable that a Fordist labour–capital compromise prevails. In terms of macroeconomic modelling, this means that the accumulation regime is *a priori* not Fordist. It may be a fairly classic case of growth led by profits (Boyer, 1988b).

3   Finally, national growth may be based on the extraversion of an export sector supplying the resources to feed consumption and internal investment. In this case the national growth loses its autonomy, since it is constrained by trends in the world economy and the ability of countries to benefit from possible changes in the international division of labour (Mistral, 1986). This is certainly the case of less advanced countries that do not have a sufficient technical base. As a result, the accumulation regime no longer has anything in common with that of the central economies and it is in fact a sheer contradiction to use minor variants of Fordism to describe it (Lanzarotti, 1992).

Even though their expertise and industrial bases are considerably stronger, since the end of the 1960s many OECD countries have experienced both extraversion and specialisation so that the internal accumulation regime has become highly dependent on their insertion into the international division of labour. This factor may even be enough to bring about the shift of Fordism towards an intensive regime governed by exports. This would explain the decay of the Fordist wage–labour nexus, since the remuneration of workers becomes a cost which penalises competitiveness instead of an element of the dynamism of consumption as it was in the past (Bowles and Boyer, 1995).

Thus the concept of Fordism should be located in a series of accumulation regimes defined by the origin of productivity gains, the principles of division of income and the degree of extraversion of the economy. Many regimes can therefore be derived, although theoretical analysis must examine micro and macroeconomic viability and empirical studies must confirm their existence. At the end of this process, which requires painstaking and systematic efforts, using both econometrics and institutional analysis, it is important to suggest a classification of accumulation regimes on solid foundations and without recourse to the facility of mere prefixes attached to Fordism. This work is far from done, but the present volume is a stage in it.

Many different national trajectories*

The following chapters offer an interesting panorama. The term 'trajectory'* refers to the strong inertia in the economic dynamic, which is caused by a national configuration of institutional forms that are often to a great extent idiosyncratic.

All the old industrialised countries appear to be, or to have been, hit by a crisis in the mode of *régulation*, which was strongly influenced by contrasted institutional configurations. Paradoxically, although the United States seems to have found a new growth regime, it is one that no longer allows a rise in the standard of living without an extension of the hours worked by American families (Chapter 31). This trend was maintained in the 1990s thanks to an unprecedented surge of finance. Such is not the case in France, where accumulation is still intensive. However, internationalisation has had a drastic effect on the institutional architecture that is the foundation of the Golden Age, and so far no alternative to Fordism has emerged (Chapter 32). By way of contrast, in Sweden, which had long been characterised by intensive accumulation governed by exports, a spectacular collapse of the social democratic institutions occurred (Chapter 33). Since the 1990s Japan, which in the 1980s was a reference model in terms of intensive accumulation based on mass consumption and product differentiation, has suffered from a deep crisis of its mode of *régulation* (Chapter 34). This has been aggravated by the financial fragility revealed by the bursting of the financial bubble (Boyer and Yamada, 2000).

The collapse of Soviet-type economies provides a fine example of the extension of the regulationist method to a context where mass production never managed to establish itself (Boyer, 1995a). It therefore becomes clear that the concepts of a wage–labour nexus, monetary regime and form of competition are ultimately well adapted to describing largely extensive accumulation, directed by *régulation* through shortage,* which is the opposite dialectic to the over production tendencies of canonical capitalist economies (Chapter 35). But studies of the sequence of reform attempts that have taken place since the 1960s show that the Polish, Hungarian and Czech economies are far from being an identical reproduction of the same mode of *régulation* through shortage.

The Soviet Union is a key example in so far as it reflects a major structural crisis involving slow erosion of the surplus, more severe rationing and the inability of the political authorities to lead the reforms required to enable the economic crisis to be overcome. Most of the institutions that would allow the state to direct the reconstruction of the structures of production have been taken apart, so that the Russian economy is trapped in a series of vicious circles which appear to be very difficult to escape from (Chapter 36). Furthermore, old forms of company organisation may emerge again (Peaucelle, 1995), but their survival is difficult in the prevailing context of structural uncertainty (Sapir, 1998).

Underdeveloped countries are another field of application and renovation for *régulation* theory. Compared with Carlos Ominami's (1986) synthesis, which is already dated, conceptualisation of the origins of underdevelopment has advanced. While in some countries the disparity of the wage–labour nexus is the origin of structural unbalances, in others it is the extreme international dependence caused by the lack or weakness of the section of the means of production (Talha, 1995). Even in a situation of external dependence, Latin American countries are characterised by a wage–labour nexus, a state form and degrees of competition which are sufficiently distinct to produce different national trajectories (Chapter 37).

The differences are even greater in countries where the wage–labour nexus is still at an embryonic stage. The merit of analyses of the Maghreb is that they have attempted to adapt the theory to part of the African continent, which until now has been particularly resistant to *régulation* theory. This is an invitation to rework categories and methods in order to make them relevant to that context (El Aoufi, 1995). For the time being there is also a severe lack of regulationist research on the newly industrialised countries of South East Asia. Paradoxically, the establishment of a wage-based society and the absorption/adaptation of technical innovation should make *régulation* theory more relevant and easy to adapt to this context.

Will bad *régulations* drive out the good ones?

Does the combination of national trajectories define a viable configuration for the international economy as a whole? The perspectives presented by the different chapters highlight a major contradiction (Boyer, 1994b). Until the late 1980s it could be claimed that the stiffening of international competition in fact meant a competition between different methods of reconstructing the mode of development. Fundamentally, the emerging regime pursued intensive accumulation on new terms. On the one hand, the speed of reaction to market variations, differentiation by quality and the ability to mobilise innovation in production were characteristics of a new configuration of scientific management. On the other hand, the accumulation regime was increasingly governed by external competitiveness and exports, a trend that affected economies of average size in addition to small open economies (Cassiers, 1989).

Nevertheless, these principles were able to be embedded into differing institutional architecture: the social market economy in Germany, social democracy in the Scandinavian countries and micro- or meso-corporatism in Japan. The advantage of these solutions was that they combined moderate inequalities with economic efficiency (Boyer 1992a). The differences between these institutional configurations evoked political choices, since the imperative of competitiveness did not seem to dictate a 'single best way'. It was clear, for example, that Sweden was not a variety of Japanese society! In fact, in this battle of '*régulation* versus *régulation*', the economies that were most governed by a market logic and individualism, such as the United States, Great Britain and Canada (Drache and Gertler, 1991), appeared to fall behind in international competition.

In the late 1990s the situation seems to have been the opposite. The rapid rise in speculation, the globalisation of financial markets and the flow of financial innovations have created an international system which is more uncertain than ever, and whose movements destabilise the previously most effective institutional constructs. Diversity in the development of financial innovations and their rapid international diffusion have upset the conditions of international competition, since the movements of exchange rates and interest rates have been far greater than differences of structural competitiveness linked with the adoption of new production principles. In this new context the forms of capitalism dominated by an Anglo-American style market-led logic seem to come out better than those where the market was channelled and subjected to controls, through the impact of large companies, the bargaining between labour and management or the state (Amable *et al.*, 1997). The Swedish economy collapsed, German reunification brought a major weakness to the heart of Europe and eventually Japanese economic dynamism became exhausted owing to the combined effect of the drastic evolution of the yen, the slowdown in international trade and the surge in financial innovation.

Thus in the late 1990s, the economies that gave way to the charm of a 'return to the market' prevailed over economies of organised capitalism. Hence a threatening paradox: were these tendencies of the international economy to be prolonged, it is highly likely that *bad 'régulations' would drive out the good ones* and that eventually the risk of stagnation or instability would increase, following the model of the inter-war period. Markets have been globalised, but political power has not. Contemporary societies could suffer painfully from the widening gap.

31 The United States

Goodbye, Fordism!

Robert Boyer and Michel Juillard

The United States is to *régulation* theory what England was to Marx. There are several reasons why the United States has acted as a special laboratory for numerous economic theories. They include the fact that it was formed more recently, on a market basis, that it has played a hegemonic role since the Second World War, and that its economy was fairly independent of international trade until the mid-1960s. In a study of the US economy since the Civil War, Michel Aglietta (1974, 1976) revealed the key concepts of *régulation* theory. The concept of Fordism* and analyses of the contemporary crisis are therefore heavily influenced by the United States.

Fordism

Why were the years following the Second World War not affected by a repeat of the catastrophic events of the 1930s? Why did this period enjoy strong and relatively stable growth? The enduring long-term trends in terms of production organisation are then linked with major transformations in the wage–labour nexus, forms of competition, the monetary regime and insertion into a special international regime, the *Pax Americana*. As a whole, these transformations define an accumulation regime later described as Fordism. The allusion is to Henry Ford, the Detroit entrepreneur who saw himself as a social reformer, as well as to Antonio Gramsci's analysis of the integration of the American proletariat.

Fordism is first the widespread use of a way of organising the work process which develops the logic of scientific management inherited from Taylorism. Its natural field of application is large assembly firms (Hounshell, 1984), but it extends to banking, insurance and the distribution sector, where there is great division of labour and mechanisation is the guiding principle.

The second aspect of Fordism was more original. It was the result of a post-1945 labour–capital compromise that codified the principle of sharing the productivity gains created by scientific management. A rise in union power allowed negotiations for collective bargaining for agreements in companies or typically Fordist sectors such as the automobile industry. Corresponding wage increases then diffused to the rest of the private sector, and by extension to an increasing number of employees in the public sector. This combination of 'connective' and 'collective' bargaining (Piore, 1982) transformed the determinants of the nominal wage, which was less sensitive to unemployment but was indexed on anticipated productivity gains, lagging slightly behind changes in the cost of living (Boyer, 1989; Leroy, 1995; Baslé *et al.*, 1999).

This accumulation regime still required the guidance of an adequate mode of *régulation*. All institutional forms experienced major changes, first at the time of the New Deal and then at the end of the Second World War. Although the dominance of large companies and financial concentration were somewhat obstructed by anti-trust laws, they nevertheless led to some pacification of competition, which occurred more through advertising and cosmetic differences between products than through price wars. As the American school of administered prices has already emphasised, the result was that companies set prices by applying a mark-up rate to estimated unit costs, depending on the volume of investment to be financed for a complete product cycle. Very few sectors continued to show complete price flexibility, which would have ensured an instantaneous balance of supply and demand.

Thus the degree of cyclical fluctuation was reduced because the institutional forms of Fordism provided codification of growth in parallel with production and consumption. One final essential change involved the durable institution of a monetary regime founded on the legal tender currency and a debt economy (Chapter 7). As a result, inflation tended to be permanent, since it was the means of ensuring the homogeneity of wage rises, even in sectors with weak productivity growth, as well as constantly relaunching accumulation through credit and consumption. The two World Wars, and especially the Second World War, transformed relations between the state and the economy, since the state could then legitimately intervene in the codifying and management of almost all institutional forms. Only social insurance remained partial or limited to particular groups (Weir *et al.*, 1988). Finally, the international Bretton Woods system was based on the clearly understood aims and interests of the United States. This meant not only that American economic policy was free of any international constraints, but it was also compatible with the diffusion of the US' growth model to other large industrialised countries, at least until the late 1960s.

The crisis of Fordism

In a dialectical fashion the very success of the accumulation regime introduced elements of blockage and crisis, beyond 'external' events (oil shocks, the Gulf war), which were superimposed on to largely endogenous development. This view is shared by theoreticians of the social structure of accumulation,* who consider the slowdown in productivity and the loss of structural stability of earlier adjustment processes to have been the origin and cause of the American crisis that began in 1967. However, their interpretations of the crisis are very different.

For American radicals (Bowles *et al.*, 1986a) the productivity slowdown can be explained by a rise in management costs allocated to the control of production workers. Furthermore, the growth of direct wages and productivity difficulties may have originated in the development of social security, which reduced the cost of job loss. The conservative policies that tried to reverse these structural changes managed only to accentuate inequalities and restore profits to the detriment of full employment (Bowles *et al.*, 1988).

Regulationist researchers have developed a set of interpretations that can be combined but among which it is difficult to establish a hierarchy. In Michel Aglietta's (1976) founding work the accelerated obsolescence of capital is seen to cause inflation and eventually to block accumulation in real terms. Aglietta argues that in Fordism structural crisis is expressed through inflation, causing a destabilisation of relations between oligopolistic competition and the monetary regime. However, later research emphasises contradictions produced by changes in the Fordist wage–labour nexus.

The nature of a productivity regime may be to follow a logistic curve, since excessive mechanisation can prove to be counterproductive in terms of global productivity (Boyer and Mistral, 1981). Alternatively, the repetitive nature of Fordist work causes the repeated conflicts challenging earlier principles which are manifested in serious productivity and quality problems (Coriat, 1994). In a third interpretation, the crisis of Fordism occurred during the over-accumulation of the 1960s, which later collapsed amid a fall in investment returns. As a result of the fall in the profit rate, a period of under-accumulation began, leading to a productivity slowdown. In other words, a particularly extreme economic and social cycle – the Vietnam War – pulled the economy out of its long-term trajectory and subsequently on to a path of reduced growth (Boyer and Juillard, 1992).

This unfavourable development was reinforced still further by the temporal discrepancy between the productivity slowdown which took place after 1967 and the modification of wage formation that appeared in 1971 (Juillard, 1993: 149–56). The shock to investment returns was resolved through a reconsideration of Fordist wage formulas, as shown by the long-lasting break in the evolution of the real wage (Figure 31.1). Thus one of the engines of post-war growth was obstructed.

Whatever the original triggers of the crisis in Fordism, the crisis was followed by various cumulative mechanisms. First of all, the very weak growth of productivity caused a virtual stagnation of real wages. This in turn caused companies to develop intensive labour-techniques. In parallel, the consumption of American households was supported only by increasing the number of hours worked (Schor, 1991) or by an increase in the number of active workers per household, and temporarily by a massive use of credit.

From the point of view of wage earners, there was little incentive to make an effort, given the mediocre pay, which is not necessarily compensated by the decline of unemployment benefits. The low investment rate of the subsequent fifteen years reflects a fall in competitiveness compared with most other industrialised countries. As a result, the American economy is losing market shares in exports as well as in the domestic market, especially in terms of capital goods (Julliard, 1993: 195).

Finally, during the first phase of the crisis, in other words until the late 1970s, the break in growth led to an upsurge in distribution conflicts, which emerged through steady inflation. Faced with the danger of a meltdown of the financial system, a violently anti-inflationary monetary policy was introduced by the Federal Reserve Board in the early 1980s. An unprecedented period then began, breaking with earlier macroeconomic patterns. Longer and more severe recessions than in the past ensued, with uncertain periods of recovery. Whatever the negative consequences, the austerity policies were maintained for more than a decade, showing a reversal of power relations between debtors and creditors (Aglietta and Orléan, 1982). This was another sign of increasing distance from the earlier Fordist regime, which was favoured by very low, or even negative, real interest rates.

All these factors combined to cause large public deficits, since the growth of the fiscal base slowed down while public spending was maintained in accordance with previous social entitlements and institutionalised compromises. Their persistence marked the end of Keynesian principles of contra-cyclical policy, reinforced conservative calls for a reduction in the role of the state, and also reduced the margins for manoeuvre of fiscal and budgetary policies. In parallel, a large foreign deficit and the extent of direct investment changed the conditions of American economic policy. This was seen both in trade (the North American Treaty on Free Trade; protectionist threats to Japan and Europe) and in the management of interest rates that were caught between the needs of the domestic situation and developments in the exchange rate of the dollar. Thus a series of vicious circles were set into motion, from productivity difficulties to persistently high interest rates, including the apparent irreducibility of public and foreign deficits and rising debt.

An extensive accumulation regime with fragmented mass consumption

The decay of the Fordist regime gradually led to the emergence of new adjustment principles that differed from those of the 1960s, so that retrospectively the equivalent of a new accumulation regime emerged from developments that had taken place since the early 1970s. Its main characteristic was the return to more extensive forms of growth, combining job creation, extended working hours and low growth in productivity and wages. However, this regime is still based on mass consumption, offering an element of continuity with typical Fordism. Perhaps the relevance of regulationist analyses lies in their insistence on the novelty of the regime. Most American researchers, with some exceptions (Harrison and Bluestone, 1990), still emphasise the long-term invariability of American economic trends. They refer to a succession of long waves (Bowles *et al.*, 1983b) and the repetition of over-accumulation crises (Brenner and Glick, 1991).

An increasing number of institutional and statistical indicators confirm that since 1971 at least there has been one extensive accumulation with increasing differentiation of mass consumption (Appendix 31.1). First of all, the Fordist sector is contracting and jobs are shifting *en masse* towards the service sector, which is characterised by a very different wage–labour nexus (Petit, 1985, 1994a, 1998a). In parallel, the traditional bastion of the unions is weakened, so that wage impetus no longer diffuses through the same key sectors. Furthermore, in sectors where there is strong internal or international competition wage earners are forced to make concessions, so that their pay falls behind that of highly qualified professionals, who are in strong demand in the finance and high-technology sectors.

It is therefore not at all surprising that the *régulation* of wages is becoming increasingly competitive. This is shown partly by greater sensitivity to unemployment (Mistral and Kempf, 1988; Boyer, 1991) and partly by fragmenting of the income hierarchy. Since 1970 the poorest 20 per cent of American households have experienced virtual stagnation in their real income, while the richest 20 per cent continued to experience gains that conformed to long term trends (Figure 31.2). As a result, the consumption norm has become fragmented (Steinberg, 1982), breaking with the gradual diffusion from the richest to the poorest Americans (for example, black minorities during the 1960s). Professionals have an increasingly internationalised and differentiated life style, while some minorities have experienced absolute pauperisation and no longer even have access to typical Fordist goods. The production and demand circuit has thus changed fundamentally.

Each household has to increase its sources of income in order to sustain the standard of living which was previously provided by the male bread-winner under Fordism. Contrary to some claims, Americans work more than ever (Schor, 1991), and when they do not manage to ensure their standard of living through their income they make massive use of credit. The worst positioned among them discovered that in the 1990s, even given the same social status, they did not attain the same standard of living as their parents (Levy, 1988).

Not only are the wage–labour nexus and sources of technical change different from Fordism, but the monetary regime and insertion into the international economy have also undergone major changes since 1971. The aim of the Federal Reserve Board is essentially to fight inflation. The instruments available to the central bank have been transformed by deregulation, the sophistication of new financial instruments and the globalising trend of financial markets.

On the other hand, the American territory is now in competition with others in terms of productive investment, production and financial investment. Direct Japanese investment is a response to the closure threats of the American market: jobs (only very few) are thus created, but the transplants exert a new competitive pressure on American companies. As entire sectors have virtually disappeared, the consumption of many durable goods and company investment have fed a dramatic growth in imports (Figure 31.3) which the yo-yoing of the dollar only partially manages to curb. Wall Street is still the great centre of financial intermediation but, in the 1980s, the rise in the regime of Japanese banks showed clearly how much the American dynamic depends on worldwide savings, especially those from Japan.

An American decline or renaissance?

The fact that the United States was the first country to emerge from the great recession of the early 1990s may convey the impression that American growth and hegemony are established once again on new bases. In response to the question of whether this is 'Fordism as usual', regulationist analyses suggest a simple diagnosis. First, a major break occurred between 1967 and 1971, taking the United States far from the virtuous circle that once formed the charm and cohesiveness of the 'American way of life'. There was stagnation of productivity, exacerbation of inequalities and increasingly different living standards, competition (with Japan and Mexico), expansion of the service sector and an increased role of finance in the economy, all of which define an unprecedented historical regime. Next, the constraints of the international economy affected the American economy and limited the available options in terms of economic policy, while large American companies adopted increasingly cosmopolitan behaviour and inevitably exported some jobs, for example to Mexico.

In the 1980s it was not obvious that the extensive accumulation regime would be capable of restoring the lost economic hegemony of the United States. Japan and European nations were exploring new variants of intensive accumulation which were apparently more promising, while newly industrialising countries (including Mexico) posed a threat to its status as a high wage economy. At that time there was a great risk that ultimately islands of high competitiveness would coexist with an ocean of unqualified, illegal and informal activities often found in developing economies.

The events of the 1990s have brought a few but significant correctives to this previous pessimistic assessment. The United States has reclaimed a dominant role in terms of information technologies and financial inno-vation, to say nothing of the impact of its foreign policy on the global geopolitical situation. The vigour and duration of this expansion phase seem to confirm these changes, generating the idea that a 'new economy' has emerged. Is a new accumulation regime at work? Not necessarily, in view of the extremely concentrated nature of the productivity gains (*Economist*, 1999), the persistence of great inequalities and the determining role of credit in the financial and economic euphoria – which has so often preceded major crises!

A century later, will America follow the painful trajectory of Great Britain (Elbaum and Lazonick, 1987; Farnetti, 1994)? Or, on the contrary and in an unprecedented manner, will it show that it is possible for the most advanced economy to renew the bases of its hegemony in the first half of the twenty-first century? The boom that took place between 1992 and 2000 seems to tip the balance in favour of the second hypothesis, but we must wait to see the turn of this cycle in the American economy to know whether the first possibility has been excluded.

Appendix 31.1 Goodbye, American Fordism

Since 1967–71 productivity and real wages have experienced a permanent slowdown (Figure 31.1). Income inequalities are increasing: the rich are becoming richer and the poor are staying poor (Figure 31.2). The economy is increasingly pressured by external competition, including in the capital goods sector (Figure 31.3). The United States is exploring an unprece-dented accumulation regime: extensive accumulation with a fragmentation of mass consumption (Table 31.1).

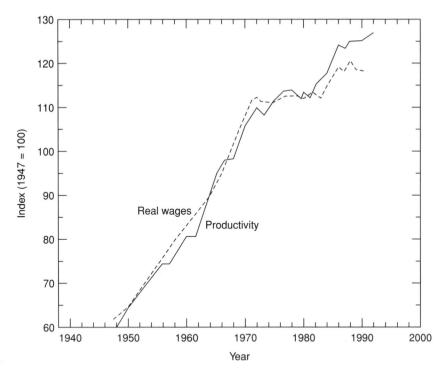

Figure 31.1 The movement of productivity and real wages since the Second World
War

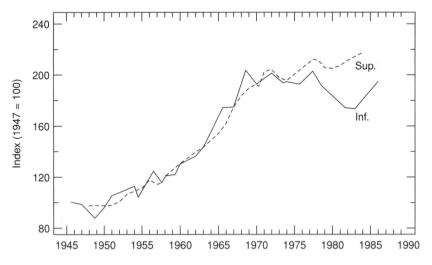

Figure 31.2 Income inequality since the Second World War

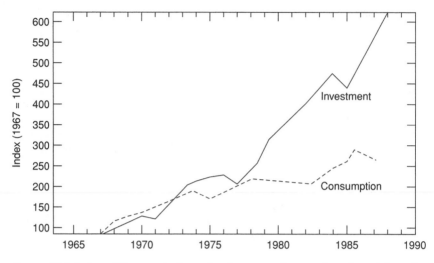

Figure 31.3 Index of the penetration rate of consumption goods and capital goods
Source: after Juillard (1993)

Table 31.1 Four types of accumulation regime

Type of consumption	Type of accumulation: primarily	
	Extensive	*Intensive*
Very little integration with capitalism	1 British economy, eighteenth and early nineteenth centuries	2 American economy, nineteenth century
Closely integrated with capitalism	4 American economy, last third of the twentieth century	3 OECD economy after 1945

32 France

The end of Fordism ... and no successor in sight

Benjamin Coriat

Traditionally, the Fordist *régulation* '*à la française*' was characterised by the extensive involvement of public authorities in both industrial policy (cf. the importance of the 'public' industrial sector) and social policy (high levels of publicly managed social expenditure in relation to GNP). This *régulation* was based on relatively stable rules as regards wage/profit sharing, based on centralised collective bargaining agreements guaranteed by public authorities. Since the mid-1980s, this edifice has been affected by a series of major national and international changes which eventually led to commitment to a highly original strategy of competitive disinflation. Thus the management of the wage–labour nexus and monetary policy, the two pillars of *régulation*, underwent profound transformations whose consequences will be examined in this chapter.

Chronicle of a future death: the end of Fordist *régulation*

The changes started with a major break with the international monetary system following the unilateral declaration of the end of the convertibility of the dollar to gold announced by the Nixon administration in August 1971. This decision, which in fact signalled the abandonment of fixed exchange rates and the dawn of a system of floating exchange rates, removed one of the essential pillars of the French strategy for strong growth – the use of regular devaluations to sustain the competitiveness of exports.

The 1973 oil crisis, accompanied by the most serious recession in post-war history, signalled the end of the virtually unlimited availability of energy at low prices and struck at the other pillar of French growth. This led to major reconsiderations, since France was highly dependent on energy.

Another major event occurred in the mid-1980s, supported by the American authorities. This was a steep rise in interest rates. This situation inverted the growth rate/interest rate differential, adding a major burden to constraints on financing for companies as well as for the national budget.

In this context the wave of deregulation of large international services (airlines, transport, telecommunications), and especially financial services, completely overturned the environment of firms, introducing major changes in the 'rules of the game' that had previously prevailed at the international level.

Finally, and mainly owing to the changes analysed above, the surge of 'globalisation' implied the end of post-war *régulation*. This series of major events resulted in the creation of large regional blocs on a worldwide scale. For France, the choice in favour of Europe, confirmed by every government, implied a tightening of constraints on budgetary and monetary policy.

1974–83: missed opportunities

The global context thus changed drastically, putting the entire world under pressure in what was certainly a 'major crisis' of the international regime. But the French elite least understood this change and they were among the last to perceive the importance of the changes for the future. The series of adjustments that were made in practice proved extremely detrimental from the point of view of French strategic interests.

Unlike Germany and Japan, the French response to the oil shocks was not to use energy more economically. Instead France undertook a large and costly nuclear energy programme whose profitability depended on strong growth in consumption, which in fact did not occur at all during the 1980s. In addition, the cost of the oil shock was borne almost entirely by companies. Taking into account wage indexation and the continued rise in indirect costs due to increasing unemployment, there was a sharp fall in profitability.

Consequently, in the early 1980s the country's competitive position had seriously deteriorated, particularly compared with Germany and Japan, which emerged as the strongest contenders during this period. Moreover, in 1981–2 the change of government was accompanied by a reflationary policy that was not well received in the European context of austerity and general recession. From 1983 France found itself in an urgent situation requiring a dramatic change of economic policy (Taddei and Coriat, 1993).

1983–94: the good and the bad in competitive disinflation

The adoption of a strategy of maintaining a strong franc (in practice this meant linking the franc with the mark at the cost of very high interest rates) was a radical change in French strategy. It implied a virtually complete reversal by public authorities, shifting from a strategy of regular devaluation to one of competitive disinflation.

Its origin lies in the impossibility of continuing on the previous path of regular devaluation.

The realignment of parities within the European Monetary System no longer allowed *ex ante* competitive gains, but only compensated a degraded *ex post* competitiveness. . . . The liberalisation of capital made devaluation gains more uncertain, since the cost of the non-credibility of parity rapidly became prohibitive in terms of interest rates.

(Muet, 1993)

In practice, competitive disinflation aimed to create a price advantage over the main competitors who were involved in less stringent strategies for fighting inflation. The success of this policy assumed deindexation of wages, a decrease in employer costs and strict control of budgetary expenditure. It was hoped that competitive gains would cause a correction of market shares (domestic and foreign) and thereby have a favourable effect on employment. This policy was resolutely maintained for a decade, with the only interlude the realignment effected by the Chirac government in 1986, which caused a devaluation of the franc and a revaluation of the mark. Ultimately the policy produced conflicting results.

At the end of 1992 competitive disinflation produced positive results for 'fundamental' areas: inflation was reduced dramatically, the budgetary deficit was absorbed and the substantial foreign trade surplus was back in balance. Company profitability returned, but there was also a dramatic slowdown in growth, and rather than dropping, or even stabilising, the unemployment rate grew rapidly and continuously. The unfavourable international environment, including Germany's decision to finance the reconstruction of the eastern *Länder* through loans, maintained an economic cycle of high interest rates that were extremely detrimental to growth and employment. In this context, the crisis of the European Monetary System in 1993, and speculation against the franc, introduced doubt into the heart of an arrangement that had been based on a strong franc.

All in all, the mode of insertion of the French economy into the global economy was totally overwhelmed by this series of shocks and adjustments. Deregulation from the United States contributed to the ineffectiveness of domestic *régulation* principles. Seen as the cornerstone of European stability, economic policy focused on the defence of a strong currency and fixed parity with the mark. However, the resulting benefits (rapid disinflation, stability of European exchange rates) did not compensate for the rise in unemployment.

Partial and late adjustment to the new industrial order: the dangers of dualism

As well as the traditional parameters of macroeconomic policy, the conditions and sources of company and national competitiveness were overturned. Gradually a 'new industrial order' (Taddei and Coriat, 1993) was established, characterised by support for three main tendencies. First, under the influence of financial deregulation, the world economy became even more integrated and globalised. At the same time, a profound revolution that was both organisational ('Toyotism') and technological (especially for microelectronic products) gave all forms of innovation a key role. Finally, and partly as a result of these two tendencies, there was a great increase in the complexity of competitive relations. Many new aspects were added to the essential feature of cost competitiveness, for instance product differentiation, rapid delivery and 'quality' (Asencio and Mazier, 1991).

Large or very large companies became actively involved in adjustments to new constraints created by a different competitive environment. Large groups were heavily redeployed in the world economy. Their performance, measured in terms of acquisitions, take-overs and alliances, speaks for itself, as most non-French commentators are quick to point out (Jacquemin, 1993). However, a different perspective emerges from a consideration of the qualitative dimensions of French adjustments.

First, the organisational changes in companies were very belated: the prevailing company model in France was Taylorian, that is, a strong hierarchy and compartmentalisation. This was especially detrimental in the new competitive environment, and changed only very slowly (Bauer and Bertin-Mourot, 1991). Only a few large concerns tried to innovate in this field ('qualifying training' at Péchiney, 'project groups' at Renault and the ACAP 2000 agreements of Usinor).

Apart from a few small innovative companies, small and medium-size firms suffered tremendously from the restrictions accompanying macroeconomic policy, which appears to have benefited only large exporters. After two decades of tremendous change, there was also a clear slackening of the inter-industrial fabric (Passeron, 1993). Such was the case, for example, in the complementary relationship between industry and services. Although in global terms French service sector companies did not appear to suffer any particular handicap, their relations with industrial companies were not very efficient and this was felt by those involved (de Bandt and Petit, 1993). Similar observations can be made of relations between industry and distribution (which are very conflictual in France), or in an even larger and more important area, in relations between industry and the financial system.

This weakness was all the more debilitating since France had a high mortality rate for small- and medium-size firms. This was the case both among newly established firms and among those lacking a successor upon the founder's retirement. This no doubt relates to the fact that there was a large gap in terms of 'large-, small- and medium-size firms'. Faced with international competition, large companies (employing more than 500 employees) supplied only about 40 per cent of the total salaried work, as opposed to nearly 50 per cent for small- and medium-size firms (ten to 499 employees). Yet it was the small- and medium-size firms that bore the brunt of the crisis.

The creation of a 'capitalism of financial centres' is no panacea

The role of mass privatisation between 1986 and 1987, and the privatisation that has taken place since 1993, should be viewed in this context. One of the main features of the French model was a very large public sector, which provided a basis of support for industrial policy, particularly in the typically French form of the famous 'major programmes'. This was also a link with priorities in economic policy. This model is currently being dismantled.

As a result of privatisation, the core of the French productive system is in the process of reconstruction, with a view to ensuring a move by the economy towards a 'capitalism of financial centres' arranged around three key poles (Morin, 1994). Financial and banking institutions have a dominant position at the centre of each pole. A set of industrial groups is connected with them through participatory interaction.

This situation would not be worrying if there were not at least two troublesome elements. The first is the absence of countervailing powers. After the era of civil service mandarins acting hand-in-glove with large state (or parastatal) companies, are we entering an era of industrial barons, an unquestioned and unassailable charmed circle which will determine the essence of the French economy? The second concern is that the new order seems clearly to favour financiers, to the detriment of industry. In an economy that has shown a relative withdrawal of industry and which, given its crucial role, needs large industrial revitalisation above all, the rise to power of financiers is hardly an encouraging sign.

Compared with Japanese-style 'co-operative' models of industrial organisation (where many *keiretsus* used to guarantee strong and stable links between companies) or the German model (where *Hausbank* and *Länder* act as collective organisers), there can be no doubt about the weakness of the 'French model' (Chandler, 1990; Caves, 1989). The construction of micro-patterns required by a move towards 'post-Fordism' in order to ensure effective dissemination of innovation and activities between large groups and small- and medium-size firms, as well as between industries and services, clearly remains to be done. Yet, the current creation of three large financial poles dominated by private actors seems to deprive France of its traditional means of action in industrial policy without providing a satisfactory substitute for the previous system.

The end of Fordist contracts and fragmentation of the wage relation

After a commendable but brief attempt to find a way out 'at the top', by strengthening mechanisms for dialogue and negotiations for change (the Auroux laws), the adoption of competitive disinflation has resulted in a gradual but thorough questioning of all typical *régulations* in the Fordist wage relation.

From 1983 to 1984 the deindexation of wages was implemented and its effects were soon felt (Ralle, 1993). In response to employment difficulties, the co-ordinated policy of a reduction in working hours introduced at one point (the adoption of the thirty-nine-hour week) was eventually abandoned and left to the discretion of partners who had little inclination to adhere to it. Likewise, after the spectacular failure of a management attempt to negotiate flexibility, gentle but constant deregulation continued. It moved into a new stage in 1986–7 with the removal of the requirement of prior public authorisation for redundancies. Called for by the Conseil national du patronat français, or CNPF, the national employers' union, according to its advocates this would lead to the creation of some 200,000–300,000 jobs in three years. In fact, unemployment continued to rise inexorably.

Under the weight of deregulation and rising unemployment, the Fordist wage relation gradually fell apart. Typically, the relation had consisted of an employment relation giving access to a wage and to associated entitlements to monetary social transfer (via indirect benefits), which gradually developed and increased through many different arrangements over time. Currently there is a dramatic rise in 'weak', weakened or incomplete employment relations through many forms of insecure, part-time or fixed-term jobs. But the most remarkable aspect has been the appearance of a 'suture' relationship between non-wage earners and wage earners, in an attempt to manage mass unemployment.

In fact this is an assertion and strengthening of a 'training relation' as substitute and 'suture' for a failing employment relation. In most cases the relation is a sort of 'bet' on future endorsement of the training, which is effective only if the market sanctions the training by recruitment to a job that gives access to the true employment relation.

But since this strategy is not enough, public authorities have taken the initiative to create an unconditional monetary transfer relation, conceived of as a deliberate substitute for the broken down employment relation. This involves the *revenu minimum d'insertion* (minimal income support assumed to help access to a job) and other types of benefit income. By lending some credence to the principle that it is possible to receive 'income without a job', this tendency represents a return to the past as compared with the consistent aims of all social policies since Speenhamland (Polanyi, 1983).

A profoundly different wage relation that has become mainly differentiated and fragmented is thus formed and reinforced. Are these temporary forms and are they merely the transition from Fordism to post-Fordism? Or do they now reflect the structural forms of post-Fordism? The question is not easy to answer.

France's lack of institutional innovation

Finally, the joint burden of the breakdown of the International Monetary System, extensive deregulation from the United States and constraints imposed by adherence to the European Union (the Single Act, Maastricht and Amsterdam treaties) have had a cumulative effect, setting France on a radically new accumulation trajectory. The mechanisms of Fordist *régulation 'à la française'* have been eroded and appear to be largely inefficient in the new global context that governments have resolutely chosen for insertion.

All in all, the series of adjustments made on the basis of choices by public authorities has not been accompanied by the institutional creations that would enable the economy to move in new virtuous circles. Nor until 1997 had they even managed to deal effectively with rising unemployment, which threatens both the economic equilibrium and the social cohesion that Fordist growth provided with such remarkable coherence.

33 The Nordic countries

A *régulation* perspective on small countries

Lars Mjøset

Régulation theory was adopted in the Nordic countries in the early 1980s among small groups of academics whose interest in political economy dated back to the student revolt of the late 1960s (but an interesting precursor of *régulation*-type institutionalism exists in the work of the Swedish economist J. Åkerman, 1954, 1955). For these researchers the idea that post-war capitalism was very different from that which Marx had analysed came as a refreshing breath of unorthodoxy.

The wage–labour nexus: Fordist production methods and life styles

The twentieth century, especially its post-war Fordist phase, was the main area of interest for Nordic research in political economy. It was generally assumed that competitive *régulation* predominated during the nineteenth century. There were, however, few efforts to investigate this topic using data and methods from economic history. The exception is a study of wage formation in Norway (Kiel and Mjøset, 1990) although the data for the competitive period are of poor quality. Mechanisms demonstrated in France (Boyer, 1979a) could be only partially identified. This research indicated the influence of factors that had not been emphasised by the *régulation* school, at least not in its early work. For example, the stratification between a skilled male labour aristocracy and female workers, or the paternalistic attitude of employers who might bid wages up to keep skilled workers with the firm. Another conclusion was that economic dualism should be brought more explicitly into the *régulation* models of wage formation under liberal capitalism (as in a study of Germany, Lutz, 1984).

In the Nordic region the transformation of the wage–labour nexus also occurred under the influence of social democratic parties and strong trade union confederations from the late nineteenth century to the present. The first sector-based collective bargaining agreements (in the engineering industry) were signed in Denmark in 1900, in Sweden in 1905, in Norway in 1907, in 1940 in Finland and in 1942 in Iceland. The first laws governing collective bargaining agreements date back to 1910 in Denmark, 1915 in Norway, 1928 in Sweden, 1924 in Finland and 1938 in Iceland (Korpi, 1981). In the late 1930s the various collective bargaining agreements were co-ordinated as 'national bargaining agreements'.

In this respect the Nordic institutional frameworks were well prepared to assimilate the spread of Fordist production and consumption norms from the Marshall Plan (1948) onwards. Such assimilation was unconnected with the foreign policy preferences of each country. Denmark, Iceland and Norway were members of NATO, Sweden was neutral and Finland had a treaty of friendship and co-operation with the Soviet Union. However, none of these countries acquired the complete set of Fordist industries, even though American methods of work organisation (Taylorism, time and motion studies, etc.) spread throughout their manufacturing industries. The Fordist assembly line was introduced to sectors where it seemed most appropriate (mainly the Swedish automobile industry, Danish abattoirs, etc.). As the most diversified Nordic economy, Sweden played a role like that of the United States for the Nordic area, having the largest market and employing a surplus Finish labour force. It was also the pioneer in social innovations such as the universalist welfare state.

While the Fordist production norms were only partly assimilated, Nordic society imitated Fordist consumption norms completely. 'The American way of life' played an important role, both in terms of economic demand and as a point of ideological identification, even though the Nordic political context was very different from that of the United States.

Different types of organised capitalism

In terms of forms of competition, there are no empirical studies of competitive pricing during the period of liberal capitalism in the Nordic area. It is, however, clear that a hypothesis of oligopolistic pricing in the post-war Fordist period cannot be accepted without reservation (cf. Chapter 13). Crucial in post-war Nordic economic planning are macroeconomic 'inflation models' in which the main exporting firms are assumed to be price takers in international markets. International inflation and the pace of productivity determine wages in this sector. The wages are later generalised to all sectors. In sheltered sectors, it is assumed, employers determine a mark-up price that leaves the wage–profit distribution constant.

So far as *régulation* of the monetary system is concerned, in the late nineteenth century a monetary union existed between Denmark, Norway and Sweden, while the inter-war period saw liberal deflationary policies at their worst, particularly in Norway and Denmark. In the post-war period all the Nordic countries (with the partial exception of Denmark) developed various versions of a state-interventionist, credit-based financial system relatively closed to international influences by means of capital controls.

Interest rates were managed and kept low, and consequently credit was rationed. Under this system the influence of banks and the stock exchange was marginal.

All in all, the results available are too sparse to suggest a stylised version of competitive capitalism. For the post-war period, however, the ideal type of monopolist or 'administered' *régulation* – or simply organised capitalism – is also useful in studying Nordic countries.

An original insertion into the international division of labour

The two dimensions added to *régulation* theory by Boyer (1986a) – insertion into the international division of labour, as well as the state – were crucial in that they brought out a number of specific features of Nordic trajectories.

The insertion of the small Nordic economies into the international division of labour is based on a few dominant export sectors. Given this one-sided integration into the world economy, the concept of an accumulation regime is difficult to apply, in so far as the circuit of economic reproduction extended beyond each of the small economies. To analyse the Nordic area, the staple goods theory of economic development, initiated by Harold Innis (1967) and developed by Albert Hirschman (1977) was a better starting point. This focus has later been refined through the inspiration of neo-Schumpeterian studies of national innovation systems (Lundvall, 1992).

The development of the Nordic economies was not based on a fully fledged Fordist production system. Their economic structures evolved as various manufacturing branches interacted with the transformations of the dominant export sectors, which were originally linked with staple exports (Mjøset, 2000a). *Finland,* for example, was initially an exporter of timber, adjusting towards paper/pulp, and emerging finally, from the late 1960s, as an exporter of turnkey paper-making factories. *Iceland's* exports were essentially based on fishing but after the 1980s there was an addition of specific items based on microelectronics. Icelandic engineers developed a 'niche' in installations and sophisticated computer programmes for fishing vessels. Historically the *Norwegian* economy was based on fishing, wood, naval construction, semi-finished products based on furnace processes requiring cheap energy (supplied by hydro-electric plants) and, since the 1970s, on oil. *Denmark* is characterised by its food industry complexes, and *Swedish* development is a combination of industries involved in forestry, metallurgy and the production of Fordist consumption goods (Edquist and Lundvall, 1993).

As for the state, there is a long research tradition dealing with social mobilisation, the structuring of civil society and state formation. Much of this has been synthesised by the German social scientists Ulrich Menzel and Dieter Senghaas (1986) in their studies of modern European development and its relevance to development in contemporary Third World countries. A survey of this approach (Mjøset, 1992b) suggested both that elements of the *régulation* approach may serve to improve this framework, and that *régulation* studies have something to learn from the broader taxonomy of institutions provided by Senghaas and Menzel. The taxonomy was also used in a historical comparative study of Ireland and several small Alpine and Nordic countries (Mjøset, 1992a).

Economic policy models: diversity followed by fragmentation

As for economic policies, decision makers became used to a number of standard routines during the Golden Age (Mjøset, 1987). These defined the Golden Age economic policy models. In Norway, Sweden and partly in Denmark these models were variations on Keynesianism, while Finland and Iceland used non-Keynesian pro-cyclical models involving devaluation cycles (Pekkarinen, 1989). No homogeneous Nordic economic policy model could be traced.

In the early 1970s, owing to greater domestic and foreign pressure, these rules and norms of economic policy produced unexpected results (Mjøset, 1987, 1993). Consider Norway and Sweden as examples. Both in the mid-1970s and in the mid-1980s, overshooting of several economic policy targets produced very expansive booms. Throughout the period of fiscal and incomes policy austerity (the late 1970s) following the first boom, full employment was defended by soft monetary policies, involving devaluations and political-institutional resistance to an increase in interest rates. The inflationary effects of these policies undermined the regulatory systems that had worked well in the Golden Age. Deregulation followed, most notably of the housing market and of the domestic financial systems. There were also major changes in incomes policies, particularly in Sweden.

In this setting, the mid-1980s boom followed. In Norway the boom ended abruptly in 1986–8, an effect of declining oil prices and the dollar exchange rate, the two major variables influencing Norwegian business cycles since the early 1970s (Mjøset *et. al.*, 1994). In Sweden the boom continued, in line with international cycles. As the downturn came in the early 1990s, both countries tried to make the European Monetary System an anchor of price stability by pegging to the ECU, also anticipating entry into the European Union. (For other aspects of relations with the EU, see Kosonen, 1992; Mjøset, 1992c.) This commitment was bolstered by the removal of all capital controls.

Full employment was thereby downgraded from first to second priority. Unemployment rates, which never exceeded 3 per cent during the period 1973–88, shot up towards the much higher European average, where Denmark had been for a long time. The hard currency policy, however, depended on the success of EU monetary integration. But the European Union experienced setbacks during the monetary crises of 1992 and 1993.

These transformations destroyed much of the old regulatory framework. In most countries there was no new stable economic policy model. Through the 1990s, however, it seems that new models stabilised in Denmark and Norway.

Nordic 'welfare states': active employment policies and expansion of the social services

The Western European welfare states set up during the 'Golden Age' reflected the spread of Fordism in the area (Esping-Andersen, 1990, 1999). The welfare states took account of social needs and insured against risks for a labour force that was essentially industrial and male, with a single family wage, a lifetime income, very little mobility and a guaranteed suitable social wage. The welfare state contributed at the beginning (education) and end (pensions) of individuals' lives.

The weakening of the Fordist growth model implied profound and enduring transformations in the labour market. Two particularly important changes were the fall in the share of the industrial labour force among the active population and the growth in both private and public administrative activities and the service sector, which were by nature more diverse.

The Nordic welfare states can be analysed in comparison with other Western European countries, particularly in their different responses to changes in the structure of the labour market. In continental Europe the Catholic tradition restricted the role of the welfare state to social reproduction that was traditionally linked with the family; it cared for children, the aged and the sick. It also led to the creation of differences in professional status. In contrast, the Nordic welfare states were universalist and explicitly redistributive (Esping-Anderssen, 1990, 1999).

The continental European welfare states tried to maintain full employment by reducing activity rates, particularly through early retirement. Given the logic of a family wage (high payroll taxes and labour costs) and the Catholic emphasis on the housewife staying at home, an extensive increase in private and public social services was out of the question. The result was jobless growth, and the reproduction of the Fordist welfare state, but with an increasing group of 'outsiders'.

In contrast, *the Nordic* countries could resort to active manpower policies and growth in social services. The latter was a major source of job creation, given that high fixed labour costs and egalitarian wage policies limited the growth of personal consumer services. Nordic systems of social security insurance were thus made to cover more needs during individuals' lives, for instance child care.

Many social services required female skills. Since they were secure, well paid and flexible in terms of working hours, women found these state jobs attractive. The expansion of social and family services also contributed to greater gender equality. In this way the Nordic welfare states not only maintained full employment, but also generated a large growth in female employment in the 1980s, creating the double income/dual career family.

Three future scenarios

While the issue for continental Western European countries is conservation of the Fordist welfare state, the dilemma for Nordic countries is the high cost of the wages of state employees. The wage claims of these employees follow industrial rates of pay, despite the fact that their jobs are marked by low (or rather, unmeasurable) productivity growth. Temporarily extra tax revenues can counteract the squeeze on the state finances, in so far as high tax rates can be borne by dual-income families.

But in the long term a conflict could arise between the welfare state and the egalitarian norms dominatant in the Nordic countries. Either the state will force wages down in the many low-skilled social security jobs or it will have to privatise such services, thereby creating a private sector with low wages (the British solution). If this diagnosis is correct, the Nordic trajectory of leaving Fordism threatens to destroy the three main rights from this period: full employment, a universalist welfare state and egalitarianism. This is the *liberal* scenario.

Other less pessimistic scenarios have also been suggested (Andersson and Mjøset, 1987; Andersson, 1994). Following Karl Polanyi (1946) the above-mentioned transformations may be seen as calling for popular movements defending non-market aspects of land, labour and money. Many would like to see the European Union organise a response – this is the *federalist* vision – but so far the European Union has not replaced the national welfare states (Mjøset, 2000b)

Andersson (1994) argues that there is no way the Nordic countries can revitalise their classical 'Golden Age' models, given the present pressures of internationalisation. He thus launches a more radical vision, suggesting a 'red–green' mode of development, involving (1) reliance on the micro-electronic revolution to establish a less materials and energy-intensive economy, (2) the re-establishment of economic borders for capital and goods (e.g. taxing capital movements), and (3) a restructuring of the welfare states and labour markets through a citizens' income system (see also Andersson, 1996). This is the *radical* vision, which, however, for the time being seems to lack the support of any broad social movement.

34 Japan

Demythologising *régulation*

Yasuo Inoué and Toshio Yamada

Régulation theory was introduced to Japan in the second half of the 1980s, later than in other countries. It is therefore a recent arrival, which, right from the start, caused many academic controversies. These produced a strand of analysis of Japanese capitalism based on the regulationist approach. It began with a reconsideration of the interpretation of accelerated growth (1955–73). The question was whether the concept of Fordism is applicable to post-war Japanese growth. In attempting to answer this question from an econometric and institutional point of view, Japanese regulationists seek a closer understanding of their changing economy. This chapter presents the current state of research on Japan (*Mondes en développement*, 1992; *Japon in extenso*, 1994; Nadel, 1994b; Boyer and Yamada, 2000), and focuses on the problematic, assumptions and themes that require further development. This is followed by a presentation of the trajectory of the Japanese economy throughout the post-war period.

Was modern Japanese capitalism Fordist?

In regulationist analyses of the post-war Japanese economy the most controversial issue is whether the accelerated growth period can be described in terms of Fordism. Here we shall be discussing essential aspects of the debate, whose synthesis is offered elsewhere (Miyamachi and Peck, 1993).

According to statistical data, the Japanese economy of this period experienced parallel growth in the capital goods and consumption goods sectors, a virtuous cycle in mass production and mass consumption, as well as conforming to the Kaldor law that links growth with productivity. This is the Fordist aspect. However, investment was pulled by profit rather than demand and wages were influenced by economic cycles that remained large. Furthermore, the growth rate of real wages was slower than productivity growth. Wage formation was not indexed to productivity. This suggests that the Japanese accumulation regime during this period was both Fordist and non-Fordist.

In terms of the wage–labour nexus, it is commonly recognised that typical Taylorism–Fordism was not established in Japan. Certain elements of production organisation that conformed to Taylorian and Fordist methods were introduced, but without the use of 'separation of conception and execution', which is the essence of Taylorism. In other words, the Fordist compromise of accepting Taylorism and bargaining for an indexed wage did not occur in Japan and the mode of *régulation* was not typically Fordist.

If such is the case, then was the mode of development of Japanese growth truly Fordist? There are different interpretations of the core of Fordism. Itoh (1992) points to the presence of a Fordist accumulation regime by emphasising various facts, while Uni (1991) views the Japanese economy (1962–73) as 'Fordism without the Fordist wage compromise'. What then is 'a wage compromise that is not Fordist'? It is the non-separation of conception and execution, on which the famous 'multi-functionality' of Japanese manufacturing workers is based. From the end of the Second World War, a wage compromise very different from the one in the United States was established. Trade unions were unwilling to give up the opportunity to intervene in work organisation problems, and employers accepted workers' claims, since they viewed worker participation as an asset to management. While it was rejected on some occasions, this non-Fordist compromise during the tense power relations of the 1950s was definitively re-established in the early 1960s. Furthermore, the accumulation regime involved highly developed mechanisation in the consumption goods sector (the Bertrand 1998 model) and the Fordist consumption norm was formed owing to progressive growth in the real wage.

Other analyses question these 'Fordist theses'. According to Tohyama (1990), accelerated growth was directed by a sharing of productivity gains in favour of capital and thus by investment pulled by profits. Furthermore, at this time, there was still a large agricultural sector, as well as traditional professional relations.

Despite the apparent opposition of these points of view, there is no fundamental difference in the interpretation of the facts by the authors. They differ in terms of which facts they focus on, and on what is the core of the concept of Fordism. At the current stage of research 'stylised facts' must be created and the very concept of Fordism must be reconsidered on the basis of the experience of the Japanese economy (Hirata, 1993).

Developing the concept of Fordism

Various authors have contributed to this conceptual renewal. While pointing out the lack of simultaneous growth in productivity and the real wage, Hirano (1993) emphasises what he views as a medium term wage compromise, which is based on the following implicit agreement. From the point of view of wage earners, jobs are stabilised within a domestic labour market. Wages evolve in a pro-cyclical manner. However, since the wage share develops in a contra-cyclical manner following the principle

Table 34.1 A chronology of institutional forms and *régulation* research

Japanese-style Fordism, 1955–73	Changes 1974–84	Transformation from 1985
1 Flexibility in the division of labour in the workshop. Less separation between conception and execution	Consolidation of the production system with earlier factors and wage earner involvement	Continuity of the production system but also partial reconsideration due to stagnation in the market
• More differentiated mass production than in the United States	• Deepening of differentiated mass production	• Increased need for industrial competitiveness through quality and innovation
2 Priority of the domestic market (stable formation of domestic demand in the medium term)	Growth directed by exports (stagnation, lowering of the wage share)	Return to a bipolar domestic market
• Lower wage growth than productivity growth	• Stabilisation of the explosion, then of wage rises	• Weakening of 'Shunto'
3 Wage compromise achieved through collective bargaining ('Shunto')	Stagnation of wage rise to the benefit of investment and job security during the cycle	Wage compromise shaken by the destabilisation of employment, caused by the violent bursting of the bubble
4 Financial system closely linked with industrial development	Beginning of financial liberalisation	Financing of the economy and 'wealth effect'. Bubble boom (1987–90) triggered by demand for property and lax financial policy
• Real exchange rate initially undervalued, then overvalued over time	• Re-evaluation of the yen (*endaka*), favouring a reduction in the cost of raw materials	• Re-evaluation of the Yen, reinforcing delocalisation. Search for productivity and restructuring
5 Stabilisation of the international framework favouring domestic economic development	International destabilisation through the floating exchange system	Restructuring of the branch circuit especially in South East Asia
6 Decentralised companyist *régulation* mediated by hierarchical structural forms	Extension and implicit reinforcement of compromises; *régulation* interiorised by each individual economic actor	Deep crisis rather than recession, leading to a search for a new form of *régulation*

of a share economy, the consumption demand of households remains stable and large enough to develop a domestic market in durable consumption goods. Meanwhile, companies establish a medium term, rather than short term, profit maximisation strategy. This strategy guarantees a very high level of investment in the medium term. This compromise is dependent on the institutional intermediation provided by Shunto, a form of collective bargaining to determine annual wage growth. One of the specific features of Japanese *régulation* comes from the fact that wage levels are determined in a flexible manner, taking the annual economic cycle into account and therefore diffusing among sectors and firms in a decentralised manner. This decentralised *régulation* was extremely effective in so far as the size of the cake to be shared in the national economy grew almost consistently during the period of accelerated growth.

The move from micro-*régulation* to macro-*régulation* was also ensured by the system described by Uemura and Ebizuka as a 'hierarchical market–firm nexus'. No doubt inspired by Coriat's (1991) thesis (efficiency through Ohnism and social injustice marked by ostracising exclusion), as well as by Lipietz (1993c) (the aristocracy of large company trade unions and the social exclusion of women) and Boyer (1992c) (meso-corporatism), Uemura and Ebizuka (1994) emphasise the structural compatibility of firms, the labour market and inter-firm relations. This compatibility is illustrated by the downward mobility of wage earners towards small and medium-size firms (less than a thousand employees). In other words, the medium term wage compromise outlined above only functions with a penalty (quite large unemployment costs in the segmentation of the labour market) and a stabilising system (subcontracting and casual workers).

After this brief examination of the main results of research into the application of the concept of Fordism to Japan, what lesson is to be learnt? A common view is that diversity in the wage compromise reflects the nature of the prevailing accumulation regime and mode of *régulation*. In this context, parallel development of productivity and the real wage does not seem to be the sole reference point for Fordism. This brings us to the claim that the concept of Fordism could be refigured on the basis of a variety of examples of economic growth, starting with Japan and the newly industrialising countries in Asia (Yagi, 1992).

After the first oil shock: changes and transformations in the Japanese model

The Japanese economy was severely affected by the oil shock of 1973. The shock led to a fall in the growth rate, rising inflation and a drop in the profit rate. Japan therefore suffered from stagflation, like other Western countries in the second half of the 1970s. However, because it was increasingly oriented towards export-led growth, Japan became an 'economic power'. During the 1970s and 1980s it has attracted the attention of foreign countries by its impressive performance. Leaving aside the issue of assessing this performance, Japan continues to provoke reflections and research into its economic mechanisms.

In this context, since 1989 an international debate on whether 'Japanese management is post-Fordist' has developed. It was instigated by Kenney and Florida (1988), who showed that Japan is one of the front runners in the race towards post-Fordism, thanks to its new methods of obtaining productivity gains. In contrast, Kato and Stevens (1993) claim that Japan is still in a pre-Fordist stage, or ultra-Fordism, given remaining pre-modern factors. This debate interested many Japanese and foreign researchers and also involved the regulationist problematic. While the debate is not yet over, it has had the advantage of clearing up many misunderstandings about the concept of *régulation*.

Stimulated by this situation, Japanese regulationists began to study the national trajectory of contemporary Japan. With respect to the wage–labour nexus, research has developed studying the specific nature of wage formation in Japan. Hirano (1993) suggests a thesis of the 'seniority wage combined with personal merit evaluation'. According to him, Japanese society cannot be reduced to groups. Merit-based individualism reinforces both equality and competition between wage earners. More detailed analyses can also be mentioned in this field, such as a comparison of pay slips at Peugeot and Nissan (Hanada, 1994), and a detailed analysis of Toyota's wage system (Shimizu, 1994). In terms of sectors, since 1975 meso-corporatism at the inter-sector level has caused a decrease in the role of the diffusion of wages between sectors through Shunto (Tsuru, 1992).

This research all points to the fact that the accumulation regime of the period prior to 1973 experienced a qualitative change. The industrial goods market was increasingly directed abroad. In order to control product unit costs, employers imposed a stagnation or lowering of growth on the wage share in the second half of the 1970s. In return, workers were guaranteed stable employment, if only in large companies. However, this compromise reached its limit after the boom period in the second half of the 1980s. The famous Japanese development model then came under serious reconsideration. Research based on the regulationist approach offered a variety of diagnoses.

For the mode of *régulation*, a hypothesis of *régulation* based on firms, that is to say, a companyist *régulation*, was suggested (Coriat, 1991; Yamada, 1992). Isogai (1994) presents an institutional analysis of Japanese firms. He argues that the Japanese economy is characterised by *régulation* that is neither competitive nor monopolistic. Rather, it is centred on large companies. This is ensured by internal and external flexibility, which avoids the institutional rigidity of monopolistic *régulation*. Japanese companies do integrate economic and social aspects (Wakamori, 1991). This is the price of the effectiveness of decentralised *régulation* (Hirano, 1993).

Furthermore, Japan is increasingly encountering problems whose solutions are difficult to find at the level of individual companies – for instance, health, education and the environment.

It is therefore time to construct a general schema for the companyist *régulation* with the set of features found in this mode of organisation. This seems to be necessary if a long term alternative for Japan is to be suggested. Is not utopia the direction needed by our times (Saito, 1991)?

What is the trajectory of the future?

To conclude, three main questions appear to be key in identifying the national trajectory and envisaging a future: productive and financial globalisation and ecology.

1   Companies, and hence also the Japanese economy, are becoming increasingly globalised. This is mainly an effect of transplants to Western countries, where there is varying resistance to traditions of local worker movements. Is Japanese management transferable to Western societies? It has already been stressed that the question of transferability is the background to the international debate on post-Fordism in Japan.

An interesting configuration emerges when the model of Japanese management is introduced in collective bargaining with trade unions. It seems that in some cases (Boyer, 1992c) traditional collective bargaining has been forced to change, just as Japanese management as such was not directly transferred (Boyer *et al.*, 1998). So long as these are the elements of new management, providing alternatives to Taylorism or to classic Fordism, then they are accepted in transplants. On the other hand, the incentive principle that causes a marked differentiation of wages is not always accepted by trade unions.

2   It is impossible to think about the future of the Japanese economy without analysing the financing system. It is agreed that a lax financial policy coinciding with the high demand for real estate created a speculative explosion in the late 1980s. An excess of capital therefore flooded on to the property market and stock exchange. So long as land and share prices continued to rise, the problem of joining the esoteric to the exoteric did not arise, to use Alain Lipietz's (1979) expression. However, the price fall was all the more violent owing to the sudden rise. As a consequence there was an accumulation of bad loans. According to estimates, they amounted to between 30 per cent and 50 per cent of total mortgage loan liabilities. Even if this did not lead to an open financial crisis, banks and manufacturing businesses had to undertake a massive stabilising programme.

Owing to a domestic recession, the Japanese currency is increasingly oriented towards a redefinition (Aglietta, 1992a). On a worldwide scale this seems to imply the weakening of Japan as a financial inter-mediary.

3   Finally, the globalisation of the Japanese economy is inseparable from the growth of newly industrialising countries in East Asia. This is the famous pole of world economic development. But in the early twenty-first century is this pole of development also an ecological threat (Inoué, 1994)? As we know, the paradigm of Fordist development involves radical changes in production and consumption norms, but the environmental norm is not taken into account. The cost to the envi-ronment has hardly been included in the process of industrialisation, which aims to catch up with the highly developed countries. Owing to its extremely high growth rate in the late 1960s, Japan was con-fronted with the problem of damage from industrial pollution. Although contention over the responsibility and indemnities of polluting indus-tries has not yet been settled, the ecological problem has altered in the meantime. Instead of the industrial pollution of yesterday, it is now a matter of general pollution as a consequence of individual daily consumption. The East Asian countries have been indeed the devel-opment pole of the early 1990s, but the region may also have aggravated pollution through its accelerated industrialisation. To avoid the risk, a principle of international *régulation* must be established in the Asian region to define and implement an international norm governing the living conditions of nations as well as individuals, thus avoiding the facile solutions proposed by so-called free trade (Chapter 29).

In short, the experience of the Japanese economy as well as that of neighbouring countries leaves many questions open, to which the *régula-tion* approach has yet to give appropriate answers – fortunately! For it is only by engaging fully with the complexities of reality that the regula-tionist approach, born in the West, will be enriched by its adopted lands.

35 Institutions, *régulation* and crisis in socialist economies

Bernard Chavance

In the 1980s *régulation* theory contributed to the formulation of new questions and a reinterpretation of the classic problems of socialist economies. In France this produced a vast body of literature, reviewed below (see also Chavance, 1990, 1995).

What wage–labour nexus?

Initially, methodological differences over what constitutes a socialist system, inherited from issues discussed in the 1970s, divided those who believed in the radical distinctiveness of socialist systems and those who supported a thesis of state-led capitalism. The first group claimed that the concept of wage labour did not apply to the Soviet Union, owing to the lack of 'free' buying or selling of labour power and because of workers' 'absolute right' to employment (job security and a guaranteed wage). The work constraint was therefore seen as political rather than economic (Andreff, 1984). The other group advanced the opposite thesis, arguing for an original form of the freedom/constraint duality of the wage labour system in general, so that paradoxically Soviet-style wage labour appeared closer to Marxian representation than contemporary Western wage labour. In this system the labour constraint is not only economic but also political (an obligation to work), while the employment guarantee is linked with a *régulation* form that causes shortages in the labour market (Chavance, 1984a). A minimal consensus between advocates of a 'particular type of wage labour' (non-capitalist), such as Wladimir Andreff and Marcel Drach, and those in favour of a 'particular form' of wage labour (capitalist) such as Bernard Chavance and Jacques Sapir later emerged. This explains the degree of similarity in the themes studied.

URGENSE (a collective directed by Wladimir Andreff) analysed 'arhythmic Taylorism in the context of a diminished wage–labour nexus', emphasising the obstacles to Fordism in centrally planned economies. These include lack of continuity and regularity in the work process (due to supply disturbances), impediments in the system to a move towards world technical production norms and an endogenous limit on social consumption norms (URGENSE, 1982). In several studies, Marcel Drach examined the 'non-occurrence of Fordism' in the east as being linked with 'precarious Taylorism' and a 'non-Fordist accumulation regime' (Drach, 1983, 1984).

The limits of central control over the 'labour market' in the Soviet Union, owing to high mobility and to workers' wage push, which was partly accepted by managers, has been emphasised (Chavance, 1983). The contrast between Taylorian and Fordist industrial time and the time of Soviet industry, which was more discontinuous and heterogeneous, explains differences in forms of labour alienation and methods of worker resistance, as well as the specific difficulty encountered in the establishment, rationalisation and stability of production norms. A survey of various aspects of the wage–labour nexus in the Soviet Union, including labour force shortages, mobility, work time, income formation and modes of consumption, work organisation, institutions and individual practices (clientism) was undertaken by Sapir (1984).

Between an intensive and an extensive accumulation regime

Wladmir Andreff (1978a) drew a distinction between extensive and intensive modes of accumulation, classic concepts in the literature. The 'progressive' mode that includes both is characterised by a constant stream of technological innovation enabling flexible adaptation by the production apparatus. According to this approach, the Soviet Union experienced an intensive (from 1928), rather than an extensive, accumulation crisis, owing to difficulties encountered in moving towards a 'progressive' regime.

A 'Marxist regulationist' interpretation was put forward by Lafont and Leborgne (1979) and Leborgne (1992). They describe Soviet accumulation as apparently intensive yet extensive in reality, and as relatively 'dual', since the organic composition of capital, productivity and employment tended to grow in sector I more than in sector II. Crises were caused by over-accumulation and manifested in an inverted form as shortage crises (Charles Bettelheim, 1982, 1983, formed this thesis with regard to the 1930s.) But the roots of crises are the same as in all capitalist countries: 'the tendency of the mode of production to accumulate, thus exceeding the limits that the fall in the profit rate sets for the valorisation of capital' (Lafont and Leborgne, 1979).

In the work cited above (Chavance, 1983) the Soviet 'development model' is described in terms of extensive growth and its exhaustion, the structural disequilibrium of accumulation (in favour of sector I), impediments to Fordism, militarisation and a mode of *régulation* through shortage. This analysis was extended in terms of expansion drive and braking mechanism, cumulative asymmetry in industry and a residual tendency in consumption growth (Chavance, 1989).

Drach (1988) developed a concept of 'outsize accumulation'. This refers to the 'excessive' aspects of an accumulation regime based on the maximum growth of physical quantities and the priority given to a group of 'fundamental goods'. It also suggests the lack of a measuring standard typical of bureaucratic order as opposed to the monetary order.

A systemic crisis

Referring to a distinction between *régulation* through shortage* and crisis proposed in 1983, Bernard Chavance (1984b) examined the question of why cyclical *régulation* and *régulation* through shortage became blocked in the late 1970s, giving way to a genuine crisis. In the 1970s the impact of openness to the West changed from a stimulus to growth to a hardening of the external constraint. 'It was through the combination of a worsening of internal systemic difficulties, choices in economic policy and the impact of the crisis in the West, that socialist economies are plunged into a crisis which aggravates inflationary tensions and tendencies to shortage.' Thus according to the distinction suggested by Boyer, the European socialist countries and the Soviet Union underwent a crisis of the mode of *régulation* (major crisis), rather than within the mode of *régulation* (minor crisis). Hence the dire need for economic reform.

For small Eastern European countries (the Soviet Union was a different case) Andreff and Graziani (1985) argued that it was necessary to identify the origin of external constraints (1965–77) and their activation (after 1978). They claimed that this activation led governments to adjustment policies and industrial restructuring that revealed the structural difficulties of the accumulation regime. Wladimir Andreff (1987) highlighted a degree of consensus among the various analyses, describing the 'crisis in the accumulation regime'. This was 'the connection between a *régulation* crisis, difficulties in technical change and the industrial adaptation of an economy that was increasingly open to the outside, and a crisis in the work process'. He concluded that there was a 'latent structural crisis' through the combination of the rigidity of productive structures in these economies and constraints caused by their participation in the world economy.

Specific aspects of the crisis phenomena of socialist economies were emphasised by Drach (1984, 1985). He suggested a Braudel-style interpretative model for the interaction of three 'crisis time frames' (1987). Short time refers to investment cycles, long time is linked with a secular decline in growth and efficiency, and stochastic time is that of political crises (1956, 1968, 1980). The varying configurations created by the intersection of these different time scales explain different aspects of crisis seen in the history of the socialist economies.

Jacques Sapir's (1986) thesis on the Soviet Union since the war suggests a cyclical model for the Soviet economy and points to a clean break in 1976 in the already declining macroeconomic development of the country, with a final period of near industrial stagnation. Against a background of complex interactions in long term developments, endogenous movements and exogenous shocks, he argues that in the late 1970s the Soviet Union experienced one of the harshest post-war cycles before entering a real crisis (Sapir, 1990), which was still ongoing in the late 1990s (Sapir, 1998). This crisis was a consequence of the attempt and failure in the second half of the 1960s to leave voluntarist *régulation* behind and move towards consensual management (Sapir, 1989)

Bureaucratic and/or money-based co-ordination?

A fairly clear division appeared on this topic between advocates of an approach based on a particular market system, who attributed some importance to monetary phenomena in socialist economies, and those in favour of a non-monetary definition of the economy, who emphasised quantitative, real phenomena.

In this debate Wladimir Andreff (1984) declared that the rouble was not a 'capitalist currency' since it did not act as a general equivalent because of the juxtaposition of two 'hermetic' monetary circuits. Cash money was exchanged only for consumption goods while non-cash money was exchanged only for production goods. Nor was it a 'private means of accumulation'. According to Bernard Chavance (1984a) there is a connection between the monetary form of exchange for consumption goods, labour power and the means of production. This explains why the two moneys are in fact one, the rouble, and that this connection is the blind spot of the 'political economy of socialism' (Chavance, 1980). Cash and non-cash money are not entirely hermetic; they do in fact transfer from one to the other. It is important not to confuse 'private' and 'individual' in terms of accumulation, since the theoretical problem is whether or not there is any accumulation in a monetary form or a value form of surplus. In short, this is a monetary system (market and wage based), but with entirely original institutional forms and *régulation*, which explain the relatively passive nature of money in the state sector.

Belief in a relevant monetary moment encouraged Jacques Sapir to emphasise the role of short term credit in cyclical mechanisms, studying the phenomenon of hidden inflation through fictive classifications of some production as 'new products' and analysing links between investment and financial movements in the Soviet Union (Sapir, 1986, 1989). Inversely, the symmetrical contrast between a 'bureaucratic economy' and a 'monetary economy' was at the centre of Drach's research (1988). Here the notion of an 'apparatus' plays a role in centrally planned economies analogous to that of money in market economies, the latter's role being interpreted in a similar fashion as Aglietta and Orléan (1986). This approach emphasises the interpenetration of '*régulation*' and 'deregulation' in socialist economies. Crisis is thus seen as a 'collapse of the sociability of the apparatus' or as a 'demonetisation of the apparatus' (Drach, 1987). An accumulation regime based on the maximisation of the production of physical quantities predominated. The objective function is expressed in terms of use value with a preference for goods that is symmetrical to a Keynesian preference for liquidity.

Régulation through shortage and asymmetrical cycles

Interpretations of dominant modes of *régulation* have been influenced by socialist cycle theories, and particularly by the analysis of investment cycles of Hungarian authors (J. Kornai, T. Bauer).

According to Bernard Chavance (1984b) *régulation* through shortage predominated in Eastern European countries from the 1950s to the late 1970s. It was founded on a 'chain of spillovers of shortages' based on investment impulses that have repercussions on the market for consumption goods, the labour market (or the holding back of labour performance) and possibly foreign trade. Successive variations in the intensity of different shortages is an original mode of *régulation* that characterises the growth and the normal operation of these economies, unlike genuine crises where shortages become generalised and the cycle does not include endogenous recovery. China is obviously a different case, even though there is a surprising cycle of industrial investment that is virtually analogous to the one found in Eastern European countries, and which has remained even after the reforms (Chavance, 1987).

In a study of the Soviet Union, viewed as a 'centrally managed' rather than a 'centrally planned' economy, Gérard Roland (1987a) stated that a theory of *régulation* through shortage provides a satisfactory explanation of fluctuations in investment growth, but not of relations between the investment and the consumption sector. This is because planners' control of the intensity of shortages in the consumption sector is fairly direct and effective. Roland considers that *régulation* through shortages has a stabilising effect on growth by absorbing fluctuations. More generally, centralised planning and chronic shortages influence each other. The 'balancing process' can be analysed through six '*régulation* forms': centralised (by the plan or through shortages, at both the macroeconomic and the sector level), by flexible Ministry actions, and finally decentralised (by a fall in quality or through parallel activities) (Roland, 1989). Drach (1988) attached greater significance to the role of information in *régulation* and fluctuations around 'norms', as well as studying investment cycles in East Germany.

Jacques Sapir (1986) suggested an original model for cyclical *régulation* in the Soviet Union between 1950 and 1970. There is a critical rate of investment growth beyond which production develops inversely with investment. The cycle is asymmetrical, with a slow rise and rapid fall. Through an analysis of conflicts between the various agents, the centre, managers and workers, Sapir broadens the Hungarian approach by including *régulation* school analyses and advancing a complex explanation of the investment–consumption–productivity–employment cycle. He thus emphasises the importance of workers-consumers' behaviour and the role of agriculture in industrial fluctuations, beyond the internal conflicts of the management and planning hierarchy in this sector.

According to one last thesis, the socialist economies experienced 'mixed, planned and market *régulation*' (Andreff, 1990, 1993) but here the term *régulation* is used simply in the sense of co-ordination.

An enduring institutional and systemic heritage

For Wladimir Andreff (1978b) the Soviet Union was 'in fact a monopoly with massive state intervention', in other words a 'state monopolism'. In more general terms, there was 'congruence' but no convergence between Western capitalist systems and Soviet-type systems. Indeed, similar processes produce different results, such as scientific research and development, production internationalisation, individual income expenditure and inflation, while different processes produce fairly similar results, such as industrial concentration, cheating, a parallel economy, wage forms and forced labour (Andreff, 1981).

Bernard Chavance (1985) argues that the original institutional foundation of traditional (unreformed) socialist economies is a combination of the single party system and state ownership with centralised planning. In the definition of capitalism in general as an economic rather than a social system, which is both market and wage-based, three principal forms can be identified: competitive, monopolistic and statist. Statist capitalism, found in Soviet-type systems, is neither successive nor progressive by comparison with the other two forms, it is simply different from them.

Jacques Sapir, on the other hand, qualifies the importance of state ownership. The 'guaranteed sale' in a shortage economy has a greater effect than ownership forms in what he describes as state capitalism. It is first and foremost a 'mobilised economy', analogous to wartime economies (1985, 1990). High 'degrees of economic mobilisation' are compatible with various forms of ownership. For example, the institutional conditions of the cycle lie in pseudo-validation, labour force shortages, quantity maximisation and the organisation of the tax and budgetary system, rather than state ownership (Sapir, 1985). This then is a 'non-commercial market system' (Sapir, 1989).

For Marcel Drach (1988) the fundamental institution of 'bureaucratic order' is the 'apparatus'. This concept is close to Weber's notion of bureaucracy, but is also influenced by the analyses of the Budapest school (especially G. Markus). In keeping with his thesis of the institutional symmetry of money and the apparatus, Drach compares financial intermediation with bureaucratic intermediation. Anton Brender (1977) suggested an analogous concept in a comparison of Japan and the Soviet Union.

Gérard Roland (1989) argues that the 'Soviet mode of production' involves a fundamental contradiction between use value and index value, that is, the quantitative index of the plan. The end purpose of maximising index values causes a reproduction of the full global employment of resources, chronic shortages, waste, the centralisation of power, the exogenous nature of technical innovation and extensive growth. Roland thus implicitly makes central planning the essential institutional characteristic of the system.

The many different approaches inspired by *régulation* theory are a real contribution to the analysis of socialist systems for themes such as the wage–labour nexus, the mode of development and crisis. The research has emphasised the rise in economic and social tensions in the decade that preceded the violent destruction of the socialist systems. This is a step forward for the study of the complex and historically uncharted process of post-socialist transformation, in which the systemic and institutional inheritance plays a far from insignificant role.

36 Crisis and transition in the Soviet Union and Russia

Jacques Sapir

The interpretation of the crisis and collapse of the Soviet system is one of the greatest challenges for economic analysis, provoking a debate over the nature of the transition, its aims and what is at stake.

The crisis and an understanding of the Soviet economic system

Two alternative interpretations were put forward to explain the crisis in the Soviet Union. For some it was the result of the fundamental inefficiency of centralised planning, especially its inability to establish a growth regime based on an intensive rather than an extensive use of resources. Others saw the crisis as the result of more cyclical factors, varying from the pressure of Western countries (through the arms race or the restriction on importing advanced technologies) to a perversion of reforms undertaken since 1965, or even a result of *perestroika*. There is therefore a conflict between one discourse in which the crisis is inevitable and another where it is accidental. This divergence of opinion is based largely on an uncritical use of statistical and documentary sources. It also reflects certain biases, for instance a refusal to recognise the crisis, still ongoing at the turn of the millennium.

A more systematic analysis of available data, particularly the elements that enable the construction of a deflator of the Soviet growth rate in the 1960s and 1970s, produces a very different view of the trajectory of the Soviet economy since 1945. First it shows the relative stability of growth until the mid-1970s, even if it is at a lower level than official statistics. Only in the mid-1970s was there a real collapse in growth leading to economic stagnation from 1978–9. It also reveals the existence of regular cyclical fluctuations affecting not only production but also investment, productivity, consumption and even the employment distribution between sectors.

It therefore turns out that, like market economies, the form of the historical movement of growth in the Soviet Union was cyclical. But the cycle, or rather one specific cycle, broke the mechanism and set the economy on a new trajectory.

Two major phenomena: cycles and shortages

This immediately suggests several areas of investigation. The first concerns the nature of cyclical fluctuations. These were partially described in the late 1950s by Alexandre Gerschenkron. Their frequency does not correspond to political changes in the Soviet Union, thus dismissing a purely political explanation. The cyclical fluctuations apparently combine endogenous economic dynamics with the effects of modes of decision making and action under the Soviet system. The key role of bargaining illustrates the importance of understanding the rules and conventions governing the traditional Soviet system. These rules and conventions also relate to institutions (some of which are political, such as hierarchical modes in and outside companies) and to inherited practices structuring society and economic practices, such as guaranteed sales, a centralised financial system and rationing through quantity and prices.

The cyclical mechanism matches labour market phenomena. For example, it matches the role of relative revenue between sectors in distributing recruitment. This explains the uneven transfer of the labour force from the agricultural sector to the manufacturing sector, as well as fluctuations in the distribution of recruitment within the manufacturing sector among its branches. Nevertheless, it assumes incomplete market mechanisms, particularly regarding the role of prices in resource allocation. Shortages in the consumption goods market produced temporary, followed by permanent, effects as a production disincentive. As a result, company directors and employees used local bypassing strategies. In this sense, the work organisation system was incomplete and undermined by a structural crisis because of inability to secure and stabilise forms of incentive that were in keeping with these institutions and their effects, despite many attempts.

This observation prompts a second investigation of the interpretation of shortage. It is easy to view shortages simply as repressed inflation. However, this explanation ignores the entire dimension of inter-company exchanges, where it is manifested principally as uncertainty affecting upstream of the production unit, which compensates for the lack of uncertainty downstream due to the sale validation of the product in a market economy.

A reformulation of the question of shortage in the terms of information theory, with varying levels of uncertainty and the emergence of rumours in a system that is regularly destabilised, is an alternative to reducing shortage to being seen as a consequence of the quantitative theory of money. It allows an understanding of the strategic behaviour of agents in response to this uncertainty. It also leads to internalisation practices at the level of companies, ministries and networks in different forms of stocking and in an emerging technological culture. These aspects lead to the reproduction of excess demand and to rendering monetary creation endogenous.

It is therefore necessary to consider how the reproduction of fluctuations, which gave the system a dynamic, eventually caused it to break. This third area of investigation can be approached in two ways.

The origins of a break in the mode of *régulation*

An empirical study of available data shows a weakening of some endogenous mechanisms during the 1960s, with greater difficulty for the manufacturing sector in attracting new workers, and increasingly harsh effects on productivity through phases of intensification in shortages on the consumption goods market. Gradually the fluctuations began to arise not in the peripheral branches of the accumulation schema of the Soviet model, but in central ones such as mechanical construction. Historically this coincided with the exhaustion of labour force resources and the beginning of a drastic labour shortage in the Soviet economy, partly for demographic reasons. Furthermore, the process of modernising the productive apparatus, which began in 1965, heightened the vulnerability of companies to the effects of shortages.

A second complementary approach views the gradual disintegration of explicit and implicit modes of co-ordination as the effect of an important social change. In the 1960s and 1970s Soviet society stopped evolving through violent changes and started to replicate itself identically. The exhaustion of integrating mechanisms of upward social movement implied an increase in wealth concentration, which was an added pressure on the economy. They also created an obstacle to the rise of the technical authority required by modernisation. Planning mechanisms, whose regulating role was far from negligible, became increasingly inefficient as the share of implicit information in total necessary information rose. Both the mechanisms of internalisation and network creation, and the development of bargaining practices, reduced the role of explicit signals, relative prices and central orders. This situation was probably aggravated by the increasing complexity of production after the early 1960s.

It is therefore possible to interpret the late 1970s crisis as a true *régulation* crisis. It reflected an increasing disconnection between microeconomic behaviour and institutions, rules and conventions. This disconnection was a result of the relative success of the system, in other words, its ability to transform a rural country into an industrial power. It was aggravated by errors in economic policy and particularly by Brezhnev's refusal to react to early signs of crisis. His administration deliberately gave priority to the perpetuation of the social and political forms on which his legitimacy was based. By so doing, it provoked a latent political crisis which, given the constraints of the Soviet political and social system, resulted in increased evasive attitudes (exit, in Hirschman's 1970 terms). They took the form either of engagement in parallel activities or simply discouragement and withdrawal into the private realm.

As in all *régulation* crises, it is reductive to consider only its economic aspect. The Soviet crisis of the 1970s was also a political, social and moral crisis. Insight into the nature of the transition comes mainly from an analysis of the system and its crisis. It is hardly surprising that those who viewed shortages merely as repressed inflation and thought that planning was limited to a distortion of relative prices made suggestions that were ultimately very similar to the stabilisation policies applied in the Third World.

Transition policies: a combination of perverted effects

The sequence of liberalisation, opening, stabilisation and structural adjustment derives from a simplistic view of the Soviet system. The emphasis on relative prices simply ignores other channels for the transmission of information, especially the fact that they were frequently implicit. This was responsible for an inability to understand the effects of harsh price liberalisation policies associated with the opening of economies almost overnight. The depressive effects of these measures are underestimated. What is more, the emergence of perverse restructuring policies, in other words raw materials and semi-finished products specialisation, was the opposite of predictions and forecasts.

In a similar fashion, focus on state ownership as the principal characteristic of Soviet-type economies produces a naïve approach towards privatisation processes. The emphasis is then on the fastest modes of privatisation possible, in the hope that it will provoke microeconomic restructuring. The real situation soon demonstrated how misconceived this notion is. The coupon privatisation system that was widely used did not lead to any restructuring. It merely perpetuated a situation in which property rights were fuzzy and weakly enforced in both the private and the public sector.

This created a situation where commercial mechanisms were freed, sometimes even more than in Western market economies, although there were no institutions to ensure market discipline. One of the first problems that arose immediately was a loss of payment discipline through outstanding payments between companies and increasingly fragile fiscal systems. This made it extremely difficult to implement traditional macroeconomic policies and ran the risk of rebounding in the form of a massive banking crisis, threatening the stability of the system.

A second problem was an extensive production of 'rumours' and rising transaction costs. These caused a structural blockage of investment and a harnessing of savings by speculative activities. This situation also blocked the emergence of small private companies in the productive sector. The deformations of the manufacturing sector self-replicated, and networking and internalisation behaviour did not disappear. A situation of structural rigidity in the productive apparatus then arose in a context of massive supply and demand shocks. This only aggravated the depression, while also creating the conditions for high inflation. This was reflected in a high residual level of inflation once the shock of price freeing had been absorbed and despite recurrent applications of stabilisation policies.

A third problem arose from the first two combined. The maintenance of a heavily unbalanced situation in which monetary instruments (interest rates) were fairly ineffective, and where there was limited flexibility in the productive sector, did not allow governments engaged in IMF-type stabilisation policies any alternatives to budgetary policy. The reduction of public spending soon became an obsessive objective with destructive effects. The collapse of public investment set back a take-off in private investment. But, above all, there was a dire lack of public action, which seriously added to the disorder of the institutional system. Conditions of legality became unclear and corruption developed. The harsh reduction in transfers caused a serious social crisis in addition to an interregional crisis that threatened to destroy the unity of the country.

Priorities in a different policy

The policies outlined above precluded a stable and balanced growth trajectory. Serious economic and social disorder led to the overthrow of politicians who had initiated the transition, to the advantage of powers from the old system and nationalist bids.

The analysis of the mechanisms of the Soviet economy that has been presented gives an indication of how the transition should have been managed.

1   The reconstruction of a robust and flexible payment system, which does not confuse solvency and liquidity constraints, and which creates the necessary conditions for good payment discipline is a top priority.
2   The development of an equally sound banking system is another. This is not only because of the role of this sector in the system of payments, but also on account of its role in supervising companies. In an economy where financial markets are forced to remain limited and uncertain for several years, relations between bankers and entrepreneurs, and between bankers and the central bank, are crucial elements in market discipline.
3   The reconstruction of a budgetary and fiscal system is an obvious third priority. It is pointless to hope to control the budget deficit when the fiscal system is in ruins. It is just as illusory to hope to undertake microeconomic restructuring so long as the tasks of the public authorities are still left to companies owing to budgetary inability to take responsibility for them. The re-establishment of large-scale public intervention is one of the first conditions for liberating a flexible framework for microeconomic agents. But, by lapsing in its own payment

discipline in the second half of 1993, the Russian government accelerated the dismemberment of the fiscal and budgetary system.

4   Finally, no transition is possible without the establishment of new rules, norms and conventions, which necessarily involves the consent of a consensus or majority. In this regard, the fall-back on the executive power which liberal Russians imposed, with the explicit support of Western advisers and governments, resulted in a replication of the authoritarian and arbitrary practices of the Soviet system.

In more general terms, any economic policy during a period of transition must take the lack of market institutions into account, at least in the early stages, as well as the structural rigidity of the production apparatus during supply and demand shocks.

Under these conditions, it seems that the adjustment of such shocks over time, through pricing procedures and customs duties, conforms to the instituting of a restructuring process for the productive apparatus. This would imply that priority is given to the conditions of public and private investment formation in order to allow a microeconomic transformation. This requires a stabilisation of the informational framework, through the establishment of programmes of action in the medium term and the emergence of stabilised public demand.

37 Regulationist approaches and accumulation in Latin America

Jaime Aboites, Luis Miotti and Carlos Quenan

When applied to Latin American economies, regulationist approaches are defined in terms of a critique of dependence theories and the structuralism of the Commision Economica para America Latina y el Caraibe (CEPAL). While recognising the influence of the international context, exerted via many different channels, *régulation* approaches have sought to understand, in a national framework, historical variations in accumulation regimes and examples of *régulation* found in Latin America. Regulationists show the same concern to identify the specific features of each Latin American society and economy as that which inspired the work of Anibal Pinto and other researchers studying different 'styles of development' from the 1960s to the mid-1970s (Pinto, 1976; Calcagno, 1990).

In order to develop a more rigorous chronology of growth, the first generation of research therefore sought to analyse the main institutional forms present in Latin American countries.

The wage–labour nexus: between institutionalisation and the informal sector

In most studies of individual countries, the wage–labour nexus is the heart of an analysis seeking to identify the principal mechanisms of overall *régulation*. Thus in *Argentina* the establishment of an 'administered' *régulation* of the labour market during the 1930s and 1940s is intimately linked with the introduction of new mechanisms for harnessing agricultural rent and a recentring of growth on the domestic market (Hillcoat, 1986). From the late 1950s a burst in intensive accumulation was accompanied by a consolidation of a wage–labour nexus that was similar to Fordism, along with increases in social security spending and the institutionalisation of wage formation. Wages were increasingly indexed to living costs and linked with productivity gains (Miotti, 1991).

Likewise, in *Chile* there was a precocious institutionalisation of the wage–labour nexus, which gradually moved away from competitive *régulation* and contributed to industrialisation (Ominami, 1980, 1986). In *Mexico* during the Cardenist period monopolistic *régulation* in wage

Table 37.1 Specific aspects of the wage–labour nexus and its impact on post-war growth regimes in Latin America

Country, time period and authors	Wage–labour nexus and other institutions	Impact on growth regimes
Chile 1932–82 Ominami (1980, 1986)	1 Precocious institutionalisation of the wage–labour nexus 2 Large mining industry	1 Stabilisation of consumption but pressure on profits 2 Model based on raw material exports
Mexico 1939–85 Gutierrez-Garza (1983) Aboites (1985) Hernandez and Aboites (1994)	1 Strong state interventionism and very advanced labour legislation 2 Specific institutions for agriculture 3 Role of the informal sector	1 Attenuated competitive mechanisms 2 The dynamism of agriculture plays a key role in the operation of the growth regime (until 1970)
Venezuela 1943–83 Hausmann (1981) Hausmann and Marquez (1986)	1 Collective conventions, minimum wage and significant institutionalisation for regular workers 2 Informal sector with competitive adjustments 3 Compatibility between public expenditure, monetary creation, imports and oil receipts	1 Relative stabilisation of consumption in urban areas 2 Shocks transmitted from the modern sector to the informal sector 3 Marked dependence on the circulation process of oil rents
Brazil 1955–80 Cartier Bresson and Kopp (1981) Coriat and Saboia (1987) Saboia (1987) Mota Veiga (1989)	1 State-based *régulation* and collective conventions in the industrial sector 2 Competitive wage–labour nexus, considerable wage differences and large informal sector 3 Key role of the state in promoting the integration of the production mechanism and the modification of international insertion	1 Dynamism and 'plasticity' of the modern industrial sector 2 Role of inequality in demand stratification 3 Strong connections between productive sections
Peru 1970–85 Huanacune Rosas (1991)	1 Large informal sector 2 Role of the informal sector in both income and consumption formation	1 Possible functionality of the informal sector 2 Competitive mechanisms very important
Argentina 1860–1990 Hillcoat (1986, 1989) Miotti (1991)	1 Precocious institutionalisation of a monopolistic wage–labour nexus. Homogeneous wage increases. Lack of an informal sector 2 Weak dynamic in agricultural productivity	1 Intensive accumulation, based on self-centred industrial development 2 Unfavourable impact on growth and very wide cycles

Source: Based on Boyer (1994a).

formation was also established. Following heavy state intervention this resulted in the application of highly advanced work legislation (Gutierrez Garza, 1983; Aboites, 1985).

However, in most Latin American countries the development of configurations in the wage–labour nexus similar to those in Europe during the same period was not common. In *Brazil*, for example, the wage–labour nexus was characterised by competitive methods of *régulation* without any stable indexing of wages to prices or productivity, so that the pay range remained wide and variable. Furthermore, Brazil had a vast informal sector (Coriat and Saboia, 1987; Mota Veiga, 1989).

The informal sector is one of the major features of labour markets in many Latin American countries. It raises the question of the connection between the formal and informal sectors and their role in processes of capital accumulation. Again many different instances are possible. Indeed, in *Peru* wage formation in the formal sector appears to be influenced by fluctuations in the informal sector. Given its extensiveness, the informal sector has a key position in terms of both income formation and demand (Huanacune Rosas, 1991).

On the other hand, during the 1970s in *Mexico,* when unemployment began to rise, the institutional complex that was essentially created during the 1930s and 1940s sought to 'isolate' the modern sector from the informal sector. As a result, industrial wages continued to depend on productivity while average incomes in the informal sector remained low. During the 1980s, when the previous accumulation regime was in crisis and adjustment policies were opening the way to structural change, institutions governing work gradually adjusted wage levels to match the total labour force supply and the new conditions of an increasingly open economy (Aboites and Hernandez Laos, 1994).

Besides their specific effects on methods of wage-earners reproduction, different configurations of the wage–labour nexus influence other institutional forms and growth regimes in the semi-industrialised economies of Latin America (see Table 37.1).

Subordinate international insertion with national features

Insertion into the international regime is an essential factor in explaining accumulation dynamics. The 'truncated' industrialisation that took place in Latin America – in other words, expansion of section II (consumption goods) but weak development of section I (means of production) (Fajnzylber, 1983) – accounts for the subordinate position of the region in international economic relations.

That said, the specific regime of international insertion can either stimulate or permanently handicap a growth regime. In terms of commercial insertion, import substitution processes are a common characteristic. Owing to the lack of competitiveness of a protected industrial sector, these processes are financed by primary exports. However, the complexity of relations governing the connection between the domestic dynamic and the type of international insertion reveal many different national situations.

In *Mexico*, given the weakness of the sector producing capital goods, imports of necessary investment goods for the prevailing accumulation regime from 1940 to 1970 were financed essentially by exports of raw materials, which were made possible by agricultural expansion (Aboites, 1989).

In *Argentina*, on the other hand, the stagnation of agricultural exports and the resulting disequilibria in the foreign sector led to repeated applications of stabilisation policies, and gave rise to the characteristic 'stop/go' movements of the economy. Thus in the early attempts to move from extensive accumulation to an intensive regime, industrial growth encountered external constraints (Hillcoat, 1986, 1989).

It should be recognised that the persistence of 'peripheral' commercial insertion is not inevitable. Voluntarist strategies could lead to a substantial modification of the export structure, as demonstrated by the example of *Brazil*.

Different accumulation regimes

Various studies have sought to understand both the regular patterns that enable accumulation developments and the factors from which major crises originate. In some cases the study of accumulation regimes in Latin America examines the relation with the evolution of non-capitalist forms of production.

Mexico is a good illustration of this. Alongside the wage–labour nexus there is an important structural form determining the connection between the (non-capitalist) peasant economy and the modern agricultural sector. State management of this connection allowed agriculture to play a key role in post-war expansion. At the same time as favouring increases in real wages for the urban population and a cheap supply of agricultural raw materials for industry, the growth of production and productivity in agriculture gave rise to exportable surpluses which were used to finance growth. It was therefore the agricultural crisis and the withering of this structural form, in the second half of the 1960s, that sounded the death knell of an accumulation regime based on the domestic market (Aboites, 1989).

Venezuela is a typical example of a *rentier* accumulation regime in which the state occupies a central position in overall *régulation*. Growth and accumulation were based on a dynamic compatibility between oil exports, public spending and imports, while the mechanisms of monetary creation countered the destabilising effects of fluctuations in oil rents (Hausmann, 1981). The deregulation of these adjustments was thus the basis of the endogenous crisis that paradoxically manifested itself during the prosperous

Table 37.2 Accumulation, crises, *régulation*: a synthetic presentation of Argentina's trajectory

Institutional forms and accumulation features	1870–1929	1944–75	1991–[1]
Wage-labour nexus	Competitive Lack of indexation on the cost of living Income distribution unbalanced	1 Monopolistic 2 Collective bargaining agreements. Strong state intervention 3 Indexation based on the cost of living, distribution of productivity gains 4 Increasing homogeneity in wage increases 5 High level of wage earners in working population. Labour market little influence on wage levels. Distribution of income uneven in the short term but relatively balanced in the medium term	1 Towards a competitive relation 2 Fragmentation of collective forms of wage negotiation 3 Prohibition of indexation on living costs 4 Increasing diversity of wages (in levels and variations) 5 De-salaried economy (informal urban sector develops) Strong segmentation of the labour market Attempts to institutionalise labour market flexibility (negotiation at individual companies level and part time work) Very uneven income distribution; increased poverty (1970 = 5%, 1990 = 27%)
Role of the state	Passive in *régulation* Automatic adjustments Active industrial policy	Active in *régulation* and accumulation Arbiter in income distribution Fiscal reform (efficiency) Fiscal weakness and ineffectiveness	Deregulation and mass privatisation Balanced budget ideal Lack of industrial policy
Forms of competition	Large export companies Small and medium sized firms and industries in the domestic market Open to the world market	Transnational companies Oligopolistic forms Small- and medium-size firms and industries Protected economy	Large diversified national groups Oligopolistic forms Small- and medium-size firms and industries Reopening to the world market economy

Monetary regime	Gold standard and large opening to the world market	Administered market Virtual absence of a capital market Monetary policy based on domestic objectives	Financial extraversion Bi-monetary regime (dollar/peso) Development of capital markets
Insertion in the world economy	Export of raw materials Absolute advantages Open economy Foreign Direct Investment (FDI) associated with the infrastructure and financing of primary export production	Export of primary products: initially meat, later cereals and oils Industrial exports towards the end FDI in dynamic sectors: automobile; other metal-mechanical areas; chemicals and pharmaceuticals	Industrial exports with strong economies of scale and intensive use of natural resources: steel, aluminium, petrochemicals, vegetable oils Exports of primary products Open economy and regional integration (MERCOSUR) Insertion associated with service sectors: water, gas, electricity, communications, transport, banks, insurance
Accumulation regime	Agricultural rents (nineteenth century – 1920), then displacement of dynamic core towards industry	Inward-looking industry, under external constraints Extensive and then intensive accumulation	Outward looking specialisation (commodities) with a strong development of modern services
Main instability factors of the mode of development	Exogenous shocks Increasing inadequacy of *régulation* for industrial accumulation at end of period	Endogenous: Income distribution Increasing inflationary pressures Low rates for industrial exports/imports	Exogenous: Extreme external financial fragility Endogenous: Fragile specialisation Technical progress can destabilise growth Tensions generated by increasing inequality

Source: Based on research on Argentina cited above.

Note

1 The current period has seen the establishment of new modalities of *régulation* but the new accumulation regime is not yet consolidated. As in earlier periods, most of the expected features emerge during the crisis.

petrodollar years, even before it was aggravated by the collapse of the international oil market and a foreign debt crisis (Hausmann and Marquez, 1986).

Mexico and *Venezuela* are both characterised by a weak development of section I, to differing degrees. However, accumulation developments in *Brazil* were accompanied by increased interaction between the two sections (Cartier-Bresson and Kopp, 1981; Coriat and Saboia, 1987). To a great extent state intervention contributed to this, by means of its production commitments and sector-based policies governing forms of competition and causing profound changes in its international insertion. However, the external financial constraints of the 1980s completely destabilised the regulating action of the state.

During the 1960s in *Argentina* there was also an increasingly close relationship between productive sections, together with the consolidation of intensive accumulation. The origin of productivity gains in Argentina showed a Kaldorian cumulative growth dynamic. However, the model was in fact characterised by increasing imbalance in public finance and experienced strong inflationary tensions and fluctuations which, even if less extreme than those of the 1950s, were a contrast to the stabilisation cycle introduced by Fordism in developed countries (Miotti, 1991). The fragility of the accumulation regime was shown when, in the mid-1970s, disequilibria in the balance of payments converged with a productivity slowdown and increased pressure for real wage rises. The soaring inflation that resulted was the first element of a major crisis. This crisis formed a lengthy break in the economic trajectory of Argentina and brought with it a potential new mode of development (Table 37.2).

These different national situations, in both Latin America and other developing regions, were already obvious in initial case studies. Since then, the research of Alain Lipietz (1985) and Carlos Ominami (1986), in particular, has made it possible to move towards a classification of Third World accumulation regimes as pre-industrial, *rentier*, introverted industrialisation, Taylorist or mixed regimes. This categorisation drew criticism on the grounds of a need for more extensive and rigorous use of analyses in terms of productive sections (Lanzarotti, 1992).

The new challenges of structural reforms

The general structural crises of the 'lost decade' (the 1980s) and the policies of openness, deregulation and state withdrawal (adjustment policies) applied since then have extended these changes. How have the changes affected relations between productive sections? What is the effect of transformations in monetary regimes, particularly in economies that have experienced hyperinflation with dollarisation and financial openness? What new forms of competition have resulted from commercial openness, the cornerstone of reforms seeking to put extraverted regimes back in place?

Finally, what is the position of national *régulation* mechanisms in the case of open economies which, as well as experiencing radical transformations in their international insertion, are also engaged in new processes of regional integration?

A large area of potential research arises: what is the impact of the structural reforms recommended by the IMF and the World Bank on national specificity? This would allow an examination, as in the case of *Venezuela*, of both the inertia that has resulted from old *régulation* methods and the difficulties that must be overcome in order to suggest other *régulations* (Hausmann, 1988; Quenan *et al.*, 1994; Miotti *et al.*, 1996, 1999). This is an invitation for prospective analyses that will try to untangle approaches to re-establishing a stable growth regime despite uneven economic cycles (Miotti, 1991, 1994, with regard to Argentina). It would then be possible to undertake a systematic reconstruction of national trajectories along with their structural crises.

At the same time as it supports the development of a new wave of comparative studies, this research could open up new areas of collaboration and discussion with neo-structuralism and other critical Latin American approaches (Rosales, 1988; Sunkel, 1990; Sàinz and Calcagno, 1992). The common research aim will be to suggest a renewal of economic analysis that goes beyond the limits of neo-liberal approaches.

Part VI

Future prospects for *régulation* theory

38 *Régulation* theory among theories of institutions

Marie-Claire Villeval

According to Langlois (1988), the problem with the old American institutionalist school was that it sought an understanding of the economy with institutions but without theory, while neoclassicists wanted an economic theory without institutions. The question is therefore how to construct an economic theory of institutions. Many research programmes today share this ambition. Have institutions, which once acted as a watershed, now become a meeting point?

Régulation theory is intended as a reflection on the economic dynamic of capitalism and the transformation of institutional spheres. Using a basic cartography, the frontiers and lines of communication between *régulation* theory and other research programmes concerned with the status of institutions will be mapped. On this basis the potential contribution of the dialogue between *régulation* theory, convention theory and institutionalist theory will be reviewed, suggesting new areas of debate on the subject of institutional change and development.

Are institutions the 'focal point' of contemporary economic debate?

The contemporary focus on institutions masks a mass of different definitions, theoretical references and justifications. The international revival of interest since the late 1970s includes both reflections on limited rationality (Simon) and on the need to palliate market failures (Arrow), which partly explain the success of NIE (Williamson and North's New Institutional Economics, to be distinguished from neo-institutionalism). Following Coase, Williamson places institutions within the contract-based problematic of transaction costs, including opportunism and associating the firm, viewed as an alternative institution to the market, with a group of inter-individual contracts. Rules make up contractual arrangements. Although the categories of institution and transaction are formally adopted from old American institutionalism (Commons), the two approaches prove to be irreconcilable (Dutraive, 1993).

By appealing to game theory, new institutional economics (Lewis, Schelling, Schotter, Shubik) makes a greater contribution to convention theory. From a historical perspective, Morgenstern perceived that the short-sightedness of the neoclassical model was caused by difficulty in taking strategic interactions into account. He therefore distinguished various institutional arrangements and equilibrium prices according to types of arrangement. The relation between institutions and game theory was then adopted terminologically, with Shubik referring to 'mathematical institutionalist theory' (Schotter, 1992). In static games, conventions act as a means of co-ordinating actions and as a criterion for choosing between several Nash equilibria. In dynamic games, conventions act as regular behaviour patterns produced in a process of rule selection.

Without wishing to obscure their differences, generally the Austrians support a substantial approach to social institutions (money, language, etc.). In Menger there is a degree of similarity between social institutions and natural organisms in that their origin is outside all deliberative activity (with the exception of 'pragmatic' institutions) and they can be accounted for precisely (Garrouste, 1994). In response to constructivist rationalism, Hayek shows that institutions are made up rules of conduct that are not decided by men 'but which eventually govern individuals' action because, when they apply them, their actions are more efficient and successful than those of competing groups' (Hayek, 1973: 21).

Unlike these previous approaches, the 'neo-institutionalists' (Galbraith, Gruchy, then Hodgson, Ramstad, Rutherford and Samuels) follow in the heritage of old American institutionalism (from Veblen, Commons, J. M. Clark and Mitchell to Ayres). They should not be confused with the 'new institutionalists' of the New Institutional Economics: unlike NIE they do not propose an alternative to the market as an institution, but instead use institutions as a category in the analysis of coherence. They refer to Veblen's definition of an institution as a 'set of thought patterns shared by most men' and to Commons's definition as 'the collective action that controls, liberates and promotes the expansion of individual action'. Commons's institutionalism is based on a process of social negotiation (Perlman, 1991) and the concept of transactions (exchange, managing and distribution). While in NIE 'institutions are a 'variable explained' by the choices of agents who, for reasons of efficiency, prefer contract-based inter-actions to market exchange' (Dutraive, 1993), in this instance they provide an explanatory variable of action.

In France the renewed interest in institutions also dates back to the 1970s, to the contributions of *régulation* theory. It is viewed as a break with neoclassical theory, rather than as an amendment, as it is in the United States. Analysis of the economic dynamic is based on a theorisation of institutional forms, defined as a codification of fundamental relations. The purpose of these institutional forms is to consider the reproduction and transformations of a system that is built on antagonistic social relations, in a process of making compromises coherent. The opposition of state versus market is thus left behind.

A classification of many different approaches

The research referred to above reflects the great variety of conceptions of institutions and calls for organisation. The following classification is suggested on the basis of three criteria: methodology, the principles of institutional development and the functions of institutions. Two major groups of approaches can be identified. While there is convergence between Menger, Hayek, new industrial theory and NIE ('Group 1'), they are clearly very different from other approaches ('Group 2': old and neo-institutionalism, *régulation* theory).

The two groups use different methods. Group 1 is associated with methodological individualism; social phenomena are interpreted through an analysis of individual interactions (Elster). Group 2 is holistic. Institutions, seen as the result of collective processes for resolving problems in a historical framework, form the basic unit; the market therefore constitutes an institution. Old institutionalism was based on Pragmatic philosophy (Peirce, James, Dewey), and emphasised the relation between a value system and the reasons for collective action.

The principle of institutional development is also a basis for distinctions. Customs are included in Group 1, as an expression that depends on stable preferences in a neoclassical framework. Institutions result from individual actions, but once they are established they merely constrain choices, they do not shape individuals' behaviour (Hodgson, 1989).

For Menger, 'organic' institutions (as opposed to pragmatic ones) emerge unintentionally from frequent interactions between individuals in the pursuit of self-interest as their skills develop (learning by imitation). But Menger is not particularly interested in the mechanisms of institutional development (Garrouste, 1994). In contrast, while Hayek is not really interested in the origins of institutions, he bases the adjustment of socially efficient institutions on an invisible hand mechanism (a spontaneous order), seeing them as the object of natural selection. NIE views institutions as explaining market failures, as the consequences of constrained optimisation and transaction costs. These costs, incompleteness and informational asymmetries play an important role in institutional development. This development is compatible with improvements in economic efficiency (Rutherford, 1986) by including partial intentionality (Williamson, 1985) or by referring to the selection of efficient institutions through market mechanisms (North, 1966).

For Shubik, in the new institutional economy institutions are *ad hoc* rules constraining the market, while Schotter sees conventions as the result of meta-games, that is, processes of rational decisions (Mirowski, 1986). Once established, conventions are self-enforcing (Nash's equilibrium in

Harsanyi and Aumann) and lasting thanks to the pressure to conform, even if they are no longer socially optimal. In the evolutionary approach found in Axelrod's (1986) games, three reasons explain the maintenance of only efficient norms: natural selection of the most efficient, a process of trial and error (revision of beliefs) and imitation of players with the best results.

In Group 2 the institutional dynamic and connections between technical and institutional changes are viewed as the product of social conflict, learning curves, tensions between customs and innovating pressures that cause a loss of coherence in the system, conflicts between existing institutions and discoveries.

The position of *régulation* theory and proximity to American institutionalists

In *régulation* theory the principles of action for institutional forms are the law, compromises and the value system on which routines are based, but their mode of production remains unclear. The origins of institutions lie in major crises, conflicts, wars, etc. Six evolutionary principles have been identified (Boyer, 1994b). Institutional viability is made possible through the many bases of support. The social coherence of an institution is not immediate, it is attained only through learning. An institution is viable only if it is consonant with the overall institutional architecture of society. The hierarchy of institutional forms is neither permanent nor universal. Globalisation does not lead to a geographical or historical convergence of institutional architecture and institutional optimality does not guarantee stability. The learning process that participates in the redefinition of these architectures in crisis not only relates to selection through economic efficiency, it also involves the question of the social compatibility of compromises that are not immediately institutionalised (Billaudot, 1994b). This brings up issues of the relations between the economy, law and ethics.

A possible link then appears to the study of the development of institutions in Veblen, resulting from a group of 'cumulative causes' linked with tensions between ceremonial and instrumental values, and between financial and industrial rationales. In Commons the negotiation principle is essential, revealing the artificial selection of institutions, which is ethically necessary, especially in order to move towards 'reasonable capitalism' (Commons). For neo-institutionalists 'the analysis of institutions cannot be based on a single cost calculation; it must refer to categories such as customs and rules proposed by 'old institutionalists' as well as uncertainty and the knowledge most recently taken into account by the economy' (Dutraive, 1993).

Finally, there is no agreement on the function of institutions, which is often overdetermined. From a functional perspective, Group 1 concentrates on a solution to problems of 'satisficing', reducing uncertainty and transaction costs, compensation for market malfunction, the range of agents'

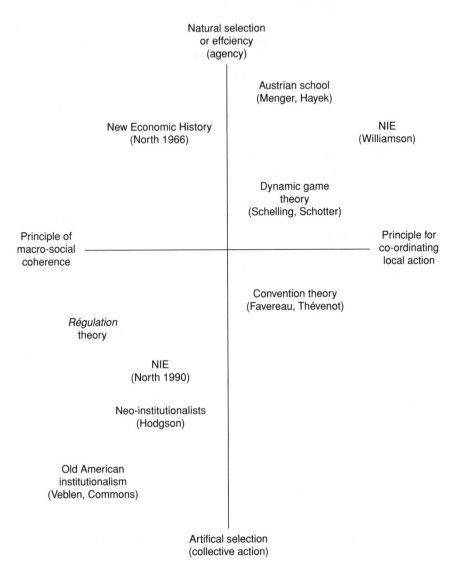

Natural selection
or effciency
(agency)

Austrian school
(Menger, Hayek)

New Economic History
(North 1966)

NIE
(Williamson)

Dynamic game
theory
(Schelling, Schotter)

Principle of
macro-social ——————————————— Principle for
coherence   co-ordinating
                                                              local action

Convention theory
(Favereau, Thévenot)

Régulation
theory

NIE
(North 1990)

Neo-institutionalists
(Hodgson)

Old American
institutionalism
(Veblen, Commons)

Artifical selection
(collective action)

Figure 38.1 A cartography of theories of institutions

computational failings, and, in wider terms, their function in co-ordinating
inter-individual activities. In game theory, 'the role of institutions is to
resolve precise co-ordination problems, particularly the results of absence,
multiplicity or the non-optimality of spontaneous equilibria' (Walliser,
1989). For Menger and Hayek, institutions make progress possible in so
far as their origins are truly unintentional.

In Group 2 institutions act as guides for action, allowing risk taking and structuring of society within a context of asymmetrical powers. They act as stabilisation modes for expectations or compromises on rules for collective action. They supply a framework for the selection and transformation of information into knowledge (old and neo-institutionalism). Routines provide a support structure for incremental technical change. Institutions participate in the shaping of regular accumulation patterns and they are the basis for the reproduction of the mode of *régulation* in *régulation* theory.

Figure 38.1 presents a synthesis of this analysis. The horizontal axis represents functionality. On the left, the institutions – which are meaningless if separated from each other – that contribute to macro-social coherence require a holistic methodology. On the right, the function of institutions is based on the resolution of local co-ordination problems for inter-individual actions whose analysis is based on an individualist methodology, so that evaluative criteria vary with each institution. The vertical axis represents the evolutionary dynamic: it contrasts natural selection or selection on the basis of economic efficiency with artificial selection, including power and social legitimisation. A third axis, which is not represented, could indicate a historical view, contrasting *ex ante* coherence with *ex post* coherence of institutions with respect to the economic and social dynamic.

This diagram should not be construed as a fixed representation. None of these groups is a homogeneous whole. Complementary relationships between the 'fathers' of 'institutionalist' research programmes can be identified (Vanberg, 1989; Samuels, 1989). There are also 'methodological alliances'. For instance, in order to extend the analysis of institutional generation, which is still not deeply explored in *régulation* theory, co-operative relations have been established between it and convention theory, through game theory (Boyer and Orléan, 1992).

What is the connection between *régulation* theory and convention theory?

The meaning and coherence of institutions towards each other is observed *ex post* in *régulation* theory, implying that it has no predictive value. The desire to understand how conventions develop led to shared reflections with convention theory, through the tools provided by game theory. Yet the initial foundations of convention theory and game theory link them more closely with Group 1 (conventions as solutions produced by co-ordination problems).

The dialogue between *régulation* theory and convention theory is potentially fruitful in terms of an analysis of principles of action for some institutions (Favereau, 1993b). It is useful to compare these research programmes in order to understand the dynamic interplay of formal organised institutions and informal institutions (value systems, collective representations, norms). While convention theory tends to emphasise informal institutions in its analysis, *régulation* theory does not shed much light on them. Institutions are neither pure conventions nor mere organisations. Finally, a comparison of these research programmes enables a deeper understanding of the dynamic of collective learning in transitional societies.

However, there are limits to this comparison, both methodological (holism versus methodological individualism) and analytical (an initially macroeconomic or microeconomic approach). Even if there is an area of agreement on some functions (mode of homogenisation, reduction of uncertainty) and even if both research programmes place the emergence of collective actors at the heart of the dynamic, the relations between conflict and co-operation are not identical. Convention theory appears to dissolve conflict into convention, learning into compromise and tension into instituted co-ordination, while in *régulation* theory institutional forms are a codification of contradictory social relations and cannot form equivalence models. Finally, game theory does not necessarily provide the means of theorising the simultaneous genesis of an institution and of its coherence with other changing institutions.

The endogenous dynamic of institutions and economic performances: dialogues with other research programmes

This dynamic interweaving of research calls for a more structured dialogue between *régulation* theory and different institutionalist theories. This is not a forced dialogue; there is a similarity of concerns even with old institutionalism, which coincides with *régulation* theory's institutional forms. These include an analysis of the dynamics of capitalism (especially in the rise of collective representation), an analysis of money (the artificial and institutional measure of scarcity in Commons), the forms of companies (Berle and Means (1932) on 'collective capitalism') and the wage relation (Commons). Old institutionalism was based on pragmatic philosophy and a holistic, historical and evolutionary perspective. It includes power asymmetries and views institutions as the substance of social life and the collective action of the basic unit of analysis. Emphasis is placed on the genesis and action of laws, conventions and routines in a 'path-dependence' framework. In Commons the principle of 'part–whole relationships' mediated by institutions enables a theorisation of the interplay of micro and mesoeconomics within a social whole. A connection is therefore possible even if the question of macroeconomic closure is not addressed in old institutionalism. The analysis of the dynamics of capitalism is undertaken at a disaggregated level, while analysis of regular patterns and crises at the macroeconomic level is an important contribution derived from *régulation* theory.

The call for a dialogue between *régulation* theory and other institutionalist research programmes seeks to develop an analysis of the endogenous dynamic of institutions as well as evaluating economic performance, viewed in terms of an evaluation of institutional performance. Empirically, this involves the following procedures. Levels of performance depend partly on the density of interactions, intra- and inter-company learning ability, and hence the quality of underlying institutional arrangements. To avoid both economic and institutional determinism in the evaluation of performance, it is necessary to analyse contemporary forms of collective action, the search for new compromises promoting co-operation and the production of new social orders, at the world and national level as well as at a disaggregated level. A re-examination of interacting collective actors and the dynamic of industrial relations, in order to analyse institutional innovation and new arrangements between the law, compromises and routines, is necessarily part of an analysis that combines ethics, law and economics. This is a condition for renewed responses to the fundamental questions of unemployment in OECD countries, endogenous technological accumulation in developing countries and the construction of the wage–labour nexus in Eastern Europe.

Progress has been made thanks to the debate between *régulation* theory and British and American neo-institutionalist analyses (flexibility and institutional 'ossification'; Hodgson), the German approach to institutions (institutional rigidity as a possible support for offensive mechanisms during crises; Streeck, 1992), and Scandinavian approaches seen in the National Innovation Systems (the emergence of a 'learning economy'; Lundvall, 1992). Does institutional efficiency lie in the ability of collective actors to generate coherent innovative institutional arrangements, the capacity of these arrangements to solidify, thereby benefiting long term risk taking, or in institutional learning skills?

Rethinking this evaluation requires an analysis of the move from institutional innovation to normalisation, the dynamic between differentiation and standardisation, and the connection between selection and learning, so as to understand differences in the rhythms and modes of institutional reconstitution.

39 *Régulation* and the American radical school

Allan Coban

The United States has been the homeland of economics and the active centre for redefining research programmes since the Second World War. The Keynesian-classical synthesis, monetarism, the supply side school, the new classical school, neo-Keynesianism and, more recently, endogenous growth, have spread throughout the world in rapid succession. This activity and the revival of the Extended Standard Theory (EST) tend to obscure the contributions of other schools such as institutionalism, the radical school and particularly the social structure of accumulation (SSA)* theory.

This research programme, which agrees with *régulation* theory on many points, has an original approach that could enrich and renew French and European research in two ways. First of all, institutional macroeconomics must take power relations in capitalist societies into account. Second, the synergy of Marxian intuitions and advances in new microeconomic tools opens the way to an original theory of institutions.

Strikingly similar aims and basic concepts

For many years now the American radicals associated with the Union of Radical Political Economists (URPE) have had a similar project to regulationists. It is to understand the origin of the exceptional growth of the post-Second World War period, and to analyse the mechanisms and consequences of the structural crisis that struck the United States in the late 1960s (URPE, 1978). Their initial theoretical framework is strikingly similar, making critical use of Marxist theory in order to understand features and transformations of contemporary capitalism.

Indeed, crises did not occur everywhere, nor did they always take the same form. This is because the combination of problems of valorisation, realisation and legitimisation appears in different configurations (Bowles *et al.*, 1986a: 10–15). Radicals also share with regulationists a desire to modernise the language of Marxist theory through the eclectic but rigorous use of the tools of macroeconomic modelling, econometrics and, more recently, game theory and microeconomics in a situation of asymmetrical and imperfect information.

The parallel between these two theoretical constructs also relates to basic concepts and their general architecture (Boyer, 1986c; Kotz, 1990). Thus the concept of capital/labour agreement is counterpart to the wage–labour nexus. SSA and *régulation* theory both emphasise the original nature of the post-Second World War compromise, whereby wage earners accepted managerial prerogatives in company management in return for their demands for a stable and sometimes larger share of income. In both cases the power relation and the wage relation are closely connected. There is a similar emphasis on the social division of labour, but SSA's originality is in showing that productivity problems are connected with rising monitoring costs (Bowles *et al.*, 1983a) while *régulation* theory concentrates on work conflicts and the maturity of Fordism (Chapter 30).

The determining role of large companies (SSA) and monopolistic competition* (*régulation* theory) both reflect the consequences of concentrating on the prices and profit dynamic (Boyer and Mistral, 1981: 254–5; Bowles *et al.*, 1986a: 334–5). Likewise, the Pax Americana (SSA) is reminiscent of the international regime (*régulation* theory). On the other hand, there is no equivalent of the concept of a monetary regime in SSA, which ascribes a large degree of autonomy to government authorities. An example of this autonomy is found in the making of monetary policy, unlike the strongly endogenous tendency in *régulation* theory, which privileges the concept of configuration (Chapter 15) or a state intervention regime (Chapter 16).

The concept of a capital/citizen agreement corresponds to the concept of institutionalised compromise* (Chapters 12 and 15). Both approaches recognise that the political process has the power to institute some groups as holders of economic rights that are quite separate from the private wage relation (Chapter 16). Hence a social and economic dynamic that differs from nineteenth century capitalism. While it acts as a stabilising element for economic cycles during periods of strong growth, it can also accentuate financial disequilibria once the virtuous circle of growth is broken.

The structural crisis of American capitalism

This configuration of capitalist social relations and relations with the state defines the essential characteristics of the accumulation process, viewed as a dynamic balancing of tensions that are constantly created by the alteration of the negotiating power of capital and labour. If capital is too strong, underconsumption crises may occur, but if labour takes the initiative the fall in the profit rate results in the need to increase the exploration rate in the Marxist sense (Bowles *et al.*, 1986c). The parallel with *régulation* theory's presentation of accumulation regimes is striking. Likewise, the reasons for the Golden Age (Marglin and Schor, 1990) are reminiscent of the causes of the *trente glorieuses*: due to the introduction of a series of original compromises, the contradictions of accumulation were contained in an original configuration.

But the same factors at the root of the absence of a re-run of the inter-war depression explain why America entered a period of crisis. *Régulation* theory and SSA agree on the diagnosis of a structural crisis, understood as a loss of accumulation stability. However, the exact description of the crisis varies. *Régulation* theory views it as an expression of the techno-logical and social limits of Fordism: the investment boom of the late 1960s came up against a drastic fall in returns (Chapter 31). For SSA, the crisis concerned capitalist social relations, which required increasingly large monitoring costs in the company (a rise in indirect labour) as well as in society (police, army, criminality) (Bowles *et al.*, 1983a). The crisis there-fore involved both economics and politics. This was especially the case since it was part of the economy of waste. The concept of a waste economy is not found in *régulation* theory.

Thus the problems of labour and its monitoring occupy a central posi-tion, which conforms to a long American tradition (Braverman, 1974; Marglin, 1974). In this regard, two other branches of the radical family that *régulation* theory has collaborative links with should be mentioned. Some radicals have constructed a macroeconomic theory which frees itself from the stagnationist views of Keynesianism, and accounts for the novelty of post-war accumulation where capital and labour had a shared interest in expansion. This is another helpful formalisation of Fordism (Marglin, 1984; Marglin and Schor, 1990).

Other American researchers who have been more directly influenced by *régulation* theory have explored institutional configurations which made it possible to overcome the crisis of mass production (Piore and Sabel, 1989). Flexible production required local institutions fostering trust and co-operation, and which replaced the Keynesian state of the Fordist era. In return, this hypothesis of the future gave rise to a critical evaluation by *régulation* theory, emphasising, for example, the persistence of returns of scale, combined with extensive product differentiation for the consumer (Boyer and Coriat, 1986).

Beyond these general areas of similarity, the two approaches have symmetrical strengths and weaknesses, on which to found a research programme for the 2000s.

Long-term historical studies for *régulation* theory; subversion of neo-Walrasian theory by SSA

One initial difference is the proportion of historical studies to theory. A collection and comparison of long-term historical studies has been the main means of theoretical progress for *régulation* theory. This process is also present in SSA, which, for example, provided a panorama of labour transformations in the United States (Gordon *et al.*, 1982), which paral-leled exactly studies of the wage–labour nexus over the long term. But the period 1950–70 is analysed differently. It is analysed in terms of the homogenisation and diffusion of a Fordist wage–labour nexus by *régulation* theory, and as the consolidation of a labour segmentation and wage status by SSA. On the other hand, the periodisation of productivity regimes for both *régulation* theory (Chapter 31) and SSA (Gordon, 1991) presents a contrast between two main periods – before the First World War and after the Second World War. The most rigorous statistical test of a structural crisis is found in SSA (Bowles *et al.*, 1983a), while *régulation* theory makes use of a combination of institutional and statistical analyses which are often less acute.

But since 1985 the radicals' research has taken an important theoretical direction that is without equivalent in *régulation* theory. Several neoclassical theorists have studied the origin of firms and the limits of the market in new analyses of information asymmetries. For radicals these asymmetries, far from being exogenous, are the direct consequence of the very particular nature of labour, which the capitalist must constantly extract from labour power. Paradoxically, efficiency wage theories find one of their strongest justifications in the Marxist theory of labour power.

It is thus possible to base Marxist models of production processes on microeconomics. A firm's production possibilities are determined not only by technology, but also by the nature of direct work monitoring, whether this involves installations, supervision by foremen or incentive wage formulas (Bowles, 1985). The analysis can be extended to debtor/creditor relations, which similarly involve conflicts of interest and strategic behaviour so that arrangements and contracts distort the optimal solution that should prevail for the economy as a whole (Bowles and Gintis, 1993).

The SSA researchers are therefore involved in a large contemporary project to construct an economic theory of institutions (Appendix 39.1). SSA forwards a set of propositions with a paradoxical but key conclusion: 'The anonymity of market exchange promotes unfavourable norms for an efficient solution to co-ordination difficulties.'

The difference between radicals and EST is not the same for convention theory (Chapter 41). A hypothesis of substantial rationality is maintained and the starting point of the theory is power asymmetries, rather than the co-ordinating difficulties of independent economic units. The tremendous difficulty of constructing an alternative to EST is clear. Many distinct alternatives exist, which are not necessarily mutually compatible, especially since even the base camp of economic theory has shattered into a myriad of largely incompatible sub-programmes (Amable *et al.*, 1995).

These advances in SSA opened perspectives for *régulation* theory. While convention theory explores some difficulties with the market, the contested exchange theory shows the complemenarity* between hierarchical and market relations in terms of a dialectic which is at the very origin of the problematic, while also renewing it with an unexpected microeconomic foundation. Furthermore, while *régulation* theory has spent a good deal of time studying the endogenous nature of technical change and the historical evolution of consumption norms, despite its essential role, it has barely considered this second endogenous source, which SSA theorists have started to explore (Bowles, 1997).

Macro-econometric modelling in SSA versus international comparisons in *régulation* theory

A second point of comparison concerns the respective role of these two methods in research advances. Macroeconomic modelling is present in *régulation* theory (Chapter 18), but *régulation* theory never sought to construct a canonical model of administered *régulation* and to extend it and estimate it to make it comparable to offerings by other macroeconomic theorists and econometricians. This gap is all the more surprising and regrettable given that its founding thinkers began as builders of macro-economic models for economic administration.

In contrast, SSA constructed this type of model for the American economy in a far more systematic manner. A framework was presented in the mid-1980s (Bowles *et al.*, 1986a: 329–35) and has evolved through constant comparison with alternative approaches, including Nicholas Kaldor's cumulative growth theory (Gordon, 1991). The properties of this model differ greatly from those of *régulation* theory. Furthermore, the evaluation of this type of model is then used to analyse the impact of past economic policies, for example Ronald Reagan's policies. Although they were intended to restore the hegemony of capitalists by weakening the position of wage earners, these policies led to such underutilisation of production capacities that they failed to restore the previous dynamic of profits (Bowles *et al.*, 1988). The relevance of this type of modelling is twofold. First of all it weighs up contradictory effects that only an econometric exercise can assess, and second it contributes to debates on economic policy according to the norms of a profession which has become highly technical since the 1970s. This type of arrangement is sorely lacking in *régulation* theory and an important, or even top-priority, task could be to gradually construct this type of tool. It would also be a means of synthesising and diffusing a new generation of regulationist models.

On the other hand, while *régulation* theory has sought to free itself from its initial specifically French features through systematic international comparison, SSA has retained its American-centred bias. It has certainly formed schools by example in Japan (Tsuru, 1991) and provoked international comparisons verifying, for example, whether the cost of job losses has been as great elsewhere as it has been in the United States (Weisskopf, 1985). Some of these studies have been undertaken by regulationists (Peaucelle and Petit, 1988). However, it appears that not all economies are as Hobbesian as the United States, and that Germany and Japan in particular do not match the canonical model, which consequently requires amendment. In a similar fashion, the suggestions of economic policy focus on wage increases, a reduction in inequalities and the democratisation of economic institutions in the United States (Gordon, 1996). This strategy would not necessarily suit medium-size economies, or even small or social democrat economies, as the comparative research of *régulation* theory has emphasised (Chapters 32 and 33). In other words, SSA could benefit from the lessons of *régulation* theory's many international comparisons and amend or revise its economic model on that basis.

Constructing an institutional macroeconomics, placing power in the centre of a theory of institutions

In the light of this rapid survey, it is clear that the different paths of the 1980s and 1990s could eventually contribute to future joint research. At a time which is still dominated by Panglossian optimism with respect to the efficiency and neutrality of markets, it is essential to develop an original theory of institutions concentrating on the interaction between power and economics (Knight, 1992), thus continuing Marxian and radical analyses. But it is also important to derive a macroeconomic theory that takes full account of the variety and sophistication of institutional forms at work in contemporary societies. This second area of study has already been examined in collaborations between SSA and *régulation* theory (Bowles and Boyer, 1988, 1990b, 1995), and these joint studies should be enhanced and developed in the future. The most promising project, however, is a theory of institutions that will share in the inheritance of the founding fathers of political economy. EST neglects this approach, even though it is essential for understanding societies in which power, conflicts and contradictions are still omnipresent.

Appendix 39.1 The radicals' vision and programme for the theory of institutions

The originality of the radicals is to have considered that market exchange is not a given and that it assumes power relations which must be constantly maintained by various institutional arrangements. This is unlike EST, which believes either that the problem does not exist or is overcome by a third party independently of those involved in the exchange (Bowles and Gintis, 1993). This is an initial line of differentiation between the theories (Figure 39.1). The second area of difference relates to the exogenous or endogenous nature of preferences and norms. Radicals believe that these are the result of previous interactions between agents (Bowles, 1997), unlike the microeconomics of imperfect information (Stiglitz, 1987), but similar to the propositions of Amartya Sen.

This original classification has the advantage of reintroducing the question of economic rights and their central place in institutional analysis. In one sense it is faithful to classical and Marxist approaches, even though its proximity to George Akerlof (1984) and Douglass North (1990) is surprising. It also reintroduces an interesting connection between power and economics in a general proposition: 'The general competitive equilibrium of a set of contested exchanges attributes power to agents on the short side of markets, which by definition are no longer in equilibrium.' There is an interesting application of this in the concept of the cost of job loss, which becomes a determinant in work intensity (Bowles *et al.*, 1983a).

	Exogenous implementation of rights	Endogenous implementation of rights
Exogenous preferences and norms	*Walrasian exchange*	*Contested exchange*
	Ricardo Walras Arrow-Debreu Coase/welfare theory	Solow/Shapiro/Stiglitz Holmstrom/Ross/Shavell Williamson Hurwicz/Groves
Endogenous preferences and norms	*Cultural change and contractual exchange*	*Cultural change and contested exchange*
	Mill Hayek Marshall Sen	Smith Marx Akerlof North

Figure 39.1 The four varieties of economic theory
Source: Bowles and Gintis (1993: 99)

40 Evolution and *régulationary* theories

Similarities and differences

Benjamin Coriat and Giovanni Dosi

Despite very different starting points and relatively diverse objects of enquiry, from the mid-1980s it has become increasingly evident to a few practitioners from both camps that the evolutionary and regulationist research programmes share some important 'building blocks' and that a more systematic comparison of the two types of analysis would be mutually enriching. (See also Coriat and Dosi, 1998, for a more detailed discussion of what follows.)

Two research programmes with apparently different interpretative motivations

Régulation theory was developed essentially to study a very challenging specific issue. In fact it was intended to furnish theoretical tools and interpretative constructs to account for a particular form of crisis (stagflation) in the 1970s and the transition from sustained growth to 'structural crises'. The challenge of such an interpretation has been that *crises had to be analysed in their endogenous drivers*, and not only as outcomes of external shocks (Boyer, 1986a; Coriat, 1994b). Conversely, the contemporary 'evolutionary' research programme emerged in the late 1960s as an attempt to account for processes of economic growth fuelled by endogenous technical innovation and grounded in 'bounded rational' notion of agency.

The term *evolutionary theories* will be used here to refer to a group of conceptualisations and models with a *common emphasis on economic dynamics* in terms of their 'disequilibria' features, within decentralised processes of novelty generation (*in primis,* technological innovation).

The classic early reference is Nelson and Winter (1982), and a later collective contribution is Dosi *et al.* (1988). These are complemented by a growing collection of empirical analyses of the 'anatomy' of capitalist innovation systems (cf., among others, Freeman, 1982; Rosenberg, 1976, 1982; Nelson, 1993) and by different attempts to formalise, in this perspective, various aspects of macroeconomic growth, innovation diffusion and industrial dynamics (cf. the discussion in Coriat and Dosi, 1994, and references therein).

Evolutionary theory is concerned primarily with the micro-foundations of economic dynamics grounded first on processes of research, adaptation and generally 'bounded rational' learning and second on the mechanisms of environmental selection (e.g. on financial and product markets). In turn, the selection mechanism, for 'populations' of heterogeneous behaviour, technology, etc., has been analysed in terms of its analogies with and differences from a 'biological metaphor' (for early contributions cf. Winter, 1964, 1971). 'Bounded rationality' – in the broadest sense – is commonly acknowledged to be the general characteristic of decision making in complex, non-stationary environments, and goes together with changing distribution of behavioural repertoires, 'cognitive frames' through which agents imperfectly interpret their environments, and problem-solving capabilities. On these grounds, the general interpretative hypothesis is that observed statistical regularities in aggregate variables (e.g. productivity, incomes, employment, etc.) should be interpreted as *emerging properties* stemming from far-from-equilibrium interactions.

Note also that the modelling methodology of evolutionary theory operates on the grounds of some stylised. 'phenomenological' generalisations about technology, behaviour, interactions, etc. So, for example, there has been an attempt to identify historical regularities in innovation processes (defining and specifying the basic features of 'technological paradigms', 'regimes', 'trajectories' are among these endeavours), and in organisational practices (trying to operationalise notions such as 'routines' and 'organisational' capabilities, etc.). Conversely, the basic methodology of *régulation* theory is grounded in the search for historically specific *structural forms* encompassing basic institutional invariables in relationships among diverse types of actors ('firms', 'workers', 'banks', etc.) and among markets (of labour, finance, products, etc.). In the regulationist approach, institutions and institutional 'forms' are of crucial importance in as much as they contribute to the shaping of the behaviour of agents by creating 'regularities'.

Thus stated, the two research programmes would not seem to have much in common except for a general concern with long-term dynamics. However, in our view, they display more profound overlaps and complementary features. To begin with, they obviously share a lack of dogmatic commitment to any 'natural' self-regulating properties of markets as such, as well as a search for the institutional foundations allowing them to operate in a relatively orderly fashion.

The nature and role of institutions are indeed a fundamental domain where fruitful complementary areas – but also possibly important theoretical differences – are likely to emerge.

Institutions, corporate organisations and micro-behaviour: complementary features, tensions and challenges

The *institutional embeddedness* of economic processes – shared in principle by both research programmes – is in fact often interpreted along different lines.

On the one hand, evolutionary theories – in keeping with their largely microeconomic orientation – have directed most of their attention to specific organisational forms and organisational routines. There is, of course, ready acceptance of the underlying institutional foundations of the latter, but so far not much attention has been paid to the nature of institutions as such, with the exception of the specific institutions supporting technological change and 'national systems of innovation'. (Cf. Lundvall, 1992; Freeman, 1995; Nelson, 1993; however, for more general discussions see Nelson and Sampat, 1998, and Part V of Dosi, 2000.)

Conversely, *régulation* theory has attempted since its origins to identity some basic *macro* institutions capable of shaping markets' dynamics and agents' behaviour in ways yielding 'virtuous circles' of accumulation and growth (Aglietta, 1976; Boyer and Mistral, 1981). In this perspective, at least in work published in the 1980s, the style of analysis is far more *holistic,* going from historically dominant institutions to the archetypal behaviour of institution-specific 'representative agents', e.g. the 'Fordist firm', the 'Keynesian state', etc., even if many 'typologies' emphasise different 'variants' of a given dominant form.

These differences in focus of the two approaches reveal, in fact, somewhat symmetrical difficulties and challenges. With regard to *régulation* theory, the overwhelming emphasis on the internal consistency conditions of discrete types of socio-economic structures typified as 'regimes of accumulation' makes it somewhat difficult to account for transitions between one regime and another, linked as they are with *micro*economic changes in organisational forms (Coriat, 1990; Coriat and Weinstein, 1995). Moreover, the focus on 'regularities' shaped by a given set of institutions in a given regime offers a difficult account of the essential *diversity* underlying competition and economic change, even in an invariable *régulation* regime.

Evolutionary theory faces almost the opposite difficulty. How can micro-investigations on the formation and development of elementary routines, technologies, etc., be linked with broader, inevitably more 'macro'-analyses of evolution in the very long term and the specific institutional arrangements all that entails? How does one account for the long-term co-evolution of technologies, routines, forms of corporate organisations and institutions? Despite different points of departure, it is clear here where the two research programmes present strong actual or possible complementarities.

Indeed, one possible area of convergence is the search for (unorthodox!) microeconomic foundations of macroeconomics. In regulationist terms this question involves the *identification of micro-behaviours* to support each *régulation* regime or to open the way to new 'regularities' during a period of transition between one 'regime of accumulation' and the next. This applies in general and in particular with reference to the painstaking contemporary explorations for 'post-Fordist' combinations of new organisational forms, new technologies and yet-to-be-explored forms of institutional governance (Boyer and Durand, 1997; Taddei and Coriat, 1993).

Another crucial issue concerns the very nature of organisational arrangements, organisational behaviour and individual behaviour within organisations of various kinds (e.g. as workers, citizens, investors, consumers, etc.).

It was mentioned earlier that both evolutionary and *régulation* approaches share the idea that a good deal of individual and collective behaviour is 'bounded rational', context-dependent (the agents act largely from 'habit') and relatively inert over time, shaped as they are by the equally inert institutions in which they are embedded.

Moreover, both approaches share the view that a good deal of the reproduction of the socio-economic fabric rests on the development and implementation of organisational routines. However, as is discussed at much greater length in Coriat and Dosi (1998), most organisational routines involve a dual nature. On the one hand, they store and reproduce problem-solving competence, while they also act as mechanisms of governance of potentially conflicting relations. As it happens, the evolutionary approach has focused almost exclusively on the 'cognitive' aspects of routines (by so doing it has opened interesting avenues of dialogue with disciplines such as cognitive psychology and artificial intelligence), but it has largely neglected the dimensions of power and control intertwined in the routines themselves, a field extensively covered by the *régulation* approach in its analysis of work organisation. Thus whilst the *régulation* approach has tended to emphasise the requirements of social coherence implied by routines, it has not paid much attention to their knowledge content.

This may suffice as a first approximation but it is clearly unsatisfactory as an end result for either approach. Pushing it to extremes, in the former perspective, an answer to the question of 'how Renault (or GM or United Biscuits . . .) behaves' is inclined to account for operating procedures, mechanisms of knowledge accumulation, learning strategies, and so on. This leaves in the shadows phenomena such as the conflict between different social groups, the links of particular organisational rules with income distribution and the exercise of power (well beyond knowledge content). Conversely, by putting most of the emphasis on the latter phenomena, the regulationist answer tends to convey the idea that governance is the paramount role of routines, irrespective of the fact that Renault or GM have to know how to produce cars and United Biscuits cakes, and they have got to do it well, and improve over time. The risks of one-sided accounts are particularly acute when accounting for the *origins* of routines themselves, with an evolutionary inclination to trace them back to cognitive dynamics only, and regulationists feeling too comfortable with a reduction of the problem to a selection of dynamics among well specified menus of actions/strategies/conventions.

In Coriat and Dosi (1998) we argue that the dual nature of routines and, in conjunction, their double origin, are challenging points of encounter between the evolutionary and institutionalist research programmes.

Some conclusions

Notwithstanding a series of important analytical issues – which may indeed be a source of serious interpretative conflict, and some illustrations of which have been provided – there is an ideal sequence of modes of interpretation and levels of description in which both the evolutionary and regulationist programmes could ambitiously fit. As discussed at greater length in Coriat and Dosi (1998), these run from a sort of 'nano-economics' – wherein the abandonment of any belief in the magic of a perfect and invariant rationality forces a dialogue with cognitive and social psychology, organisation theory and sociology – all the way to grand historical conjectures on the long term destinies of contemporary forms of socio-economic organisation. Even a quick evaluation of the state of the art highlights enormous gaps between what we know and what such an ideal evolutionary-institutionalist research programme would demand. These gaps are wide at all levels, but in our view four issues are particularly urgent for the agenda.

A first issue concerns co-evolutionary processes. The essence of the co-evolutionary point is that what happens in each partly autonomous domain of the socio-economic system (for example, technology or institutional structures) shapes and constrains what is going to happen in others. Hence the overall dynamics is determined by the way each domain evolves but also by the ways the various domains are connected with each other.

Co-evolutionary issues appear at all levels of interpretation. For example, the emergence and development of each industry ought to be seen as a co-evolutionary process between technologies, corporate organisation and supporting institutions (Nelson, 1993). Analogously, the origins of organisational routines (cf. above) are a closely co-evolutionary process, shaped by diverse and probably conflicting selection criteria, that is, problem-solving versus governance requirements (Coriat, 2000).

A second, related item that is high on the research agenda refers to the transition across different socio-economic regimes of growth: for example, at which level can such a transition be detected? What are the effects of 'higher-level' changes (for example, in institutional set-ups or in the policy environment) on microeconomic behaviour? And, conversely, under what circumstances does non-average micro-behaviour become 'auto-catalytic' and eventually induce higher-level phase transitions? What kind of co-evolutionary processes do particular classes of transition entail?

A third priority item, in our view, concerns what could summarily be called the relationships between emergence and embeddedness, or, to put it another way, the role of 'bottom-up' processes shaping/generating higher-level entities (or at least aggregate statistical patterns) versus 'top-down' processes by which higher-level entities (for example, institutions, established mechanisms of interaction, etc.) shape/generate 'lower-level' behaviour. One of the claims underlying this entire chapter is that the link works both ways and that the 'macro-foundations of the micro' ought to be taken into account as well. But how does one get beyond suggestive metaphors and elaborate, more rigorous, albeit highly simplified models that nonetheless capture the intuition? Note that what we mean is some-thing more than feedback between a system-level state variable (for instance, a price or market share) and the argument of an individual algo-rithm (for instance, pricing or investment rules). At a somewhat deeper level, we believe it is possible to develop models in which micro decision algorithms themselves are shaped by macro-states and, conversely, possibly non-linear interactions among agents change collective interaction rules/constraints/opportunities.

Fourth, we suggest that the nature of learning processes, too, deserves priority attention. A crucial task here is to account for the formation and collective establishment of cognitive categories, problem-solving proce-dures (routines?) and expectations about the identities and behaviour of social actors.

Needless to say, these are enormous tasks. In a nutshell, they demand nothing short of sound institutionalist analyses robustly coupled with equally sound micro-founded accounts of learning, market interactions, adaptation and innovation.

41 Conventions and *régulation*

Olivier Favereau

In the 1990s *régulation* theory and convention theory can be seen as two institutionalist research programmes which, despite their differences, are similar and involved in the same project of exploring the uncertain future of a resurgence of the institutionalist tradition.

Any system of rules with some coherence (manifested in different ways) will be referred to here as an 'institution'. By 'institutionalism' we mean any research philosophy in economic theory characterised by two principles. First, regular micro- or macroeconomic patterns can be causally connected with the systems of institutional rules that organise transactions. Second, the theoretical model is used to explain the system of institutional rules itself. In a word, institutions are essential, endogenous variables. The discussion therefore centres on the similarities and differences between *régulation* theory and convention theory within the institutionalist movement.

The method: new economic theories or renewal of economic theory?

One similarity between *régulation* theory and convention theory (CT) is that they are both a critique of 'standard theory' (ST) and 'extended standard theory' (EST). These labels refer to current transformations of the dominant 'neoclassical' theory (Favereau, in Dupuy *et al.*, 1989). Standard theory reduces rationality to constrained optimising and deals with the co-ordination only through market prices. It is a general equilibrium theory, stemming from Walras.

Extended standard theory agrees with and emphasises this reduction of rationality to constrained optimisation, and extends the arena of choice available to economic agents to the contractual devices of their interactions. Any effective organisational rule can be deduced from a dynamic game in which it provides the non-co-operative solution.

Régulation theory totally rejects this explanation of institutional forms, which ascribes too great a role to individual rationality and obscures social relations. Convention theory also rejects it, on the basis that the cognitive resources with which economic agents are endowed are unrealistic, or because the properties and mechanisms of institutional forms are closely linked with the limits of individual rationality (Simon, 1983). An associated similarity is systematic openness to other social sciences – an approach that is unheard of in mainstream economics.

That said, *régulation* theory and convention theory differ from mainstream economics through opposing methods. This source of difference is not just theoretical. *Régulation* theory's critique is fundamentally external, while convention theory's is deliberately internal – hence the fallacious but quite understandable impression that convention theory is simply a hypocritical variation of the neoclassical tradition. A simple characterisation of convention theory's research programme is the equation:

CT = EST + Bounded rationality

Despite its extreme simplicity, this characterisation is acceptable because the founding insight of proponents of convention theory is that the direct and indirect consequences of conversion to a 'realist' (rather than 'instrumentalist'; Friedman, 1953) methodology in terms of individual rationality would be devastating for the orthodox construct. This is especially the case in that methodological individualism must now recognise the existence and strategic importance of collective objects for individual rationality.

Beyond the 'internal/external' distinction, *régulation* theory's aim is to construct a new economic theory as an alternative to orthodoxy; in other words, to change economic theories. Convention theory has a different philosophy in that years of experience have shown that any attempts to refound economic theory by a complete rejection of the prevailing dominant orthodoxy have failed. The ability to adapt and renew the orthodoxy is always tied to contesting and reforming critical heterodoxies. The aim of convention theory is therefore to provoke a change in the language of theoretical economics (enabling it to speak effectively about institutional phenomena), a task which, by definition, is collective and implies extensive critical collaboration. It would therefore be a poor critique of convention theory to reproach it for lacking an explicit conventionalist theory of inflation or unemployment, for example, since this reproach turns back on itself. Are we to believe that the hypothesis of bounded rationality has no effect on the validity of the mainstream theses concerning inflation or unemployment? To argue either way is to enter the logic of convention theory.

A similar difference is found in relation to openness to other social sciences. This openness is one instrument among others for *régulation* theory in its extensive use of history. It is not depreciatory to refer to this feature, since such instrumentality is, after all, an innovation when compared with the traditional attitudes of economists, and is a radical critique of them. The openness of convention theory has this function incidentally, especially in the cognitive sciences. However, its primary inspiration is very different: economists involved in convention theory view problems in economics in a way which suggests that other social sciences deal with the same problems using different terms and approaches. The classic issue of co-ordinating economic activities is linked with the founding question of sociology and political philosophy, that is, production and co-operation between beings endowed with reason and which are therefore autonomous. Where economists examine conditions of equilibrium, sociologists and political philosophers study ways of reaching an equitable and legitimate agreement.

There is therefore a second way into convention theory, not by way of dominant economic theory, but through other social sciences. But does it mean giving up economics in favour of these other disciplines? Not necessarily: the economist's discovery of his relation to sociology and philosophy colleagues leads him to review their results in the light of the discovery. This involves a shift from a logic of explanation to a logic of understanding, where the observer reconstructs mental representations of the observed subject. Consequently, this second route to convention theory can be roughly condensed in the equation:

$$CT = \text{Co-operation in sociology/Justice in political philosophy}$$
$$+ \text{Understanding}$$

To conclude, the convention theory research programme would not have been possible without the 'cognitive' and 'interpretative' turns within the social sciences.

The research that best illustrates these two aspects in convention theory is that of Jean Pierre Dupuy (1992). He traces the difficulties and internal contradictions of the standard theory of rationality and demonstrates the great difficulty, or impossibility, of deducing collective objects from the individual behaviour found in standard rationality. Laurent Thévenot (Boltanski and Thévenot, 1991) made the important discovery that it is well worth reinterpreting major works of sociology and philosophy as economic works, and vice versa.

But that is not all. A careful examination of areas of difference reveals that *régulation* theory and convention theory are not theoretical constructions at the same logical level. This implies the possibility of solidarity.

It is possible that the same type of reasoning is at work in John Rawls's theory of justice, Robert Boyer's version of the theory of Fordism and the theory of markets in Peter Doeringer and Michael Piore's work (Favereau, 1994b). In each instance there is implicit or explicit analysis of institutional rules to construct a socio-economic sphere that combines efficiency and equity, so long as they are viewed as evolving phenomena: productivity gains on the one hand, increased income on the other.

With some elaboration of the theoretical universe it is also possible to show that these three aspects are in fact a single form of reasoning. This is the 'non-standard theory' universe to which convention theory contributes. Two areas of research emerge: one is the conception of rules as a heuristic device to resolve co-ordination difficulties, and the other a conception of organisations as devices converting individual learning into collective learning.

This undertaking, which is no doubt uncertain, even hazardous, nevertheless has the advantage of revealing two developments. The first is from RT1(similar to the Marxist analysis of the capitalist mode of production) to RT2 (separate from this analysis and based on dynamic aspects of institutional forms). The other is from CT1 (centred on the coherence of complete modes of co-ordination) to CT2 (oriented towards learning dynamics associated with a given institutional whole).

Microeconomics: organised agent or collective actor?

While (extended) standard theory stipulates that individuals pursue their own self-interest (which may imply following rules), convention theory and *régulation* theory claim that individuals primarily follow rules (which does not mean that they are not thereby also pursuing their self-interest).

This fundamental proposition is not in fact stated explicitly in either *régulation* theory or convention theory. However, it is fairly clear in both cases: *régulation* theory's institutional forms would be meaningless if they did not translate into rules and regular behaviour patterns. The concept of rules is omnipresent in convention theory's entry through 'bounded rationality' (Reynaud, 1992; Favereau, 1993a, re-reading Doeringer and Piore), while it is rare in convention theory's entry through 'social sciences'. For convention theory a crucial feature of bounded rationality (which is distinctly different from standard rationality) is that it includes concern to co-ordinate with others. Rules are a natural manifestation of this involvement, and are the first illustration of the production of collective objects in methodological individualism, as revisited and corrected by convention theory.

The importance of this fundamental suggestion is shown in the theory of the firm. If there is one place where rules are followed it is in the firm, even if *régulation* theory emphasises work organisation rules and convention theory focuses on demands for coherence between personnel management, production techniques and product quality. This coherence is based on 'company models' (Eymard-Duvernay, 1987) or 'production worlds' (Salais and Storper, 1994) which are the simple, combined expression of the co-ordination models referred to above.

This area of similarity should be qualified, since *régulation* theory identifies rules via macroeconomics and convention theory via microeconomics. *Régulation* theory's 'institutional forms' are the 'codifying of one or several fundamental social relations' (Boyer, 1991), and agents reproduce these social relations by conforming to them. But does that mean that it is necessarily a classic 'top-down' holistic approach? Close examination of models of Fordism and its crisis instead suggest a surprising valorising of 'intermediary institutions' (Aglietta, 1992b). Collective negotiation in the branch is the fundamental place of *régulation* for *régulation* theory, no doubt agreeing with a clear understanding of Keynesian issues.

This then fits together. The view of rules as 'institutional forms' matches the creation of collective actors (especially trade unions and employers' associations) validated by state rules. Exogenous intervention from a higher level is in fact required, since a collective actor cannot determine both the rules that govern it and those it lays down, once it has been created. *Régulation* theory's theory of rules thus assigns a major role to collective actors and the law. The justification is far better, however, for RT1 than for RT2.

Convention theory's point of view appears to be exactly the opposite. Convention theory's aim is to construct a microeconomics of 'understanding' (in contrast to (extended) standard theory's microeconomics of 'explanation'). This difference is clearly reflected in the key term of each research programme: *régulation* points to the priority of the system over its elements; 'convention' takes the foreground in the search for agreement – which nevertheless implies at least three terms, two individuals and a point of intersection. The canonical situation studied closely by André Orléan (1987), Eymard-Duvernay (1987) and Favereau (1993b) always leads to an interpretation of concepts of rationality (individual) and co-ordination (inter-individual). Despite the unpredictability of the future (or rather because of it), co-operation can arise between non-altruistic rational economic agents if the involvement of agents in an incomplete contractual schema suiting all strategic operations reflects a serious intention to co-operate, precisely because economic agents recognise themselves as rational and non-altruistic.

The intention to co-operate is formed according to a reduced model of the social contract (which can be analysed in Boltanski and Thévenot's *cités* or in the parallel development of efficiency and equity in Rawls, Boyer and Doeringer and Piore). The social contract can be employed to decipher the partner's reactions during unexpected events that inevitably arise. This deciphering could produce the 'tests' studied by Boltanski and Thévenot, and resolve itself in confirmed participation or in the contesting ('voice') and desertion ('exit') studied by Albert Hirschman (1970).

It must therefore be concluded that there is a contrasting mechanism in the genesis of rules, at least for RT1 and CT1. In the first case they are temporary armistices of class warfare, while in the second they represent a partial co-operation agreement between agents with bounded rationality. This is a source of agreement not only between RT2 and CT2, but also between RT1 and CT1.

It is therefore very paradoxical that the most extreme forms of *régulation* theory and convention theory, that is, RT1 and CT1, are bound to each other. If *régulation* theory aspires to be more than a functionalist specification of a larger version of the Marxist theory of reproduction, it must adopt a theory of change for 'institutional forms'. As a compromise between collective actors with conflicting interests, unless there is internal theoretical contradiction, these institutional forms will change not to ensure the reproduction of the capitalist mode of production but only because it is in the selfish, local interest of the actors involved. In other words, RT1 needs a microeconomics of understanding, as developed by CT1. Conversely, convention theory needs *régulation* theory (and even RT1) if, true to its research programme, it wishes to analyse the agreements (especially compromises) that are most likely to have a general effect.

Nevertheless, the most fruitful interactions are between RT2 and CT2. In an examination of mechanisms for creating collective actors, the conventionalist concept of an organised agent is very useful. Collective decision making and representation structures are objects used by economic agents to co-ordinate with one another, when they are acknowledged as having a degree of legitimacy. The legitimacy of a collective actor can be measured by how willing economic agents are to 'lend' it intentions with which they identify (Dennett, 1990).

Compromise is a key concept for convention theory as well as for *régulation* theory. All compromises involve a co-operative and non-co-operative aspect, an element of trust and an element of suspicion.

Macroeconomics: co-ordination or reproduction?

An area common to convention theory and *régulation* theory is the fact that in both research programmes institutions produce real effects. For *régulation* theory it is wrong to see institutions as belonging to the superstructure, to use Marx's terminology. According to convention theory, standard theory and extended standard theory are wrong to allow an influence to institutional relations (which are in fact contract-based) only in so far as they lead to moving away from the first-best optimum. It is necessary to go even further: the real 'positive' effect of institutions is dynamic (regular growth, for RT2; collective learning, for CT2). This suggests an original proposition in the field of theoretical economic research: institutions produce a social dynamics, and hence institutions are unintelligible without reference to a social dynamics.

A second similarity is that convention theory and *régulation* theory agree that in theoretical modelling institutional rules must have constraint status if a sufficiently short time scale is adopted (even through convention theory emphasises the margin of interpretation surrounding all rules, even laws). If the time horizon is sufficiently distant they must have the status of fully fledged endogenous variables.

Can this agreement about the dual nature of dynamics extend to the *régulation* theory thesis about the duality of crises? It cannot, and this is where a major disagreement arises. The set of constraints alluded to above form a system in *régulation* theory, which is the capitalist mode of production. Regulationist macroeconomics is without question a macroeconomics of reproduction for RT1. What about convention theory? A false symmetry would suggest matching 'reproduction' with 'co-ordination'. But that makes no sense: if convention theory emphasises the limits of individual rationality at the microeconomic level so strongly, it can only imply recognition of non-co-ordination at the macroeconomic level. Conventionalist macroeconomics is a macroeconomics of diversity.

Convention theory has studied this topic extensively. Research by Eymard-Duvernay into business firm models, and by Salais-Storper into production worlds, is mentioned above. With respect to the question of diversity of rules in wage formation (an awkward issue for *régulation* theory), it is appropriate to add the theoretical and empirical research of Bénédicte Reynaud and the working hypothesis (typical of CT2) suggested by Favereau (1993a). An important consequence of this macroeconomics of diversity is a new perspective on the efficiency of economic policy (Eymard-Duvernay *et al.*, 1994; Bessy, 1993). Business firms have very different approaches to national policies on employment, and local 'executants' of these measures in fact have a creative function owing to the need to interpret general texts in their application to a specific context. This point is often neglected in references *régulation* theory makes to the law. In the future it should prove to be a productive area of interaction between convention theory and RT2.

Although the important differences between a macroeconomics of reproduction and a macroeconomics of diversity should not be underestimated, it is important to recognise the blind alleys in which both may be locked.

The shift from RT1 to RT2, which has not been extensively theorised by regulationists (prior to this book), threatens *régulation* theory's macroeconomic project. If the umbilical cord to the Marxian theory of value is cut, the definition of social relations codified by 'institutional forms' is brought into question. To put it bluntly, there are no more social classes, there are only pressure groups. Likewise, convention theory faces the risk that the macroeconomics of diversity is in fact a non-macroeconomics. However, it is possible to envisage a way out for both, for two reasons.

The first reason is simply that economic agents are not indifferent to macroeconomics. Some data can serve as public indicators (for example, the unemployment rate or the growth rate) for judging the overall situation, and especially for evaluating the probability that the interdependence created by payment conventions will result either in greater respect for conventions (a situation which is more plainly called economic growth) or, at times of greater difficulty and even impossibility, in satisfying it (a situation referred to as 'systemic risk' for the financial community) (Aglietta, 1993; Cartelier, 1990). What is the macroeconomic result of microeconomic rules of the game? Growth, stagnation or crisis? A suitable concept of 'equilibrium' suggests itself in response and is defined as follows: the equilibrium of rules, namely intervals of variation in the unemployment and growth rate for which rules of adjustment to disequilibria, which are legitimate, are not questioned (Thévenot and Favereau, 1995).

The second reason relates to the internal structure of aggregate results. It is here that diversity plays an analytical role. Macroeconomic trajectories must also be evaluated in terms of stability or the lack of it in the statistical distribution of relevant variables (for example, household income or business firm size). These arguments clarify underdevelopment both as a deadlock in collective learning (Favereau, 1995a) and competitive relations (Biencourt *et al.*, 1994).

Since the combination of these two elements is equally interesting for RT2 and CT2, it does not so much lead us away from Marx as bring us closer to the classical economists. The distribution of income reveals the game rules of society, and social groups are identified through the rules by which they take their share of national income. What sort of growth regime produces the rules? A pessimistic diagnosis calls for society to transform itself, while respecting the principles of a democratic state. This was the research programme of economists at the end of the eighteenth century and in the early nineteenth century; it may be that of the beginning of the twenty-first century as well.

42 Is *régulation* theory an original theory of economic institutions?

Robert Boyer

To conclude this panorama of research, it may be useful to measure the distance covered since the programme outlined by an earlier work of synthesis (Boyer, 1986) and the Barcelona colloquium (*Économie et Sociétés,* 1989, 1990). The proposal was to undertake new case studies in order to extend *régulation* theory's area, to formalise the macroeconomic mechanisms underlying Fordism and to investigate again the origins of major crises. This programme of research led to an analysis of crises in real time and made an appeal for a more assertive contribution to the theory and history of economic institutions.

Many different analytical methods confirm the impact of institutions

Case studies undertaken in many countries (Japan, Scandinavia, newly industrialised countries in South East Asia, etc.) did reveal the existence of different national trajectories. This supported the hypothesis of extensive variation in institutional forms, as well as an emphasis on variations in performance linked with different modes of *régulation* (Chapter 30).

The 1980s and 1990s also experienced a re-emergence of dynamism in financial innovation (Aglietta, 1986a, 1995; Aglietta *et al.*, 1990; Boyer, 1999a), the active diffusion of market mechanisms (Boyer, 1995a), and the importance of forms of competition in the dynamics of technical change (Petit, 1998a). In other words, while the rapid rise of Fordism was based fundamentally on a precise codifying of the wage–labour nexus, in the 1990s finance appeared to govern the dynamics of other institutional forms. This includes the wage–labour nexus, implying a significant change in the hypotheses on which a stabilised growth regime is based (Boyer and Durand, 1998).

The fact that financial, technical and organisational innovations now go beyond national frontiers presents *régulation* theory with two questions. As a result of privileging analyses of institutional forms on a national basis, has it neglected the more international aspects of the division of labour (Robles, 1994), and hence accumulation? Consequently, what autonomy does the nation state still have for implementing strategies for overcoming the crisis (Drache and Gertler, 1991; Drache and Boyer, 1995)? Similarly, can local (Benko and Lipietz, 1992, 1999) and sector-based organisational forms (Allaire and Boyer, 1994) explain increasing national competitiveness? This is one of the difficult areas of work opened in the 1990s (Part IV) which must now be explored.

From a more methodological perspective, research has suggested formalisations, often borrowed from game theory, that show how rules, conventions and even institutions emerge from the strategic interaction of agents (Boyer and Orléan, 1991; Lesourne, 1991; Orléan, 1994). This provides a theoretical and direct justification for the impact of institutions on the economy, as well as their total dependence on the prevailing mode of *régulation* (Corneo, 1993; Greenan and Guellec, 1992; Boyer, 1999a).

Furthermore, an individual organisation, such as a union, can have very different objectives, means and consequences, depending on its context and country (Boyer, 1995b). Conversely, very different organisational forms may play an identical role, in spite of their name or official function. Such is the case, for example, in professional training, which is organised differently in Germany, Japan and Sweden, yet fulfils the same function of continuously improving skills and knowledge in economies with high value added and high wages (Boyer and Durand, 1997). This demands rigour and precision in analysing economic institutions.

The endogenous shift from growth to crisis

Endogenous structural change is one of the distinctive features of *régulation* theory. In neoclassical approaches a succession of random shocks propel economic dynamics, so that a structural crisis can arise only from the divorce of an organisational form and destabilising external disturbances. This can be seen, for example, in the effect of the oil shocks on productivity trends. *Régulation* theory agrees that these factors are involved, but also believes that they have no claim to be the exclusive cause. Since the emergence of industrial capitalism, the accumulation process launches expansion phases, but usually also provokes a reversal, since cumulative disequilibria appear from within the system, in an endogenous manner. In some cases they can be reabsorbed by the established mode of *régulation* – these are minor crises – while in others it sets off a destabilisation process of an institutional form and then of the general architecture ensuring their coherence.

It is not easy to keep this insight rigorous, since the illusions of language mask difficult methodological problems. An application of techniques of the non-linear dynamic to regulationist models offered a precise definition of just what a structural crisis is (Lordon, 1993a, b, 1997a). It was possible to draw up a classification involving a shift from 'high' equilibrium to 'low' equilibrium, transition through catastrophe, alteration in the cyclical pattern, and transition from regular to chaotic evolution (Chapter 23). This is a useful counterpoint to the fashion that reduces macroeconomics to analyses of the impact of a set of random shocks operating on a linear model, with a very poor dynamic and limited economic content. In actual analysis endogenous determinist dynamics, random shocks and conflict are combined in the explanation of the move from growth to crisis. The advantage of *régulation* theories is that they are a reminder that stochastic aspects alone do not suffice.

The transformation from one mode of *régulation* to the next: a subtle alchemy?

The research assembled in this volume suggests that these transformations are not an easy, automatic transition between two well defined equilibria. Instead, conflicts, strategic behaviour and political intervention play a crucial role. Hence a difficult methodological problem: should researchers wait for the dust of history to settle and for conflicts to give rise to a new institutional architecture, or can they provide some general results of elements governing this process? In the first alternative, they will be accused of being scholars *post factum*, in other words, describing rather than theorising. In the second case, their ambition to grasp the laws of history will be denounced as a hopelessly Promethean task: once upon a time Leninist Marxism tried – and failed.

Between these two extremes is research into the processes of overcoming structural crises, which is important because it makes a theoretical development of founding notions and tools of analysis necessary.

1   Any analysis of future modes of *régulation* presumes sufficiently general formalisations to enable an analysis not only of extensive growth, but also of intensive growth, without mass consumption, as well as Fordism and historically unprecedented regimes. In parallel, international comparisons, for example including Japan, have stressed the originality of some of the modes of *régulation* that have appeared since the 1970s. In particular, mass consumption may be a process that does not presume an *a priori* contract codifying productivity sharing (Boyer, 1992c; Ebizuka *et al.*, 1997).

2   It is easier to identify the complex processes of emerging from a crisis through a historical analysis of previous periods, for example the Great Depression of the inter-war period. Consequently, the conjunction of individual strategies, even early precursors, as in the case of Henry Ford's $5 a day, are not enough to propel an economy from one mode of co-ordination to the next (Boyer and Orléan, 1991, 1992, 1994). As it happens, collective actors, public intervention, laws and collective conventions eventually brought about the shift to Fordism, but through institutional arrangements that were quite the opposite of those imag-

ined by Henry Ford (Boyer and Orléan, 1991). Once again, it is important to stress how the mode of *régulation* that eventually emerges is largely unintentional, since the compatibility of a group of compromises, which are naturally partial or sector-based, is basically ensured *ex post* (Chartres, 1995).

3   Finally, it is necessary to examine the reasons why the crisis of Fordism which began in the United States in the late 1960s lasted far longer than the Great Depression of the 1930s. The enquiries of *régulation* theory point to an important insight: the interdependence and complementarity of contemporary institutional forms* explain why it is so difficult to synchronise their overall transformation. In contrast, the compromises encouraging growth during the Golden Age were part of claims by social groups or related to long term structural changes. Furthermore, in this context the relative flexibility of market relations was not an obstacle to an institutionalisation of the fundamental social relations that favour the emergence of a new mode of development.

This is why even though regulationist research makes no claims to predict the future the real-time analysis of the crisis of Fordism, reconsideration of the Great Depression of the 1930s and the theory of modes of development open new perspectives for developing and refining the founding concepts presented in this volume. It is significant that similarities with convention theory have been drawn in this field (Salais and Storper, 1994; Orléan, 1994). This is the early stage of a theory of organisational forms, conventions and institutions.

The results obtained, which are still provisional, can be summarised in six main statements.

Markets need a complete institutional network to be effective

Until recent years, economists believed they knew what a market was (Bourdieu, 1997): many viewed the general market of general equilibrium theory and the definitions of actual decentralised market mechanisms as a continuum. Unfortunately, modern microeconomics has shown that these two conceptions are not at all the same, and that it is therefore impossible to extrapolate the two welfare theorems to market economies that really exist (Boyer, 1997).

Régulation theory emphasises the fact that markets are not self-established, in so far as their daily operation presumes a complete network of rules and external enforcers to ensure honest transactions. It is also necessary for third party organisations or regulations to define quality criteria for each market and for there to be an authority to determine which actors can enter the market (otherwise it would be destroyed by opportunistic behaviour on the part of agents for whom it is rational to be dishonest).

Similarly a monetary system has to guarantee future payments in a juridical context which allows legal sanctions for failure to pay, etc.

In other words, *régulation* theory emphasises the fact that the market is one institution among others, rather than an alternative to an economy without institutions. Without a legal system, the state's power of coercion, a well organised system of payments, a codifying of the quality and rules of entry, markets cannot function effectively.

The state is not only predatory, it can also be developmentalist

Just as it is important to distinguish the market in general from its various configurations, the state is also manifested through a mass of interventions and forms, so that it would be wrong to maintain a dichotomy between the state and the market as two alternative co-ordination mechanisms. Neither of these pure forms can exist alone, nor is it possible *a priori* to award either of them the palm for efficiency at all times and places. *Régulation* theory concludes that the ratio of these two principles of economic action depends on the context – in other words, the economy and period considered.

Public choice theory has propagated the notion that the state is naturally inefficient, since administrators in charge of promoting the general interest in fact pursue their own private interests, to the detriment of the community they claim to serve. But this is to forget the determining role the state can have – even in the hands of bureaucrats – in implementing the rules of the game (law, police). Such is all the more the case in the supply of collective services that it alone can provide. The state may have a longer term horizon; it has to correct positive and negative externalities that result from the conjunction of private strategies; it has a role in preserving the social link, based on principles that the generalisation of purely market relations tends to destroy. No doubt Karl Polanyi's (1946) message is still worthy of consideration today (Hollingsworth and Boyer, 1997).

There are some cases in which adequate public intervention has encouraged the adoption of a more efficient growth regime than any that would have resulted from trusting pure market mechanisms (Wade, 1990). France during the Golden Age, Japan and by extension the newly industrialised countries suggest that it is less the size of the state that governs growth performance than its ability to promote the emergence of institutional forms and support for an adequate accumulation regime. This message still stands in the design of development strategies (Boyer, 1999c) and clarifies our understanding of the transformation difficulties of Soviet-type economies (Chavance, 1997; Sapir, 1998).

There are various forms of co-ordination alternatives to state and market

But there is a third, even more important, conclusion that modifies the canonical opposition between state and market in economic theory. On this point *régulation* theory joins the teachings of neo-corporatist analyses, especially developments since 1980 (Schmitter, 1990). Sociological and historical research on economic institutions (Hollingsworth *et al.*, 1994) yields a classification that is very close to the principles of co-ordination, bridging political and economic spheres (Hollingsworth and Boyer, 1997). Besides the market and the state, already discussed, these enquiries suggest four other intermediary forms (Figure 42.1).

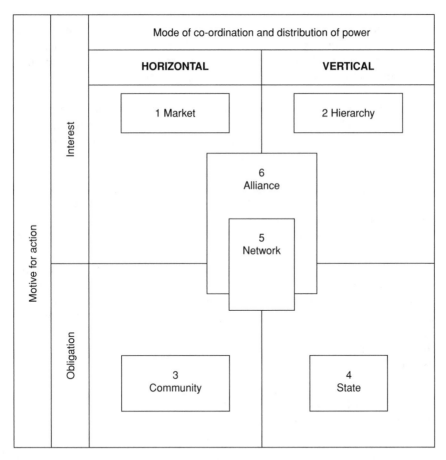

Figure 42.1 Synopsis of different modes of co-ordination and institutional arrangements

1   *Alliances* are a mode of governance maintained initially through the agreement of the parties concerned while also operating in the sphere of economic logic, just like the market. Their advantage is that they share the uncertainties associated, for example, with new technologies.
2   *Private hierarchies*, as found in large vertically integrated firms, are another form whose role has increased continuously throughout capitalism's long history. They optimise production and transaction cost dynamics, as well as encouraging some forms of innovation.
3   *Communities* group together communes, clans, districts and clubs, establishing a form of cohesion that derives from the adherence of actors to valuable rules of the game at the small group level. Their main advantage is linked with establishing trust, which is necessary for most modern economic activities.
4   *Networks* are made up of professional associations, unions and private interest governance bodies, in other words, the dismemberment of some of the traditional activities of a centralised state. Constructed in the field of social relations (family, group, etc.) these networks can also be used in economic competition and innovation.

The somewhat simplistic dichotomy between market and state reflects a classification based on two criteria. First, motives for action, in other words, self-interest privileged by economists or the sense of obligation that sociologists bring to the fore, and, second, horizontal and egalitarian aspects versus hierarchical, unequal aspects of co-ordination processes. Furthermore, it is apparent that each of these institutional arrangements requires particular conditions, and generally shows as many strengths as weaknesses. There is therefore no *a priori* optimal arrangement, whatever the configuration of the problem. Empirical observation and comparative studies largely endorse this.

A final advantage of this classification should be stressed. Institutional arrangements ensure a bridge from the micro to the macro and vice versa, since they operate at an intermediate level between actors and the economic system viewed from a more general level. *Régulation* theory concepts can be used in analysing operating regimes* at the sector level and not just the macroeconomic level. The initial insights of sector analysis are thus extended to more general use (Chapters 24 and 27).

Institution, organisation, convention, routine . . . necessary clarification

The explosion in institutionalist research in the 1990s was often founded on a contract between market and institution, with the implication that anything that is not a pure economic adjustment is an institution, obeying a single, supposedly non-market logic. Diversity in institutional adjustments has already disproved this hypothesis, but an additional stage is necessary, particularly since the aim is to identify the factors that shape the evolution of institutions.

A semantic clarification is therefore necessary. Research from the 1990s suggests a set of interrelated definitions and distinguishes six configurations that range from the most general to the most local (Table 42.1).

1   *The constitutional order* was introduced by political science (Sabel, 1997) and economic history (North, 1990) research, thus transforming the meaning given to it by Friedrich von Hayek (1973). Operating in the sphere of legitimacy and instituting deliberation, the constitutional order defines the rules making it possible to resolve conflicts between contradictory partial rationales. This is essentially a political and juridical process.

2   *Institutions* define a generally immaterial means that often appeals to the law of structuring interactions between organisations (and possibly individuals), so reducing the uncertainty associated with the deployment of many different strategic behaviours in a sphere that would be devoid of any rule. Institutions govern both the political and the economic spheres. Many historical studies suggest the significant dependence of institutions on the constitutional order (North, 1990). This research also offers a valuable lesson about the nature and functioning of markets (Fligstein, 1996).

3   *Organisations* are radically different from institutions, since an explicit power structure instigates a set of routines to co-ordinate individual strategies and control opportunistic behaviour within the boundaries of the organisation. This type of entity may be either a company or a non-profit organisation. Control processes and economic incentives are combined to ensure the coherence of each organisation. Thus the contrast between the firm and the market foregrounded by transaction cost theory (Coase, 1937) and contemporary derivatives (Williamson, 1975, 1985) is generalised.

4   *A routine* defines a rule of action obtained by converting frequently tacit skills into codified knowledge, which is thus transmissible and accessible to a group of agents belonging to the same organisation or facing the same problems. The principle of action is essentially cognitive and inter-individual, but immaterial; it distinguishes routine from habitus and organisations. The concept of routine was suggested by evolutionary theories, particularly to identify the nature of the firm as a set of routines and, by extension, skills (Nelson and Winter, 1982; Dosi and Salvatore, 1992; Chapter 40). The importance of this semantic clarification becomes clear here as an attempt to identify each theory precisely in relation to the type of problem posed.

5   *A convention* results from the frequently unintentional convergence of a set of expectations and interdependent behaviour, through a series of entirely decentralised interactions, with no explicit co-ordination

Table 42.1 The need for precise definitions of the various institutional entities

Nature / Component	Definition	Principle of action	Factors of change
Constitutional order	A set of *general rules* to settle lower level conflicts among institutions, organisations, individuals, implying heterogeneous rationales	*Legitimacy* via deliberation	Large inertia in democratic states Role of *political* process in redesign
Institution	An immaterial method of *structuring interactions* among organisations	Reduces or removes the *uncertainty* associated with strategic behaviour	Structural *crises* Low efficiency is not a *sufficient* reason for change
Organisation	A *structure of power and a set of routines* to overcome co-ordination failures among agents or control opportunistic behaviour	*Carrot* and *stick* (i.e. the pay and control system) are related to external institutions or conventions	Poor outcomes in the *competition* with other organisations Major crises trigger redesign
Routine	A set of *rules for actions* derived from the conversion *from tacit to codified knowledge* that can be shared by several actors belonging to the same entity	*Standardisation* makes complex processes simpler, allowing a *shared understanding and reaction*	Adverse *evolution of the environment* *Inconsistency* in a set of routines or shift from *technè to epistémé*
Convention	A *self-enforcing set of shared expectations and behaviour*, emerging from decentralised interactions	*Lost memory* of the origins of the convention which seems 'natural'	*General crisis, invasion, translation,* etc Efficiency is rarely a selection criterion
Habitus	A set of *embodied behaviour patterns*, forged during an individual's socialisation process	*Adaptation* to a given field; possible disequilibria out of this field	Shift to a new field of a habitus forged in another New *learning*, even if quite difficult

procedure. This process is therefore directly social and is not exclusively cognitive. Once established, the convention appears 'natural' to all agents involved, so that the forgotten origin of the convention is its principle of action. Conventionalist research is evident here, and its relation to *régulation* theory has already been emphasised (Favereau, 1989a, 1993b, 1997; Boltanski and Thévenot, 1991; Orléan, 1994; Salais and Storper, 1994). Unlike a routine, a convention cannot be easily exported outside its area of emergence. The dynamic of these two forms is consequently different *a priori*.

6   *The habitus* reflects the consequences of the socialisation process for the formation of representations and individual behaviour. It employs a key concept from the sociology of Pierre Bourdieu (1980), which is useful, since it demonstrates the possibility of a regular pattern in the behaviour of individuals from the same social group, apart from any explicit coercive or organisational forces. Thus the institutional order is incorporated in individuals (Douglas, 1986), which for economists implies that what they term preferences are not exogenous data but rather the result of previous interactions (Bowles, 1997). The *habitus* may be an essential ingredient of the viability of some institutional forms, such as the Japanese wage–labour nexus (the division of labour between the sexes) or the monetary regime implemented by the Bundesbank (the trauma of hyperinflation).

New research must restructure and widen the institutional forms of *régulation* theory on the basis of a combination of the 'elementary bricks' described above. This is a necessary stage in understanding the emergence, maturity, crisis and disappearance of different institutions.

Towards a theory of complementarity and institutional hierarchy

This question involves an examination of the conditions under which the conjunction of a set of institutional forms and modes of governance define a long term socio-economic evolutionary path. The neoclassical theory of institutions has a simple answer: the competitive mechanism ensures the spread of the most efficient institutions, since they will be imitated by worst placed firms, regions and nations. But the logical conclusion of this analysis is that central banks should have a status similar to the Bundesbank (to promote price stability), labour markets should have North American flexibility (to promote employment), internal organisation should be based on Japanese firms (to develop skills, the basis of product quality) and states should adopt a French administrative structure (which has, or used to have, a reputation for being relatively efficient in public management).

Régulation theory examines the viability of this type of combination of institutions whose rationales may conflict and eventually produce detrimental results. First, it ignores the fact that institutions are founded as a result of conflicts and specific national compromises. Second, the impact of the same organisational form may be favourable or unfavourable depending on its compatibility with other modes of co-ordination. If, for example, the principles of the Bundesbank were introduced to an economy that usually resolved conflicts over income distribution through inflation, then a rise in unemployment might be the penalty of a mismatched monetary and wage regime (Boyer *et al.*, 1994).

It is prudent, and no doubt more fruitful, to search for functional equivalents of the most efficient foreign institutions, in a subtle alchemy between old principles and the requirements of a new model, so as to obtain fairly similar results by very different means. Any institutional innovation begins a process of trial and error, so that a perfect replica of a foreign institution is rarely the point of equilibrium in the process. This theme is important in evolutionary theories, as well as in a variant of convention theory focused on learning through practice. This is the advantage of the concept of hybridisation, in the sense that new and old, native and cosmopolitan, social and economic are combined. Clearly this brings up the question of the principles and forces capable of ensuring the coherence of an institutional architecture. The observation of changes in the 1990s compared with the period of monopolistic *régulation* in the Fordist era suggested the need for new concepts in *régulation* theory. Originally the Fordist period was analysed as a fortunate but unexpected conjunction of a set of innovations, institutionalised compromises and institutional forms. On reflection, this explanation appeared simplistic and was supplemented by reference to four other processes.

1   *The co-evolution of institutions** acts on the model of what evolutionary theories formalise in terms of the technology and organisation of firms. Indeed, even if initially different institutional forms are not entirely adjusted to each other, the resulting developments introduce the elements of a reconfiguration. It penalises architectures that are incapable of reproducing founding institutionalised compromises and provides a minimum performance as identified in the related institutional architecture (Boyer and Orléan, 1991; Orléan, 1994; Boyer and Freyssenet, 2001). It is necessary, however, to emphasise that the market, and the competitive imperative that it instigates, are not applicable as such to the selection of and learning about institutional forms that evolve just as much under the influence of power relations as with economic performance. Furthermore, this process is extremely slow, as seen in British history and more generally by the long term lack of convergence between institutions (Berger and Dore, 1996).

2   *Institutional complementarity** governs the compatibility of two institutional forms and explains the frequency of their co-occurrence in

international comparisons, for example. In more precise terms, complementarity signifies that the conjunction of two institutional forms supplies an adaptability and performance that is superior to alternative configurations in which only one of the forms is present. Furthermore, actors may recognise *ex ante* the need for this complementarity and implement it even before an unfavourable evolution causes them to look for such a configuration. This mechanism therefore differs from the one that ultimately implies co-evolution, and many examples can be seen in historical studies. Thus the gold standard of the nineteenth century goes together with an atomised organisation of labour markets and a competitive wage–labour nexus. The contract-based nominal wage under the Fordist regime is associated with a credit economy in which the national money supply is endogenous and the constraints imposed by the international system are limited (Boyer, 1993).

3   *An institutional hierarchy** extends the notion of complementarity by linking it with the dominance of one institutional form over another, owing to the nature of political coalitions at the heart of institutionalised compromises, on which each regime is based. The adjustment of one institutional form to another is no longer linked with evolutionist trial-and-error processes or a miraculous compatibility to be discovered by actors. Rather it is linked with the interplay of power relations, implying the ability of some collective actors to generate restructuring compromises beyond their direct sphere of influence. To refer to two previous examples, the competitive *régulation* of the nineteenth century expressed the dominance of industrial capitalism, while post-Second World War monopolist *régulation* reflected the need for compromise with the wage-earning class, which had become an essential political force (Boyer, 1999a). The 1990s have seen the rise to power of internationalised financial capital, imposing its logic on the state (in search of credibility), the wage–labour nexus (subject to the flexibility imperative) and the monetary regime (responsible for economic and financial stability) (Aglietta, 1998).

4   *An economic paradigm** is the matrix through which economic representations are legitimised, and consequently also the hierarchy of institutions and institutional forms. This fourth mechanism extends the ideas and theories of the previous mechanism, which it justifies, particularly in economic policy discourse. In the contemporary period, it acts through beliefs and by incentives or constraints on behaviour (Lordon, 1997a; 1999). Thus in the 1960s, modernising political and economic coalitions were based on concepts of progress, catching up and growth. In contrast, the 1990s were marked by the victory of a culture of monetary stability, efficient markets and the power of shareholders. In this intellectual and ideological context, the hierarchy of institutional forms was redefined (Boyer, 1999a).

The originality of *régulation*'s tune in the institutionalist concert

At the beginning of the twenty-first century economists appear to be convinced of the importance of institutions, so that this theme, neglected for so long, has become the focus of many studies in most research programmes. This includes contract theories, the microeconomics of imperfect information, the transaction costs approach, an extension of game theory, and the analysis of relations between law and economics. What then is the source of the individuality of the regulationist programme? The previous reflections have outlined the basis of a response that calls for a few additional closing comments.

First of all, *régulation* theory has always been characterised by an overt desire to identify the institutions that constitute capitalism through an approach that challenges the dominance of a purely microeconomic approach to this system. The term *hol-individualism* should be recalled, signalling the desire to establish a link between the macro and micro through reflections on institutional forms. The emergence of a monetary regime, such as the euro, is better understood by taking political processes into account than through the 'horizontal' interaction of economic agents in search of stability and predictable exchange rates.

Régulation theory is interested in re-structuring *relations between the political and economic spheres* by recognising the varied interactions at work in contemporary societies. Economic logic must be combined with political goals although they are fundamentally different. Many institutional compromises emerge from this tension, and hence also institutional forms and, eventually, new modes of *régulation*. This approach is different from methodological individualism and from the concepts of self-interest and rationality that neoclassical economists extend to the political sphere.

Indeed, at a time when economists are discovering the diversity and importance of institutions, regulationists, who have long shared this conception and produced results related to it, are concentrating their efforts on explaining elements in the *transformation of institutions*. In contrast, most theorists tend to emphasise the optimality of institutions, without history, and regret that they are naturally more inert than markets. The inertia of institutions is often attributed to the irrationality of agents or the inability of the political authorities to implement the 'right' solutions recommended by economists.

This is not at all the case with regulationists, whose concerns for long term history and comparative analyses emphasise the endogenous factors that govern the evolution of institutions, as well as the variety in relations between politics and economics. The central theme, how the very success of an institutional architecture ultimately causes its downfall, bears witness to the Marxian inheritance of *régulation* theory, as well as its originality and relevance. By recognising the complementarity and hierarchy of institutions and the effort to define the elements that contribute to the emergence and viability of institutional forms, these themes are considered afresh.

A large area of research is opening up, one which involves defining the *macro-social and institutional bases of a microeconomics* that grasps the reality of behaviour at work in the contemporary world. This is quite the opposite of the seemingly positive, but actually normative, analysis which has long been the strength of neoclassical theory but which could ultimately call for a radical reconsideration of its hypotheses, concepts and methods.

For further research in *régulation* theory

Readers can consult the web site of the *Association Recherche et Régulation* http://www.upmf-grenoble.fr/irepd/docregul.htm, where the following resources are available:

- An online publication, *La lettre de la régulation*, listing information about publications, seminars, colloquia and other research activities relating to *régulation* theory.
- A bibliographical data bank, *Babireg*, tracing research undertaken since 1970 classed by subject, period, author and geographical area.
- Announcements of seminars, colloquia and research documents.

Fundamental articles to supplement and update the present volume are published annually in *L'Année de la régulation*, published by Editions La Découverte, 9 bis, rue Abel-Hovelacque, 75013 Paris until 2000 and then by Editions de Sciences politiques.

Glossary

Accumulation regime   The set of regularities that ensure the general and relatively coherent progress of capital accumulation, that is, which allow the resolution or postponement of the distortions and disequilibria to which the process continually gives rise. These regular patterns relate to:

1   The evolution of the organisation of production and of the workers' relationship to the means of production.
2   The time horizon for the valorisation of capital, which offers a basis for the development of principles of management.
3   A distribution of value that allows the reproduction and development of the different social classes or groups.
4   A composition of social demand that corresponds to the tendencies in the development of productive capacity.
5   A manner of articulation with non-capitalist economic forms, when they hold an essential place in the economic formation under study.
(Boyer, 1986a: 46, trans. Charney, 1990: 35–6)

Accumulation, extensive/intensive   There are two opposite situations for accumulation regimes:* they may be either dominantly extensive or intensive. Extensive accumulation relates to the capitalist development that conquers new branches and new markets, spreading its production relations to new spheres of economic activity, without however altering the conditions of production and the efficiency of labour or capital in any significant manner. In contrast to this, in a regime of intensive accumulation, the conditions of production are systematically transformed with a view to increasing the productivity of labour. New investments are primarily in the form of an increase in capital stock per worker. This is obviously a logical distinction more than a type of historical identification since it is common knowledge that the transformation of the conditions of production is an intrinsic characteristic of capitalism (Chapter 20).

Capitalist mode of production   This is characterised by the very specific form taken by relations of exchange and production. In the first place, the exchange relation takes on the commodity form. The creation of the obligation of payment in money simultaneously institutes monetary constraint and the merchant subject. In the second place, the separation of the direct producers from their means of production and their obligation to sell their labor power define the nature of capitalist relations of production, or more generally, the nature of the wage relation (*sic*, i.e. wage–labour nexus) (Boyer, 1986a: 44, trans. Charney, 1990: 33).

Co-evolution of institutional forms   A process of trial and error through which a series of institutional forms* that are initially disconnected and formally independent (since they result from institutionalised compromises among diverse agents in different fields) adjust to one another until a viable institutional configuration emerges. The economic adjustments then become part of a mode of *régulation* and appear coherent retrospectively. This notion extends to institutional analysis a concept developed by neo-Schumpeterian theories in relation to the joint evolution of technology and organisation (Chapter 40). However, the mechanisms at work may differ: in one case it may depend on market selection, while in another political processes play the determining role.

Complementarity of institutional forms   This is a configuration in which the viability of an institutional form* is strongly or entirely conditioned by the existence of several other institutional forms, such that their conjunction offers greater resilience and better performance compared with alternative configurations. For example, the Fordist wage–labour nexus and a credit-based monetary regime proved to be complementary, as were the competitive wage–labour nexus* and the gold standard regime. This definition concurs with the theory of supermodularity for organisations in relation to the propagation of the model of just-in-time and total quality (Milgrom and Roberts, 1990). It also agrees with the lessons of 'comparative institutional analysis' with regard to the complementarity of *keiretsu*, employment stability and the main bank in Japan (Aoki, 1995).

Convention   A convention should be understood both as the result of individual actions and as a context of constraint for its subjects since it is both an agreed arrangement and a product of this agreement, endowed with a compulsory normative force (Dupuy *et al.*, 1989: 143). *See* Theory of Conventions.

Crisis   *Régulation* theory distinguishes five types of crisis, classified by their increasing degree of severity in as much as they concern organisational forms of increasing significance.

1   *Exogenously triggered crisis*   An episode during which the continued economic reproduction of a given geographical entity is blocked, owing to shortages linked with natural or climatic disasters, or to an economic collapse originating in external events or wars (Boyer, 1986a: 61, trans. Charney, 1990: 49).

2   *Endogenous or cyclical crisis*, resulting from the operation of the mode of *régulation*   A phase in which tensions and disequilibria accumulated during periods of expansion are wiped out. The cyclical crises take place within the existing economic mechanisms and social patterns, and thus within the prevailing mode of regulation in a given country and era. In this sense, the recurrence of phases favourable and unfavourable to accumulation is the direct consequence of the reigning institutional forms, which cyclical crises affect only very slowly and partially (Boyer, 1986a: 62, trans. Charney, 1990: 50).

3   *Crisis of the mode of* régulation   An episode in which the mechanisms associated with the prevailing mode of *régulation** prove incapable of overcoming unfavourable short-term tendencies, even though the regime of accumulation* was at least initially viable (Boyer, 1986a: 64, trans. Charney, 1990: 52). Such a crisis can be recognised by at least three characteristics. First one (or several) institutional forms are eroded and destabilised by the very pattern of economic activity. Second, the expectations of the economic actors, even the best informed, recurrently turn out to be wrong, because they rely on the previous regularities. Third, in many instances social conflicts emerge out of the detrimental and adverse economic evolution and they give rise to a variety of proposals for reshaping one or more of the institutional forms.

4   *Crisis of the accumulation regime*   This is defined by the attainment of the limits of the most essential institutional forms – those that shape the regime of accumulation* – and the rise of contradictions within them. It implies in due time the crisis of the system of regulation (*sic*, i.e. mode of *régulation*), and thus of the whole mode of development (Boyer, 1986a: 68, trans. Charney, 1990: 56). It is to be distinguished from a crisis in the mode of *régulation* because when an institutional form reaches its limits there is negative spillover upon others and so the disequilibria are propagated from one sphere to another. Generally speaking, the macroeconomic pattern becomes uneven, growth problematic and uncertain.

5   *Crisis of the production mode*   The collapse of the specific set of social relations that characterises a mode of production.* In other words, such a crisis occurs when an economic formation reaches the limits of one arrangement of institutional forms, precipitating challenges to and the abolition of the most fundamental aspects

of the prevailing set of social relations (Boyer, 1986a: 70–1, trans. Charney, 1990: 58).

Cumulative growth The principle of cumulative causality is thus to identify, within the creation/distributing circuit of productivity gains for each growth regime, the intensity of retroactive effects between the methods of production organisation and demand formation. The schema of cumulative growth applies to the analysis of both intensive and extensive accumulation regimes.* The endogenous dynamic that these retroactive effects exhibit may result from increasing returns to scale as a positive factor in the economic system under consideration (Chapter 22).

Economic paradigm A purportedly coherent set of theories, representations and principles of action which acts as justification and clarification for both public and private decisions (Lordon, 1995; 1997). Economic history suggests that one of these principles dominates every major historical period. This is especially noticeable in the administration of the state and the orientation of economic policy. Examples are the developmentist paradigm, Keynesian principles of short-term economic stabilisation, the ideal of monetary stability, incentive theory and the plea for economic value added (EVA). The hierarchy* governing many institutional configurations is often legitimised by this type of economic paradigm (Chapter 42), as is the orientation of economic policy (Chapter 17).

Endometabolism Essentially, endometabolism is the interdependence of operation and development within a socio-economic system. *Endogenous structural change* means that a structure draws the motor forces of its 'development' from its own 'operation'. Thus endometabolism is the process by which the functioning of the structure alters the structure itself. The simple fact that a structure exists, that its existence 'unfurls', may be a sufficient motive for its alteration (Lordon, 1993: 504).

Fiscal and financial regime Three major forms of the state* are connected in the cycle of its operational metamorphoses: first, the pure political forms of sovereignty . . . next, legal forms of legitimacy . . . and lastly fiscal forms. These three operating forms gradually converge in what is termed the organic circuit of the state. In demonstrating how, in a given historical situation, this organic circuit effectively 'forms a loop' by authorising the financial growth of the state and the development of political power, a fiscal and financial regime and the mode of *régulation* of the corresponding political order emerge. A fiscal and financial regime ensures a functional connection between the legal and public spending forms of legitimacy of the state through the intermediary process of levying taxes (Théret, 1992).

Fordism   Fordism may be defined as an accumulation regime* that combines three characteristics.

1   An organisation of work which, starting from Taylorism, pushes even further the division of labour into separate tasks, the mechanisation of production processes and a complete separation of conception and production.

2   Next, employees obtain institutionalised sharing of productivity gains, in a manner other than through the effects of labour shortages that appear when accumulation becomes too extreme. These two characteristics together define the Fordist wage–labour nexus.

3   But this is not sufficient in itself, since it must be linked with compatible institutional forms, whether it occurs within oligopolistic competition* or a monetary regime* based on credit. In addition, an essential characteristic is that the process of adjustment of production and demand occurs mainly within a single nation. . . . In other words, intensive accumulation is governed by internal consumption (Chapter 30).

Form of competition   This refers to the way in which relations are organised among a set of centres of accumulation who *a priori* make decisions independently of each other (Boyer, 1986a: 50, trans. Charney, 1990: 39). Several very different cases may be identified: competitive mechanisms are at work when the fate of privately produced goods is determined by a confrontation on the market *after* production. Monopoly reigns when certain rules of socialisation prevail *before* production through the maintenance of a social demand whose quantity and composition are largely geared to supply (Boyer, 1986a: 50, trans. Charney, 1990: 39).

Form of co-ordination   In order to respect the many possible forms of co-ordination, as well as the solid foundation that provides the evidence of a natural presupposition, it was initially assumed that relevant action is situated in a varied universe. . . . In this perspective, we suggest that a company may be conceived of as an arrangement of compromises intended to manage the tensions between several different aspects and involving at least commercial and industrial elements. This definition emphasises the multiplicity of worlds implied in the operation of what is termed a company, and this multiplicity requires the development and maintenance of a compromise arrangement. . . . Of all the composite combinations, the trade and industrial elements are specified in what are commonly referred to as companies. The prominence of a given order (commercial, industrial, domestic, etc.) brings about types referred to as a 'production model' or a 'company model'. . . . Domestic co-ordination takes place with reference to tradition and the domestic order may be described in three ways: *temporal* (through custom and precedence), *spatial* (by local proximity) and *hierarchical* (in terms of authority) (Thévenot, 1989: 1160, 179 and 185).

Form of insertion into the international regime   Its position is defined by the set of rules that organise the nation state's relationship with the rest of the world, in terms of both commodity exchanges and the localisation of production, via direct investment or through financing of capital inflows and external deficits (Boyer, 1986a: 51, trans. Charney, 1990: 40).

Form of the state   The group of institutionalised compromises . . . [that,] . . . once they are made, create rules and patterns in the evolution of public spending and revenue, as well as the orientation of regulations. *See also* Fiscal and financial regime.

Governance   In contrast to neoclassical theory models which concentrate on the behaviour of isolated agents in the market, we consider each industry as a matrix of interdependent social exchange relations or transactions that intervene individually or collectively within organisations, in order to develop, produce and market goods and services. . . . Transactions take place among a large group of actors that includes producers and suppliers of raw materials, researchers, manufacturers, distributors and many others. These actors must resolve a series of problems on a daily basis, for instance obtaining credit, determining salaries, standardising products and fixing sales prices, in order for economic activity to continue . . . (Campbell *et al.*, 1991: 5–6).

Hierarchy of institutional forms   A configuration in which, for any given era and society, particular institutional forms* impose their logic on the institutional architecture as a whole, lending their dominant tone to the mode of *régulation*. One point of view is that during the conception of an institutional form the constraints of another central, and hence superior, institutional form are explicitly or implicitly taken into account. According to a second interpretation, the transformation of an institutional form guides the development of one or more other institutional forms through the range and intensity of its repercussions. In Fordism* the wage–labour nexus* played this role, because of the founding compromise from which it originates. In the 1980s this hierarchy was replaced by the monetary and financial regime,* which tends to dictate many developments in other areas.

Institutional (or structural) form   Any kind of codification of one or several fundamental social relations (Boyer, 1986a: 48, trans. Charney, 1990: 37). Five fundamental institutional forms are identified:

1   The forms of monetary constraint (*see* Monetary regime).
2   The configurations of the wage–labour nexus (*see* Wage–labour nexus).

3   The forms of competition (*see* Forms of competition).
4   The methods of insertion into the international regime (*see* Form of insertion into the international regime).
5   The forms of the state (*see* Form of the state).

Institutional arrangement at the sector level   This notion refers to the set of institutions producing the norms, processes and interventions that frame and direct the operation of economic regimes (at the level of a sphere of activity). They make it possible to avoid an exclusively state-based approach to public policy or institutions by taking into account more complex configurations of relations between the state and professionals (Bartoli and Boulet, 1990: 19).

Institutionalised compromise   The compromise originates from a situation of tension and conflict between socio-economic groups. The conflict of interests vary, depending on how much is at stake. . . . When none of the forces present manages to dominate the opposing forces sufficiently to enable it to impose its own interests entirely, a compromise ensues. Institutionalised compromises are different from an authoritarian institutionalisation of public order. . . . Institutionalisation refers to the instituting of a form of organisation, creating rules, rights and obligations for creditors, imposing discipline in regard to the institution which then takes on the appearance of a given fact for each individual agent or group, through which behaviour and strategy are gradually adapted. One of the remarkable results of institutionalised compromises is the essential robustness of the constructions that are set up. Institutionalised compromises impose themselves as frameworks in relation to which the population and concerned groups adapt their behaviour. It is not therefore surprising that the true securing of positions and acquired interests illustrated by institutionalised compromises later tend to become the object of increasing tension (Delorme and André, 1983: 672–4).

Institutionalism   Any research philosophy of economic theory characterised by two principles. First, micro or macro-economic patterns can be causally connected with the systems of institutional rules that organise transactions. Second, the theoretical model explains the systems of rules. In short, institutions are essential, endogenous variables (Chapter 41).

Limited state/embedded state   Long-term analysis of public interventions in France has led to the conclusion that since the early nineteenth century there have been two configurations, characterised by the different relations of the state to the economy*, i.e. two forms of the state*. The first developed on the basis of the rules that came out of the Revolution, and lasted until the First World War. This is the notion of a 'limited' state that relates to an economy that is seen as an autonomous space. The Second World War marked the change to a state that is 'embedded' in the economic sphere. In France this truly involved an assumption of responsibility owing to two major innovations: the institutionalising of benefits and the concept of co-ordinating monetary administration and general economic policy under the aegis of the public authorities. The welfare state is most closely associated with the embedded state configuration (Chapter 12).

Mode of development The conjunction of an accumulation regime* and a type of *régulation*.*

Mode of production Any particular form of relations of production and exchange, that is, the social relations governing the production and reproduction of the material conditions required for human life in society (Boyer, 1986a: 43, trans. Charney, 1990: 32).

Mode of *régulation* The set of procedures and individual and collective behaviours that serve to:

1 Reproduce fundamental social relations through the mode of production* in combination with historically determined institutional forms.
2 Support and 'steer' the prevailing regime of accumulation*.
3 Ensure the compatibility over time of a set of decentralised decisions, without the economic actors themselves having to internalise the adjustment principles governing the overall system (Boyer, 1986a: 54–5, trans. Charney, 1990: 43).

Mode of *régulation* at the sector level This is the combination of economic regimes of operation and institutional arrangements.* The combination should be viewed as a process rather than as a fixed state, and it should therefore be studied as a dynamic (Bartoli and Boulet, 1990: 19).

Monetary regime The monetary form (is) the specific form of the fundamental social relation (of a given country and era) that establishes the merchant subjects . . . money . . . is not a particular type of commodity, but a means of establishing relations between the centre of accumulation, wage earners and other merchant subjects (Boyer, 1986a: 48, trans. Charney, 1990: 37).

National trajectory This is the consequence of the endogenous dynamic and responses associated with a mode of development* and specific institutional forms.* In so far as they are irreversible once they have emerged, these distinctive features can generally be observed over relatively long periods of two to three decades. The national aspect of trajectories results from the fact that conflicts and compromises are largely specific to a given geographical area; this is the case even when institutional forms arise from international conflicts.

Furthermore, it is possible to distinguish two types of trajectory, depending on the degree of persistence shown by institutional forms and procedures when confronted with attempts to reform them.

1   We refer to a trajectory in the *weak* sense when the dynamic processes of adjustment relate to a single mode of development.
2   By extension, a trajectory in the *strong* sense is when a common style directs the dynamics generated by the succession of two or more different regimes. For example, compared with other industrialised countries, France is characterised by a high level of institutionalisation in economic relations. This explains why the crisis of the 1930s, like the crisis that began in the 1970s, showed far more regular macro-economic developments than in the United States, a country which is affected by a different role for the state and the predominance of market logic. Institutional co-evolution,* complementarity* and hierarchy* contribute to the development of these trajectories.

Neoclassical theory   In general terms, neoclassical theory is based on three hypotheses: the restriction of pure economics to the principle of *homo economicus*, substantial rationality and the concept of equilibrium as the guarantor of the compatibility of a group of decentralised strategies thanks to a complete set of markets. It is however possible to identify two variants of neoclassical theory (Amable *et al.*, 1995).

Neoclassical theory, fundamentalist   This approach claims that only one model of general equilibrium provides an adequate theoretical framework. It believes that fundamentally prices depend only on consumer preferences and technical capability. Above all, the key question is the efficiency of a market economy, which culminates in the two welfare theorems that assess the links between market equilibrium and Pareto optimum. A more ideological variant exists in which the market economy is always and everywhere the only effective and viable economic system (Amable *et al.*, 1995).

Neoclassical theory, methodological   This theory is defined by a set of tools to be adapted to the problem posed. The basic hypotheses can be liberated from the hypotheses of the theory of general equilibrium. The hypotheses of rationality and optimisation within constraints are central to this approach, but methodological neoclassical theory also accepts the relevance of partial equilibrium, which may depend on the given informational context (the asymmetry of information) and institutional context (the existence of markets, the nature of the firm, etc.). A market equilibrium is often then no longer Pareto-optimal. The theory is diffracted among a myriad of models based on *ad hoc* hypotheses which are often linked to contradictory conclusions (Amable *et al.*, 1995).

Operating economic regime   This is defined as the set of economic mechanisms that guarantee the reproduction of a sphere of activity for a period of time. This notion is of most interest in situations where it is possible to identify a relatively enduring cohesion between production, consumption and exchange rationales, making it possible to describe a type of operating economic regime endowed with some stability in its reproducibility. The analysis of an operating economic regime is based on the conditions of supply, demand, price formation and, more generally, the conditions of exchange between producers, distributors and consumers (Bartoli and Boulet, 1990: 19).

Regime of governance   Governance mechanisms do not exist in isolation; rather they act together in different combinations, in other words in 'regimes of governance' which vary depending on the industry and era. Furthermore, at every point in time actors tend to organise themselves, adopting exchange rules and using control methods that correspond to the particular mode of governance. In this sense, some governance mechanisms dominate within a mode of governance (Campbell *et al.*, 1991: 32).

Régulation   The *régulation* of a mode of production expresses the way in which the determining structure of a society's general laws is reproduced. . . . A theory of social *régulation* provides an alternative to the theory of general equilibrium. . . . Studies of the *régulation* of capitalism do not look for abstract economic laws. *Régulation* is the study of the transformation of social relations that creates new economic and non-economic forms, organised in structures and reproducing a determining structure, the mode of production (Aglietta, 1976).

***Régulation* through shortage**   This type of *régulation* predominated in eastern European countries from the 1950s to the late 1970s. It is founded on a 'chain of rationing' based on investment patterns that have repercussions on the market for consumption goods, the labour market (or company bankruptcy) and possibly foreign trade. Successive variations in the intensity of different rationing is an original mode of *régulation* that characterises the growth and normal operation of these economies, unlike true crises, where there is generalised rationing and the cycle does not include endogenous recovery (Chapter 35).

Rule in wage formation   This is defined as a normative statement of the kind: 'if *x*, then *y*'. But not all statements of this kind are rules. In fact the rule in wage formation is defined as a lasting relation between a hypothesis or presupposition and its economic effect. It must therefore be abstract, hypothetical and permanent. The hypothesis or presupposition refers to a type of situation, not to people or events. This is what makes the rule abstract. The structure of the rule is hypothetical. The hypothesis or presupposition refers to a type of situation, not to facts or particular individuals, since this would imply that it was no longer abstract. Finally, the rule presents a permanent relation between a hypothesis and its consequence; it defines what must happen if the conditions of a hypothesis are realised. There are three types of consequences: order, permission and entitlement. Thus the rule is not necessarily linked to a sanction (Reynaud, 1992: 49).

Social structure of accumulation (SSA)   This term refers to the specific institutional environment within which the capitalist process of accumulation is organised. This accumulation is present in particular historical structures: the credit and monetary system, the type of involvement of the state in the economy, the nature of class conflicts, etc. The SSA is the conjunction of these institutions. ... Each long period is associated with a distinctive social structure of accumulation that defines the successive stages of capitalist development (Gordon *et al.*, 1982: 9).

Capitalist economies experience periods of rapid and relatively stable growth once all the socio-economic institutions of a SSA are established. But every SSA is subject to both exogenous shocks and endogenously created tensions. These frictions eventually erode the SSA, generally after several decades, compromising its ability to promote returns, investments and growth. The social order then enters a period of crisis during which political disputes develop. What is at stake is the institutional restructuring necessary to re-establish the conditions for successful accumulation (Bowles *et al.*, 1986: 2).

Strategic area   All the possibilities offered by the international regime for each geographical area, along with the constraints involved (Mistral, 1986).

The state as relational, integrated and complex (ERIC)   The state is relational in that it is perceived not as a substance defining an intrinsic essence by disjunction, but rather through a conjunction of phenomena indicating strong geographical patterns. It is integrated in the sense that nowhere is there a duality between the state seen only as structure in contrast to the state seen only as actor. All in all, we are faced with the ubiquity and multiple nature of the state, and the theory accounts for this. In this sense the state is certainly a complex category, which suggests that the market economy may be perceived more as a composite than in terms of a state–market couple (Chapter 15).

Theory of conventions   According to an early statement – based on orthodox economic theory – the theory of conventions* pursues the traditional research programme of methodological individualism in economics (namely the issue of co-ordinating economic activity) but including a hypothesis of limited rationality.

According to a second statement – based on social sciences other than political economy – the theory of conventions pursues the traditional research programme of political philosophy or fundamental sociology (namely the issue of co-operation between subjects endowed with the faculty of reason). However, it emphasises an 'understanding' of the actions, texts and objects which agrees with the 'interpretative turning point' of the social sciences.

These two approaches are complementary in as much as they share similar hypotheses. First, the co-ordination of interdependent situations with a positive outcome works through institutional arrangements that blend efficiency and equity; second, the multiplicity of areas of justification is not compatible with universal optimising rationality (Favereau, 1993: 1).

Wage–labour nexus   This is the configuration of mutual relations among different types of work organisation, life-styles and ways in which the labour force is reproduced. Analytically speaking, there are five components to the historically observable configurations of the capital–labour relation: the type of means of production; the social and technical division of labour; the ways in which workers are attracted and retained by the firm; the direct and indirect determinants of wage income; and, lastly, the workers' way of life, which is more or less closely linked with the acquisition of commodities and the use of collective services outside the market (Boyer, 1986a: 49, trans. Charney, 1990: 38).

Bibliography

Aboites Jaime (1985) 'Industrialisation et développement agricole au Mexique: une analyse du régime d'accumulation de long terme, 1939–1985', CEPREMAP 8727, Paris.

―――― (1989) *Industrialización y desarrollo agrícola en México*, Ed. Plaza y Valdés/ UAM, Mexico City.

Aboites Jaime and E. Hernandez Laos (1994) *La mobilidad de la mano de obra en México*, STPS-Banco Mundial, Mexico City.

Aglietta Michel (1974) 'Accumulation et régulation du capitalisme en longue période. Exemple des Etats-Unis (1870–1970)', thesis, Université de Paris I.

―――― (1976) *Régulation et crises du capitalisme*, Calmann-Lévy, Paris; second edition 1982; third edition, Odile Jacob, Paris, 1997.

―――― (1980) 'La dévalorisation du capital: études des liens entre accumulation et inflation', *Economie appliquée*, 33 (2), 387–423.

―――― (1986a) *La fin des devises-clés*, La Découverte, Paris.

―――― (1986b) 'Etats-Unis: persévérance dans l'être ou renouveau de la croissance', in Boyer Robert (ed.) *Capitalismes fin de siècle*, Presses Universitaires de France, Paris.

―――― (1987) 'La crise financière et ses conséquences', *Revue d'économie financière*, 3 (4), 4–29.

―――― (1991) 'Le risque de système', *Revue d'économie financière* 17 (3), 61–89.

―――― (1992a) 'Les dérapages de la finance japonaise', *Economie prospective internationale*, 51, 9–29.

―――― (1992b) 'Le risque de système et la *régulation* des économies de marché', *La Lettre de la régulation*, 3, 1.

―――― (1993) 'Crises et cycles financiers: une approche comparative', *Revue d'économie financière*, 26, 5–56.

―――― (1995) *Macroéconomie financière*, Collection Repères, La Découverte, Paris.

―――― (1998) 'Le capitalisme de demain', *Notes de la Fondation Saint Simon*, Paris.

Aglietta Michel and Bauland Camille (1994) 'Contrainte extérieure et compétitivité dans la transition vers l'Union économique et monétaire', *Revue de l'OFCE* 48, 7–51.

Aglietta Michel and Boyer Robert (1982) 'Une industrie compétitive en France et dans le monde', in *Une politique industrielle pour la France*, La Documentation Française, Paris.

Aglietta Michel and De Boissieu Christian (1998) 'Problèmes prudentiels', *Conseil d'analyse économique*, 5, Documentation française, Paris.

Aglietta Michel and Brénder Anton (1984) *Les métamorphoses de la société salariale. La France en projet*, Collection Perspectives de l'Economique, Calmann-Lévy, Paris.

Aglietta Michel and Moutot Philippe (1993a) 'L'évolution des structures financières des grand pays et la prévention du risque de système dans l'union économique et monétaire', *Cahiers économiques et monétaires*, 41, 55–81.

—— (1993b) 'Redéployer les réformes. Comment adapter la stratégie de transition', *Economie internationale*, 54 (2), 67–103.

Aglietta Michel and Orlean André, (1982) *La violence de la monnaie*, Presses Universitaires de France, Paris.

—— (eds) (1998) *La monnaie souveraine*, Odile Jacob, Paris.

Aglietta Michel, Brender Anton and Coudert Virginie (1990) *Globalisation financière. L'aventure obligée*, Economica, Paris.

Aglietta Michel, Orlean André and Oudiz Gilles (1980) 'Contraintes de change et régulations macroéconomiques nationales', *Recherches économiques de Louvain*, 46 (3), 175–206.

—— (1981) 'Des adaptations différenciées aux contraintes internationales: les enseignements d'un modèle', *Revue économique*, 32 (4), 660–710.

Akerlof George (1984) *An Economic Theorist's Book of Tales*, Cambridge University Press, Cambridge.

Åkerman Johan (1954) 'Economic plans and causal analysis', *International Economic Papers*, 4, 33–81 (first published in Swedish 1942).

—— (1955–7) *Structures et cycles économiques*, 3 vols, Presses Universitaires de France, Paris.

Allaire Gilles (1988) 'Le modèle de développement agricole des années 60', *Economie rurale*, 184–6, 171–81. Reprinted in Allaire and Boyer, *La grande transformation de l'agriculture* (1994).

Allaire Gilles and Boyer Robert (eds) (1994) *La grande transformation de l'agriculture. Lectures conventionnalistes et régulationnistes*, INRA-Economica, Paris.

Amable Bruno (1989) 'Economies d'échelle dynamiques, effet d'apprentissage et progrès technique endogène: une comparaison internationale', *Revue de l'IRES*, 1, 31–54.

—— (1993a) 'Effets d'apprentissage, compétitivité hors prix et croissance cumulative', *Economie appliquée*, 45 (3), 5–31.

—— (1993b) 'Catch-up and convergence: a model of cumulative growth', *International Review of Applied Economics*, 7 (1), 1–25.

—— (1992) 'Effets nationaux d'apprentissage, spécialisation internationale et trajectoires de croissance' in Foray D. and Freeman C. (eds) *Technologie et richesse des nations,* Economica, Paris.

Amable Bruno, Barré Rémi and Boyer Robert (1997) *Les systèmes d'innovation à l'ère de la globalisation*, OST-Economica, Paris.

Amable Bruno and Boyer Robert (1992) 'The R&D productivity relationship in the context of new growth theory', in Capron Henri (ed.) *Proceedings of the Workshop on Quantitative Evaluation of the Impact of R&D Programmes*, Commission of the European Communities, Brussels.

Amable Bruno, Boyer Robert and Lordon Frédéric (1995) 'Le paradoxe de l'*ad hoc* en économie', in Cartelier Jean and D'Autume Antoine (eds) *L'économie est-elle une science dure?* Economica, Paris.

Amin Ash and Robins Kevin (1992) 'Le retour des économies régionales? La géographie mythique de l'accumulation flexible', in Benko G.B. and Lipietz A. (eds) *Les régions qui gagnent*, Presses Universitaires de France, Paris.

Amin Ash and Thrift N. (1993) 'Globalisation, institutional thickness and local prospects', *Revue d'économie régionale et urbaine*, 3, 453–78.

Andersson Jan Otto (1994) 'Economic integration, the Nordic models and unemployment', in Fagerberg Jan and Lundberg Lars (eds) *European Economic Integration. A Nordic Perspective,* Avebury, Aldershot.

—— (1996) 'Fundamental values for a third Left', *New Left Review,* 216, 66–78.

Andersson Jan Otto and Mjøset Lars (1987) 'The transformation of the Nordic models', *Co-operation and Conflict,* 22 (4), 523–58.

André Christine and Delorme Robert (1982) 'Matériaux pour une comparaison internationale de l'évolution de longue période des dépenses publiques', *Statistiques et études financières*, red series, 390, 3–56.

—— (1989) 'Analyse comparée des interventions publiques en économie entre la France et la République Fédérale d'Allemagne', CEPREMAP 8914, Paris.

Andreff Wladimir (1978a) 'Structure de l'accumulation du capital et technologie en URSS', *Revue d'études comparatives Est–Ouest*, 9 (1), 175–203.

—— (1978b) 'Capitalisme d'Etat ou monopolisme d'Etat en URSS? Propos d'étape', in Lavigne Marie (ed.) *Economie politique de la planification en système socialiste*, Economica, Paris.

—— (1981) 'Vers une théorie de la congruence des systèmes', in Lavigne Marie (ed.) *Travail et monnaie en système socialiste*, Economica, Paris.

—— (1984) 'Marxisme en crise cherche sociétés socialistes: à propos des thèses de P. M. Sweezy et de B. Chavance', *Babylone*, 2–3, 277–305.

—— (1987) 'Bilan comparatif de la crise économique en URSS et dans les six pays européens du CAEM: de la réalité à l'emphase théorique', in Chavance Bernard (ed.) *Regulation, cycles et crises dans les économies socialistes*, Editions de l'Ecole des hautes études en sciences sociales, Paris.

—— (1990) 'Crise, *régulation* et réforme dans les économies socialistes', *Revue d'économie politique*, 100 (1), 1–42; 100 (2), 143–206.

—— (1993) *La crise des économies socialistes. La rupture d'un système*, Presses Universitaires de Grenoble, Grenoble.

—— (1997) 'Pays de l'Est et Union européenne: convergence ou congruence?' in J-P. Faugère, Caire G. and Bellon B (eds), *Convergence et diversité à l'heure de la mondialisation*, Economica, Paris.

—— (1999) 'Multi-faceted East–West economic convergence in Europe', *Economic System*, 23 (2), 4–9.

Andreff Wladimir and Graziani G. (1985) 'Contrainte extérieure et politiques d'adaptation', in Lavigne Marie and Andreff Wladimir (eds) *La réalité socialiste*, Economica, Paris.

Annandale Denise and Bertrand Hugues (1990) *La gestion des ressources humaines dans les banques en Europe*, Economica, Paris.

Antonelli Cristiano, Petit Pascal and Tahar Gabriel (1992) *The Economics of Industrial Modernization*, Academic Press, London.

Aoki Masahiko (1986) 'Horizontal *v.* vertical information structure of the firm', *American Economic Review*, 76 (5), 971–83.

—— (1988) *Information, Incentives and Bargaining in the Japanese Economy*, Cambridge University Press, New York.

—— (1990) 'Toward an economic model of the Japanese firm', *Journal of Economic Literature*, 27, 1–27.

—— (1991) *Information, motivations et marchandage,* trans. Aoki M. 1988, Economica, Paris.

—— (1995) 'Towards a Comparative Institutional Analysis: Motivations and some Tentative General Insights', working paper, Stanford University, Stanford CA, 4 October.

Appay Béatrice (1992) 'Individuel and collectif: questions à la sociologie du travail', unpublished MS.

Arena Richard (1991) 'Approches théoriques et économie industrielle' in Arena R., Benzoni, De Bandt J. and Romani P.-M., *Traité d'économie industrielle*, second edition, Economica, Paris.

Arnold V. (1988) *Equations différentielles ordinaires,* Mir, Moscow.

Asensio A. and Mazier Jacques (1991) 'Compétitivité, avantages coûts et hors-coûts, et spécialisation', *Revue d'économie industrielle*, 55 (1), 84–107.

Aumann Robert J. (1987) 'Game theory' in *The New Palgrave: A Dictionary of Economics*, vol. 2, ed. J. Eatwell, M. Milgate and P. Wexman, Macmillan, London, 460–82.

Axelrod Robert (1986) 'An evolutionary approach to norms', *American Political Science Review*, 80 (4), 1095–111.

Aydalot Philippe (1980) *Dynamique spatiale et développement inégal*, Economica, Paris.

—— (ed.) (1984) *Crise et espace*, Economica, Paris.

—— (ed.) (1986a) *Milieux innovateurs en Europe*, GREMI, Paris.

—— (1986b) 'Les technologies nouvelles et les formes actuelles de la division spatiale du travail', *Dossier 47*, Centre Economie, Espace, Environnement, Paris.

Ayres, C. (1944) *The Theory of Economic Progress*, University of North Carolina Press, Chapel Hill NC.

—— (1952) *The Industrial Economy. Its Technological Basis and Institutional Destiny*, Houghton Mifflin, Boston MA.

Bagnasco Arnaldo and Trigilia C. (1993) *La construction sociale du marché. Le défi de la troisième Italie*, Ed. de l'ENS–Cachan, Cachan.

Bairoch Paul (1989) 'European trade policy 1815–1914', in Mathias, P. and Pollard, S. *The Cambridge Economic History of Europe*, VIII, Cambridge University Press, Cambridge.

Banuri Tariq (1992) 'Quel espoir pour les pays du Sud?' in Barrere Martine (ed.) *Terre, patrimoine commun*, La Découverte, Paris.

Bardissa J. (1976) *Cent ans de guerre du vin*, Théma, Paris.

Barkai, H. (1989) 'The old historical school: Roscher on money and monetary issues', *History of Political Economics*, 21 (2), 179–200.

Barral P. (1968) *Les agrariens français de Méline à Pisani*, Armand Colin, Paris.

Bartoli Pierre (1990) 'L'érosion d'une *régulation* sectorielle: le cas du vin' in Coulomb P. *et al.* (eds) *Les agriculteurs et la politique*, Presses de la Fondation nationale des sciences politiques, Paris.

Bartoli Pierre and Boulet Daniel (1989) 'Dynamique et régulation de la sphère agro-alimentaire. L'exemple viticole', 3 vols, doctoral thesis, Université de Montpellier I, INRA ESR.

—— (1990) 'Conditions d'une approche en termes de *régulation* sectorielle: le cas de la sphère viticole', *Cahiers d'économie et sociologie rurales*, 17, INRA-ESR, Paris, 7–38.

Baslé Maurice (1993) 'Mise en perspectives de l'institutionnalisme de quelques économistes allemands et américains', *Économie appliquée. Archives de l'ISMEA*, 46 (4), 159–76.

Baslé Maurice, Mazier Jacques and Vidal Jean François (1993) *Quand les crises durent . . .*, Second edition, Economica, Paris. *When Economic Crises Endure*, Sharpe, New York, 1999.

Basle Maurice, Dufourt D., Heraud J. A. and Perrin J. (eds) (1994) *Changement institutionel et changement technique. Evaluation, droits de propriété intellectuelle et système national d'innovation*, Editions du CNRS, Paris.

Baudry B. (1992) *Contrat, autorité, confiance. La relation de sous-traitance est-elle assimilable à la relation d'emploi?* Presses de la Fondation nationale de sciences politiques, Paris.

Bauer M. and Bertin-Mourot B. (1987) *Les 200 en France et en Allemagne. Deux modèles contrastés de détection – sélection – formation de dirigeants de grandes entreprises*, Seuil, Paris.

Bazzoli Laure, Kirat Thierry and Villeval Marie-Claire (1994) 'Règles, contrat et institutions dans la relation salariale: pour un renouveau institutionnaliste', *Travail et emploi*, 1 (58), 94–110.

Beaud Michel (1989) *L'économie mondiale dans les années 80,* La Découverte, Paris.

Beccatini Giacomo (1992) 'Le district marshallien: une notion socio-économique', in Benko G. B. and Lipietz A. (eds) *Les régions qui gagnent*, Presses Universitaires de France, Paris.

Beffa Jean-Louis, Boyer Robert and Touffut Jean-Philippe (1999) 'Employment relationships in France', *Notes de la Fondation Saint Simon* 106, Paris.

Bell D. (1973) *The Coming of Post-industrial Society. A Venture in Social Forecasting*, Basic Books, New York.

Benassy Jean-Pascal, Boyer Robert and Gelpi Rosa-Maria (1979) '*Régulation* des économies capitalistes et inflation', *Revue économique*, 30 (3), 397–441.

Benetti Carlo and Cartelier Jean (1980) *Marchands, salariat et capitalistes*, Maspéro, Paris.

Benhabib J. (1992) 'Effets nationaux d'apprentissage, spécialisation internationale et trajectories de croissance' in Foray D. and Freeman C. (eds) *Technologie et richesse des nations*, Economica, Paris.

Benko Georges (ed.) (1990) *La dynamique spatiale de l'économie contemporaine*, Editions de l'espace européen, La Garenne-Colombes.

Benko Georges (1991) *Géographie des technopoles*, Masson, Paris.

Benko Georges and Dunford Michaël (eds) (1991) *Industrial Change and Regional Development*, Belhaven/Pinter, London.

Benko Georges and Lipietz Alain (eds) (1992) *Les régions qui gagnent*, Presses Universitaires de France, Paris.

—— (1999) *La richesse des régions*, Presses Universitaires de France, Paris.

Berge P., Pomeau Y. and Vidal C. (1992) *L'ordre dans le chaos,* Hermann, Paris.

Berger Suzane and Dore Ronald (eds) (1996) *National Diversity and Global Capitalism*, Cornell University Press, Ithaca NY and London.

Berlan J-P. and Rosier Bernard (1986) 'Les nouvelles technologies agricoles comme production sociale', *Économie rurale*, 192–3, 23–8.

Berle Adolf and Means Gardiner (1933) *The Modern Corporation and Private Property*, Commerce Clearing House, New York.

Berliner Joseph (1957) *Factory and Manager in the USSR*, Harvard University Press, Cambridge MA.

Bertoldi Moreno (1989) 'The growth of the Taiwanese economy, 1949–89: success and open problems of a model of growth', *Review of Currency Law and International Economics*, 39 (2), 245–88.

Bertramsen René B., Peter Jens, Thomsen Frølund and Torfing Jacob (1991) *State, Economy and Society*, Unwin Hyman, London.

Bertrand Hugues (1978) 'Une nouvelle approche de la croissance française de l'après-guerre: l'analyse en sections productives', *Statistiques et études financières*, orange series, 35, 3–36.

—— (1983) 'Accumulation, régulation, crise: un modèle sectionnel théorique et appliqué', *Revue économique*, 34 (6), 305–43.

—— (1990) *Etude comparative des systèmes d'emploi en Europe*, Office de Publication officiel des Communautés européennes, Brussels.

Bertrand Hugues, Mazier Jacques, Picaud Y. and Podevin Gilles (1982) 'Les deux crises des années 1930 et des années 1970', *Revue économique*, 33 (2), 234–73.

Bessy Christian (1993) *Les licenciements économiques. Entre la loi et le marché*, Editions du CNRS, Lyon.

Bettelheim Charles, (1974–83) *Les luttes de classes en URSS (1917—1941)*, 4 vols, Seuil–Maspéro, Paris.

Bhaskar V. and Glyn Andrew (eds) (1994) *The North, the South, and the Environment*, Earthscan, London.

Biencourt Olivier, Eymard-Duvernay François and Favereau Olivier (1994) 'Il faut définir le marché à partir de l'entreprise et non l'inverse', research paper, Forum-Laedis.

Biesmans Francis (1988) 'Un schéma d'accumulation intensive: théorie et application économétrique à la Belgique', mimeo, Centre d'histoire quantitative, Université de Liège. June.

Billaudot Bernard (1976) 'L'accumulation intensive du capital', thesis, Université de Paris I.

—— (1994a) 'Modélisation historique et institutionnelle de la dynamique macroéconomique', working paper IREPD, Grenoble.

—— (1994b) 'Théorie économique et espace du politique: confrontation entre la théorie néo-libérale et la théorie historique et institutionnelle de la régulation', *Note de l'IREPD*, 21, Grenoble.

—— (1996) *L'ordre économique de la société moderne*, Harmattan, Paris.

Boismenu Gérard and Daniel Drache (eds) (1990) *Politique et Régulation. Modèle de développement et trajectoire canadienne*, Montreal, Méridien; Harmattan, Paris.

Boismenu Gérard and Jalbert Lisette (eds) (1991) '*Régulation* et problème contemporains', *Cahiers de recherche sociologique*, 17, 583–612.

Boismenu Gérard, Gravel Nicolas and Loranger Jean Guy (1994) 'Régime d'accumulation et *régulation* fordiste: estimation d'un modèle à équations simultanées', working paper, Université de Montréal.

Boltanski Luc and Ciapello Eve (2000) *L'esprit du capitalisme,* Gallimard, Paris.

Boltanski Luc and Thévenot Laurent (1987) *Les économies de la grandeur*, Presses Universitaires de France, Paris.

—— (1991) *De la justification*, Gallimard, Paris.

Bordo M. and Eichengreen B. (eds) (1993) *A Retrospective on the Bretton Woods System*, NBER, University of Chicago Press, Chicago.

Borelly R. (1990) 'L'articulation du national et de l'international: concepts et analyses', *Economie et sociétés*, Theories of *Régulation* series, 24 (12), 67–96.

Boulin J-Y. (1992a) 'Les politiques du temps de travail en France: la perte du sens' *Futuribles*, special issue, 165–6, 41–62.

—— (1992b) 'L'organisation sociale du temps' *Futuribles,* special issue, 165–6, 239–52.

Bourdieu Jérôme (1997) 'Le marché, cet asile d'ignorance ', *La Lettre de la Régulation*, 23, 1–4.

Bourdieu Pierre (1980) *Questions de Sociologie*, Minuit, Paris.

—— (1986) 'Habitus, code et codification', *Actes de la recherche en sciences sociales*, 64, 40–4.

Bourdieu Pierre (1995) 'L'Etat et la concentration de la violence symbolique', in Théret Bruno *L'Etat, la finance et le social. Souveraineté nationale et construction européenne*, La Découverte, Paris.

Bourdon M. (1990) 'L'agriculture française dans la récession économique', in Coulomb P. *et al.* (eds) *Les agriculteurs et la politique*, Paris: Presses de la FNSP.

Bourguinat H. (1987) *Les vertiges de la finance internationale*, Economica, Paris.

Bouvier Jean (1989) *L'historien sur son métier,* Editions des archives contemporaines, Paris.

Bowles Samuel (1985) 'The production process in a competitive economy: walrasian, neo-Hobbesian and Marxian models', *American Economic Review*, 75 (1), 16–36.

—— (1997) 'Endogenous Preferences: The Cultural Consequences of Economic Organization', mimeo, University of Massachusetts, Amherst MA.

Bowles Samuel and Boyer Robert (1988) 'Labor discipline and aggregate demand: a macroeconomic model', *American Economic Review*, 78 (2), 395–400.

—— (1990a) 'A wage-led employment regime: income distribution, labour discipline and aggregate demand in welfare capitalism', in Marglin Steve and Schor Juliet (eds) *The Golden Age of Capitalism*, Clarendon Press, Oxford.

—— (1990b) 'Notes on employer collusion, centralized wage bargaining and aggregate employment', in Brunetta Renato and Dell'Aringa Carlo (eds) *Labour Relations and Economic Performances*, Macmillan, London.

—— (1995) 'Wages, aggregate demand, and employment in an open economy: a theoretical and empirical investigation', in Epstein Gerald and Gintis Herbert, (eds) *Macroeconomic Policy after the Conservative Era. Studies in Investment, Saving and Finance*, Oxford University Press, Oxford.

Bowles Samuel and Gintis Herbert (1993) 'The revenge of *homo economicus*: contested exchange and the revival of political economy', *Journal of Economic Perspectives*, 7 (1), 83–102.

Bowles Samuel, Gordon David M. and Weisskopf Thomas E. (1983a) *Hearts and Minds. A Social Model of US Productivity Growth*, Brookings Papers on Economic Activity 2, Brookings Institution, Washington DC.

—— (1983b) 'Long swings and the non-reproductive cycle', *American Economic Review*, 73 (2), 152–7.

—— (1986a) *L'économie du gaspillage. La crise américaine et les politiques reaganiennes*, La Découverte, Paris. Trans. of *Beyond the Waste Land*, Doubleday, New York, 1983.

—— (1986b) 'Power and profits: the social structure of accumulation and the profitability of the postwar US economy', *Review of Radical Political Economy*, 18 (1–2), 132–67.

—— (1988) 'Business ascendancy and economic impasse: a structural retrospective on conservative economics, 1979–87', *Journal of Economic Perspectives*, 3 (1), 107–34.

Boyer Robert (1978) 'Les salaires en longue période', *Economie et statistique*, 103, 27–57. Trans. 'Wage formation in historical perspective: the French experience', *Cambridge Journal of Economics*, 3, 99–118, 1979a.

—— (1979) 'La crise actuelle: une mise au point en perspective historique. Quelques réflexions à partir d'une analyse du capitalisme français en longue période', *Critiques de l'économie politique*, new series, 7–8, 5–113.

—— (1986a) *La théorie de la régulation: une analyse critique,* La Découverte, Paris. Trans. Craig Charney as *The Regulation School*, Columbia University Press, New York, 1990.

—— (ed.) (1986b) *The Search for Labour Market Flexibility*, Oxford University Press, Oxford, 1988.

—— (1986c) 'La crise américaine, les radicaux et nous', in Bowles Samuel *et al.* (eds) *L'économie du gaspillage*, La Découverte, Paris.

—— (1988a) 'Technical change and the theory of "régulation"', in Dosi Giovanni, Freeman Christopher, Nelson Richard, Silverberg Gérald and Soete Luc (eds) *Technical Change and Economic Theory*, London, Pinter.

—— (1988b) 'Formalizing growth regimes', in Dosi Giovanni, Freeman Christopher, Nelson Richard, Silverberg Gérald and Soete Luc (eds) *Technical change and Economic Theory*, London, Pinter.

—— (1989) 'Wage labor nexus, technology and long run dynamics: an interpretation and preliminary tests for the US', in Di Mateo M, Goodwin R.M. and Vercelli A. (eds), *Technological and Social Factors in Long Term Fluctuations*, Lecture Notes in Economics and Mathematical Systems 321, Springer, Berlin.

—— (1990a) 'The impact of the single market on labour and employment', *Labour and Society*, 15 (2), 109–42.

—— (1990b) 'Les problèmatiques de la *régulation* face aux spécificités sectorielles: les perspectives ouvertes par la thèse de Pierre Bartoli et Daniel Boulet', *Cahiers d'économie et de sociologie rurales*, 17, 40–76.

—— (1990c) 'Le bout du tunnel? Stratégies conservatrices et nouveau régime d'accumulation', *Economie et Sociétés*, R Series 5, 5–66.

—— (1991) 'Capital–labor relations and wages formation: continuities and changes of national trajectories among OECD countries', in Mizoguchi T. (ed.) *Making Economies More Efficient and More Equitable*, Oxford University Press, Oxford; Kinokunya, Tokyo.

—— (1992a) 'Justice sociale et performances économiques: de la synergie au conflit?', in Affichard Joëlle and De Foucauld Jean-Baptiste (eds) *Justice sociale et inégalités*, Esprit, Paris.

—— (1992b) 'La capitalisme français et ses concurrents 1945–1991: du miracle au blocage', in *L'Etat de la France 1994,* La Découverte, Paris.

—— (1992c) 'Rapport salarial et régime d'accumulation au Japon: émergence, originalités et prospective. Premiers jalons', *Mondes en développement*, 20 (79–80), 1–30.

—— (1992d) 'Les alternatives au fordisme: des années 1980 au XXIe siècle', in Benko G.B. and Lipietz A. (eds) *Les régions qui gagnent*, Presses Universitaires de France, Paris.

—— (1993) 'D'une série de "National Labour Standards" à un "European Monetary Standard"?' *Recherche économiques de Louvain*, 59 (1–2), 119–53.

—— (1994a) 'Do labour institutions matter for economic development? A "régulation" approach for the OECD and Latin America with an extension to Asia', in Rodgers Gerry (ed.) *Workers' Institutions and Economic Growth in Asia*, ILO Publications, Geneva.

—— (1994b) 'Les capitalismes vers le XXIe siècle: des transformations majeures en quête de théories', *Notas Economicas*, 8–39.

—— (1995a) 'The great transformation of Eastern Europe: a "regulationist" Perspective', *Emergo: Journal of Transforming Economies and Societies*, 2 (4), 25–41.

—— (1995b) 'The future of unions: is the Anglo-Saxon model a fatality, or will contrasting national trajectories persist?', *British Journal of Industrial Relations*, 33 (4), 545–56.

—— (1997) 'About the role and efficiency of markets: history, theory and policy in the light of the nineties', in Hollingsworth Roger and Boyer Robert (eds) *The Embeddedness of Capitalist Institutions*, Oxford University Press, Oxford.

—— (1998a) 'An Essay on the Political and Institutional Deficits of the Euro', CEPREMAP 9813, Paris.

—— (1998b) 'The changing status of industrial relations in a more interdependent world: an interpretation and agenda for further research', in Wilthagen Ton (ed.) *Advancing Theory in Labour Law and Industrial Relations in a Global Context*, North-Holland, Amsterdam.

—— (1999a) 'Le politique à l'ère de la mondialisation et de la finance: le point sur quelques recherches régulationnistes', *L'Année de la régulation 1999*, III, 13–75. Trans. 'The political era of globalisation and finance: focus on some *régulation* school research', *International Journal of Urban and Regional Research*, 24 (2), 274–322.

—— (1999b) 'Deux enjeux pour le XXIe siècle: discipliner la finance et organiser l'internationalisation', *Techniques financières et développement*, 53–4, Epargne sans frontière 8–19.

—— (1999c) 'State and market: towards a new synthesis for the twenty-first century', in UNESCO *World Social Science Report*, UNESCO, London.

—— (chairman) (1999d) *Le gouvernement de la zone Euro*, Rapport du Groupe de Travail du Commissariat Général du Plan 'Co-ordination des politiques macroéconomiques en Europe', Documentation Française, Paris.

Boyer Robert and Caroli Eve (1993) 'Changement de paradigme productif et rapport éducatif', mimeo, CEPREMAP, Paris. Trans. 'Production Regimes, Education and Training Systems: From Complementarity to Mismatch ?', mimeo, CEPREMAP, Paris.

Boyer Robert and Coriat Benjamin (1984) 'Les *greenbacks* "revisités": innovations dans les institutions et l'analyse monétaires américaines (1860–1913)', working paper, CEPREMAP. 8420, Paris.

—— (1986) 'Technical flexibility and macro stabilization', *Ricerche economiche*, 40 (4), 771–835.

Boyer Robert and Drache Daniel (1996) *States against Markets. The Limits of Globalization*, Routledge, London.

Boyer Robert and Durand Jean-Pierre (1993a) *Comment naissent le nouveaux systèmes productifs*, Harmattan, Paris.

—— (1993b) *L'après-fordisme*, Syros, Paris. New edition 1998. Trans. *After Fordism*, Macmillan, London, 1997.

Boyer Robert and Freyssenet Michel (forthcoming) *The World that will Change the Machine*, Oxford University Press, Oxford.

Boyer Robert and Juillard Michel (1992) 'The New Endogeneous Growth Theory versus a Productivity Regime Approach: One Century of American Economic History Revisited', working paper, CEPREMAP, 9210, Paris.

Boyer Robert and Mistral Jacques (1978) *Accumulation, inflation, crises*, Presses Universitaires de France, Paris. Second edition 1983.

Boyer Robert and Orlean André (1991) 'Les transformations des conventions salariales entre théorie et histoire', *Revue économique*, 42 (2), 233–72.

—— (1992) 'How do conventions evolve?' *Journal of Evolutionary Economics*, 2, 165–77.

—— (1994) 'Persistance et changement des conventions', in Orlean André (ed.) *Analyse économique des conventions*, Presses Universitaires de France, Paris.

Boyer Robert and Petit Pascal (1981) 'Progrès technique, croissance et emploi: un modèle d'inspiration kaldorienne pour six industries européennes', *Revue économique*, 32 (6), 1113–53.

—— (1984) 'Politiques industrielles et impact sur l'emploi: les pays européens face à la contrainte extérieure', *Revue d'économie industrielle*, 27, 108–21.

—— (1989) 'The cumulative growth model revisited', *Political Economy, Studies in the Surplus Approach*, 4 (1), 75–101.

—— (1991) 'Kaldor growth theories: past, present and prospects for the future', in Nell Edouard and Semmler Willy (eds) *Nicholas Kaldor and Mainstream Economics: Confrontation or Convergence?* Macmillan, London.

Boyer Robert and Ralle Pierre (1986) 'L'insertion internationale conditionne-t-elle les formes nationales d'emploi?' *Economie et sociétés*, P29 series, 117–68.

Boyer Robert and Schmeder Geneviève (1990) 'Division du travail, changement technique et croissance: un retour à Adam Smith', *Revue française d'économie*, 5 (3), 125–94.

Boyer Robert and Yamada Toshio (eds) (2000) *The Crisis of Japanese Capitalism*, Routledge, London.

Boyer Robert, Chavance Bernard and Godard Olivier (1991) *Les figures de l'irréversibilité en économie*, Editions de l'EHESS, Paris.

Boyer Robert, Dore Ronald and Mars Zoe (eds) (1994) *The Return to Incomes Policy*, Pinter, London.

Boyer Robert, Charron Elsie, Jürgens Ulrich and Tolliday Steven (eds) (1998) *Between Imitation and Innovation*, Oxford University Press, Oxford.

Braverman Henry (1974) *Le travail dans le capitalisme monopoliste*, Maspéro, Paris.

Brender Anton (1977) *Socialisme et cybernétique*, Calmann-Lévy, Paris.

Brenner Robert and Glick Mark (1991) 'The regulation approach: theory and history', *New Left Review*, 188, 45–120.

Cahuc Pierre (1993) *La nouvelle micro-économie*, La Découverte, Paris.

Calcagno Erique (1990) 'Evolución y actualidad de los estilos de desarrollo', *Revista de la CEPAL* (Santiago), 42.

Campbell John L., Hollingsworth Roger J. and Lindberg Leon N. (1991) *Governance of the American Economy*, Cambridge University Press, Cambridge.

Campinos-Dubernet M. (1984) 'Emploi et gestion de la main-d'oeuvre dans le BTP', *Dossier du CEREQ*, 34, 15–63.

Campos de Mello (1982) *La puissance du faible: les rapports Nord–Sud dans la négociation forêt de la CNUCED*, DEA, Université de Paris I.

Cappellin R. (1988) 'Transaction costs and urban agglomeration', *Revue d'économie régionale et urbaine*, 207–31.

Cartelier Jean (ed.) (1990) *La formation des grandeurs économiques*, Presses Universitaires de France, Paris.

Cartelier Jean and De Vroey Michel (1989) 'L'approche de la régulation: un nouveau paradigme?', *Economie et sociétés*, 23 (11), 63–87.

Cartier-Bresson Jean and Kopp Pierre, (1981) L'analyse sectionnelle: approche du système productif en Amérique latine', thesis, Université de Picadie.

Cassiers Isabelle (1989) *Croissance, crise et régulation en économie ouverte. La Belgique entre les deux guerres*, De Boeck Université, Brussels.

Castells Manuel and Hall P. (1994) *Technopoles of the World. The making of Twenty-first Century Industrial Complexes*, Routledge, London.

Caves Ronald (1989) 'International differences in industrial organisation', in Schmalensee R. and Willig R., *Handbook of Industrial Organization*, North-Holland, Amsterdam and New York.

CEPREMAP–CORDES, (1977) *Approches de l'inflation: l'exemple français*, ed. Benassy J-P., Boyer R., Gelpi R-M., Lipietz A., Mistral J. and Munoz J., Ominami C., Report of the Research Convention 22/176, December.

—— (1978) *Approches de l'inflation. L'exemple français*, Recherches Economiques et Sociales 12, Documentation française, Paris.

Cette Gilbert and Taddéi Dominique (1992) 'Les effets économiques d'une réduction–réorganisation du travail', *Futuribles*, 165–6, 171–92.

—— (1997) *Réduire la durée du travail. De la théorie à la pratique.* Collection Inédit, Sciences Sociales, Librairie Générale Française, Le Livre de Poche, Paris.

Chandler Alfred D. Jr (1990) *Scale and Scope The Dynamics of Industrial Capitalism*, Belknap Press of Harvard University Press, Cambridge MA.

Chartres Jacques-André (1995) 'Le changement de modes de régulation: apports et limites de la formalisation', in Boyer Robert and Saillard Yves (eds) *Théorie de la régulation. L'état des savoirs*, La Découverte, Paris.

Chavance Bernard (1980) *Le capital socialiste. Histoire critique de l'économie politique du socialisme (1917—1954)*, Sycomore, Paris.

—— (1983) *Le système économique soviétique*, Sycomore, Paris.

—— (1984a) 'Pourquoi le capitalisme étatique? Réponse à W. Andreff', *Babylone*, 2–3, 225–45.

—— (1984b) 'Les formes actuelles de crise dans les économies de type soviétique', *Critiques de l'économie politique*, 26–27, 225–45.

—— (1985) 'Economie et politique dans la dictature sur les besoins', *Les Temps modernes*, August–September, 205–37.

—— (ed.) (1987) *Régulation, cycles et crises dans les économies socialistes*, Éditions de l'École des hautes études en sciences sociales, Paris.

—— (1989) *Le système économique soviétique de Brejnev à Gorbatchev*, Nathan, Paris.

—— (1990) 'L'analyse des systèmes économiques socialistes et la problématique de la régulation', *Revue d'études comparatives Est–Ouest*, 21 (2), 277–308.

—— (1995) 'Hierarchical forms and co-ordination problems in Socialist Systems', *Industrial and Corporate Change*, 4 (1), 271–91.

Chavance Bernard (1997) 'De la réforme du socialisme à la transformation post-socialiste: la Chine en perspective comparative', in Duménil Gérard and Lew R. (eds) *Où va la Chine? Actuel Marx*, 22, 69–90.

Chiaromonte Fiorella, Dosi Giovanni and Orsenigo Luigi (1992) 'Innovative learning and institutions in the process of development: on the microfoundations of growth regimes', in Thomson R. (ed.) *Learning and Technological Change*, Macmillan, London.

Clerc Denis, Lipietz Alain and Satre-Buisson Joël (1988) *La Crise*, Syros, Paris. Second edition 1985.

Clio Jean (1998) '*Régulation* et histoire: Je t'aime, moi non plus', in Boyer Robert and Saillard Yves (eds) *Théorie de la régulation. L'état des savoirs*, La Découverte, Paris.

Coase R. H. (1937) 'The nature of the firm', *Economica*, 4 (16), 386–405.

Cohen B.J. (1997) *Organizing the World's Money. The Political Economy of International Monetary Relations*, Basic Books, New York.

Commissariat Général du Plan, (1993) *L'économie face à l'écologie*, La Découverte/Documentation Française, Paris.

Commons, J.R. (1913) *Labor and Administration*, Macmillan, New York.

—— (1924) *Legal Foundations of Capitalism*, Macmillan, New York.

—— (1934) *Institutional Economics. Its Place in Political Economy*, Macmillan, New York. Reprinted Transaction, New Brunswick NJ, 1990.

—— (1951) *The Economics of Collective Action*, Macmillan, New York.

Commons, J.R. *et al.* (1910) *A documentary history of American Industrial Society*, 10 vols, Arthur Clark, New York.

Contamin Rémy and Lacu Cyrille (1998) 'Origines et dynamiques de la crise asiatique', *L'Année de la Régulation 1998*, II, La Découverte, Paris.

Cooper R.N. (1987) *The International Monetary System. Essays in World Economics*, MIT Press, Cambridge MA.

Coriat Benjamin (1979) *L'atelier et le chronomètre,* Bourgois, Paris.

—— (1980) 'Ouvriers et automates. Trois études sur la notion d'industries de processus', CREST, Paris, mimeo.

—— (1982) 'Relations industrielles, rapport salarial et régulation', *Communication*, 3, Dunod, Paris.

—— (1990) *L'atelier et le robot. Essai sur le fordisme et la production de masse à l'age de l'électronique*, Bourgois, Paris.

—— (1991) *Penser à l'envers*, Bourgois, Paris.

—— (1992) 'L'entreprise et l'approche en termes de régulation, premiers jalons', Cahiers de l'IREPD mimeo, University of Grenoble.

—— (1994a) 'Taylor, Ford et Ohno: nouveaux développements de l'analyse du ohnisme', *Japon in extenso*, 31, 7–23.

—— (1994b) 'La théorie de la régulation: origines, spécificités, perspectives', *Futur antérieur*, special issue *Ecole de la Régulation et critique de la raison economique*, Harmattan, Paris.

—— (2000) 'The abominable system of Mr Ohno: competence, routine and control in the Japanese production system', in Dosi G., Nelson R.R. and Winter, S. (eds) *The Nature and Dynamics of Organisational Capabilities,* Oxford University Press, Oxford.

Coriat Benjamin and Dosi Giovanni (1994) 'Learning how to Govern and Learning how to Solve Problems: on the Co-evolution of Competences, Conflicts and Organizational Routines', presented at the Prince Bertil Symposium, Stockholm,

June. Reprinted in Chandler A., Hagström, P. and Sölvell Ö. (eds.) *The Dynamic Firm*, Cambridge University Press, Cambridge.

—— (1998) 'The institutional embeddedness of economic change: an appraisal of the "evolutionary" and the "regulationist" research programme', in Nielsen K. and Johnson B. (eds) *Institutions and Economic Change*, Edward Elgar, Cheltenham, Reprinted in Dosi G., *Innovation, Organization and Economic Dynamics*, Edward Elgar, Cheltenham, 2000.

Coriat Benjamin and Saboia Joao (1987) 'Régime d'accumulation et rapport salarial au Brésil (from the 1950s to the 1980s): un processus de fordisation forcée et contrariée', GERTTD 87–01, Paris.

Coriat Benjamin and Taddei Dominique (1993) *Entreprise France. Made in France*, Livre de Poche, Hachette, Paris.

Coriat Benjamin and Weinstein Olivier (1995) *Les nouvelles théories de l'entreprise. Une présentation critique,* Livre de Poche, Hachette, Paris.

Corneo Giacomo (1993) 'Syndicat, négociations et marchés internes. Essais en économie du travail', thesis, EHESS, Paris.

Cornwall John (1977) *Modern Capitalism. Its Growth and Transformation*, Martin Robertson, Oxford.

Corolleur F. (1994) *Dynamiques industrielles et institutionnelles localisées*, IREPD, Grenoble.

Coulomb P., Delorme H., Hervieu B., Jollivet M. and Lacombe P. (1990) *Les agriculteurs et la politique,* Presses de la Fondation nationale de sciences politiques, Paris.

Courlet Claude and Pecqueur Bernard (1991) 'Systèmes locaux d'entreprises et externalités: un essai de typologie', *Revue d'économie régionale et urbaine*, 3–4, 391–406.

—— (1992) 'Les systèmes industriels localisés en France: un nouveau modèle de développement', in Benko G. B. and Lipietz A. (eds) *Les régions qui gagnent*, Presses Universitaires de France, Paris.

Da Mota Veiga Pedro (1989) La *régulation* au Brésil: contribution à l'étude du rapport salarial et du rapport Etat–économie, working paper 16, ESLAC, Paris.

Davidson Paul (1978) *Money in the Real World*, second edition, Macmillan, London.

Davis Christopher and Wojciech Charemza (1989) *Models of Disequilibrium and Shortage in Centrally Planned Economies*, Chapman & Hall, London.

Daynac M. and Dupuy C. (1991) *Reconversion. Théorie et pratiques*, DATAR, Paris.

De Bandt Jacques and Gadrey J. (1994) *Relations de service, marchés de services*, Editions du CNRS, Paris.

De Bandt Jacques and Petit Pascal (1993) 'Compétitivité: la place des rapports industrie/services', in Coriat B. and Taddeï D. (eds) *Entreprise France. Made in France* II, Livre de poche, Hachette, Paris.

De Bernis G. (1987) *Relations économiques internationales*, Dalloz, Paris.

De Brunhoff Suzanne (1971) *L'offre de monnaie. Critique d'un concept*, Maspéro, Paris.

—— (1979) *Les rapports d'argent*, Presses Universitaires de Grenoble Maspéro, Paris.

—— (1982) *Etat et capital*, Maspéro, Paris.

De Vroey Michel (1984) 'A regulation approach interpretation of the contemporary crisis', *Capital and Class*, 23, 45–66.

Debailleul Guy (1990) *Evolution de la politique agricole américaine: Une approche régulationniste*, thesis, Institut National Agronomique, Paris–Grignon.

Dehem R. (1978) *De l'étalon sterling à l'étalon dollar*, Calmann-Lévy, Paris.

Dehove Mario (1997) 'L'Union européenne inaugure-t-elle un nouveau grand régime d'organisation des pouvoirs publics et de la société internationale?', *L'Année de la Régulation 1997* I, La Découverte, Paris.

Delavaud André and Neffa Julio Cesar (co-ordinators) (1994) *L'Argentine à l'aube du troisième millenaire*, Editions de l'IHEAL, Paris.

Delorme Robert (1984) 'Compromis institutionnalisé: état inséré et crise de l'état', *Cahiers d'économie politique*, 26–7, 149–60.

—— (1991) 'Etat et hétérogénéité: ERIC et le MPPE', *Cahiers de recherche sociologique*, 17, 153–84, special issue *Régulation et problèmes contemporains*, Montréal.

—— (1994) 'Economic diversity as cement and as a challenge to evolutionary perspectives', in Delorme R. and Dopfer K. (eds) *The Political Economy of Diversity. Evolutionary Perspectives or Economic Order and Disorder?* Edward Elgar, Cheltenham.

—— (ed.) (1996) *A l'Est, du nouveau. Changement institutionnel et transformations économiques*, Harmattan, Paris.

Delorme Robert and André Christine (1983) *L'Etat et l'économie. Un essai d'explication de l'évolution des dépenses publiques en France 1870–1980*, Seuil, Paris.

Dennett Daniel (1990) *La stratégie de l'interprète*, Presses Universitaires de France, Paris.

Donzelot Jacques (1984) *L'invention du social*, Fayard, Paris.

Dosi Giovanni (1984) *Technical Change and Industrial Transformation,* London, Macmillan.

—— (1988) 'Sources, procedures and microeconomic effects of innovation', *Journal of Economic Literature*, 26 (3), 1120–71.

—— (2000) *Innovation, Organization and Economic Dynamics. Selected Essays*, Edward Elgar, Cheltenham and Northampton MA.

Dosi Giovani and Salvatore Roberta (1992) 'The structure of industrial production and the boundaries between firms and markets', in Storper M. and Scott A. J. (eds) *Pathways to Industrialization and Regional Development*, Routledge, London.

Dosi Giovanni, Freeman Christopher, Nelson Richard R., Silverberg Gérald and Soete Luc (eds) (1988) *Technical Change and Economic Theory*, Pinter, London.

Dosi Giovanni, Marengo Luigi, Bassanini A. and Valente M. (1993) 'Norms as Emergent Properties of Adaptive Learning. The Case of Economic Routines', Center of Research in Management working paper, University of California, Berkeley CA.

Douglas Mary (1989) *Ainsi pensent les institutions*, SOGEDIM, Editions Usher, Paris.

Drach Marcel (1983) 'Crise du travail et non-lieu du fordisme dans les économies de type soviétique', *Revue d'études comparatives Est–Ouest*, 14 (1), 13–38.

—— (1984) *La crise dans les pays de l'Est*, La Découverte, Paris. Second edition 1987.

—— (1985) 'Les trois crises', in Lavigne Marie and Andreff Wladimir (eds) *La realité socialiste*, Economica, Paris.

—— (1987) 'Temps court, temps long, temps stochastique: l'articulation des différentes temporalités de crise dans les économies de type soviétique', in

Chavance Bernard (ed.) *Régulation, cycles et crises dans les économies social-istes*, Editions EHESS, Paris.

—— (1988) 'Monnaie et appareil. *Régulation* et dérèglements dans les économies centralement planifiées', thesis, Université de Paris I.

Drache Daniel and Boyer Robert (1995) *The Power of Nations, The Limits of Markets*, McGill-Queen's University Press, Montreal.

Drache Daniel and Gertler Meric S. (eds) (1991) *The New Era of Global Competition*, McGill-Queen's University Press, Montreal.

Du Tertre Christian (1988) *Flexibilité organisationnelle et productivité dans le Bâtiment*, Editions Plan construction et architecture, Paris.

—— (1989) *Technologie, flexibilité, emploi. Une approche sectorielle du post-taylorisme*, Harmattan, Paris.

—— (1992) *Travail, technologie, organisation*, Editions de l'IRIS, Université Paris-Dauphine.

—— (1994a) 'Le changement du travail: le rôle majeur des "relations de services"', *Document IRIS*, Paris.

—— (1994b) 'Dynamique du BTP et nouveaux dispositifs institutionnels pour une sortie de crise', presented at the colloquium 'L'innovation en chantiers', Editions Plan construction et architecture, Paris 14 and 15 September.

—— (1999) 'Les services de proximité aux personnes: vers une *régulation* conven-tionnée et territorialisée?', *L'Année de la Régulation 1999*, La Découverte, Paris.

Du Tertre C. and Santilli G. (1992) *Automatisation et travail*, Presses Universitaires de France, Paris.

Dufourt Daniel (1994) 'Arrangements institutionnels et explications du processus de changement: les enjeux d'une réflexion renouvelée sur les institutions', in Basle M. *et al.* (eds) *Changement institutionnel et changement technologique*, Editions du CNRS, Paris.

Dumenil Gérard and Levy Dominique (1993) 'Les régulationnistes pouvaient-ils apprendre davantage des classiques? Une analyse critique de quatre modèles', *Economie et sociétés*, 'Théories de la Régulation', series 27 (6), 117–55.

Dunford M. (1988) 'Grenoble and Central Scotland's Regional Electronics Industries', working Paper 18, University of Sussex, Brighton.

Dunmore Timothy (1980) *The Stalinist Command Economy*, Macmillan, London.

Dupuy C., and Gilly Jean-Pierre, (eds) (1993) *Industrie et territoires en France. Dix ans de décentralisation*, Documentation Française, Paris.

—— (1994) 'Apprentissage organisationnel et dynamique territoriale', Colloque International de SORIA, in Pecqueur Bernard and Soulage Bernard (eds) *Dynamiques territoriales et mutations économiques*, La Découverte, Paris.

Dupuy Jean Pierre (1992) *Introduction aux sciences sociales. Logique des phénomènes collectifs*, Ellipses, Paris.

Dupuy Jean Pierre, Eymard-Duvernay François, Favereau Olivier, Orlean André, Salais Robert and Thévenot Laurent (1989) *Revue économique* 40 (2), special issue *Convention Theory*.

Dutraive, Véronique (1993) 'La firme entre transaction et contrat: Williamson épigone ou dissident de la pensée institutionnaliste ?', *Revue d'économie poli-tique*, 103 (1). 83–105.

Ebizuka Akira, Uemura Hiroyasu and Isogai Akinori (1997) 'L'hypothèse de "la relation hiérarchisée marché–firme" et l'économie japonaise de l'après-guerre' *L'Année de la Régulation 1997*, I, La Découverte, Paris.

Economie et Societes (1989) *Le Colloque de Barcelone*, 11 (R4) Presses Universitaires de Grenoble, Grenoble.

Economie et Societes (1990) *Le Colloque de Barcelone* 12 (R5), Presses Universitaires de Grenoble, Grenoble.

The Economist (1999) 'The new economy: work in progress', 24–30 July, pp. 19–21.

Edquist Charles and Lundvall Bengt-Åke (1993) 'Comparing small Nordic systems of innovation', in Nelson Richard (ed.) *National Innovation Systems*, Oxford University Press, Oxford.

Edwards Richard (1979) *Contested Terrain*, Heinemann, London.

Eichengreen Barry (ed.) (1985) *The Gold Standard in Theory and History*, Methuen, London.

El Aoufi Noureddine (1995) 'Trajectoires nationales au Maghreb', in Boyer Robert and Saillard Yves (eds) *Théorie de la régulation. L'état des savoirs*, La Découverte, Paris.

Elbaum Bernard and Lazonick William (1987) *The Decline of the British Economy*, Clarendon Press, Oxford.

Esping-Andersen Gösta (1990) *The Three Worlds of Welfare Capitalism*, Polity, Cambridge.

—— (1999) *The Social Foundations of Post-industrial Economies,* Oxford University Press, Oxford.

Eymard-Duvernay François (1987) 'Les entreprises et leurs modèles', *Cahiers du Centre d'études de l'emploi*, Presses Universitaires de France, Paris.

Eymard-Duvernay François, Bessy Christian, Gomel Bernard and Simonin Bertrand, (1994) 'Les agents du service public de l'emploi dans leurs relations avec les entreprises', research paper, Centre d'études de l'emploi, Paris.

Fagerberg Jan (1991) 'Technology and *régulation* in a classical model of economic growth', *European Journal of Political Economy*, 7, (3), 299–312.

Fajnzylber F. (1983) *La industrialización trunca*, Nueva Imagen, Mexico City.

Farnetti Richard (1994) *L'économie britannique de 1873 à nos jours*, Armand Colin, Paris.

Favereau Olivier (1989a) 'Marchés internes, marchés externes', *Revue économique*, 2, 273–328.

—— (1989b) 'Organisation et marché', *Revue française d'économie*, 4 (1), 65–86.

—— (1993a) 'Suggestions pour reconstruire la théorie des salaires sur une théorie des règles', notes for the CNAM seminar 'Le travail: marché et organisation', 2 April.

—— (1993b) 'Théorie de la *régulation* et économie des conventions: canevas pour une confrontation', *La Lettre de la Régulation*, 7, 1–3.

—— (1994a) 'Contrat, compromis, convention', unpublished MS.

—— (1994b) 'Co-ordination par les règles et apprentissage collectif: application à la théorie des salaires', research paper, University of Paris X.

—— (1995a) 'Développement et économie des conventions', in Hugon Guy *et al.*, *L'Afrique des incertitudes*, Presses Universitaires de France, Paris.

—— (1995b) 'La science économique et ses modèles', in Cartelier Jean and D'Autume Antoine (eds) *L'économie est-elle une science dure?* Economica, Paris.

—— (1997) 'L'incomplétude n'est pas le problème, c'est la solution', in Reynaud Bénédicte (ed.) *Les limites de la rationalité* II, La Découverte, Paris.

Fligstein Neil (1996) 'Markets as politics', *American Sociological Review*, 61, 656–73.

Flora Peter (1986) 'Introduction', in Flora Peter (ed.) *Growth to Limits. The Western European Welfare States since World War I*, II, de Gruyter, Berlin and New York.

Freeman Christopher (1982) *The Economics of Industrial Innovation* second edition, Pinter, London.

—— (1994) 'The economics of technical change', *Cambridge Journal of Economics*, 18, 463–514.

—— (1995) 'The national system of innovation in historical perspective', *Cambridge Journal of Economics*, 19, 5–24.

Freyssenet Michel, Mair Andrew, Shimizu Koïchi and Volpato Guiseppe (1998) *One Best Way? Trajectories and Industrial Models of the World's Automobile producers*, Oxford University Press, Oxford.

Friedberg E. (1993) *Le pouvoir et la règle*, Seuil, Paris.

Friedman Milton (1953) *Essays in Positive Economics*, University of Chicago Press, Chicago.

—— (1968) 'The role of monetary policy', *American Economic Review*, 58 (1), 1–17.

Funabashi Y. (1988) *Managing the Dollar from the Plaza to the Louvre*, Institute for International Economics, Washington DC.

Gadrey J. (1990) 'Rapports sociaux de service: une autre *régulation*', *Revue économique*, 41 (1), 49–69.

—— (1992) *L'économie de services*, La Découverte, Paris.

—— (1994) 'La modernisation des services professionnels: rationalisation industrielle ou rationalisation professionnelle?', *Revue française de sociologie*, 35 (2), 163–95.

Gaffard Jean-Luc (ed.) (1990) *Economie industrielle et de l'innovation*, Dalloz, Paris.

Gandois R. (chairman of the commission on 'French competitiveness' in preparation for the Eleventh Plan) (1993) *France: le choix de la performance globale*, Documentation Française, Paris.

Gardner R.N. (1980) *Sterling–Dollar Diplomacy in Current Perspective*, Columbia University Press, New York.

Garrouste Pierre (1994) 'Carl Menger et Friedrich A. Hayek à propos des institutions: continuités et ruptures', in Basle M, Dufourt D. *et al.*, *Changement institutionel et changement technique*, Editions du CNRS, Paris.

Gerschenkron Alexandre (1962) 'Industrial enterprise in Soviet Russia', in *Economic Backwardness in Historical Perspective*, Harvard University Press, Cambridge MA.

Gervais M., Jollivet M. and Tavernier Y. (1976) 'La fin de la France paysanne de 1914 à nos jours', in Duby G. and Wallon A. (eds) *Histoire de la France rurale* IV, Seuil, Paris.

Giddens Anthony (1984) *The Constitution of Society*, Polity Press, Cambridge.

Gilly Jean-Pierre (1987) 'Innovation et territoire: pour une approche méso-économique des technopoles', *Revue d'économie régionale et urbaine*, 5, 603–47.

Gilly Jean-Pierre and Grossetti M. (1993) 'Organisation, individus et territoires: le cas des systèmes locaux d'innovation', *Revue d'économie régionale et urbaine*, 3, 449—68.

Goddard Olivier (1992a) 'Stratégies industrielles et conventions d'environnement: de l'univers stabilisé aux univers controversés', *INSEE-Méthodes, Environment et Economie*, 39–40, 145–74.

—— (1992b) *La réduction des émissions de gaz à effet de serre au moyen de taxes*, OECD, Paris.

Goodwin Richard (1967) 'A growth cycle', in Feinstein C. H. (ed.) *Socialism, Capitalism and Economic Growth,* Cambridge University Press, Cambridge.

Gordon David M. (1997) From the drive system to the capital–labour Accord: econometric tests for the transition between productivity regimes', *Industrial Relations*, 36 (2), 125–59.

Gordon David M. (1996) *Fat and Mean*, Martin Kessler Books, Free Press, New York.

Gordon David M. (1991) 'Kaldor's macro system: too much cumulation, too few contradictions', in Nell Edward J. and Semmler Willi (eds) *Nicholas Kaldor and Mainstream Economics*, Macmillan, London.

Gordon David M., Edwards Richard and Reich Michael (1982) *Segmented Work, Divided Workers*, Cambridge University Press, Cambridge.

Gouin D.M., Hairy D. and Perraud D. (1985) *Crise laitière et transformation des modes de régulation sectoriels,* INRA ESR, Paris and Grenoble.

Grando Jean-Marc, Margirier Gilles and Ruffieux Bernard (1980) 'Rapport salarial et compétitivité des économies nationales', thesis, Université de Grenoble II.

Granou André, Baron Yves and Billaudot Bernard (1979) *Croissance et crise*, Maspéro, Paris.

Grasman J. (1987) *Asymptotic Methods for Relaxation Oscillations and Applications,* Applied Mathematical Sciences 63, Springer, Berlin.

Greenan Nathalie and Guellec Dominique (1992) 'Co-ordination within the Firm and Endogenous Growth', discussion paper, INSEE, Division des Etudes Economiques, G series 9206.

Gregory Derek and Urry John (eds) (1985) *Social Relations and Spatial Structures*, Macmillan, London.

Guibert Bernard (1986a) *L'ordre marchand. Structures de la vénalité*, CERF, Paris.

—— (1986b) *La violence capitalisée. Essai sur la politique de Marx*, CERF, Paris.

Gutierrez Garza Esthela (1983) 'L'accumulation de capital et le mouvement ouvrier au Mexique 1950–1960', thesis, Université de Paris–VIII.

Guttmann Robert (1984) 'Stagflation and credit-money in the USA', *British Review of Economic Issues*, 6 (15), 79–119.

—— (1989) *Reforming Money and Finance. Institutions and Markets in Flux*, Sharpe, Armonk NY.

—— (1990) 'The regime of credit-money and its current transition', *Economie et sociétés*, 24 (6), 81–105.

—— (1994) *How Credit-Money Shapes the Economy. The United States in a Global System*, Sharpe, Armonk NY.

Haggard S. and Simmons B.A. (1987) 'Theories of international regimes', *International Organisation*, 41 (3), 491–517.

Haken H. (1983) *Advanced Synergetics,* Springer, Berlin.

Hale Jack and Huseyn Koçak (1991) *Dynamics and bifurcations,* Springer, Berlin.

Hall Peter (1989) *The Political Power of Economic Ideas*, Princeton University Press, Princeton NJ.

Hamouda O., Rowley R. and Wolf B. (eds) (1989) *The Future of the International Monetary System*, Edward Elgar, Aldershot.

Hanada Masanori (1994) 'Modalité de la fixation des salaires au Japon et en France', *Japon in extenso*, 32, 23–41.

Harvey David (1989) *The Condition of Postmodernity*, Oxford, Blackwell.

Harrison Bennett and Bluestone Barry (1990) *The Great U-turn*, Basic Books, New York.

Harsanyi John C. (1962) 'Measurement of social power, opportunity costs and the theory of two-person bargaining games', *Behavioural Science,* 7, 67–81.

Hatzfeld Henri (1971) *Du paupérisme à la sécurité sociale (1850–1940)*, Armand Colin, Paris.

Hausmann Ricardo (1981) State Landed Property, Oil Rent and Accumulation in the Venezuelan Economy', thesis, Cornell University, 1981.

—— (1988) 'Sobre la crisis económica venezolana', presented at an international colloquium on *Régulation* Theory, Barcelona.

Hausmann Ricardo and Márquez Gustavo (1986) 'Du bon côté du choc pétrolier', in Boyer Robert (ed.) *Capitalismes fin de siècle*, Presses Universitaires de France, Paris.

Hayek Friedrich A. (1973) *Droit, législation, liberté*, Presses Universitaires de France, Paris.

Heintz W. (1992) 'Modèles d'entreprises et conventions de qualité. Les entreprises de collecte-stockage sur le marché du blé', thesis, Institut national agronomique, Paris and Grignon.

Héritier Pierre (1991) *Les enjeux de l'Europe sociale*, La Découverte, Paris.

Hillcoat Guillermo (1986) 'La crise des modèles de développement en Amérique latine. De la substitution d'importations à l'économie tournée vers l'extérieur: une discussion théorique illustrée par l'expérience argentine', thesis, Université de Paris VIII.

—— (1989) 'L'évolution du rapport salarial en accumulation intensive. L'expérience argentine', Problèmes d'Amérique latine 95, Documentation Française.

Hirano Yasuro (1993) 'Economic growth and the wage–labour nexus in post-war Japan', in Boyer R. and Yamada T. (eds) La Collection de la *Régulation* I, *Crises du capitalisme*, Fujiwara Shoten, Tokyo.

Hirata Kiyoaki (1993) *Civil Society and Régulation*, Tokyo: Iwanami Shoten.

Hirsch A. (1970) 'Mitchell's work on Civil War inflation in his development as an economist', *History of Political Economy*, 2 (1), 118–32.

Hirsch M. and Smale S. (1974) *Differential Equations Dynamical System Linear Algebra*, Academic Press, New York.

Hirschman Albert (1970) *Exit, Voice and Loyalty*, Harvard University Press, Cambridge MA.

—— (1977) 'A generalised linkage approach to development, with special reference to staples', *Economic Development and Cultural Change*, 25, supplement.

—— (1978) *Passion et intérêt*, Minuit, Paris.

Hodgson Geoffrey (1988) *Economics and Institutions*, Polity / Blackwell, Oxford.

—— (1989) 'Institutional rigidities and economic growth', *Cambridge Journal of Economics*, 13 (1), 79–101.

Hollard M. and Margirier G. (1986) 'Nouveaux procès de production et implications macroéconomiques: contribution au débat sur la flexibilité', *Formation Emploi*, 14, Documentation française, Paris.

Hollingsworth Roger J. and Boyer Robert (eds) (1997) *Contemporary Capitalism. The Embeddedness of Institutions*, Cambridge University Press, Cambridge.

Hollingsworth Roger, Schmitter Philippe and Streeck Wolfgang (1994) *Governing Capitalist Economies*, Oxford University Press, Oxford.

Hounshell David A. (1989) *From the American System to Mass Production, 1800–1932*, Johns Hopkins University Press, Baltimore MD.

Hourcade Jean Claude (1993) 'Les arguments économiques de la négociation internationale autour de l'effet de serre', in Commissariat Général du Plan, Documentation française, La Découverte, Paris.

Hourcade Jean Claude and Baron R. (1992) *Réduire les émissions de gaz à effet de serre au moyen de permis négociables*, OECD, Paris.

Howell Chris (1992) *Regulating Labor*, Princeton University Press, Princeton NJ.

Huanacune Rosas Francisco (1991) 'Jalons d'une proposition sur le rôle fonctionnel du secteur informel: le cas péruvien 1970–1985', dissertation, EHESS, Paris.

Innes Harold (1967) 'The importance of staple products', in Easterbrook W. T. and Watkins M. H. (eds), *Approaches to Canadian Economic History*, McClelland & Stewart, Toronto.

Inoué Yasuo (1994) 'Trajectoires nationales d'industrialisation de la Corée du Sud et de Taïwan', *Japon in extenso*, 32, 80–9.

Isogai Akinori (1994) 'An "institutional" analysis of a Japanese type of economic system', *Keizaigaku-kenkyu*, 59 (3–4), 483–517.

Itoh Makoto (1992) 'The Japanese model of post-Fordism', in Storper M. and Scott A. (eds) *Pathways to Industrialization and Regional Development*, Routledge, London.

Jacquemin Alexis (1993) 'L'industrie française face à ses défis', in Coriat Benjamin and Taddei Dominique, *Entreprise France*, Le livre de Poche, Hachette, Paris.

Japon in extenso (1994) 31–32, Paris. Japanese contributors: Hanada M., Hirano Y., Inoue Y., Shimizu K., Uemura H. and Ebizuka A.

Jessop Bob (1989) '*Régulation* théories in retrospect and prospect', *Economies et sociétés, Théorie de la régulation*, 23 (11) 7–62.

—— (1990a) '*Régulation* theories in retrospect and prospect', *Economy and Society*, 19 (2).

—— (1990b) *State Theory. Putting the Capitalist State in its Place*, Polity Press, London.

—— 'Twenty years of the (Parisian) *régulation* approach: the paradox of success and failure at home and abroad', *New Political Economy*, 2 (3), 503–26, 1997.

Jobert Bruno (1999) 'Des états en interactions', *L'Année de la Régulation 1999*, La Découverte, Paris.

Journal of Post-Keynesian Economics (1983) special issue on Kaldor, ed. Thirlwall, introduction, 2–18.

Juillard Michel (1993) *Un schéma de reproduction pour l'économie des Etats-Unis 1948–1980. Tentative de modélisation et de quantification*, Publications Universitaires Européennes, Peter Lang, Paris.

Julla E. (1991) 'Espace, territoire et régulation des économies locales', thesis, Université des Sciences Sociales de Toulouse.

Kaldor Nicholas (1970) 'The case for regional policies', *Scottish Journal of Political Economy*, 17 (3), reprinted in *Further Essays on Economic Theory*, Duckworth, London, 1970.

—— (1972) 'The irrelevance of equilibrium economics', *Economic Journal*, 82, 176–201. Reprinted in *Further Essays on Economic Theory*, Duckworth, London, 1978.

—— (1981) 'The role of increasing returns, technical progress and cumulative causation in the theory of international trade and economic growth', *Economie appliquée*, 34 (4), 593–617.

Kaldor N. and Mirrlees J.A. (1962) 'A new model of economic growth', *Review of Economic Studies*.

Karpik L. (1989) 'L'économie de la qualité', *Revue française de sociologie*, 30, 187–210.

Kato Tetsuro and Steven Rob (eds) (1993) *Is Japanese Management post-Fordist?*, Mado-sha, Tokyo.

Kébabdjian Gérard (1998) 'La théorie de la *régulation* face à la problématique des régimes internationaux', *L'Année de la Régulation 1998* II, La Découverte, Paris.

—— (1999) *Les théories de l'économie politique internationale*, Seuil, Paris.

Kenen P. (1989) *Exchange Rates and Policy Co-ordination*, University of Michigan Press, Ann Arbor MI.

—— (1994) *Understanding Interdependence. The Macroeconomics of the Open Economy*, Princeton University Press, Princeton NJ.

Kenney Martin and Florida Richard (1993) *Beyond Mass Production: The Japanese System and its Transfer to the US*, Oxford University Press, Oxford.

Kenney Martin, Curry J. and Goe W.R. (1988) 'Contextualizing Agriculture within Postwar US Society. Fordism as an Integrative Theory', international colloquium on *régulation* theory, Barcelona, 16—18 June.

Kenwood A.G. and Lougheed A.L., (1971) *The Growth of the International Economy, 1820—1960*, Allen & Unwin, London.

Kéohane Robert (1982) 'The demand for international regimes', *International Organisation*, 36 (2), 285–313.

—— (1984) *After Hegemony*, Princeton University Press, Princeton NJ.

Keynes John Maynard (1936) *The General Theory of Employment, Interest and Money*, Macmillan, London.

Kiel Arne and Mjøset Lars (1990) 'Wage formation in the Norwegian industry 1840–1985', *Scandinavian Economic History Review*, 38, (1), 19–49.

Kindleberger C.P. (1986) 'International public choice without international government', *American Economic Review*, 76 (1), 1–13.

Kirat T. (1993) 'Innovation technologique et apprentissage institutionnel', *Revue d'économie régionale et urbaine*, 3, 357–93.

Knies K. (1873–9) *Geld und Kredit*, 3 vol, Berlin.

Knight John (1992) *Institutions and Social Conflict*, Cambridge University Press, Cambridge.

Korpi Walter (1981) 'Labour movements and industrial relations', in Allardt Erik (ed.) *Nordic Democracy*, Nordiske Selskab, Copenhagen.

Kosonen Pekka (1992) 'National welfare state models in the face of European integration', *History of European Ideas*, 15 (1–3), 285–317.

Kotz David M. (1990) 'A comparative analysis of the theory of regulation and the social structure of accumulation theory', *Science and Society*, 1, 5–28.

Krasner Stephen (1982) 'Regimes and the limits of realism: regimes as autonomous variables', *International Organization*, 36 (2), 301–33.

—— (ed.) (1983) *International Regimes*, Cornell University Press, Ithaca NY.

Krätke Stefan (1997) 'Approche régulationniste des études régionales: une revue de littérature', *L'Année de la Régulation 1997* I, La Découverte, Paris.

Krugman Paul (1991) *Currencies and Crises*, MIT Press, Cambridge MA.

Kundig Bernard (1984) 'Du taylorisme classique à la flexibilisation du système productif: l'impact macroéconomique des différents types d'organisation du travail', *in Critique de l'économie politique*, 26–7, 53–70, La Découverte, Paris.

Lacroix Anne and Mollard Amédée (1988) 'Durée et intensité du travail des agriculteurs dans la crise économique', *Actes et communications*, 3, 45–82.

—— (1993) 'Environnement et théorie de la *régulation:* une approche à partir de l'agriculture', summer school 'Economie des institutions', INRA, Hyères, 27—30 September working paper EAEPE, fifth annual conference, Barcelona, 28–30 October. Working paper 93–05, Département d'économie et de sociologie rurale, Université de Grenoble.

—— (1994) 'L'approche sectorielle de la régulation: une problématique à partir de l'agriculture', in Allaire G. and Boyer R. (eds) *La grande transformation de l'agriculture. Lectures conventionnalistes et régulationnistes,* INRA-Economica, Paris.

Lafont Jean and Leborgne Danièle (1979) 'L'accumulation du capital et les crises dans l'URSS contemporaine: une première approche', CEPREMAP 7910, Paris.

Langlois Richard N. (1989) 'What was wrong with the "old" institutional economics (and what is still wrong with the "new")?' *Review of Political Economy*, 1 (3), 270–99.

Lanzarotti Mario (1986) 'L'industrialisation en Corée du Sud: une analyse en sections productives', *Revue Tiers Monde*, 27 (107), 637–59.

—— (1992) *La Corée du Sud. Une sortie du sous-développement*, IEDES Presses Universitaires de France, Paris.

Laurent C. (1992) '*L'agriculture et son territoire dans la crise*', thesis, Université de Paris VII.

Lavigne Marie and Andreff Wladimir (eds) (1985) *La réalité socialiste. Crise, adaptation, progrès*, Economica, Paris.

Laville J.-L. (1993) 'L'évolution du travail', *Travail*, 29, 13–21.

Lavoie Marc (1982) 'Les post-keynésiens et la monnaie endogène', *L'actualité économique*, 58 (1–2), 191–219.

—— (1984) 'Endogenous flows of credit and the post-Keynesian theory of money', *Journal of Economic Issues*, 18 (3), 771–97.

Leborgne Danièle (1982) '1930–1980: cinquante ans de croissance extensive en URSS', *Critiques de l'économie politique*, 19, 71–98.

Leborgne Danièle and Lipietz Alain (1988) 'L'après-fordisme et son espace', *Les Temps modernes*, 43 (501), 75–114.

—— (1990) 'Pour éviter l'Europe à deux vitesses', *Travail et société*, 15 (2), 189–210.

—— (1991) 'Idées fausses et questions ouvertes de l'après-fordisme', *Espaces et sociétés,* 66–7, 39–68.

—— (1992) 'Flexibilité offensive, flexibilité défensive: deux stratégies sociales dans la production des nouveaux espaces économiques', in Benko G.B. and Lipietz A. (eds), *Les régions qui gagnent*, Presses Universitaires de France, Paris.

Lelart M. (1991) *Le système monétaire international*, La Découverte, Paris.

Leroy Claude (1995) 'Les salaires en longue période', in Boyer Robert and Saillard Yves (eds) *Théorie de la régulation. L'état des savoirs*, La Découverte, Paris.

Lesourne Jacques (1991) *Ordre et désordre*, Economica, Paris.

Lesourne Jacques and Orléan André (eds) (1998) *Advances in Self-organization and Evolutionary Economics*, Economica, Paris.

Levy Frank (1998) 'Incomes, families, and living standards', in Litan Robert E., Lawrence Robert Z. and Schultze Charles L. (eds) *American Living Standards*, Brookings Institution, Washington DC.

Lichtenberger Yves (1993) 'Ressources humaines, formation et qualification: renouveler les approches', in Coriat Benjamin and Taddéi Dominique (eds) *Entreprise France. Made in France II*, Livre de Poche, Hachette, Paris.

Lipietz Alain (1974) *Le tribut foncier urbain*, Maspéro, Paris.

—— (1975) 'Quelques problèmes de la production monopoliste d'espace urbain', in *Note méthodologique de l'Institut de l'environnement* 5, Paris.

—— (1977) *Le capital et son espace*, Maspéro, Paris.

—— (1979) *Crise et inflation, pourquoi?* Maspéro–La Découverte, Paris.

—— (1983) *Le monde enchanté. De la valeur à l'envol inflationniste*, La Découverte–Maspéro, Paris.

—— (1984a) *L'audace ou l'enlisement,* La Découverte, Paris.

—— (1984b) 'A Marxist approach to urban ground rent', in Ball M. (ed.) *Land Rent, Housing and the Planning System*, Croom Helm, London.

—— (1985) *Mirages et miracles. Problèmes de l'industrialisation dans le tiers monde*, La Découverte, Paris.

—— (1986) 'New tendencies in the international division of labor: regimes of accumulation and modes of regulation', in Scott A. J. and Storper M. (eds) *Production, Work, Technology*, Allen & Unwin, London.

—— (1988) 'La trame, la chaîne et la régulation: un outil pour les sciences sociales', CEPREMAP 8816, Paris.

—— (1990) 'Le national et le régional: quelle autonomie face à la crise capitaliste mondiale?', in Benko G.B. (ed.) *La dynamique spatiale de l'économie contemporaine*, Editions de l'espace européan, La Garanne.

—— (1991) 'Les rapports capital–travail à l'aube du XXIe siècle', in Chaumont C.Y. and Van Parijs P. (eds) *Les limites de l'inéluctable*, De Boeck-Wesmael, Brussels.

—— (1992a) 'Une économie à reconstruire', in Barrere Martine (ed.) *Terre, patrimoine commun*, La Découverte, Paris.

—— (1992b) *Berlin, Bagdad, Rio. Le XXIe siècle est commencé*, Quai Voltaire, Paris.

—— (1993a) *Vert-espérance. L'avenir de l'écologie politique*, La Découverte, Paris.

—— (1993b) 'Postfordism and the international debate around Toyotist Japan' (in Japanese), *Kansai University Keizai Ronshu*, 42–1, 9–31.

—— (1995) 'Enclosing the global commons: global environmental negotiations in a North–South conflictual approach', in Bhaskar V. and Glyn A. (eds) *The North, the South, and the Environment*, Earthscan, London.

—— (1996) 'Les nouvelles relations Centre–Périphérie: les exemples contrastés Europe–Amérique du Nord', trans. in Naastepad C. W. M. and Storm S. (eds) *The State and the Economic Process*, Edward Elgar, London.

—— (1998) *La société en sablier*, La Découverte, Paris.

—— (1999) *Qu'est-ce que l'écologie politique? La grande transformation du XXIe siècle*, La Découverte, Paris.

Lipietz Alain and Radane Pierre (1993) 'Energie: élargir les marges de liberté', in Commissariat Général du Plan, *L'Economie face à l'écologie*, Documentation français–La Découverte, Paris.

Livet Pierre (1994) *La communauté virtuelle*, Eclat, Paris.

Livet Pierre and Reynaud Bénédicte (1997) 'L'interprétation des règles: un obstacle à la politique économique', in Reynaud Bénédicte (ed.) *Les limites de la rationalité*, La Découverte, Paris.

Lordon Frédéric (1991) 'Théorie de la croissance: quelques développements récents', *Observations et diagnostics économiques*, 37, 193–243.

—— (1993a) '*Irrégularités des trajectoires de croissance, évolutions et dynamique non-linéaire. Vers une schématisation de l'endométabolisme*', thesis, EHESS, Paris.

—— (1993b) 'Endogenous structural change and crisis in a multiple time-scale growth model. A stylized formalization of the exhaustion and crisis of the Fordist growth regime', working paper, CEPREMAP, 9324, Paris.

—— (1994a) 'Modéliser les fluctuations, le changement structurel et les crises', *Revue d'économie politique*, 104, (2–3), 264–73.

—— (1994b) 'Periodic and aperiodic fluctuations in a Goodwinian/Kaldorian model of endogenous growth', mimeo, CEPREMAP, Paris.

—— (1994c) 'La *régulation* et la politique économique: d'une négation originelle à une réintégration théorisée', mimeo, CEPREMAP, Paris.

—— (1997a) *Les quadratures de la politique économique*, Albin Michel, Paris.

—— (1997b) 'Endogeneous structural change and crisis in a multiple time-scales growth model', *Journal of Evolutionary Economics*, 7 (1), 1–21.

—— (1999) 'Croyances économiques et pouvoir symbolique', *L'Année de la Régulation 1999*, III, La Découverte, Paris.

Lorenz Hans-Walter (1989) *Nonlinear Dynamical Economics and Chaotic Motion*, Lecture Notes in Economics and Mathematical Systems 334, Springer, Berlin.

Lucas Robert E. Jr (1984) *Studies in Business Cycle Theory*, MIT Press, Cambridge, MA.

Lundvall Bengt-Ake (1992) *National Systems of Innovation. Towards a Theory of Innovation and Interactive Learning*, Pinter, London.

Lutz Burkart (1990) *Le mirage de la croissance marchande*, Editions de la Maison des Sciences de l'Homme, Paris. German edition 1984.

Lyon-Caen Antoine and Jeammaud Antoine (1986) *Droit du travail, démocratie et crise*, Actes Sud, Arles.

MacKinnon R. (1993) 'The rules of the game: international money in historical perspective', *Journal of Economic Literature*, 31 (1), 1–44.

Maillat D. and Perrin J-C. (eds) (1992) *Entreprises innovatrices et développement territorial*, EDES, Neuchâtel.

Maillat D., Crevoisier O. and Lecoq B. (1993) 'Réseaux d'innovation et dynamique territoriale: le cas de l'Arc Jurassien', in Maillat D., Quevit M. and Senn B. (eds) *Réseaux d'innovation et milieux innovateurs: un pari pour le développement régional*, GREMI III, Edes, Neuchâtel.

Marengo Luigi (1992) 'Co-ordination and learning in the firm', *Journal of Evolutionary Economics*, 2 (4), 313–26.

Marglin Stephen A. (1974) 'What do bosses do? Their origins and functions in capitalist production', *Review of Radical Political Economics*, 6 (2), 60–112.

—— (1984) *Growth, Distribution and Prices*, Harvard University Press, Cambridge MA.

Marglin Stephen A. and Schor Juliet B. (1990) *The Golden Age of Capitalism*, Oxford University Press, Oxford.

Marris S. (1987) *Les déficits et le dollar. L'économie mondiale en péril*, Economica, Paris.

Martinelli Flavia and Schoenberger Erika (1992) 'Les oligopoles se portent bien, merci! Eléments de réflexion sur l'accumulation flexible', in Benko G.B. and Lipietz A. (eds) *Les régions qui gagnent*, Paris: Presses Universitaires de France.

Massey Doreen and Meegan Richard (1982) *The Anatomy of Job Loss. The How, Why and Where of Employment Decline*, Methuen, London.

Maucourant, J. (1993) 'Au coeur de l'économie politique, la dette: l'approche de J. R. Commons', *La revue du Mauss*, second semester, 209–18.

—— (1994) 'La monnaie dans la pensée institutionnaliste (Veblen, Mitchell, Commons, Polanyi)', thesis, Université Lumière-Lyon II.

Mazier Jacques (1992) 'Intégration économique et monétaire en Europe et régimes d'accumulation', *Mondes en développement*, 20 (79–80), 191–212.

—— (1995) 'L'intégration européenne', in Boyer Robert and Saillard Yves (eds) *Théorie de la régulation. L'état des savoirs*, La Découverte, Paris.

—— (1997) 'L'Europe: enlisement ou transition vers un nouveau régime de croissance?', *L'Année de la Régulation 1997*, I, La Découverte, Paris.

Mazier Jacques, Baslé Maurice and Vidal Jean-François (1993) 'Répartition des revenus, sections productives et reproduction d'ensemble', in *Quand les crises durent*, second edition, Economica, Paris.

McDowell Linda (1993) 'Doing gender: feminism, feminists, and research methods in human geography', *Transactions of the Institution of British Geographers*, new series, 17, 399–416.

Menzel Ulrich and Senghaas Dieter (1986) *Europas Entwicklung und die dritte Welt. Eine Bestandsaufnahme*, Suhrkamp, Frankfurt.

Mermet L. (1991) 'Dans quel sens pouvons nous gérer l'environnement?', *Gérer et comprendre. Annnales des mines*, 22, 165–93.

Merrien François-Xavier (1990) 'États-providence: l'empreinte des origines', *Revue française des affaires sociales*, 44 (3), 43–56.

Michon François (1991) 'Les formes institutionnelles du travail et de l'emploi', unpublished MS.

Miles M. (1984) *Beyond Monetarism. Finding the Road to Stable Money*, Basic Books, New York.

Milgrom P. and Roberts J. (1990) 'The economics of modern manufacturing: technology, strategy, and organization', *American Economic Review*, 80 (3), 511–28.

Mingat A., Salmon P. and Wolfesperger A. (1985) *Méthodologie économique*, Presses Universitaires de France, Paris.

Minsky Hyman (1982) *Can 'It' Happen Again?* Sharpe, Armonk NY.

Miotti Luis E. (1991) 'Accumulation, régulation et crises en Argentine', thesis, Université de Paris VII.

—— (1994) *Argentine. Fragilité de l'accumulation et options de la régulation*, Armand Colin, Paris.

Miotti Luis E., Nicolas Françoise and Quenan Carlos (1996) 'De la crise de la dette à l' "effet tequilla": performances comparées des économies latino-américaines', *Problèmes d'Amérique Latine*, 21, 45–68.

—— (1999) 'Argentine: chocs, crise . . . currency board . . . ou dollarisation?', *Zones Emergentes*, 6, 21–32.

Mirowski Philip (1986) 'Institutions as a solution concept in a game theory context', in Mirowski Philip (ed.) *The Reconstruction of Economic Theory*, Kluwer–Nijhoff, Boston MA.

Mistral Jacques (1986) 'Régime internationale et trajectoires nationales', in Boyer Robert (ed.) *Capitalismes fin de siècle*, Presses Universitaires de France, Paris.

Mistral Jacques and Kempf Elisabeth (1988) 'Flexibilité des salaires: l'impact des années Reagan', *Economie prospective internationale*, 36 (4), 97–113.

Miyamachi Yoshihiro and Peck Jamie A. (1993) 'Regulating Japan? Regulation theory versus the Japanese experience', SPA Working Paper, 21, University of Manchester.

Mjøset Lars (1985) 'Regulation and the institutionalist tradition', in Mjøset Lars and Bohlin Jan (eds) *Introduksjon til reguleringskolen*, working paper 21, Nordic Summer University, Aalborg.

—— (1987) 'Nordic economic policies in the 1970s and 1980s', *International Organization*, 41 (3).

—— (1992a) *The Irish Economy in a Comparative Institutional Perspective*, Report 93, National Economic and Social Council, Dublin.

—— (1992b) 'Comparative typologies of development patterns: the Menzel/ Senghaas framework', in Mjøset Lars (ed.) *Contributions to the Comparative Study of Development*, Report 92: 2, Proceedings of the Vilhelm Aubert Memorial Symposium 1990 II, Institute of Social Research, Oslo.

—— (1992c) 'The Nordic model never existed, but does it have a future?' *Scandinavian Studies*, 64 (4), 583–617.

—— (1993) 'The influence of regulation theory on Nordic studies of economic policies and social development', *La Lettre de la Régulation*, 6, 1–2.

—— (1997) 'Les significations historiques de l'européanisation', *L'Année de la Régulation 1997* I, La Découverte, Paris.

—— (2000a) 'The Nordic economies, 1945–1980' (in Italian), in Valerio Castronovo (ed.), *Storia dell'economica mondiale dall'antichita' ai giorno nostri* V, *Modernization and the Problem of Underdevelopment 1945–80*, Laterza, Rome. Available as ARENA Working Paper 6/2000.

—— (2000b) 'Employment, unemployment and ageing in the Western European welfare states' in Petit Pascal and Soete Luc (eds) *Technology and the Future of European Employment*, Edward Elgar, Cheltenham.

Mjøset Lars, Cappelen Ådne, Fagerberg Jan and Tranoy Bent Sofus (1994) 'Norway: changing the model', in Anderson Perry and Camiller Patrick (eds) *Mapping Europe's Left*, Verso, London.

Mondes en développement (1992) 79–80, Brussels. Japanese contributors: Hanada M., Hirano Y., Hirata K., Inoue Y., Miyakawa C., Nishikawa J., Shimizu k., Tsuru T., Uemura H. and Yamada T.

Mongin Philippe (1992) The 'full-cost' controversy of the 1940s and 1950s: a methodological assessment', *History of Political Economy*, 24 (2), 311–56.

Morin Pierre (1994) 'France: vers un capitalisme de coeurs financiers', *Le Monde*, journal quotidien, Paris.

Mota Veiga P. da (1989) *La régulation au Brésil. Contribution à l'étude du rapport solarial et du rapport Etat-économie*, Working paper 16, ESLAC, Paris.

Moulaert Frank and Swyngedouw E. (1988) 'Développement régional et géographie de la production flexible', *Cahiers lillois d'économie et de sociologie*, 11, 81–95.

—— (1992) 'Accumulation and organization in computing and communications industries: a regulationist approach', in Cooke P., Moulaert F. *et al.*, *Towards Global Localisation. The Computing and Telecomminications Industries in Britain and France*, UCL Press, London.

Mounier A. (1992) *Les théories économiques de la croissance agricole*, INRA–Economica, Paris.

Muet Pierre-Alain (1993) 'Contraintes et gains de la désinflation compétitive', in Coriat Benjamin and Taddei Dominique, (eds) *Entreprise France*, Livre de Poche, Hachette, Paris.

Mundell R. (ed.) (1968) *International Economics*, Macmillan, New York.

Nadel Henri (1994a) *Marx et le salariat*, second edition, Harmattan, Paris.

—— (ed.) (1994b) *Emploi et relations industrielles au Japon*, Harmattan, Paris.

—— (1998) *L'Europe des relations sociales. Institutions et économie*, Harmattan, Paris.

Nefussi J. (1987) 'Les industries agro-alimentaires en France. Croissance et financement 1950—1985. Essai sur l'intégration financière et la dynamique industrielle', thesis, Université de Paris–Nanterre.

Nelson Richard R. (ed.) (1993) *National Innovation Systems. A Comparative Study*, Oxford University Press, New York.

Nelson Richard R. and Sampat B. N. (1998) 'Making sense of institutions as a factor shaping economic performance', mimeo, Columbia University, New York.

Nelson Richard and Winter Sidney (1982) *An Evolutionary Theory of Economic Change*, Belknap Press of Harvard University Press, Cambridge MA.

Newhouse Steven, Ruelle David and Takens Floris (1978) 'Occurrence of strange Axiom A attractors near quasi-periodic flows on T^m $m \geqslant 3$', *Communications in Mathematical Physics*, 64, 35–40.

North Douglass C. (1966) *The Economic Growth of the United States, 1790–1860*, Norton, New York.

—— (1990) *Institutions, Institutional Change and Economic Performance*, Cambridge University Press, Cambridge.

Nove Alec (1981) *L'économie soviétique*, Economica, Paris.

Nutzinger Hans G. (1993) 'The firm as a social institution: the failure of the contractarian viewpoint', in Hodgson Geoffrey M. (ed.) *The Economics of Institutions*, Edward Elgar, Aldershot.

OECD (1994) *Employment Outlook*, OECD, Paris.

Ominami Carlos (1980) 'Croissance et stagnation au Chili. Eléments pour l'étude de la régulation dans une économie sous-développée', thesis, Université de Paris X.

—— (1986) *Le tiers monde dans la crise*, La Découverte, Paris.

Orléan André (1987) 'Anticipations et conventions en situation d'incertitude', *Cahiers d'économie politique*, 13, 153–72.

—— (ed.) (1994) *Analyse économique des conventions*, Presses Universitaires de France, Paris.

—— (1997) 'Jeux évolutionnistes et normes sociales', *Economie appliquée*, 50 (3), 177–98.

Oxenstierna Susanne (1990) *From Labour Shortage to Unemployment? The Soviet Labour Market in the 1980s*, Almqvist & Wiksell, Stockholm.

Oye K.E. (1985) 'Explaining cooperation under anarchy: hypothesis and strategies', *World Politics*, 38 (1), 1–24.

Padrón Alejandro (1993) 'Croissance et crise dans une économie de rente. Le cas venezuelien: une analyse en termes de régulation', thesis, Université de Paris III.

Palan Ronen (1998) 'Les fantômes du capitalisme mondial: l'économie politique internationale et l'école française de la régulation', *L'Année de la Régulation 1998*, II, La Découverte, Paris.

Palan Ronen and Gills Barry (1994) 'Transcending the state–global divide', Lynne Rienner, Boulder CO.

Palombarini Stefano (1997) 'La crise italienne de 1992: une lecture en termes de dynamique endogène', *L'Année de la Régulation 1997*, I, La Découverte, Paris.

—— (1999) 'Vers une théorie régulationniste de la politique économique', *L'Année de la Régulation 1999* III, La Découverte, Paris.

Parri L. (1993) 'I dilemmi dell'azione collectiva nell'evoluzione dei distretti italiani', *Economica e societa regionale*, 41, 213–36.

Passeron P. (1993) 'Conforter les solidarités intra-branches de la France', in Coriat Benjamin and Taddei Dominique, *Entreprise France*, Livre de Poche, Hachette, Paris.

Peaucelle Irina (1995) 'Vers un rapport salarial original en Russie', in Boyer Robert and Saillard Yves (eds) *Théorie de la régulation. L'état des savoirs*, La Découverte, Paris.

Peaucelle Irina and Petit Pascal (1988) 'Profit et formes de motivations salariales: à propos de quelques études comparatives de l'école radicale américaine', *Economie appliquée*, 41 (1), 41–71.

Pecqueur Bernard (ed.) (1989) *Le développement local. Mode ou modèle*, Syros, Paris.

Pekkarinen Jukka (1989) 'Keynesianism and the Scandinavian models of economic policy', in Hall Peter A. (ed.) *The Political Power of Economic Ideas. Keynesianism across Nations*, Princeton University Press, Princeton NJ.

Perez Carlota (1983) 'Structural changes and the assimilation of new technologies in the economic and social system', *Futures*, 15 (5), 357–75.

Perlman Mark (1991) 'Understanding the "old" American institutionalism', IVe colloque de l'Association C. Gide, Marseille, 19–20 September.

Perrin J.C. (1992) 'Pour une révision de la science régionale: une approche par les milieux', *Revue Canadienne des Sciences Régionales*, 15 (2), 155–97.

Petit Pascal (1985) '*Slow Growth and the Service Economy*', Pinter, London.

—— (1986) 'Heurs et malheurs de le *régulation* en France', in Boyer Robert (ed.) *La flexibilité du travail en Europe*, La Découverte, Paris.

—— (1990) 'Emploi, productivité et technologies de l'information dans les services', presented at IRIS, conference 'Compétence et compétitivité', Université Paris Dauphine, 5 April.

—— (1994a) 'Les dimensions tertiaires de la croissance: avantages et limites du modèle japonais', in Nadel H. (ed.) *Emploi et relations industrielles au Japon*, Harmattan, Paris.

—— (1994b) 'Les modalités de la croissance des services au Japon', *Japon in extenso*, 32–3.

—— (1998a) 'Formes structurelles et régimes de croissance de l'après fordisme', *L'Année de la Régulation 1998* II, La Découverte, Paris.

—— (ed.) (1998b) *L'économie de l'information. Les enseignements des théories économiques*, La Découverte, Paris.

—— (1999) 'Les aléas de la croissance dans une économie fondée sur le savoir', CEPREMAP 9909, Paris.

Petit Pascal and Soete Luc (1999) 'Globalization in search of a future', *International Review of Social Sciences*, 160, 47–70.

Petit Pascal and Tahar Gabriel (1989) 'La relation automatisation emploi: effet productivité et effet qualité', *Revue économique*, 40 (1), 35–54.

Pfaller Alfred, Gough Ian and Therborn Göran (eds) (1990) *Can the Welfare State Compete?* Macmillan, London.

374   *Bibliography*

Pini Paolo (1994) 'An Integrated Model of Cumulative Growth: Empirical Evidence for Nine OECD Countries, 1960–1990', draft, University of Macerata, Italy.

Pinto Anibal (1976) 'Notas sobre estilos de desarrollo en América Latina', *Revista de la CEPAL* (Santiago), 1, 157–96.

Piore Michael J. (1982) 'Convergence dans les systèmes nationaux de relations professionnelles: le cas de la France et des Etats-Unis', *Consommation*,13–30.

Piore Michael J. and Sabel Charles F. (1989) *Les chemins de la prospérité*, Hachette, Paris, Trans. of *The Second Industrial Divide*, Basic Books, New York, 1984.

Pitiot Hélène and Scialom Laurence (1993) 'Système bancaire et dérapage monétaire' *Economie internationale*, 54 (2), 137–56.

Planque B. (1991) 'Note sur la notion de réseaux d'innovation: réseaux contractuels et réseaux conventionnels', *Revue d'économie régionale et urbaine*, 3–4, 511–45.

Polanyi Karl (1946) *The Great Transformation*, French trans. (1983), Gallimard, Paris.

Posner Richard A. (1981) *The Economics of Justice*, Harvard University Press, Cambridge MA.

Postel-Vinay G. (1991) 'L'agriculture dans l'économie française: crise et réinsertion', in Lévy-Leboyer M. and Casanova J-C. (eds) *Entre l'état et le marché. L'économie française des années 1880 à nos jours*, Gallimard, Paris.

Quenan Carlos (1987) 'Eléments pour l'étude de l'endettement extérieur des pays en développement: le cas du Venezuela', thesis, Université de Grenoble II.

Quenan Carlos, Miotti Luis E. and Mila Susana (1994) 'Venezuela, potentiel de croissance et de développement', *Cahiers de l'IFRI*, 14.

Ragot Xavier and Touffut Jean-Philippe (1998) 'Le partage du profit: de la pertinence à l'échelle de la firme à la validité macroéconomique', *L'Année de la Régulation 1998* II, La Découverte, Paris.

Ralle Pierre (1990) 'Indexation des salaires: la rupture de 1983', *Economie et prévisions*, 93 (1–2), 187–95.

Rallet A. (1991) 'Théorie de la polarisation et technopoles', *Economie et sociétés*, 8, 53–64.

Raveyre M.F. and Saglio J. (1984) 'Les systèmes industriels localisés: éléments pour une analyse sociologique des ensembles de PME industriels', *Sociologie du travail*, 2, 317–48.

Reich Michael (1997) 'Social structure of accumulation theory: retrospect and prospect', *Review of Radical Political Economics*, 29 (3), 1–10.

Revue d'économie régionale et urbaine (1993) 3, special issue *Economie de proximités*.

Reynaud Bénédicte (1986) 'Règles et logiques des relations salariales', *Economie et statistique*, 192, 43–63.

—— (1990) 'Les modes de rémunération et le rapport salarial', *Economie et prévision*, 92–3, 1–15.

—— (1992) *Le salaire, la règle et le marché*, Bourgeois, Paris.

—— (1994a) *Les théories du salaire*, La Découverte, Paris.

—— (1994b) 'Les règles de salaire au Japon: un vecteur de connaissances distribuées?' *Japon in extenso*, 32, 97–105.

—— (1995) 'Questions of interpretation and collective dynamics', *Industrial and Corporate Change*, 5 (3), 699–723.

—— (1996) 'The introduction of a norm in a workshop', *Industrial and Corporate Change*, 5 (3).

—— (ed.) (1997) *Les limites de la rationalité*, La Découverte, Paris.

Reynaud Bénédicte and Najman Vladimir (1992) *Les règles salariales au concret: Enquête auprès des grandes entreprises*, La Documentation française, Paris.

Robles Alfredo C. (1994) *French Theories of Regulation and Conceptions of the International Division of Labour*, St Martin's Press, New York.

Roemer John (1981) *Analytical Foundations of Marxian Economic Theory*, Cambridge University Press, Cambridge.

Roland Gérard (1987a) '*Régulation* et fluctuations cycliques de l'investissement en URSS', *Revue d'études comparatives Est–Ouest*, 18 (2), 235–64.

—— (1987b) 'Essai sur la médiation sociale des valeurs d'usage dans le mode de production soviétique', thesis, Université Libre de Bruxelles.

—— (1989) *Economie politique du système soviétique*, Harmattan, Paris.

Rosales Osvaldo (1988) 'Relance y renovación en el paradigma estructuralista del desarrollo latinoamericano', *Revista de la CEPAL* (Santiago). 34, 213–42.

Rosanvallon Pierre (1981) *La crise de l'État-providence*, Seuil, Paris.

Roscher , W. (1857) *Principes d'économie politique*, Guillaumin, Paris.

Rosenberg Nathan (1976) *Perspectives on Technology*, Cambridge University Press, Cambridge.

—— (1982) *Inside the Black Box*, Cambridge University Press, Cambridge.

Rutherford Malcolm (1994) *Institutions in Economics: The Old and the New Institutionalism*, Cambridge University Press, Cambridge.

Sabel Charles (1997) 'Constitutional orders: trust building and response to change', in Hollingsworth R.J. and Boyer R. (eds) *Contemporary Capitalism*, Cambridge University Press, Cambridge.

Saboia João (1987) *Salario e productividade na industria. O papel da politica salarial na evoluçao dos salarios no longo prazo*, FEA/UFRJ, Rio de Janeiro.

Saillard Yves (1995) 'Le salaire indirect', in Boyer Robert and Saillard Yves (eds) *Théorie de la régulation. L'état des savoirs*, La Découverte, Paris.

Sàinz Pedro and Calcagno Alfredo (1992) 'En busca de otra modalidad de desarrollo', *Revista de la CEPAL* (Santiago) 48, 23–68.

Saito Hideharu (1991) 'Vers la création de la *régulation* démocratique' (in Japanese), in Yamada Toshio and Sudo Osamu (eds) *Postfordisme*, Tokyo: Omura Shoten.

Salais Robert and Storper Michael (1993) *Les mondes de production, enquête sur l'identité de la France*, EHESS, Paris.

Samuels Warren J. (1989) *Research in the History of Economic Thought and Methodology* VI, JAI Press, Greenwich CT.

Samuelson W. and Zeckhauser R. (1988) '*Status quo* bias in decision making', *Journal of Risk and Uncertainty*, 1, 7–59.

Sapir Jacques (1984) *Travail et travailleurs en URSS*, La Découverte, Paris. Second edition 1986.

—— (1985) 'Conflits sociaux et fluctuations économiques en URSS: l'exemple de la période 1950–1965', *Annales ESC*, 40 (4), 875–908.

—— (1986) 'Rythmes d'accumulation et mode de *régulation* de l'économie soviétique: essai d'interprétation des cycles d'investissement et de main-d'oeuvre en URSS de 1941 à nos jours', thesis, Université de Paris X.

—— (1989) *Les fluctuations économiques en URSS 1941–1985*, Editions de l'EHESS, Paris.

—— (1990) *L'économie mobilisée. Essai sur les économies de type soviétique*, La Découverte, Paris.

—— (1993a) 'Formes et nature de l'inflation', *Economie internationale*, 54 (2), 25–65.

—— (1993b) 'Les enseignements d'une transition', *Cahiers internationaux de sociologie*, 95, 919–48.

—— (1994) 'Aspects de l'évolution économique de l'ex-URSS depuis 1945', in *Economie mondiale et grandes puissances au XXe siècle*, Les Cahiers Français 265, Documentation Française, Paris.

—— (1996) 'Jalons pour un repérage méthodologique de la théorie de la *régulation*', *La Lettre de la Régulation*, 19, 1–3.

—— (1998) *Le krach russe*, La Découverte, Paris.

—— (ed.) (1991) *L'URSS au tournant. Une économie en transition*, Harmattan, Paris.

Saviotti P. and Metcalfe Stanley (eds) (1991) *Evolutionary Economics*, Harwood Academic Press, London.

Schmitter Philippe C. (1990) 'Sectors in modern capitalism: models of governance and variations in performance', in Brunetta Renato and Dell'Aringa Carlos (eds) *Labour Relations and Economic Performance*, Macmillan, London.

Schmoller, G. (1905–7), *Principes d'économie politique II*, Giard & Brière, Paris.

Schor Juliet B. (1991) *The Overworked American. The Unexpected Decline of Leisure*, Basic Books, New York.

Schotter Andrew (1992) 'Oskar Morgenstern's contribution to the development of the theory of games', in Weintraub E. Roy (ed.) *Toward a History of Game Theory*, Duke University Press, Durham NC.

Scott Allen (1988a) *Metropolis. From the Division of Labor to Urban Form*, University of California Press, Los Angeles.

—— (1988b) *New Industrial Spaces*, Pion, London.

—— (1993) *Technopolis. High-technology Industry and Regional Development in Southern California*, University of California Press, Berkeley CA.

Scott Allen, and Storper Michaël (eds) (1986) *Production, Work, Territory. The Geographical Anatomy of Industrial Capitalism*, Allen & Unwin, London.

Shimizu Koïchi (1994) 'Système du salaire toyotien ', *Japon in extenso*, 31–2, 68–85.

—— (1999) *Le toyotisme*, La Découverte, Paris.

Silverberg Gérald, Dosi Giovanni and Orsenigo Luigi (1988) 'Innovation, diversity and diffusion: a self-organization model', *Economic Journal*, 98 (393), 1032–54.

Silvestre Jean-Jacques (1990) *Encyclopédie économique*, Economica, Paris.

Simon Herbert, (1983) *Reason in Human Affairs*, Blackwell, Oxford.

Skott Peter (1991) 'Cyclical growth in a Kaldorian model', in Nell Edward and Semmler Willy (eds) *Nicholas Kaldor and Mainstream Economics: Confrontation or Convergence?* St Martin's Press, New York.

Snidal D. (1985) 'The limit of hegemonic stability theory, *International Organisation*, 39 (4), 579–614.

Sohn-Rethel A. (1977) *Lavoro intellectualle e lavoro manuale,* Feltrinelli, Milan.

Solomon R. (1979) *Le système monétaire international*, Economica, Paris.

Stackelberg, H. Von (1934) *Martform und Gleichgewicht*, Springer, Berlin.

Steinherr A. and Weiserbs D. (eds) (1991) *Evolution of the International and Regional Monetary Systems*, Macmillan, New York.

Stiglitz Joseph (1987) 'The causes and the consequences of the dependence of quality on price', *Journal of Economic Literature*, 25, 1–48.

Storper Michaël and Harrison Bennett (1992) 'Flexibilité, hiérarchie et développement régional: les changements de structure des systèmes productifs industriels et leurs nouveaux modes de gouvernance dans les années 1990', in Benko G.B. and Lipietz A. (eds) *Les régions qui gagnent*, Presses Universitaires de France, Paris.

Storper Michael and Scott A.J. (1989) 'The geographical foundations and social regulation of flexible production complexes', in Wolch J. and Dear M. (eds) *The Power of Geography. How Territory Shapes Social Life*, Unwin Hyman, London.

—— (eds) (1992) *Pathways to Industrialization and Regional Development*, Routledge, London.

Storper Michaël and Walker Richard (1989) *The Capitalist Imperative. Territory, Technology and Industrial Growth*, Blackwell, Oxford.

Strange S. (1983) '*Cave! Hic dragones.* A critique of regimes analysis', in Krasner S.D. (ed.) *International Regimes*, Cornell University Press, Ithaca NY.

Streeck Wolfgang (1992) *Social Institutions and Economic Performance*, Sage, London.

Sunkel Osvaldo (ed.) (1990) *El desarrollo desde adentro. Un enfoque neoestructuralista para América Latina*, Fondo de Cultura Económica, Mexico City.

Sylvander B. (1994) 'Formes de co-ordination et marché des produits de qualité spécifique: analyse sur le cas de la filière volaille', in Allaire G. and Boyer R. (eds) *La grande transformation de l'agriculture*, INRA-Economica, Paris.

Taddei Dominique and Coriat Benjamin (1993) *Made in France. L'industrie française dans la compétition mondiale*, Livre de Poche, Hachette, Paris.

Talha Larbi (1995) 'Théorie de la *régulation* et développement', in Boyer Robert and Saillard Yves (eds) *Théorie de la régulation. L'état des savoirs*, La Découverte, Paris.

Témin Peter (1973) *New Economic History,* Penguin Books, Harmondsworth.

Théret Bruno (1990) 'La place de l'État dans les théories économiques françaises de la *régulation*: éléments critiques et nouvelle position à la lumière de l'histoire', *Economie appliquée*, 63 (2), 43–81.

—— (1991a) '*Régulation* et topologie du social', *Cahiers de recherche sociologique*, 17, special issue *Régulation et problèmes contemporains*, 125–52.

—— (1991b) 'Apogée et déclin du rentier de la dette publique dans le "grand" XIXe siècle libéral (1815–1935). Éléments pour une réévaluation du développement historique du capitalisme en longue période', *Economie et sociétés*, série œconomia, PE 14, 87–136.

—— (1992a) *Régimes économiques de l'ordre politique. Esquisse d'une théorie régulationniste des limites de l'Etat*, Presses Universitaires de France, Paris.

—— (1992b) 'Avoir ou être? Dilemme de l'interaction entre l'État et l'économique', presented at Conférence de l'EAEPE, Paris, November.

—— (1993a) 'Les métamorphoses fiscales du capital: une approche marxiste–wébérienne des finances publiques', *Economie appliquée*, 2, 39–79.

—— (1993b) 'Hyperinflation de producteurs et hyperinflation de rentiers: le cas du Brésil', *Revue Tiers Monde* 34 (133), 37–67.

—— (1994a) 'To be or to have. On the problem of the interaction between state and economy. Toward a topological conception of the wage–labor nexus, the labor market and the welfare state', *Economy and Society*, 23 (1), 1–46.

—— (1994b) 'Finance, souveraineté et dette sociale: capital symbolique, différenciation de la société et construction européenne', in Théret B. (ed.) *L'Etat, la finance et le social. Souveraineté nationale et construction européenne*, La Découverte, Paris.

—— (1994c) 'De l'Etat-providence national à l'Etat-providence européen', *Problèmes économiques*, 2376, 15–21.

—— (1995) '*Régulation* du déficit budgétaire et croissance des dépenses de l'État en France de 1815 à 1939: une modélisation économétrique simple des régimes fisco-financiers libéraux', *Revue économique*, 46 (1), 57–90.

—— (1997) 'Méthodologie des comparaisons internationales, approches de l'effet sociétal et de la *régulation*: une lecture structuraliste des systèmes nationaux de protection sociale', *L'Année de la Régulation 1997* I, La Découverte, Paris.

—— (1999) 'L'effectivité de la politique économique : de l'autopoïèse des systèmes sociaux à la topologie du social', *L'Année de la Régulation 1999*, La Découverte, Paris.

Théret Bruno and Didier U.R.I. (1987) 'Pression fiscale limite, prélèvements obligatoires et production marchande: à propos de récentes estimations économétriques d'une courbe de Laffer pour la France', *Economie appliquée*, 40 (1).

—— (1991a), 'Six indicateurs théoriques de pression fiscale confrontés au taux usuel des prélèvements obligatoires', *Revue française de finances publiques*, 33, 213–48.

—— (1991b) 'Tax incidence, costs of production, and the impact of public transfers of resources on growth: empirical evidence from an applied departmental model for France', Conference of the Confederation of European Economic Associations (CEEA) on Taxation and Economic Growth, Amsterdam, 12–14 June, working paper IRIS-TS, Université Paris Dauphine.

Thévenot Laurent (1989) 'Equilibre et rationalité dans un univers complexe', *Revue économique*, 40 (2), special issue on *Convention Theory*.

—— (1990) 'Les entreprises entre plusieurs formes de co-ordination', in Reynaud Jean Daniel, Eyrand François, Paradeise Catherine and Saglio Jean, *Les systèmes de relations professionnelles*, Editions du CNRS, Lyon.

—— (1994) 'Des marchés aux normes', in Allaire G. and Boyer R. (eds) *La grande transformation de l'agriculture*, INRA-Economica, Paris.

Thévenot Laurent and Favereau Olivier (1995) 'Réflexions sur une notion d'équilibre utilisable dans une économie de marchés et d'organisation', in Ballot Gérard (ed.) *Marché internes. De la micro à la macroéconomie*, Presses Universitaires de France, Paris.

Thom R. (1972) *Stabilité structurelle et morphogenèse*, Benjamin, New York.

Tohyama Hironori (1990) 'Croissance rapide et crise au Japon' (in Japanese), *Keizai-Hyoron*, 39 (4), 813–37.

Tool Marc R. (1988) *Evolutionary economics*, 2 vols, Sharpe, Armonk NY.

Tordjman Hélène (1994) *Dynamiques spéculations, hétérogénéité des agents et apprentissage. Le cas des taux de change*, thesis, CEFI, Université d'Aix–Marseille II.

Touzard J-M. (1994) 'Crises sectorielles et dynamiques régionales: Les recompositions de l'agriculture en Languedoc–Roussillon', thesis, Ecole nationale supérieure agronomique de Montpellier.

—— (1995) '*Régulation* sectorielle, dynamique régionale et transformation d'un système productif localisé: exemple de la viticulture languedocienne', in Allaire G. and Boyer R. (eds) *La grande transformation de l'agriculture*, INRA-Economica, Paris.

Tsuru Tsuyoshi (1991) 'Unit labor costs, the reserve army effect and the collective bargaining system: a US–Japan comparison', in Mizoguchi T. (ed.) *Making*

Economies more Efficient and more Equitable, Oxford University Press, Oxford; Kinokunya, Tokyo.

—— (1992) 'Wage spillovers under the spring offensive system', *Mondes en développement*, 12, 21–9.

Uemura Hiroyasu (1992) 'Growth and distribution in the post-war regime of accumulation: theory and realities in the Japanese economy', *Mondes en développement*, 20, 135–51.

Uemura Hiroyasu and Ebizuka Akira (1994) 'Incentives and flexibility in the hierarchical market–firm nexus: a prelude to the analysis of productivity regimes in Japan', *Japon in extenso*, 31/32, 49–67.

Uni Hiroyuki (1991) 'Le capitalisme japonais d'après-guerre et le fordisme' (in Japanese), *Keizai-Hyoron*, 40 (11), 503–38.

Union of Radical Political Economists (1978) *US Capitalism in Crisis*, New York.

URGENSE (1982) 'Un taylorisme arythmique dans les économies planifiées du centre', *Critiques de l'économie politique*, 19, 111–36.

Valceschini E. (1993) 'Conventions économiques et mutation de l'économie contractuelle dans le secteur des légumes transformés', *Economie rurale*, 218, 19–26.

Vanberg Viktor (1989) 'Carl Menger's evolutionary and John R. Commons' collective action approach to institutions: a comparison', *Review of Political Economy*, 1 (3) 334–60.

Veblen Thorstein (1898) 'Why is economics not an evolutionary science?', *Quarterly Journal of Economics*, 12, 47–64.

—— (1901) 'La théorie économique de Schmoller', *Quarterly Journal of Economics*, 9, 83–104.

—— (1919) *The Place of Science in Modern Civilisation*, Huebsch, New York.

Veltz Pierre (1983) 'Fordisme, rapport salarial et complexité des pratiques sociales', *Critiques de l'économie politique*, 23–4, 30–42.

—— (1990) 'Nouveaux modèles d'organisation de la production et tendances de l'économie territoriale', in Benko G.B. (ed.) *La dynamique spatiale de l'économie contemporaine*, Editions de l'Espace Européen, Garenne-Colombes.

—— (1992) 'Hiérarchies et réseaux dans l'organisation de la production et du territoire', in Benko G.B. and Lipietz A. (eds) *Les régions qui gagnent*, Presses Universitaires de France, Paris.

Verley Patrick (1995) 'Histoire économie et théorie économique', in Boyer Robert and Saillard Yves (eds) *Théorie de la régulation. L'état des savoirs*, La Découverte, Paris.

Vidal Jean François (1989) *Les fluctuations internationales de 1890 à nos jours*, Economica, Paris.

—— (1998), 'La *régulation* et l'international: remarques sur l'article de R. Palan', *L'Année de la Régulation 1998* II, La Découverte, Paris.

Villey D. (1954) *Petite histoire des grandes doctrines économiques*, third edition, Genin, Paris.

Von Stackelberg H. (1934) *Martform und Gleichgewicht*, Springer, Vienna and Berlin.

Wade Robert (1990) *Governing the Market,* Princeton University Press, Princeton, NJ.

Wagner A. (1904) *Les fondements de l'économie politique*, French trans.

Wakamori Fumitaka (1991) 'Economie, société civile et Etat dans l'après-fordisme', in *Postfordisme*, Syros, Paris.

Wallerstein Immanuel (1980–4) *Le système du monde*, 2 vols, Flammarion, Paris.

Walliser Bernard (1989) 'Théorie des jeux et genèse des institutions', *Recherches économiques de Louvain*, 55 (4), 339–64.

Weir Margaret, Shola Orloff Ann and Skocpol Theda (eds) (1988) *The Politics of Social Policy in the United States*, Princeton University Press, Princeton NJ.

Weisskopf Thomas E. (1985) 'The effect of unemployment on labor producitivity: an international comparative analysis', *International Review of Applied Economics*, 1 (2), 127–51.

Williamson J. (1977) *The Failure of World Monetary Reform, 1971–74*, New York University Press, New York.

Williamson O. E. (1975) *Markets and Hierarchies. Analysis and Antitrust Implications*, Free Press, New York.

—— (1985) *The Economic Institutions of Capitalism*, Basic Books, New York.

Winter S. (1964) 'Economic "natural selection" and the theory of the firm', *Yale Economic Essays*, 4 (1), 225–72.

—— (1971) 'Satisficing, selection and the innovating remnant', *Quarterly Journal of Economics*, 85 (2), 237–61.

Wolfson M. (1986) *Financial Crises. Understanding the Postwar US Experience*, Sharpe, Armonk NY.

Yagi Kiichiro (1992) 'Approche de la *régulation* et capitalismes de l'Extrême-Orient' (in Japanese), *Chosa to Kenkyu*, Kyoto University.

Yamada Toshio (1992) 'Heurs et malheurs du mode de *régulation* japonais', *Mondes en développement*, 79–80.

You Jong-Il (1994) 'The Korean model of development and its environmental implications', in Bhaskar V. and Glyn Andrew (eds) *The North, the South, and the Environment*, Earthscan, London.

Young Allyn (1928) 'Increasing returns and technical progress', *Economic Journal*, 152, 527–42.

Zaleski Eugène (1928) *La planification stalinienne*, Economica, Paris.

Zarifian Philippe (1994) *La nouvelle productivité*, Harmattan, Paris.

Zhang Wei Bin (1991) *Synergetic Economics,* Springer, Berlin.

Zhukov Serguei V. and Vorobyov Alexandre Yu (1992) *Reforming the Soviet Union. Lessons from Structural Experience* , WP-96, WIDER, Helsinki.

Index

DEATH OF
A
VILLAGE

A Hamish Macbeth Murder Mystery

M. C. Beaton

Constable & Robinson Ltd
55–56 Russell Square
London WC1B 4HP
www.constablerobinson.com

First published in the USA by Grand Central Publishing,
a division of Hachette Book Group USA, Inc., 2003

First published in the UK by Robinson,
an imprint of Constable & Robinson Ltd., 2009

This edition published by C&R Crime,
an imprint of Constable & Robinson Ltd., 2013

A copy of the British Library Cataloguing in
Publication Data is available from the British Library

ISBN: 978-1-47210-537-0 (paperback)
ISBN: 978-1-84901-266-9 (ebook)

Printed and bound in the UK

1 3 5 7 9 10 8 6 4 2

To my friend David Lloyd of
Lower Oddington, Gloucestershire,
with affection

Hamish Macbeth fans share their reviews . . .

'Treat yourself to an adventure in the Highlands; remember your coffee and scones – for you'll want to stay a while!'

'I do believe I am in love with Hamish.'

'M. C. Beaton's stories are absolutely excellent . . . Hamish is a pure delight!'

'A highly entertaining read that will have me hunting out the others in the series.'

'A new Hamish Macbeth novel is always a treat.'

'Once I read the first mystery I was hooked . . . I love her characters.'

Share your own reviews and comments at
www.constablerobinson.com

Chapter One

*In all my travels I never met with any one
Scotchman but what was a man of sense. I
believe everybody of that country that has
any, leaves it as fast as they can.*

— Francis Lockier

The way propaganda works, as every school-
boy knows, is that if you say the same thing
over and over again, lie or not, people begin to
believe it.

Hamish Macbeth, police constable of the
village of Lochdubh and its surroundings, had
been until recently a happy, contented, unambitious man. This was always regarded, by
even the housebound and unsuccessful, as a
sort of mental aberration. And he had been
under fire for a number of years and from a
number of people to pull his socks up, get a
life, move on, get a promotion, and forsake his
lazy ways. Until lately, all comments had slid
off him. That was, until Elspeth Grant, local
reporter, joined the chorus. It was the way she

1

laughed at him with a sort of affectionate contempt as he mooched around the village that got under his skin. Her mild amazement that he did not want to 'better himself', added on to all the other years of similar comments, finally worked on him like the end result of a propaganda war and he began to feel restless and discontented.

Had he had any work to do apart from filing sheep-dip papers and ticking off the occasional poacher, Elspeth's comments might not have troubled him. And Elspeth was attractive, although he would not admit it to himself. He felt he had endured enough trouble from women to last him a lifetime.

He began to watch travel shows on television and to imagine himself walking on coral beaches or on high mountains in the Himalayas. He fretted over the fact that he had even taken all his holidays in Scotland.

One sunny morning, he decided it was time he got back on his beat, which covered a large area of Sutherland. He decided to visit the village of Stoyre up on the west coast. It was more of a hamlet than a village. No crime ever happened there. But, he reminded himself, a good copper ought to check up on the place from time to time.

After a winter of driving rain and a miserable spring, a rare period of idyllic weather had arrived in the Highlands. Tall twisted mountains swam in a heat haze. The air through the open window of the police Land

Rover was redolent with smells of wild thyme, salt, bell heather, and peat smoke. He took a deep breath and felt all his black discontentment ebb away. Damn Elspeth! This was the life. He drove steadily down a winding single-track road to Stoyre.

Tourists hardly ever visited Stoyre. This seemed amazing on such a perfect day, when the village's cluster of whitewashed houses lay beside the deep blue waters of the Atlantic. There was a little stone harbour where three fishing boats bobbed lazily at anchor. Hamish parked in front of the pub, called the Fisherman's Arms. He stepped down from the Land Rover. His odd-looking dog, Lugs, scrambled down as well.

Hamish looked to right and left. The village seemed deserted. It was very still, unnaturally so. No children cried, no snatches of radio music drifted out from the cottages, no one came or went from the small general stores next to the pub.

Lugs bristled and let out a low growl. 'Easy, boy,' said Hamish. He looked up the hill beyond the village to where the graveyard lay behind a small stone church. Perhaps there was a funeral. But he could see no sign of anyone moving about.

'Come on, boy,' he said to his dog. He pushed open the door of the pub and went inside. The pub consisted of a small whitewashed room with low beams on the ceiling. A few wooden tables scarred with cigarette burns were dotted about. There was no one behind the bar.

'Anyone home?' called Hamish loudly.

To his relief there came the sound of someone moving in the back premises. A thickset man entered through a door at the back of the bar. Hamish recognized Andy Crummack, the landlord and owner.

'How's it going, Andy?' asked Hamish. 'Everybody dead?'

'It iss yourself, Hamish. What will you be having?'

'Just a tonic water.' Hamish looked round the deserted bar. 'Where is everyone?'

'It's aye quiet this time o' day.' Andy poured a bottle of tonic water into a glass.

'Slainte!' said Hamish. 'Are you having one?'

'Too early. If ye don't mind, I've got stock to check.' Andy made for the door behind the bar.

'Hey, wait a minute, Andy. I havenae been in Stoyre for a while but I've never seen the place so dead.'

'We're quiet folks, Hamish.'

'And nothing's going on?'

'Nothing. Now, if ye don't mind . . .'

The landlord disappeared through the door.

Hamish drank the tonic water and then pushed back his peaked cap and scratched his fiery hair. Maybe he was imagining things. He hadn't visited Stoyre for months. The last time had been in March when he'd made a routine call. He remembered people chatting on the waterfront and this pub full of locals.

He put his glass on the bar and went out into the sunlight. The houses shone white in the glare and the gently heaving blue water had an oily surface.

He went into the general store. 'Morning, Mrs MacBean,' he said to the elderly woman behind the counter. 'Quiet today. Where is everyone?'

'They'll maybe be up at the kirk.'

'What! On a Monday? Is it someone's funeral?'

'No. Can I get you anything, Mr Macbeth?'

Hamish leaned on the counter. 'Come on. You can tell me,' he coaxed. 'What's everyone doing at the church on a Monday?'

'We are God-fearing folk in Stoyre,' she said primly, 'and I'll ask you to remember that.'

Baffled, Hamish walked out of the shop and was starting to set off up the hill when the church doors opened and people started streaming out. Most were dressed in black as if for a funeral.

He stood in the centre of the path as they walked down towards him. He hailed people he knew. 'Morning, Jock ... grand day, Mrs Nisbett,' and so on. But the crowd parted as they reached him and silently continued on their way until he was left standing alone.

He walked on towards the church and round to the manse at the side with Lugs at his heels. The minister had just reached his front door.

5

He was a new appointment, Hamish noticed, a thin nervous man with a prominent Adam's apple, and his black robes were worn and dusty. He had sparse ginger hair, weak eyes and a small pursed mouth.

'Morning,' said Hamish. 'I am Hamish Macbeth, constable at Lochdubh. You are new to here?'

The minister reluctantly faced him. 'I am Fergus Mackenzie,' he said in a lilting Highland voice.

'You seem to be doing well,' remarked Hamish. 'Church full on a Monday morning.'

'There is a strong religious revival here,' said Fergus. 'Now, if you don't mind . . .'

'I do mind,' said Hamish crossly. 'This village has changed.'

'It has changed for the better. A more God-fearing community does not exist anywhere else in the Highlands.' And with that the minister went into the manse and slammed the door in Hamish's face.

Becoming increasingly irritated, Hamish retreated back to the waterfront. It was deserted again. He thought of knocking on some doors to find out if there was any other answer to this strange behaviour apart from a religious revival and then decided against it. He looked back up the hill to where a cottage stood near the top. It was the holiday home of a retired army man, Major Jennings, an Englishman. Perhaps he might be more forthcoming. He plodded back up the hill, past the church, and knocked on the major's door. Silence greeted him. He knew the major lived most of the year in the south of England. Probably not arrived yet. Hamish remembered he usually came north for a part of the summer.

When he came back down from the hill, he saw that people were once more moving about. There were villagers in the shop and villagers on the waterfront. This time they gave him a polite greeting. He stopped one of them, Mrs Lyle. 'Is anything funny going on here?' he asked.

She was a small, round woman with tight grey curls and glasses perched on the end of her nose. 'What do you mean?' she asked.

'There's an odd atmosphere and then you've all been at the kirk and it isn't even Sunday.'

'It is difficult to explain to such as you, Hamish Macbeth,' she said. 'But in this village we take our worship of the Lord seriously and don't keep it for just the one day.'

I'm a cynic, thought Hamish as he drove off. Why should I find it all so odd? He knew that in some of the remote villages a good preacher was still a bigger draw than anything on television. Mr Mackenzie must be a powerful speaker.

When he returned to Lochdubh, Hamish found all the same that the trip to Stoyre had cheered him up. The restlessness that had plagued him had gone. He whistled as he prepared food for himself and his dog, and then carried his meal on a tray out to the front garden, where he had placed a table with an umbrella over it. Why dream of cafés in France when he had everything here in Lochdubh?

He had just finished a meal of fried haggis, sausage and eggs when a voice hailed him. 'Lazing around again, Hamish?'

The gate to the front garden opened and Elspeth Grant came in. She was wearing a brief tube top which showed her midriff, a small pair of denim shorts, and her hair had been tinted aubergine. She pulled up a chair and sat down next to him.

'The trouble with aubergine,' said Hamish, 'is that it chust doesnae do.'

'Doesn't do what?' demanded Elspeth.

'Anything for anyone. It's like the purple lipstick or the black nail varnish. Anything that's far from an original colour isn't sexy.'

'And what would you know about anything sexy?'

'I am a man and I assume you mean to attract the opposite sex.'

'Women dress and do their hair for themselves these days.'

'Havers.'

'It's true, Hamish. You've been living in this time warp for so long that you just don't know what's what. Anyway, I'm bored. There's really nothing to report until the Highland Games over at Braikie and that's a week away.'

'I might have a wee something for you. I've just been over at Stoyre. There's a religious revival there. They were all at the kirk this morning. Seems they've got a new minister, a Mr Mackenzie. I was thinking he must be a pretty powerful preacher.'

'Not much, but something,' said Elspeth. 'I'll try next Sunday.'

'The way they're going on, you may not need to wait that long. They've probably got a service every day.'

'Want to come with me?'

Hamish stretched out his long legs. 'I've just been. Have the Currie sisters seen you in that outfit?'

The Currie sisters were middle-aged twins, spinsters, and the upholders of morals in Lochdubh.

'Yes. Jessie Currie told me that I should go home and put on a skirt and Nessie Currie defended me.'

'Really! What did she say?'

'She said my boots were so ugly that they made everything else I had on look respectable.'

Hamish looked down at the heavy pair of hiking boots Elspeth was wearing. 'I see what she means.'

Elspeth flushed up to the roots of her frizzy aubergine hair with anger. 'I don't know why I bother even talking to you, Hamish Macbeth. I'm off.'

When she had gone, Hamish lay back in his chair, his hands clasped behind his head. He shouldn't have been so rude to her but he blamed her remarks about him being unambitious for having recently upset the lazy comfort of his summer days.

The telephone in the police station rang, the noise cutting shrilly through the peace of the day.

He sighed, got to his feet, and went to answer it. The voice of his pet hate, Detective Chief Inspector Blair, boomed down the line. 'Get yoursel' over to Braikie, laddie. Teller's grocery in the High Street has been burgled. Anderson will be there soon.'

'On my way,' said Hamish.

He took his peaked cap down from a peg on the kitchen door and put it on his head. 'No, Lugs,' he said to his dog, who was looking up at him out of his strange blue eyes. 'You stay.'

He went out and got into the police Land Rover and drove off, turning over in his mind what he knew of Teller's grocery. It was a licensed shop and sold more upmarket groceries than its two rivals. He was relieved that he would be working with Detective Sergeant Jimmy Anderson rather than Blair.

He parked outside the shop and went in. Mr Teller was a small, severe-faced man with gold-rimmed glasses. 'You took your time,' he said crossly. 'They've taken all my wine and spirits, the whole lot. I found the lot gone when I opened up this morning, and phoned the police.'

10

'I was out on another call,' said Hamish. 'How did they get in?'

'Round the back.' Mr Teller raised a flap on the counter and Hamish walked through.

A pane of glass on the back door had been smashed. 'The forensic people'll be along soon,' said Hamish. 'I can't touch anything at the moment.'

'Well, let's hope you hurry up. I've got to put a claim into the insurance company.'

'How much for?'

'I'll need to total it up. Thousands of pounds.'

Hamish looked blankly down at the shopkeeper. He had been in the shop before. He could not remember seeing any great supply of wine or spirits. There had been three shelves, near the till, that was all.

He focused on Mr Teller. 'I haven't been in your shop for a bit. Had you expanded the liquor side?'

'No, why?'

'I remember only about three shelves of bottles.'

'They took all the stuff out of the cellar as well.'

'You'd better show me.'

Mr Teller led the way to a door at the side of the back shop. The lock was splintered. Hamish took out a handkerchief and put it over the light switch at the top of the stairs and pressed. He stood on the top step and looked down. The cellar was certainly empty. And dusty.

He returned to the front to find that Jimmy Anderson had arrived.

'Hello, Hamish,' said the detective. 'Crime, isn't it? A real crime. All that lovely booze. Taken a statement yet?'

'Not yet. Could I be having a wee word with you outside?'

'Sure. I could do with a dram. There's a pub across the road.'

'Not yet. Outside.'

Under the suspicious eyes of Mr Teller, they walked out into the street.

'What?' demanded Jimmy.

'He is saying that thousands of pounds of booze have been nicked. But when I pointed out to him that he only kept about three shelves of the stuff, he said they had cleared out the cellar as well.'

'So?'

'The cellar floor is dusty. Even dust. No marks of boxes and, what's more to the point, no drag marks. It is my belief he had nothing in that cellar. He could have been after the insurance.'

'But the insurance will want to see the books, check the orders.'

'True. Well, we'd best take a statement and then talk to his supplier.'

They returned to the shop. Hamish took out a notebook. 'Now, Mr Teller, you found the shop had been burgled when you opened up. That would be at nine o'clock?'

'Eight-thirty.'

'You didn't touch anything?'

'I went down to the cellar and found everything gone from there.'

'We'll check around and see if anyone heard or saw anything. What is the name of your supplier?'

'Frog's of Strathbane. Why?'

'The insurance company will want to see your books to check the amount of the lost stores against your record of deliveries.'

'They're welcome to look at them anytime.'

'Have you seen anyone suspicious about the town?'

'Now, there's a thing. There were two rough-looking men came into the shop two days ago. I hadn't seen them before. They asked for cigarettes and I served them but they were looking all around the place.'

'Descriptions?'

'One was a big ape of a man. He had black hair, foreign-looking. Big nose and thick lips. He was wearing a checked shirt and jeans.'

'Did he sound foreign?'

'I can't remember.'

Two men in white overalls came into the shop carrying cases of equipment. 'We'll stop for a moment while you take the forensic boys through the back to check the break-in,' said Hamish.

'What do you think?' Hamish asked Jimmy when the shopkeeper had gone through to the back shop with the forensic team.

'Seems a respectable body. Still, we'll check with Frog's. If he'd had the stuff delivered, then he must be telling the truth.'

'I don't like the look o' that cellar floor.'

'Well, if there's anything fishy, the forensic boys will find it.'

They waited until Mr Teller came back. 'Now,' said Hamish, 'what did the other fellow look like?'

'He was small, ferrety. I remember,' said Mr Teller, excited. 'He was wearing a short-sleeved shirt and he had a snake tattooed on his left arm.'

'Hair colour?'

'Maybe dark but his head was shaved. He had a thin face, black eyes, and a long nose.'

'Clothes?'

'Like a told you, he had a short-sleeved shirt on, blue it was, and grey trousers.'

Hamish surveyed the shopkeeper with a shrewd look in his hazel eyes. 'I'm puzzled by the state of your cellar floor.'

'How's that?'

'There were no marks in the dust. No signs of dragging.'

'Well, maybe they just lifted the stuff up.'

Jimmy Anderson was exuding the impatient vibes of a man dying for a drink.

'Come on, Hamish,' he said impatiently. 'Let forensics get on with it while we go over what we've got.'

Hamish reluctantly followed him over to the

pub. 'Maybe I'll nip back and tell those chaps from forensic about that cellar floor.'

'Och, leave them. They know their job.' Jimmy ordered two double whiskies.

'Just the one, then,' said Hamish. 'I don't trust that man Teller one bit.'

Finally he dragged a reluctant Jimmy away from the bar. Mr Teller was serving a woman with groceries.

'I think you should close up for the day,' said Hamish.

Mr Teller jerked a thumb towards the back shop. 'They said it was all right.'

'Let us through,' said Hamish.

Mr Teller lifted the flap on the counter.

Hamish and Jimmy walked through to the back shop.

'How's it going?' Jimmy asked one of the men.

'Nothing much,' he said. 'Looks like a straightforward break-in. Can't get much outside. There's gravel there. Nothing but a pair of size eleven footprints at the top of the cellar stairs.'

'Those are mine,' said Hamish. 'But what about the cellar itself, and the stairs? When I looked down, there seemed to be nothing but undisturbed dust.'

'Then you need your eyes tested, laddie. The thieves swept the place clean and the stairs.'

'What?' Hamish had a sinking feeling in his stomach.

'Have a look. We're finished down there.'

Hamish went to the cellar door, switched on the light, and walked down the steps. He could see sweeping brush marks in the dust.

'Those weren't there before,' he said angrily. 'Teller must have done it when you pair were out the back.'

Hamish retreated wrathfully to the shop, followed by Jimmy. 'Why did you sweep the cellar?' he demanded angrily.

Mr Teller looked the picture of outraged innocence. 'I never did. I went back outside to ask them if they wanted a cup of tea. I am a respectable tradesman and a member of the Rotary club and the Freemasons. I shall be speaking to your superior officer.'

'Speak all you want,' shouted Hamish. 'I'll have you!'

'Come on, Hamish.' Jimmy drew him outside the shop. 'Back to the bar, Hamish. A dram'll soothe you down.'

'I've had enough and you'd better not have any more. You're driving.'

'One more won't hurt,' coaxed Jimmy, urging Hamish into the dark interior of the bar. When he had got their drinks, he led Hamish to a corner table. 'Now, Hamish, couldn't you be mistaken? When anyone mentions Freemasons, my heart sinks. The big cheese is a member.' The big cheese was the chief superintendent, Peter Daviot.

'I'm sure as sure,' said Hamish.

'So what do you suggest we do if the wee

man's books are in order and tie in with Frog's records of deliveries?'

'I don't know,' fretted Hamish.

'It's your word against his.'

'You'd think the word of a policeman would count for something these days.'

'Not against a Freemason and a member of the Rotary,' said Jimmy cynically.

Hamish made up his mind. 'I'm off to Frog's. You can have my drink.'

Jimmy eyed the whisky longingly. 'I should report what you're doing to Blair.'

'Leave it a bit.'

'Okay. But keep in touch. I'll see if I can sweat Teller a bit. The wonders o' forensic science, eh?'

'There's something up with that lot from Strathbane. It seems to me they're aye skimping the job because they've got a football match to go to or something.'

Hamish drove to Strathbane after looking up Frog's in a copy of the Highland and Islands phone book he kept in the Land Rover. Their offices were situated down at the docks, an area of Strathbane that Hamish loathed. The rare summer sunshine might bring out the beauty of the Highland countryside but all it did was make the docks smell worse: a combination of stale fish, rotting vegetables, and what Victorian ladies used to describe as something 'much worse'.

The offices had a weather-faded sign above the door: FROG'S WHISKY AND WINE DISTRIBUTORS. He pushed open the door and went in. 'Why, Mary,' he exclaimed, recognizing the small girl behind the desk, 'what are you doing here?'

Mary Bisset was a resident of Lochdubh, small and pert. Her normally cheeky face, however, wore a harassed look. 'I'm a temp, Hamish,' she said. 'I cannae get the hang o' this computer.'

'Where's the boss?'

'Out in the town at some meeting.'

'Who is he?'

'Mr Dunblane.'

'Not Mr Frog?'

'I think there was a Mr Frog one time or another. Oh, Hamish, what am I to do?'

'Let me see. Move over.'

Hamish sat down at the computer and switched it on. Nothing happened. He twisted his lanky form around and looked down. 'Mary, Mary, you havenae got the damn thing plugged in.'

She giggled. Hamish plugged in the computer. 'What do you want?'

'The word processing thingy. I've got letters to write.'

'Before I do that, do you know where he keeps the account books?'

'In the safe.'

Hamish's face fell.

'But you're the polis. I suppose it would be all right to open it up for you.'

'Do you know the combination?'

'It's one of thae old-fashioned things. The key's on the wall with the other keys in the inner office.'

Hamish went into the inner office. 'Where is everyone?' he asked over his shoulder.

'Tam and Jerry – they work here – they've gone into town with Mr Dunblane.'

Hamish grinned. There on a board with other keys and neatly labelled 'Safe' was the key he wanted. 'Come in, Mary,' he said. 'You'd better be a witness to this.'

Hamish opened the safe. There was a large quantity of banknotes on the lower shelf. On the upper shelf were two large ledgers marked 'Accounts'. He took them out and relocked the safe. He sat down at a desk and began to go through them. 'Keep a lookout, Mary,' he said, 'and scream if you see anyone.'

'What's this all about?'

He grinned at her. 'If this works out, I'll take you out for dinner one evening and tell you.'

Chief Superintendent Peter Daviot had finished his speech to the Strathbane Businessmen's Association. He enjoyed being a guest speaker at affairs such as these. But his enjoyment was not to last for long. He had just regained his seat to gratifying applause when his mobile phone rang. He excused himself from the table and went outside to answer it. It was Detective Chief Inspector Blair. 'Macbeth's landed us in the shit,' growled Blair.

'Moderate your language,' snapped Daviot. 'What's up?'

'Teller's shop up in Braikie was broken into and all his booze stolen. Macbeth's accusing Teller of covering up evidence and Teller is threatening to sue.'

'Dear me, you'd better get up there and diffuse the situation.'

'Anderson's up there.'

'Go yourself. This requires the attention of a senior officer. And tell Macbeth to report to me immediately.'

When Daviot returned to police headquarters, he was told to his surprise that Hamish Macbeth was waiting to see him. 'That was quick,' he said to his secretary, Helen. 'Where is he?'

'In your office,' said Helen sourly. She loathed Hamish.

Daviot pushed open the door and went in. Hamish got to his feet clutching a sheaf of photocopied papers.

'What's this all about, Macbeth? I hear there has been a complaint about you.'

'It's about Teller's grocery,' said Hamish. 'He claims to have had all his booze stolen, booze that was supplied by Frog's. These are photocopies of the account books at Frog's. They are an eye-opener. The last delivery to Teller is recorded in one set of books. But this other set shows five more shopkeepers from all over who claimed insurance and were paid fifty per cent of the insurance money.'

'How did you come by this?'

'Dunblane, the boss, and two others were out. I know the temp. She let me into the safe.'

'Macbeth! You cannot do that without a search warrant!'

'So I need one now. The temp won't talk. We'd better move fast.'

'I sent Blair up to Braikie because Teller was threatening to sue. I'll issue that search warrant and we'll take Detective MacNab and two police officers and get round there.'

It was late evening by the time Hamish Macbeth drove back to Lochdubh. He was a happy, contented man. Blair had returned from Braikie in time to hear about the success of the operation. The five other shopkeepers were being rounded up. They had claimed on supposedly stolen stock, taken it themselves and hidden it. So they gained half the insurance money and still had their stock after they had paid Dunblane.

That strange half-light of a northern Scottish summer where it never really gets dark bathed the countryside: the gloaming, where, as some of the older people still believed, the fairies lay in wait for the unwary traveller.

As Hamish opened the police station door, Lugs barked a reproachful welcome. Hamish took the dog out for a walk and then returned to prepare them both some supper. There came a furious knocking at the kitchen door just as he had put Lugs's food bowl on the floor and was sitting down at the table to enjoy his own supper.

He opened the door and found himself confronted with the angry figure of Mary Bisset's mother.

'You leave my daughter alone, d'ye hear?' she shouted. 'She's only twenty. Find someone your own age.'

Hamish blinked at her. 'Your daughter was of great help in our inquiries into an insurance fraud,' he said. 'I couldn't tell her what it was about but promised to take her out for dinner by way of thanks and tell her then.'

'Oh, yeah,' she sneered. 'Well, romance someone of your own age. You ought to be ashamed of yourself. Casanova!'

And with that she stormed off.

Hamish slammed the door. Women, he thought. I'm only in my thirties and I've just been made to feel like a dirty old man.

Chapter Two

The wife was pretty, trifling, childish, weak;
She could not think, but would not cease to
speak.

— George Crabbe

Hamish sat down at his computer in the morning to type out a full report of the insurance frauds. His long fingers flew rapidly over the keys. It was still sunny outside and he was anxious to get out and go about his normal business of sloping around and gossiping with the villagers.

The phone rang. He looked at it reluctantly for a few moments and then picked it up. 'Hamish?' said a scared little voice. 'It's me, Bella Comyn.'

'Morning, Bella. What can I do for you?'

'I'm frightened, Hamish. I want to leave him but I'm frightened of what he'll do.'

'Where is he at the moment?'

'He's down at the slaughterhouse in Strathbane.'

'Give me half an hour and I'll be over.'

Hamish typed busily, finished the report, sent it over to police headquarters, and then decided to find out what was up with Bella.

He turned over in his mind what he knew about her and her husband, Sean, while he drove out in the direction of their croft. Sean had reached the age of forty, two years before. He was a quiet, taciturn man. Then he came back from a trip to Inverness with a new bride – Bella. Bella was fifteen years younger than he, and the locals had murmured that never was there a more unsuitable crofter's wife. She wore flimsy, flirty clothes and could be seen teetering around Lochdubh in unsuitable high heels. She giggled and prattled and had seemed relatively happy.

Hamish parked his car outside their white-washed croft house and knocked on the door. Bella opened it. 'I'm right glad you've come,' she said. 'I've been wondering what to do.'

Hamish removed his cap and followed her into the kitchen.

'Would you like a cup of tea?'

'Maybe later. Tell me what's up.'

She sat down at the kitchen table. Her once-dyed-blonde hair was showing nearly two inches of black at the roots and was scraped back from her face. Her pale blue eyes were red with recent weeping.

'I can't take it any more,' she said. 'It's like being in prison. I can't go out anywhere. No movies, no meals out. Just stuck here, day in, day out.'

'Does he beat you?'

'No, he doesn't have to. He just threatens to and I do what he wants. Look at my hair,' she wailed, holding out a strand for Hamish's inspection. 'He says if I dye it again, he'll kill me.'

'What about marriage counselling?'

'Can you see Sean going to a marriage counsellor? We keep ourselves to ourselves, that's what he says, day in and day out.'

'Where would you go?'

She nervously twisted her gold wedding ring around her finger. 'I've got a friend in Inverness. I should have married him. I phoned him. He said I could come to him anytime I wanted.'

'So why do you need me?'

'Folks round here say you're prepared to bend the rules a bit to help people out. I want time to pack up my things and get out.' She looked anxiously at the clock. 'We've only got about half an hour. I can't drive. I thought you could lock him up for something and then give me a lift down to the bus in Lochdubh.'

'I cannae do that,' exclaimed Hamish, whose accent always became broader when he was upset. 'You'll need to talk to one of the women.'

'I don't know any of them.'

'And I cannae interfere in a marriage. Och, I tell you what. Leave it with me. I sometimes see you around the village. How do you get down there?'

'Sean drives me down. Then he goes off to the pub while I get the shopping.'

'So next time, just get on the bus.'

'And leave all my things? I've got my mother's jewellery.'

'You could put that in your handbag or in the bottom of a shopping bag.'

'He searches my bags the whole time in case someone's been slipping me letters. He checks the phone bill. If I'm still here when it next comes in, he'll ask me what I was doing phoning the police station. I'll need to tell him I saw someone suspicious hanging around.'

'So how did you get in touch with this fellow in Inverness?'

'Last time I was down in Lochdubh, I phoned from the telephone box on the front as soon as Sean was in the pub. A couple of pounds it took and that was the very last of my own money. He doesn't allow me any except for the shopping, and when he gets home, he ticks every item off on the list.'

'You need some friends here, women friends. Let me try to fix something.'

'It won't do any good. He'll send them off.'

Hamish suddenly grinned. 'He doesn't know Mrs Wellington, then.'

* * *

Hamish drove back to the police station and put Lugs inside. He was walking up to the manse to see Mrs Wellington, the minister's wife, when Elspeth caught up with him.

'It's about Stoyre,' she said.

'Later, Elspeth,' said Hamish curtly. 'I'm busy.'

She gave him an odd, disappointed look and turned away.

I shouldn't have been so rude to her, thought Hamish. But one thing at a time. Stoyre can wait.

He went on to the manse.

Mrs Wellington was a formidable woman dressed as usual, despite the heat, in a tweed jacket, silk blouse and baggy tweed skirt, thick stockings and brogues.

'Oh, it's you,' she said ungraciously.

'I want to talk to you about a delicate matter,' said Hamish.

'In trouble with the ladies again?' she boomed. 'Mary Bisset's mother is going around saying you're chasing her daughter.'

'That's rubbish. Can I come in?'

Hamish followed her into the manse kitchen, a gloomy room which smelled strongly of disinfectant. Manse houses were always dark, he reflected, as if light were considered unholy.

He explained Bella's problem. Mrs Wellington listened carefully and said, 'She's a flighty little thing and he should never have

27

married her, but she does need to get out a bit and the Mothers' Union always needs new members.'

'She doesn't have children.'

'Neither do the Currie sisters,' said Mrs Wellington dryly. 'But that doesn't stop them from trying to run everything. Leave it with me, Hamish.'

Hamish walked back down to the *Highland Times* office to look for Elspeth. He found her sitting at her desk, moodily stabbing a pencil into her hair.

'So what about Stoyre?' he asked.

'I took a run over there,' she said. 'Nothing. No one in the church.'

'So that's all you wanted to tell me?'

'I think you should go back. There's an odd feeling about.'

'What sort of feeling?'

'Fear.'

'It's probably the fear of some Calvinistic God. They seem to have gone all religious.'

'Could be. But I smell something else.'

Hamish suddenly felt ravenously hungry. He had not eaten any breakfast. To make up to Elspeth for his recent rudeness, he was about to ask her to join him at the Italian restaurant, but she looked up at him and grinned and said. 'What's all this about you romancing Mary Bisset?'

'There iss nothing in that,' said Hamish stiffly, and walked out. Irritating lassie.

Hamish went back to the police station and took a trout out of his freezer to defrost. Lugs let out a low grumbling sound. He did not like fish and felt his master was being selfish, but he brightened when Hamish began to fry up some lamb's kidneys for him.

Food ready, he loaded it all on to a tray and carried it out to the front garden. He placed Lugs's bowl on the grass and settled down to enjoy a meal of trout dipped in oatmeal, salad and chips.

The foxy face of Jimmy Anderson peered over the hedge. 'That looks good,' he said. He opened the gate and came in.

'I hope you've eaten,' said Hamish. 'I don't feel like cooking any more.'

'No, I'm fine.' Jimmy sank down in a chair next to him. He looked around: at the rambling roses tumbling over the front door and then over the hedge to where the loch sparkled in the sun. 'You've got the life o' Riley here, Hamish,' he said. 'Enjoy it while you can.'

'What do you mean?' demanded Hamish sharply.

'Well, because of you solving that big insurance case, Daviot's beginning to make noises about you being wasted up here, and Blair's encouraging him.'

'Why? He loathes my guts.'

'He feels if you were transferred to Strathbane, well, you'd just be another copper and he'd be more on hand to take the credit for anything you found out.'

'And what brings you up here?'

'Day off. I came to warn you about what was brewing, and I think you should be offering me something to drink.'

Hamish sighed but went into the house and came back with a bottle half full of whisky and a glass, which he set on the table. 'Help yourself.'

'Thanks.'

'So what do I do to stop getting a promotion?' asked Hamish.

'I dunno. Disgrace yourself – mildly.'

'How do I do that?'

Jimmy took a mouthful of whisky. 'You've always managed before,' he said.

'I do not want to go to Strathbane,' mourned Hamish. He waved his hand round about. 'Look what I've got to lose.'

'It's grand today, I'll give you that. But what about the long winters?'

'Believe me, long winters in Strathbane would seem worse than they do here.'

'Have it your way. Once a peasant, always a peasant. Stuck up here talking to the sheep would kill me.'

'If the bottle doesn't get to you first.'

'I can take it. Wait a wee bit: I've got an idea.'

Jimmy drank more whisky. 'There's a pet o' Blair's just joined the force. Red-hot keen. Arrest anyone on sight. Today, he's standing out on the main road afore you get to Strathbane with a speed camera. You could pelt past him at a hundred miles an hour.'

'In a police vehicle? He wouldnae do a thing. He'd think I was chasing someone.'

'Get a private car, get drunk enough, and see what happens.'

'I'd lose my licence!'

'A policeman! He'd be told to hush it up.'

Hamish snorted in disbelief. 'By Blair? Come on, Jimmy. Have some sense.'

'No, by me. He crawls to me because he wants to make CID. I'll be on hand to tell him to drop it and leak it to Daviot. Daviot hates drunken drivers but I'll tell him it'll be bad for the police image if it ever gets in the papers.'

Hamish looked at Jimmy thoughtfully and then said, 'I'll get another glass.'

PC Johnny Peters stifled a yawn. He was bored and tired. Nearly the end of his shift. Like Blair, he was originally from Glasgow and distrusted all Highlanders. He guessed that in their primitive, almost telepathic way, the news of his speed trap had spread far and wide. Cars had passed him doing a mere thirty miles an hour although it was a sixty-mile-an-hour area.

His radio crackled. 'Peters here,' he said.

'Anderson here,' came the voice. 'Just had a report of a stolen car. A white Ford Escort belonging to Mrs Angela Brodie of Lochdubh.' Peters had just taken down a note of the registration number when his sharp eyes spotted a small white car on the horizon. He signed off, ran to his car, and swung it across the road.

At first it seemed as if the approaching car, which was coming at great speed, would hit him but the driver braked about one foot from him and sat behind the wheel, smiling inanely.

Peters climbed out and approached the car and rapped on the driver's window. Hamish Macbeth wound down the window and let a strong smell of whisky out into the air.

'Out!' shouted Peters.

Hamish was breathalyzed, handcuffed, charged with being drunk and driving a stolen vehicle. He felt relieved to be out of Angela's car. He had driven painfully carefully until just before the speed trap, when he had accelerated.

As Hamish was led out of the police car, Jimmy Anderson was waiting. 'Peters,' he said. 'What are you doing arresting Hamish Macbeth? He's the hero of the hour. He's the one that solved that big insurance case.'

'I am just doing my duty,' said Peters primly. 'He is drunk and was driving a stolen car.'

'Was it that Ford Escort?'

'Yes.'

'Oh. Dr Brodie has just phoned. It was his wife who reported the car stolen, not knowing her husband had given Hamish permission to drive it.'

'Nonetheless . . .'

'Here. Take the handcuffs off. You'll learn that we try to keep things like this away from the press. I'll talk to Daviot. Let him handle it.'

Peters looked doubtful but was obviously impressed by the fact that Anderson appeared to be on easy terms with the boss. He unlocked the handcuffs on Hamish's wrists.

'Come on, Hamish,' said Jimmy.

Hamish followed him with the stiff, stork-like walk of the drunk.

'Lots of water, Jimmy,' he whispered. 'And coffee.'

'I'll leave you in the canteen while I talk to Daviot.'

Peter Daviot listened grimly to Jimmy's tale.

'I hope he has been charged,' he said.

'Well, that's why I came to see you, sir. Macbeth's a popular man with a lot o' friends in the press. If he's charged, it'll go to the sheriff's court and get in the papers. Bad for our image, sir. Besides, we don't want some reporter remembering how that drunk-driving episode of Chief Inspector Blair's was hushed up.' Blair had wrapped his car round a tree the year before after drinking heavily at a police party.

'Where's Macbeth now?

'In the canteen.'

'To think I was going to promote that man. That such ability should be allied to such dangerous behaviour.'

'May I offer a suggestion, sir?'

'Go on.'

'Macbeth manages to do very well where he is. He's never been one for the bottle. This was a one-off. Remember that fiancée o' his, Priscilla Halburton-Smythe?'

'Yes.'

'Well, he's learned she's getting married and maybe that's what upset him.'

'Send him to me. And get a police officer over to Lochdubh to pick up Mrs Brodie so that she may reclaim her car.'

Five minutes later, awash with mineral water and black coffee, a slightly more sober Hamish Macbeth faced his boss.

'Sit down,' barked Daviot. 'I am sure standing must be difficult for you. This is a bad business. You should have your licence removed and be suspended from duty.'

Hamish let out a giggle.

'And just what is so funny, Officer?'

'I couldnae help thinking o' all the cases I would solve if I were suspended. Thae detectives and policemen on the television are always being suspended from duty and that's when they solve cases.'

'Pull yourself together, man. This must be hushed up for the sake of our reputation. Do you know I was going to promote you? That's all off now. You are only fit to be a village policeman. I am sorely disappointed in you.'

'I am very sorry, sir.'

'Don't let it happen again. Get out of here. And sober up!'

'I hope it worked,' said Angela Brodie as she drove Hamish back to Lochdubh.

'Oh, it worked, all right. Thanks, Angela. Keep your eyes on the road and stop staring at me.'

'How drunk are you?'

'Nearly sober. I drank just enough to get over the limit.'

'This car reeks of booze.'

Hamish looked guilty. 'I spilled some on the seats.'

'Then when you get back, you can get some upholstery cleaner from Patel's and clean the lot.'

'Yes, Angela.'

'Mrs Wellington called on me before the police came to collect me. Seems you've launched her on a crusade to help Bella Comyn. She says she's a battered wife.'

'Not yet. But I gather her husband bullies her and won't allow her any freedom.'

'He does seem besotted with her. Do you really think he might harm her one day?'

'She seems to think so.'

'I'm going out there tomorrow with Mrs Wellington to see her.'

'Let me know how you get on.'

Back in Lochdubh, Hamish bought upholstery cleaner and diligently cleaned out the front seats of Angela's car. His mouth was dry and had a foul taste and his head was throbbing. At last he had finished. All he wanted now was two aspirin and a long sleep.

He was heading for the police station when Elspeth came running up to him. 'Hamish, there's a bit more about Stoyre.'

His headache was now dreadful. 'Is anyone dead or hurt or burgled?'

'No, it's not that. It's . . .'

'Leave it, Elspeth. Talk to me tomorrow.'

He strode off, leaving the reporter staring after him.

In the morning he awoke refreshed and with a hearty appetite. He went along to Patel's to buy bacon. As he entered the shop door, he could hear the voices of the Currie sisters, Nessie and Jessie, shrill with excitement.

'I tell you, he was cleaning out her car and stinking of the booze,' Nessie was saying. 'Why would he be doing that?'

'Why don't you ask him?' said Patel.

'Because he'll just lie, just lie,' said Jessie.

'If you want to know,' said Hamish angrily, 'I was taking some whisky to a sick friend in Strathbane and Mrs Brodie was driving me. She hit a rock and the top was loose and some of it spilled on the upholstery.'

The shop fell silent. The Currie sisters, who hated being caught out gossiping – a thing they were fond of saying that they never did – paid for their groceries and hurried out. Hamish bought a packet of bacon and headed home. He had no need to buy eggs; his hens supplied him with plenty.

He turned over the events of the day before and then remembered Elspeth. He simply must stop being rude to her. After breakfast he went to the local newspaper office, to be told she was out reporting on a flower show over at Dornoch. He wondered whether to drive over to Stoyre but then dismissed it. He had other villages on his beat to visit and it wasn't as if anything criminal had taken place in Stoyre.

He returned with Lugs in the late evening, satisfied that things on his beat were as quiet as they had been earlier that summer. He cooked a meal for himself and his dog and then was picking up the phone to call Elspeth when it rang. Mrs Wellington's voice boomed down the line. 'You've got to do something.'

'What's happened?'

'Sean's left Bella. I was up there early in the day with Angela Brodie to suggest that Bella should start attending the Mothers' Union meetings. Sean was there. He seemed pleased at the idea. Everything seemed normal. But Bella's just phoned in a state. She says he just walked out. Said he wasn't coming back.'

'I'll go right now and see her.'

'I'll meet you there.'

Bella's eyes were again red with recent weeping and she had a black eye. Mrs Wellington held her hand while she blurted out her story. Sean, she said, had pretended to be delighted at the invitation for her to join the Mothers' Union. After Angela and Mrs Wellington had left, he began to rant and say she had set it up so that she would have an excuse to slip out and meet other men, then he had blacked her eye and said he was sick of her and he was leaving her forever.

'You're better off without him,' said the minister's wife.

'How will you manage?' asked Hamish. 'For money, I mean.'

'We have a joint account. I can draw on that.'

'I thought Sean didn't let you have any money of your own.'

'He wouldn't let me draw any without his permission. But believe me, this is one time I'm not going to ask.'

'So what time did he leave?'

'About eleven o' clock.'

'But you didn't phone Mrs Wellington until this evening!'

Bella hung her head. 'I thought he would come back. I thought he'd never leave me. I'd given up the idea of running away.'

There came a long howl from outside. Bella jumped nervously. 'What's that?'

'It's my dog,' said Hamish. 'I'll see what's up.'

Mrs Wellington tut-tutted her disapproval. 'You shouldn't take that dog with you everywhere.'

Hamish went out to the Land Rover. He opened the passenger door and Lugs stumbled down to the ground. He raised his leg against the wheel.

'So that's all it was.' Hamish went back inside.

'Maybe Sean's just taken himself off to cool down,' he said. 'Mind if I have a look around the house?'

Was there a flicker of apprehension in Bella's eyes? 'Go ahead,' she said.

Hamish went through to the living room. A nearly new three-piece suite in a mushroom shade dominated the small room. There was a display cabinet with various pieces of china against one wall. No open fire; just a bar heater. Obviously the room was kept for 'best': a visit from the minister, the rare party.

He went next door to the bedroom. The double bed was covered in a blood-red shiny quilt. What was obviously Bella's side of the bed had a bedside table with film magazines and paperback romances stacked on it. He went to the table at Sean's side. On top was an alarm clock and nothing else. He jerked open the top drawer. A Gideon Bible and several packets of condoms. Hadn't Sean wanted children? He went out and through to the back of the small house and pushed open a door. This was Sean's office. There was an old-fashioned roll-top desk with neatly stacked papers beside a computer. He sifted through them. Farm accounts, sheep-dip papers, electricity and phone bills, nothing that could give him a clue to Sean's disappearance. He opened the drawers and carefully went through the contents until in the bottom drawer he found two passports, one belonging to Sean and the other to Bella. He opened Bella's. It was still in her maiden name – Bella Wilson.

He went through everything again but without finding a single clue to explain why Sean had left.

The man hadn't been gone long, he thought. It was surely a waste of police time, panicking so early over his disappearance.

* * *

He was driving back along the waterfront when he saw Elspeth Grant. He screeched to a halt. 'Want to come to the station for a cup of tea?'

'Why?'

'I've been a bit rude to you. But I've had other things on my mind.'

Elspeth swung round in the direction of the police station. 'Meet you there,' she said over her shoulder.

Hamish drove on. She was walking quickly, and by the time he had parked the Land Rover, she was waiting at the kitchen door.

He unlocked the door and ushered her into the kitchen.

'Any crime for me?' asked Elspeth as Hamish plugged in the kettle, a recent purchase. The summer had been so warm that there had been little need to light the stove every day.

Hamish told her about the insurance fraud. When he had finished, she asked, 'Do you know when that will come up in court?'

'I'll find out for you. I've just been up to see Bella Comyn.'

'Lochdubh's dizzy blonde. What's up with her?'

'Her husband's cleared off. Mind you, he only left this morning. He'll probably be back. She claims he bullied and threatened her.'

'I saw them at the Highland Games last year. He seemed besotted with her.'

'I'm sure he's all that. Maybe that's why he keeps such a strong grip on her. Here's your tea. Help yourself to milk and sugar.'

'Why is Lugs pawing at my skirt?'

'He likes tea a lot,' said Hamish. 'It's unnatural in a dog. I give him some on his birthday and at Christmas.'

Elspeth hooted with laughter. 'You treat that dog like a bairn, but then the childless always do.'

Hamish flushed with anger. 'I'm getting a bit weary of your personal remarks, Elspeth.'

'Sorry. I think you ought to take another look at Stoyre.'

'Why? Because you sense they're frightened? I need facts.'

'Well, there's a Mr and Mrs Bain from Stoyre. They've moved into a cottage up the back.'

'So?'

'They seem scared and won't talk about Stoyre.' Elspeth brushed a stray lock of hair from her face. 'Tell you what: let's go together to a church service on Sunday. Suss out the place.'

'I may be busy,' said Hamish loftily.

'You're just cross because I teased you about your dog. Come on, Hamish. Might be a laugh.'

'All right,' he said reluctantly. 'The service is usually at eleven in the morning. I'll pick you up at ten.'

'Right you are, copper. I'd best be going.'

She turned in the doorway and looked at him thoughtfully. Then she said, 'If it were me, I wouldn't believe a word Bella says.'

'And what makes you say that?'

She grinned. 'Just a feeling.'

Hamish went through to the police office after she had left and switched on his computer.

After typing in a password, he typed in the name Bella Wilson. He stared at the screen. Bella Wilson of Donnel Street, Inverness, had been charged, aged thirteen, at the juvenile court, with bullying one Aileen Hendry by repeatedly punching and kicking her. At age eighteen, she had been charged with hitting one Henry Cathcart on the head with a poker. Hamish leaned back in his chair and scowled horribly. Sean was gone and Bella was in charge of the joint account. Where was Sean?

Chapter Three

Come away, come away, death,
And in sad cypress let me be laid;
Fly away, fly away, breath;
I am slain by a fair cruel maid.
        – William Shakespeare

The next day, Hamish went up to talk to Bella. He heard her singing in the kitchen as he approached the front door. He knocked, and while he waited for her to answer, he turned and looked around. There was no garden, just sheep-cropped turf and old rusting machinery. But over by the wall was a freshly dug patch of earth.

Bella opened the door. Her hair was newly blonded and she looked fresh and pretty. 'Have you found him?' she asked.

'Not yet. Can I come in?'

'All right.' She stood back reluctantly.

Hamish walked into the kitchen and took off his cap. 'Sit down, Bella,' he said.

'What's this all about?'

45

'It iss about your police record,' said Hamish, his accent becoming more sibilant with worry.

'That was a long time ago,' she said defiantly. 'And on both occasions I was provoked.'

Hamish took a deep breath. 'Have you been battering your husband?'

'What!' she shrieked. 'A wee thing like me wi' a big man like that!'

'It does happen.'

'No, I told you the truth. He's the bully.'

'There's a freshly dug patch in the ground outside. Who dug it?'

'Me. I was going to put in some flowers.'

'So you won't mind if I take a spade and have a look.'

Bella's face hardened. 'You'll need a search warrant.'

'Oh, I'll get one. But in order to get one, I'll need to report your criminal record, and it won't just be me but the top brass from Strathbane who'll question you, and a forensic team will be going over your house.'

'Oh, dig it up, then,' she snarled. 'The spade's by the kitchen door.'

Hamish went to the door and seized the spade. He went out into the bright sunlight. He began to dig in the freshly turned earth. Only about two feet below the surface, he uncovered a dead collie. He picked out the body and laid it on the turf. It had died recently – been killed, for its head had been smashed in. He sat back on his heels, feeling sick.

He turned his head. Bella was standing by the kitchen door. 'You did this,' he said flatly.

'Sean did it,' she said. 'I didn't want you to know.'

Hamish rose and went to the Land Rover, called Strathbane, and spoke rapidly. Then he returned and stood guard over the dead dog. 'You interfering bastard,' hissed Bella, her face now ugly with rage. 'I tell you, he walked out and said he wasn't coming back.'

'You will be asked by police from Strathbane, who will be here soon, to go with them to police headquarters for questioning.'

'I thought you were the policeman here,' she jeered.

'Not when it iss a question o' murder,' said Hamish quietly.

After Bella had been taken away, he returned to the police station to type out his report. Then once he had finished, he leant back in his chair. What if Sean had really run off because he was frightened of her? He would need money. Hamish put on his cap and went out and walked along to the bank and asked to see the manager, Mr MacCallum.

'It's about Sean Comyn,' said Hamish. 'He's gone missing, feared dead. But has he drawn out any money recently?'

47

'I should not be discussing a customer's account. That's confidential.'

'A possible murder does not keep anything confidential.'

'I suppose if I don't help you, you'll get a warrant.' The bank manager switched on the computer on his desk. Hamish waited patiently while he typed in various codes. 'Ah, here we are,' said Mr MacCallum. 'Sean Comyn made out a cheque to Queen and Barrie, estate agents in Strathbane.'

'When?'

'Yesterday.'

'Anything else?'

'Two hundred pounds out of a cash machine in Strathbane the same day.'

'Well, it looks as if the man is still alive, thank God.'

Hamish went back to the police station and dialled the estate agents. He explained the police were trying to contact a Sean Comyn.

'We rented him a cottage. He wanted somewhere cheap. We got him a place in Stoyre.'

'Address?'

'Number six, the waterfront.'

'Thanks.' Stoyre again, thought Hamish as he drove off, leaving behind a sulky Lugs.

When he descended into the huddle of houses which made up the tiny village of Stoyre, he was relieved to see people moving about and men working at the nets. Elspeth and her fears! He parked outside the pub and walked along the waterfront to number 6. It had been a fisherman's cottage and had a run-down appearance, unlike its neighbours. He knocked on the door.

To his relief, Sean Comyn himself answered it. He was unshaven and red-eyed.

'What's the matter?' he asked. 'Bella?'

'A word with you. Let me in.'

Sean led him into a front room. It was dark and sparsely furnished with a few shabby chairs and a sofa.

'Before we start,' said Hamish, taking out his mobile phone, 'I'll phone police headquarters and say you've been found.'

Sean tried to say something but Hamish held up a hand for silence. 'In a minute,' he said. He reported to Jimmy Anderson that Sean had been found. 'If she's been beating him,' said Jimmy, 'will he press charges?'

'I'll see what I can do.'

Hamish rang off and turned to Sean. 'Before I begin, I want you to take this phone and call your bank manager and freeze your account or, if I'm not mistaken, she'll clean you out.'

Sean took the phone from him. He did not ask questions or protest, simply phoned the bank and did what Hamish had suggested. Then he handed the phone back and sat with his hands between his legs, slumped forward.

'Now,' said Hamish gently, 'she'd been beating you, hadn't she?'

There was a long silence and then Sean said wearily, 'How was I to know? She seemed so pretty, so fragile, like a wee bird. It started soon after we were married. She'd get this blank look in the eyes and then start hitting me with anything that was handy. The other day, I said I wasn't taking any more, I was leaving her. She laughed in my face. And then still looking at me, she punched herself in the eye – hard. "I'll say you did that," she said.'

'You'll need to file charges.'

'I cannae do that, Hamish. I'd be the laughing stock o' the Highlands.'

'She killed one of your collies.' Hamish told him about the grave.

He turned a muddy colour but said, 'I can't let folks know she was beating me.'

'They'll know soon enough. Police and forensic have been crawling over your croft house looking for your dead body.'

'But if it goes to court, it'll be in all the papers. I cannae do it.'

Hamish sighed and looked around. 'Who owns this place?'

'Some couple. They rent it out to summer visitors. They havenae been able to rent it for a while.'

'Do you have a phone?'

'Over there. It's a coin box phone. Everything's got a coin box – the gas and the electric.'

'You can't go on living here. Think of your beasts. It's hot weather and Bella's more likely to take a hammer to them than give them water.'

He shuddered. 'Give me a bit o' peace, Hamish, till I get my courage back. But I'm not pressing charges.'

Hamish took a note of his phone number. 'I'll be back,' he said.

Once outside, Hamish walked back to the Land Rover and phoned Jimmy again. 'So far, he won't press charges.'

'Well, the RSPCA will,' said Jimmy, meaning the Royal Society for the Prevention of Cruelty to Animals. 'We found a bloodied hammer. Haven't got a report back yet on where the blood came from, but it's got her fingerprints on it, and if Sean's alive, then it stands to reason it's the dog's blood. And Sean will pay her fine and be stuck in Stoyre until his croft rots.'

'Where is she now?' asked Hamish.

'Johnny Peters is driving her home.'

'Good luck to him. I'll go and see her.'

Once more to Lochdubh to file another report and out to Sean's croft. As he approached the door, he knew instinctively that there was no one at home. He tried the door. Locked. Maybe she wasn't back yet. And yet he had taken his time over the report.

He got back in the Land Rover and drove down into Lochdubh and stopped outside Patel's grocery store. A daily bus would have left for Inverness half an hour ago. He went into the shop and asked Mr Patel, 'Did anyone see if Bella Comyn left on the bus?'

Nessie Currie appeared behind him, her eyes gleaming behind thick glasses. 'The poor wee thing left on the bus with two big suit-cases. A policeman drove her to Lochdubh. What's been happening?'

Hamish didn't answer. He went back to the police station and phoned Jimmy.

'Bella Comyn left for Inverness on the bus. Johnny Peters drove her there. What was he on about?'

'I'll see if he's back yet and ring you.'

Hamish took Lugs out for a walk and then fed the dog. He was just wondering whether to ring Jimmy again when the phone rang. It was Jimmy.

'Peters didn't know anything about why she was at police headquarters,' he said. 'He'd just come on duty and was simply told to take her back to Lochdubh. She spun him a story that she had gone to report her husband missing and that she was so upset, she wanted to stay with relatives in Inverness. She packed in a short time and he drove her to Lochdubh.

She'd called the bank and whatever she heard upset her.'

'I told Sean to tell the bank to freeze the account. It was a joint account.'

'Anyway, she got on the bus and off she went.'

'You'd best phone Inverness police. We'll get her for the dog if nothing else.'

'Will do.'

'Thank God she couldnae drive or she'd have taken Sean's car as well. I'll get over to Stoyre and give him a lift home.'

'Why Stoyre?' asked Hamish as he drove the crofter towards Lochdubh.

'It was the cheapest rent I could find,' said Sean. 'I only took it for a month – holiday let.'

'Have you any idea where Bella might have gone?'

'She's an only child and her mother and father are dead.'

'What about relatives at your wedding?'

'There weren't any. We were married in the register office and two of my cousins acted as witnesses.'

'Any friends?' Hamish wondered whether to ask about the man in Inverness that Bella had said she ought to have married but decided against it.

'Not that I know of.'

'Didn't that strike you as odd?'

'No, I thought she just wanted to be with me. I couldnae get over the fact that someone so young and pretty could fancy me.'

'I hope you're over her, Sean. And if she comes back, you're to phone me immediately.'

'I'll do that. She shouldnae have killed my dog. Which one?'

'Don't know.'

'Probably Bob,' he said gloomily. 'Always was a friendly dog. Now, Queenie, the other, was mortal scared of her.'

As they approached Sean's croft, Sean said, 'It's odd. Things'll be the same as they were afore I married her. But not the same, if you know what I mean. I'll aye be frightened I'll turn round and see her standing there.'

'She's wanted on a charge for killing the dog – cruelty. She's made a run for it. I doubt if she'll be back. Get yourself a lawyer and get a divorce.'

Hamish parked the Land Rover and Sean climbed stiffly down and then heaved his suitcase out of the back. 'Thanks, Hamish.'

'I'd best come in with you,' said Hamish. 'See if she's taken anything she shouldn't have.'

Sean unlocked the door. Hamish waited in the kitchen while Sean looked around the place. 'Nothing taken but her clothes and things,' he said. He went to the door and gave a shrill whistle. A collie came bounding up to him. 'This is Queenie,' he said, fondling the animal's coat. 'I'll be all right now, Hamish.'

'Don't keep the truth of the matter to yourself, Sean. She's put it about that you were the one who was bullying her. There's no shame in it. Folks wouldn't expect you to hit back at a lassie.'

'I'll think about it.'

Hamish went back to the police station and phoned Jimmy Anderson. 'Any news?'

'Not a sight of her,' said Jimmy. 'Police were waiting at Inverness station but she never got off the bus. The driver said she got off at Dingwall. No record of her having taken another bus or even the train from Dingwall. She's gone to ground somewhere.'

'Are the police at Dingwall checking the taxi services?'

'Nobody's checking anything any more, Hamish.'

'Why?'

'Blair says it's a waste o' manpower looking for a lassie who killed a dog. He instructed us all to have nothing more to do with it.'

'Doesn't the silly cheil know she might kill a man or woman the next time?'

'He doesn't care.'

'While you're on the phone, have you heard any reports of anything going on in Stoyre?'

'Where's Stoyre?'

'It's a wee village up on the coast.'

'That's your beat. No, I haven't heard anything.'

Hamish thanked him and rang off. Then he phoned Mrs Wellington and told her the truth about Sean's marriage. At first she wouldn't believe him until he told her about the death of the dog. 'A woman who would do that is capable of anything,' said Mrs Wellington.

Hamish then phoned Angela Brodie with the same information and then asked, 'There's a new family in Lochdubh called Bain. Where's their house?'

'Up the back. The one that belonged to the dustman's wife, Martha Macleod. Remember, she and your ex-policeman moved up to live in the Tommel Castle Hotel after they got married.'

Clarry, Hamish's policeman when Hamish had last, briefly, been elevated to the rank of sergeant, had left the force to become a chef at the hotel.

'I'll call on them tomorrow,' said Hamish.

'Why?'

'Just to be friendly, that's all.'

But Hamish remembered that Elspeth in her psychic way had not trusted Bella. And Elspeth had said the Bains were frightened.

Hamish walked past Patel's and up the lane at the back to the Bains's cottage. He knocked on the door and it was answered by a small, thin woman. She had sallow skin and small black eyes, which regarded him warily.

'Mrs Bain?'

'Yes, what's happened? It's not Mairie, is it? I sent her down to the shop.'

'No, it's only a friendly call. I heard you had moved from Stoyre.'

'Yes, that's right. We're fine.' She made to close the door.

'I chust wanted a word with you,' said Hamish, not used to unfriendliness. 'Is your man at home?'

'He's asleep. He's been out all night at the fishing.'

A small voice behind Hamish piped, 'I got the milk, Ma.'

Hamish swung round. A little girl, about ten years old, stood there.

'Get in the house this minute!' ordered her mother.

The girl slid past them and vanished into the cottage.

'And is everything all right with you?' pursued Hamish.

'Yes, yes. Fine. Now, if you don't mind . . .'

'Was anything going on at Stoyre?'

She had been about to close the door but hesitated. 'No, why?'

'There was a strange atmosphere when I was there.'

'Well, ye cannae be arresting an atmosphere,' and with that she closed the door firmly.

Hamish pushed back his cap and scratched his fiery hair. He turned and walked back down to the waterfront and along to the harbour. Archie Maclean, a fisherman, was sitting on the wall outside his cottage, puffing on a hand-rolled cigarette.

'Grand morning, Archie,' said Hamish, sitting down next to him.

'Aye, it is that.'

'Don't you ever sleep?'

'I will be having a kip this afternoon. Herself is cleaning again.'

The sound of frantic activity sounded from the cottage behind them.

'I went up to see the Bains,' said Hamish.

'Aye, Harry Bain was out with us last night.'

'What's he like?'

'Quiet wee man. Nothing much to say for himself. But a good worker.'

'He's just moved here from Stoyre. Have you heard anything about Stoyre, Archie?'

'Nothing much except they seem to have a rare powerful preacher. The kirk is aye full.'

'If you get talking to Harry, see if you can find out anything.'

'I'll do that. But why? You think something criminal's going on?'

'I don't know. Just a feeling.'

Hamish went back to the police station after collecting the newspapers from Patel's. Time to relax and forget about Bella and about Stoyre. He took a deck chair out to the garden and, with Lugs at his feet, settled down to read.

The phone rang in the police station. Hamish rustled a newspaper impatiently. Let the answering machine pick it up. The window to the police office was open. The answering machine clicked on. Blair's voice broke the peace of the day. 'Get yourself over to Stoyre. Major Jennings's cottage has been blown up.'

'Where is the major?' asked Hamish as he and Jimmy stood with detectives and police officers surveying the burnt-out shell that had once been the major's bungalow.

'Flying up from the south. We'll have the anti-terrorist squad here.'

'Can't be the IRA this far north.'

'The major's retired but he was once in army intelligence. May have had something to do with Northern Ireland.'

'Are they sure it was some sort of explosive? Couldn't have been a faulty Calor gas tank?'

'Too early to say. Could just be some anti-English bastards. You mind that film *Braveheart*?'

'Of course,' said Hamish. 'And what a load of inaccurate historical rubbish it was, too.'

'Aye, but you know it caused a lot of anti-English feeling in some weak heads. Then there was that showbiz chap, Cameron

McIntosh over in Mallaig. His cottage got destroyed.'

'Well, we'll see,' said Hamish uneasily. All the while he thought, This can't be happening in Stoyre. He looked down at the calm sea and the sun-warmed stone harbour. Something evil was going on here.

Blair came marching up to him. 'Move your lazy bum, Macbeth, and see what you can get out of the local yokels.'

Hamish set off down the slope from the ruins of the major's cottage.

He decided to try the manse first. The door was eventually answered by what he at first thought was a young girl. She was wearing a short summer dress and her hair was in pigtails. Her thin legs ended in white ankle socks and black flat shoes. Her features were small but then he noticed the thin, spidery lines on her face. 'Mrs Mackenzie?'

'Yes, Officer. Won't you come in? My husband is going about his parochial duties.' Her voice was soft and lilting.

Hamish took off his cap and followed her along a stone-flagged passage to the manse kitchen. The long sash windows were open and a breeze fluttered the crystal-white net curtains. A scarlet Raeburn cooker stood against one wall and a dresser with brightly patterned plates against another. There was a scrubbed wooden kitchen table in the centre surrounded with ladder-back chairs.

'Sit down, Officer,' said the minister's wife. 'Coffee?'

'That would be grand.'

She put instant coffee in two mugs and poured boiling water from a kettle on top of the stove. 'Help yourself to milk and sugar,' she said, sitting down opposite him. 'I suppose you've come about that terrible business.'

'The major's cottage, yes. What can you tell me about it?'

'Nothing.' Her eyes were greyish blue and slightly slanted, the sort of Highland eyes which reflected everything back, in a way, without betraying their owner's feelings. 'We were woken up about dawn with this tremendous blast, and the windows of the manse rattled.'

'So you got up and went out to have a look?'

'Well, no. We were both still tired, so we went back to sleep.'

'Heavens, woman! Surely natural curiosity would ha' impelled you to go out of doors to see what had happened.'

'Odd things happen every day,' she said serenely. 'It is God's will and it is not up to us to question the will of God.'

'I would think it was up to everyone to question the will of man,' said Hamish dryly. He looked at her curiously. 'I mean, God didn't blow up the major's cottage. Some villain or villains did it.'

'It could have been lightning or a thunderbolt.'

'Meaning God zapped the major's cottage? Havers. And what do you think a douce body like the major would have done to incur the wrath of God?'

Her thin lips became even thinner as she folded them into a reproving line. 'He did not attend the kirk when he was here.'

'The kirk is Free Presbyterian. Stands to reason, the major is probably a member o' the Church of England.'

'That is as may be.'

'And what's that supposed to mean?'

She sipped her coffee in silence while Hamish gave her a frustrated look. At last he said, 'So you've nothing to tell me?'

'There's nothing I can tell you.'

He stood and picked up his cap. 'If you think of anything, let me know.'

'You can find your own way out?'

'Aye.'

Baffled, Hamish went off. He stood outside the door of the manse and looked down on the village of Stoyre, a huddle of houses before a tranquil sea. The air smelled fresh and clean. Somewhere up on the hill a sheep bleated.

He walked down into the village and into the pub. A few locals were sitting at tables. When he came in, they rose to their feet and went out. Andy Crummack, the landlord, was polishing glasses.

'I seem to be bad for business,' commented Hamish.

'We keep ourselves to ourselves in this village,' said Andy, 'and we don't like nosy coppers asking questions.'

'Then get used to it,' snapped Hamish. 'Because I'm the first of many.' He took out his notebook. 'Now, where were you when the major's cottage was blown up?'

'I was in my bed.'

'And did you go out to see what happened?'

'No, I thought it was thunder.'

'Man, the blast must have been horrendous. What time did you hear it?'

'I looked at the clock. It was just after five.'

'Andy, something's going on in this village and I mean to get to the bottom of it.'

'Aye, well, that's your job.'

The pub door opened and Elspeth came in. Hamish was relieved to see someone, anyone, from outside this strange village. 'Come and have a drink,' he hailed. He jerked a thumb at Andy. 'No use asking him anything.'

Hamish ordered a tonic water for himself and a whisky for Elspeth and carried them to a corner table. 'Got any news for me?' he asked.

'Not a thing. They all heard that blast at dawn and inexplicably no one admits to going out to see what happened or even to looking through a window.'

'Do you still think they're scared of something?'

'No, that's the odd thing. They've got carefully blank faces, but underneath they're elated about something – elated and secretive, like children hiding something.'

'Don't you think,' asked Hamish, surveying her outfit, 'that you might get a bit more out of the locals if your clothes weren't so strange?'

Elspeth was wearing a grey chiffon blouse with a pair of cut-off denim shorts and clumpy hiking boots.

'No, you old fuddy-duddy. No one is going to get anything out of this lot.'

Hamish looked across her out the window and saw a familiar figure heading for the pub door. 'Blair,' he hissed. 'Don't say you saw me.'

He vaulted the bar and made his way through to the back premises just as the detective chief inspector came through the door. There was a back storeroom with a door opening on to a weedy garden. In the middle of the storeroom, clutching a Bible and on his knees in prayer, was the landlord. Hamish edged round him and darted out into the sunlight. Andy seemed unaware of his existence.

Hamish then went diligently from cottage to cottage, asking questions and getting the same replies as Elspeth had received. He had just left one of the cottages when he heard himself being hailed by Jimmy Anderson. 'Get anything?' asked Jimmy.

Hamish sighed. 'I get the impression they all believe it was the wrath of God. They've never actually attacked anyone English up here before. I mean, they don't even like people from anywhere south of Perth.'

'See Blair?'

'He was heading for the pub. He's probably still there.'

'Well, that'll keep him away for a bit. The major should be here this afternoon. I wonder what he'll have to say. The bomb squad is combing the ruins. They think it was one of those fertilizer bombs like the IRA uses.'

'Now, why don't I believe it was the IRA?' muttered Hamish. 'There's something odd going on here, Jimmy.'

'I agree with you. I think one of them did it out of spite. Maybe the Lord told them to do it. Is there a lot of inbreeding in these parts?'

'Not now. No.'

'It would drive me daft living in a place like Stoyre. Think what it's like in the winter when the sun rises at ten in the morning and sinks at two in the afternoon.'

'It does that in Strathbane.'

'Aye, but there's life there, man. Lights, traffic, theatre, cinema, clubs.'

'And crime and drugs.'

'Maybe, but we haven't had anything as dramatic as this.'

'Oh, here's the boss,' said Hamish.

Blair, red in the face and breathing whisky fumes, came up to them. 'You,' he said to Jimmy, 'come back up to the major's with me. You, Macbeth, get back to your local duties. We've enough men here.'

Hamish trotted off. He knew that Jimmy would probably fill him in later and he also knew that he wasn't going to get anything more out of the locals.

As he drove off to Lochdubh, he noticed a cloud, a small round cloud, travelling towards the sun. The breeze through the open window felt damp against his cheek and the country-side had that waiting feeling it gets when rain is about to arrive. By the time he got back to the police station, the sky was a uniform grey, as if the clouds had sunk down rather than blowing in from the sea.

He walked Lugs and fed him and then himself. He checked on his sheep and went back indoors as the first fat raindrops began to fall. He made a pot of tea and sat down at the kitchen table to mull over the situation in Stoyre. Somehow the greyness of the day and the soft rain falling outside seemed to bring back reality to the Highlands and to his mind. He was now sure that some local had blown up the major's cottage to get rid of him. The major or some of the guests he usually invited in the summer might have offended someone, and Highland malice, as Hamish knew, ran slow and deep and took its time over getting revenge.

He carried his mug of tea through to the office and stood at the window, looking out at the rain-pocked waters of the loch. Mist was rolling down the hills opposite to hang in grey wreaths round the top of the forest trees. A small yacht sailed into view. Two figures were taking down the sails, and he could hear the chug-chug of the donkey engine.

He sat down at his desk and switched on the computer and began to type a report. The next day would be a Sunday. Hamish remembered he had promised to go to church in Stoyre with Elspeth. Might be interesting to hear one of Fergus Mackenzie's sermons and discover what it was in them that had prompted such a strong religious revival.

Jimmy Anderson arrived in the early evening. 'Blasted weather,' he said. 'Got any whisky?'

'No,' said Hamish, 'and the shop's closed. Closes early on Saturday.'

'Got anything?'

'I've got some brandy left over from Christmas.'

'That'll do.'

Hamish took down the brandy bottle from the cupboard. 'I won't join you,' he said. 'I don't like brandy much.'

'And that's why you've got it left over from Christmas. Good. All the more for me,' said Jimmy. 'Pour it out.'

Hamish poured a measure of brandy into a glass and placed it in front of him.

'Got cold in here,' complained Jimmy.

'I'll light the stove,' said Hamish. 'Any more orders?'

'No,' said Jimmy, taking a swig of brandy. 'Ah, that's better. Blair's been getting on my tits. There's bigwigs up from Scotland Yard and some bods from MI5, and Blair's been showing off by pushing me around and crawling to them.'

Hamish filled the stove with kindling and paper and struck a match. When the stove was lit, he added several slices of dark peat and a couple of logs. 'I think it was a local job,' he said.

'Well, to be sure, the dafties are all blaming it on God.'

'Did you manage to get out of them why God should be angry with Major Jennings?'

'Mrs MacBean at the general store was more forthcoming than the rest of them.'

'What did she say?' asked Hamish.

'When I asked her why God would see fit to blow up the major's cottage, she replied that God moved in mysterious ways. And believe me, that meant she was being downright talkative compared to the rest of them up in Brigadoon.'

'So long as everyone's convinced it's a terrorist attack, they'll leave the locals alone. Did the major arrive?'

'Yes, but he seemed quite unfazed. He said the cottage was insured. He said he'd had some trouble with the locals. He believes it was a piece of spite.'

'What trouble?'

'Usual trouble any incomer has up here – not getting help, plumber not turning up, no one prepared to help with the garden or building repairs, that sort of thing.'

'I'm off to the kirk tomorrow,' said Hamish. 'Maybe I'll start off by finding out why they've all gone religious.'

'Maybe you'll see the light yourself,' said Jimmy. 'Pass that bottle over.'

Chapter Four

Where we tread 'tis haunted holy ground.
                                                    – Lord Byron

Hamish's first thought when he picked up Elspeth the next day was that at least she had made the effort to dress in a more conventional manner. He had been afraid that she might have decided to turn up for church in something like hot pants. But she was wearing a long black skirt with a black sweater and had a tartan stole around her shoulders. When she climbed into the Land Rover, however, he noticed that she was still wearing her favourite clumpy boots.

'Haven't you got a pair of shoes?' he asked.

'Hamish Macbeth! Somehow you have graduated to being a grumpy husband without ever having been one. Have you seen the feet of women who have worn high heels all their lives? All bent and twisted. So just drive on and mind your own business.'

A fine drizzle smeared the windscreen. Hamish switched on the wipers, which made a grating sound. 'You need new wipers,' commented Elspeth.

'I do not,' said Hamish, who was sometimes mean about small items like windscreen wipers. 'They're chust fine when the rain's heavy.'

As if to prove his point, the rain began to pour down. 'The weather forecast's pretty good,' said Elspeth. 'It said it would get better later.'

'Do you have any idea why Major Jennings's cottage got blown up?'

'It's something to do with the villagers. I'm sure of that. There's a sort of religious mania emanating from them.'

'You mean God told them to do it?'

'Something like that,' said Elspeth vaguely. 'Oh, look, I can see a little patch of blue sky ahead.'

As they approached Stoyre, the rain abruptly ceased. Elspeth was used to the lightning-quick changes of weather in the Highlands but she still stared in wonder as the clouds rolled back and the sun blazed down on the still-black sea. Smoke rose from the cottages below them. Most villagers still had their water heated by a back boiler in the fireplace, so fires were often kept going all year round.

Up on the hill, the police tapes fluttered outside the major's cottage. The waterfront was full of cars and television vans. 'You've got competition,' remarked Hamish.

'They won't get anything out of the villagers,' said Elspeth. 'If I can't, they can't.'

'Fancy yourself as an ace reporter?'

'No, but I'm Highland and they aren't.'

Hamish parked amongst the cars. They won't get a drink here anyway,' he said. 'The pub closes on the Sabbath.'

They climbed down from the police Land Rover. There were groups of jaded press standing around. No one bothered to approach them. After their experiences trying to get something out of the villagers and failing, they probably summed up the small population as a waste of time.

Elspeth and Hamish caught up with the line of villagers making their way to the church.

'Now,' said Hamish, 'let's see what the preaching is like.'

The interior of the church was small and whitewashed. There were no religious statues, no crosses. There wasn't even an organ. A chanter, a man who struck a tuning fork on one of the front pews and sang the first note, started off the hymn singing.

They sang, 'There is a green hill far away without a city wall.'

'I used to think that meant a city that didn't have a wall,' whispered Elspeth. 'Then I learned it meant outside the city wall.'

'Shhh!' said an old lady waspishly.

The hymn was followed by two readings from the Bible, and then the minister rose to deliver his sermon. Hamish listened in surprise. Whatever had caused this religious fervour in Stoyre, it could hardly be the preachings of Fergus Mackenzie. Hamish and Elspeth were seated at the back of the church and they had to strain to hear what the minister was saying. His soft voice did not carry well. There was no passion or threat of hell-fire in his sermon. He said the villagers all knew that they were chosen by God and must live up to this privilege. He talked of Moses and the burning bush and then of the leading of the Israelites to the promised land. His soft voice and the heat of all the bodies in the church and from the sun, now blazing in through the windows, had a soporific effect on Hamish, and his head began to droop. Elspeth nudged him in the ribs. 'Pay attention.'

The service ended with the Twenty-third Psalm.

Elspeth and Hamish waited outside by the church door to see if any of the villagers said anything of interest to the minister, but all they could hear were murmurs of 'Grand service' or replies to the minister's occasional questions about health or children.

Hamish saw Mrs MacBean, who ran the general store, and taking Elspeth's arm, he fell into step beside her. 'Bad business about the major's cottage,' he remarked.

'We should not be discussing such things on the Sabbath,' said Mrs MacBean primly. 'We have our minds on higher things.' This reminded Hamish that it was a peculiarity among some Presbyterians to not even hail their best friend on a Sunday. As Mrs MacBean had said, the mind was supposed to be on higher things. They had strict observance of the Lord's Day. There would even be a member of the congregation whose duty it was to 'police' the village on a Sunday to make sure no one was doing anything sinful like watching television or hanging out their clothes.

She hurried on down the hill.

'I brought a bit of a picnic,' said Hamish to Elspeth. 'We may as well have something to eat and drink. Let's sit on the harbour wall. It should be dry by now.'

He opened the Land Rover and lifted out a basket. 'You're very domesticated,' commented Elspeth. Hamish felt a stab of irritation and wondered why even the smallest thing Elspeth said to him sounded like criticism.

Hamish had brought fruit and sandwiches and a flask of coffee. 'Now,' he said between bites of sandwich, 'what have we got?'

'Bugger all,' said Elspeth, looking dreamily over the sea.

'Think!' commanded Hamish sharply. 'Maybe the boys up the hill have found evidence of an IRA visit and so we can forget about the whole thing because whoever did it will probably be back in Ireland by now.'

'Okay, I'll think,' said Elspeth. 'At first they were afraid. Something threatened them. Then they lost that fear. Something reassured them. Let's go off on a flight of fancy. The minister talked of Moses and the burning bush. He said they were the chosen people – not the Israelites, but the people of Stoyre. They're very superstitious up here. I mean, it's not often you get weather like this right on the coast. Battered by gales all year round, poor soil to scrape a living out of, meagre fishing what with the decline in stocks and all those bloody European Union regulations.'

'We should all go and live in Brussels,' said Hamish. 'I bet they don't give a damn about rules and regulations over there.'

'Quiet! You told me to think, so I'm thinking. Maybe someone in the village has been having visions.'

'Probably the DTs.'

'Someone sees something. Can't have been the Virgin Mary. They would consider that too popish. Can't be something old and Celtic like a kelpie. That wouldn't prompt all these visits to the church. Some vision that at first frightened and then reassured. But something that told them not to talk about it.'

'Let's take it away from the supernatural,' said Hamish. 'More coffee?'

'Please.'

'Right. Say someone or some people wanted Stoyre kept sealed off. Why?'

'Nice little harbour for landing drugs.'

'True. But they would see real live men in a real live boat. I'll have another talk to Sean Comyn and then I'll try the Bain family again. There's Jimmy.'

Hamish waved to Jimmy Anderson, who was heading down the harbour towards them. Jimmy came up mopping his red, sweating foxy face with a large handkerchief. 'Didn't know it was going to be this warm,' he complained when he came up to them. 'Hello, Elspeth. Got anything to drink, Hamish?'

'There's a cup of coffee left in the flask.'

'Coffee! Yuk! There's not a dram to be found in this place.'

'How's it going?'

'Stone-faced locals without a word to say. Blair took over some of the interviewing and I thought he was going to have a stroke. Nobody saw anything. Nobody even got out of bed to see what the noise was.'

'Any news of any terrorist activity?'

'Nothing. You find out anything?'

'Only that something has prompted a religious fervour. The major usually brings up some friends for the fishing. Did he have anyone on the guest list that might excite the attentions of a terrorist?'

'No. And he only did some low-key work in Belfast ages ago. He's retired. Actually he's quite chipper about the whole thing. He planned to sell up and the insurance will bring him a lot more than he could have got from selling it.'

'Maybe he did it himself.'

Jimmy grinned. 'That's what Blair accused him of and they had to fly Daviot up to soothe the major down. This your day off?'

'Aye.'

'I might drop round to see you in Lochdubh on my way back. Got any whisky?'

'No,' said Hamish, 'and you finished the brandy.'

'Patel's open?'

'Not now. He only opens in the morning for the Sunday papers.'

'Damn! I'll be off, then.'

'How long will the police be around?' asked Elspeth.

'A good few days yet, and if there's any funny business going on in Stoyre, believe me, nothing's going to happen until they give up and leave. Say it's a local job – the major's cottage, I mean. It could just be spite but I don't think so. The man only came up in the summers. Now, the major was once in army intelligence. Perhaps someone didn't want any sharp-eyed outsider around, someone who might notice things the locals wouldn't.'

'Any word of Bella Comyn?'

'Nothing yet. I'd like that one caught before she messes up someone else's life.'

* * *

Once back at the police station after having dropped Elspeth off, Hamish fed his hens, some of whom were quite elderly as he never had the heart to kill any of them for the pot, walked Lugs, and settled down to watch television. He felt he'd done enough on his day off. Sean and the Bains could wait until the morning.

He had just untied and kicked off his heavy regulation boots, which he wore even when not wearing his uniform, when he heard the phone ringing in the office. He was just wondering whether to answer it or not when the answering machine clicked on and he heard the loud voice of Mrs Wellington. 'Clarry phoned from the hotel. He's been trying to get you. One of the maids says she saw Bella Comyn in Bonar Bridge today.'

Hamish rang the minister's wife and asked her, 'Where was she seen?'

'In that grocery shop just by the bridge.'

Hamish thanked her, retied his boots, and with a sigh set off on the long road to Bonar Bridge with Lugs beside him in the passenger seat.

'Now, Lugs,' said Hamish, 'I wonder just what is going on in Stoyre.' The dog turned his odd blue eyes reluctantly from the passing countryside and gave a slight sniff. 'Exactly,' agreed Hamish. 'I don't know either. And I don't like it. I've got some holidays owing. I've a good mind to go and stay there for a few days and see what I can find out. I could stay at that place Sean rented. Would you like Stoyre?'

Lugs sighed again.

'Me neither,' said Hamish, 'but something weird's going on there.'

Master and dog then drove in companionable silence to Bonar Bridge.

The sun had gone behind a bank of clouds when Hamish finally drove into Bonar Bridge.

The place looked deserted. He parked outside the grocery shop and went in. There were no customers. A woman behind the counter asked, 'Can I help you? It's Mr Macbeth, isn't it?'

'Aye,' said Hamish, stepping forward and removing his peaked cap. 'Have we met?'

'Up at the Highland Games at Braikie two years ago. My boy got stuck up a tree and you got him down.'

'I remember. It's Mrs Turner, isn't it?'

'That's right. What can I do for you?'

'I'm looking for a Bella Comyn, small, blonde, pretty. I heard she was in here today.'

'Oh, her! What's she wanted for?'

'Oh, just part of a general inquiry. Do you know where she lives?'

'Up in one of the Swedish houses on the council estate, number twenty-four Sutherland Lane.'

'She living on her own?'